Contents

About the Authors

David A. Crighton was educated at the Universities of Aberdeen and London. He is Deputy Chief Psychologist in the Ministry of Justice and visiting Professor of Forensic Psychology at London Metropolitan University. He has previously been Deputy Head of Psychology for HM Prison Service and the National Probation Service. Prior to that he was a Consultant Psychologist in the National Health Service, where he held a visiting position in the School of Biology, Neurobiology and Psychiatry at the University of Newcastle upon Tyne School of Medicine. He is a past Secretary and Treasurer of the British Psychological Society Division of Forensic Psychology and is currently the Chief Examiner for the Board of Examiners in Forensic Psychology. He has previously been editor of the *British Journal of Forensic Practice* and is an editorial board member of the *International Journal of Leadership in Public Services*.

Graham J. Towl was educated at the Universities of Durham and London. He is Chief Psychologist in the Ministry of Justice and visiting Professor of Forensic Psychology Chairs at the Universities of Birmingham and Portsmouth and a collaborating member of the International Centre for Research in Forensic Psychology. Previously he has been Head of Psychology for HM Prison Service and the National Probation Service, where he led a five-year process of strategic change to the delivery of psychological services. He is recipient of the British Psychological Society (BPS) award for distinguished contribution to professional psychology. He is a past Chair and Treasurer of the BPS Division of Forensic Psychology and founding Chair of the Board of Examiners in Forensic Psychology. He is editor of the *International Journal of Leadership in Public Services*. He is currently external examiner for the University of Cambridge MPhil in Criminology.

Psychology in Prisons

Second Edition

David A. Crighton and Graham J. Towl

The British Psychological Society

BPS Blackwell

© 2003, 2008 by David A. Crighton and Graham J. Towl
A BPS Blackwell book

BLACKWELL PUBLISHING
350 Main Street, Malden, MA 02148-5020, USA
9600 Garsington Road, Oxford OX4 2DQ, UK
550 Swanston Street, Carlton, Victoria 3053, Australia

The right of David A. Crighton and Graham J. Towl to be identified as the authors of this work has been asserted in accordance with the UK Copyright, Designs, and Patents Act 1988.

Designations used by companies to distinguish their products are often claimed as trademarks. All brand names and product names used in this book are trade names, service marks, trademarks, or registered trademarks of their respective owners. The publisher is not associated with any product or vendor mentioned in this book.

This publication is designed to provide accurate and authoritative information in regard to the subject matter covered. It is sold on the understanding that the publisher is not engaged in rendering professional services. If professional advice or other expert assistance is required, the services of a competent professional should be sought.

The views expressed are those of the authors and do not represent those of the Ministry of Justice or HM Government.

First published 2003 by The British Psychological Society and Blackwell Publishing Ltd
Second edition published 2008 by The British Psychological Society and Blackwell Publishing Ltd

3   2008

Library of Congress Cataloging-in-Publication Data

Crighton, David A., 1964–
  Psychology in prisons / David A. Crighton and Graham J. Towl. – 2nd ed.
    p. ; cm.
  "A BPS Blackwell book."
  Rev. ed. of: Psychology in prisons / edited by Graham Towl. 2003.
  Includes bibliographical references and index.
  ISBN 978-1-4051-6010-0 (pbk. : alk. paper)   1. Forensic psychology–Great Britain.
  2. Prison Psychology–Great Britain.   I. Towl, Graham J.   II. Psychology in prisons.   III. Title.
  [DNLM: 1. Forensic Psychiatry–methods–Great britain.   2. Prisoners–psychology–Great Britain.   W 740 C928p 2008]
  RA1148.P785   2008
  365′.6672–dc22

                                                                        2007048169

A catalogue record for this title is available from the British Library.

Set in 10 on 12.5 pt Photina
by SNP Best-set Typesetter Ltd., Hong Kong
Printed and bound in the United Kingdom
by TJ International Ltd., Padstow, Cornwall

The publisher's policy is to use permanent paper from mills that operate a sustainable forestry policy, and which has been manufactured from pulp processed using acid-free and elementary chlorine-free practices. Furthermore, the publisher ensures that the text paper and cover board used have met acceptable environmental accreditation standards.

For further information on
Blackwell Publishing, visit our website at
www.blackwellpublishing.com

The British Psychological Society's free Research Digest e-mail service rounds up the latest research and relates it to your syllabus in a user-friendly way. To subscribe go to www.researchdigest.org.uk or send a blank e-mail to subscribe-rd@lists.bps.org.uk

Foreword to
Second Edition

I am delighted to welcome this second edition of *Psychology in Prisons*. Unlike the first edition, this edition is authored, rather than edited, and it represents a great contribution to knowledge about forensic psychology. This book is based on very detailed research and wide reading and it is clear that the authors have an impressive encyclopaedic knowledge of their topics. Extremely helpful summaries are provided at the end of each chapter. As busy practitioners, I am amazed that they can find the time to read and write such high quality books. No doubt a lot of midnight oil has been burned!

This book provides valuable, insightful information about a range of key areas of application to psychology in prisons, typically reviewing the evidence base in relation to the specific areas covered and also the most effective interventions. Readers will learn a great deal about the development of criminal behaviour, the needs of prisoners, psychological assessment, groupwork in prisons, risk assessment, depression, problem drug use, post-traumatic stress, suicide and self-injury, violence and sex offenders. The chapter on risk assessment, in particular, is a really outstanding contribution to knowledge. It recommends that actuarial assessments should inform rather than direct clinical judgment and that it is important to take account of the social contexts to which offenders are released in making predictions. The authors recommend an interesting 'iterative classification tree' method.

The authors raise and discuss many important issues in forensic psychology. In particular, they point out that there has been a move from unlimited discretion to centralized prescription in psychological interventions for prisoners. The emphasis on accredited programmes was laudable in its aim to implement only interventions that have been proved to be effective. However, making the number of prisoners attending such programmes a key performance indicator or target has (according to the authors) had the perverse incentive for prisons to allocate individuals to interventions even if they were unsuitable for, or not in need of, treatment. It is clear that types of offenders should be carefully matched to types of treatments.

The emphasis on accredited (almost all cognitive-behavioural) programmes has also had the undesirable effects of converting much of the work of forensic psychologists into the mechanistic delivery of manualised programmes. The authors refer to this as deskilling psychologists and consider that such programmes can be delivered by non-psychologists. They question whether treatment in groups is better than individual treatment. They are also dubious about the value and validity of psychological tests (rather than recidivism) as measures of behavioural change. It would be useful to evaluate the impact on national recidivism rates of the introduction of accredited programmes.

The authors rightly criticise the poor quality evidence base in the UK for interventions with prisoners and recommend more systematic reviews, meta-analyses, and high quality experimental and quasi-experimental evaluations. I also think that these evaluations should include cost–benefit analyses and follow-up interviews with offenders to assess their true rate of offending in the community and different measures of their life success. Forensic psychologists are likely to be the most competent researchers in the prison service, and they should take the lead in organising and carrying out a nationally coordinated programme of research to evaluate the effectiveness of interventions.

It is clear that forensic psychology is booming in the UK and is enjoying a 'golden age'. Hopefully, this informative and thought-provoking book will set the scene for the evolution of the work of forensic psychologists from assessment and programme delivery to research on correctional effectiveness and what works. This book is a valuable source of information for all those who are interested in psychology, prisons and the treatment of offenders.

David P. Farrington
Professor of Psychological Criminology
Cambridge University

Preface

This book presents a set of reflections on psychology in prisons. It is intended to stimulate and also contribute to an ongoing discussion and debate within and beyond psychology. Over the past decade there has been unprecedented growth in the influence and application of psychology. A wider range of employers and a greater range of applied psychology expertise are seen in prisons now than ever before. Significantly, staff other than psychologists are increasingly delivering approaches based on psychological models. This shift in practice is contributing to a realization of the real and tangible benefits of psychological approaches to the improvement of the well-being of prisoners, the reduction of risk of reoffending and the interests of public protection – a public of which prisoners form an integral part.

Psychologists as a profession share a fundamental commitment to human rights, equal opportunities and the reduction of suffering. The fundamentally coercive nature of prisons therefore makes at times for an exceptionally demanding working environment. It is thus especially important that in their practice psychologists always retain a clear and informed sense of the importance of the rights of prisoners, in addition to their responsibilities. In addressing equal opportunities psychologists in prisons have had significant successes. Psychologists were amongst the first to challenge racism in prisons. Within the profession there have been clear successes as well. Women are now appropriately represented across the profession in prisons. Crucially women hold a proportionate number of the most senior positions. At the time of writing more than 90 per cent of area psychologists are women. This record compares favourably with applied psychologists working elsewhere. Problems remain though. Psychologists from lower socio-economic backgrounds remain seriously underrepresented on entry and in subsequent progression to senior levels. Indirectly related to this, black and minority ethnic psychologists are also underrepresented. Professional diversity therefore remains a significant challenge.

In this book we set out to reflect important values underpinning psychological policy and practice. In doing this we have adopted an approach that seeks to set the work undertaken in prisons in a broader context, one that draws across disciplines and seeks to set behaviour in a developmental context. In doing this we acknowledge the evidence base for psychological approaches but also its limitations. Above all, though, our aim is to encourage psychologists and others to start to actively reflect on practice in prisons. We are hopeful that this will also be of interest not only to psychologists working with prisoners, whatever their expertise or professional background, but also to anyone with an interest in psychology and its potential for improving well-being, reducing re-offending and meeting the need for improved public protection for all. Commissioners of psychological services in prisons need to have an accurate awareness of the strengths, weaknesses and costs of the various psychological interventions and therapies. Social policy makers and criminologists will also, we hope, find food for thought in this reflective set of chapters on psychology in prisons.

This edition differs significantly from the first edition, which was an edited book, designed to offer an opportunity for a range of practitioners to contribute. This edition is a co-authored text and takes a more critically reflective approach. In doing this we have stressed some of key themes. For us these include the fact that psychology in its broadest sense (both research and applied) has enormous and, as yet poorly realised potential, to reduce human suffering. That the most promising way to develop this potential is through the adoption of rigorous evidence based practices. This is likely to mean sacrificing some traditional, at times cherished, but ultimately misguided ways of working. Underpinning all of this is a need for ethical values that are so central to individual professional responsibility, whether in research or practice, delivered by psychologists or others.

We begin with four scene-setting chapters on the policy context and recent history of psychology practice in prisons. In doing this we have drawn more widely than is often the case in the public service policy literature. An understanding of this context is important in informing psychological practices in prisons, but is also imperative for psychologists who need to draw widely from the literature on psychology and not feel restricted by current fashions. Psychologists need to retain and develop a critical application of past and emerging evidence.

Chapters 5 to 7 reflect three key areas of everyday psychological practice in prisons. Each of these chapters has a comparatively wide potential application in terms of national, regional and local services. Our coverage in this respect is necessarily selective. In looking at mental health, for example, we have chosen depression, the most common of mental health problems amongst prisoners, to illustrate themes with more general application. Prisoners experience very high levels of mental health difficulties and knowledge and understanding of the issues that arise are fundamental to understanding prisoners. Drug misuse is both a health and criminal justice concern prevalent amongst prisoners. It is also an area where psychologists, as health professionals, can take a wider view than merely considering drug misuse solely in terms of the important links with the risk of reoffending.

We have chosen also to look at the issue of trauma. Regrettably this topic has been relatively neglected in the forensic psychological literature. It is something that may affect prison staff and prisoners. Prisoners frequently come from economically, socially and often emotionally impoverished backgrounds, where traumatic experiences are more common. Patterns of trauma may differ but the potential effects need to be understood if we are to maximise the impacts of such psychological work in prisons with, for example, young women prisoners who have previously suffered sexual abuse.

Despite progress over recent years the overall trend in suicide in prisons has been in an upward direction. Here there has been a regrettable comparative dearth of interest and involvement amongst psychologists with a progressive withdrawal from such work, albeit with notable exceptions. The prisoners that psychologists work most closely with will though, at a group level, have an increased risk of suicide. They will often be violent or sexual offenders, facing long (often life) sentences. Consideration of suicide risk is thus especially important when working with prisoners experiencing depression. Self-injurious behaviour is sadly all too common amongst young people and children in prisons especially amongst young women. An underpinning theme of this book is the importance of redirecting psychological approaches, interventions and therapies to work more with children and young people in prisons.

Violent and sexual offending are areas of much understandable public concern. Both areas are core concerns of the criminal justice system and present serious public health problems. Understandably psychologists working in prisons have been concerned with these areas almost since the introduction of services.

The book is rounded off with a focus on evaluation. Effective evaluation is crucial especially where, as is commonly the case, psychological interventions are experimental. Evaluations can show positive, neutral or negative effects. This is an important consideration. We need to know which of these

Preface

three categories the evidence falls into when undertaking psychological work. Evidence-based practice is key to helping policy and practice developments. Organizational pressures, intellectual and emotional investments in particular approaches can colour judgements. A more independent approach is needed and advocated.

Finally we need to say thank you to a number of people who have helped us with this task. Over the years we have both learned from and been influenced in our thinking by many colleagues, students and friends. We are keen to take this opportunity to thank them all for stimulating us to think about applied psychology and how this might be tailored to best serve real world needs. We would also like to extend particular thanks to our commissioning editor (Elizabeth Johnston) and publisher. Specific thanks also go to Jo Bailey, Pat Crittenden, David Farrington, John Geddes, Fiedrich Lösel and John Monahan who have helped us to improve the quality of the text. Any errors or omissions that remain in the book are though entirely our responsibility. In addition we wish to formally record our thanks to the Librarian and staff at the Institute of Criminology in Cambridge and Librarian and staff at the Home Office Library in London. Finally, of course, our thanks go to our families and friends.

We both very much hope that this book serves to stimulate discussion, debate and a critical understanding of much of the evidence in relation to psychological practice in prisons.

David Crighton
Graham Towl
London 2007

Part I

Context

Chapter 1

Introduction

The Context

Psychology in prisons has in recent years experienced something of a golden age, with marked increases in funding of psychologists directly employed by public sector prisons from about £12 million in 2000 to over £30 million in 2005. The number of psychologists working in prisons represents an all-time high. The influence of psychological approaches to interventions with offenders continues in large part unchallenged. It might therefore be suggested that all is well and that current trends should continue indefinitely. Politics and public service delivery are changing, though (Faulkner, 2007), as is the framework for professional regulation (Maras, 2007) and training arrangements for applied psychologists in general and forensic psychologists in particular (British Psychological Society, 2007).

There have been a significant number of helpful challenges to much of the current psychosocial intervention work being undertaken with offenders (Bottoms, 2003, 2005; Crighton, 2006a; Hedderman, 2007; Mair, 2004; McNeil, Batchelor, Burnett *et al.*, 2005; Shaw & Hannah-Moffat, 2004; Thomas-Peter, 2006a). These have urged a greater degree of eclecticism in much of the work undertaken by psychologists, a need for greater empirical rigour and a clear set of values and ethics to underpin work with offenders. Arguably, such considerations are in starkest relief in settings such as prisons where there are marked power inequalities between those providing and receiving services. In general, the greater the differential in power relations, the greater the potential for abuses, suggesting a need for psychologists to have a very clear awareness of ethical issues as these impact on practice, along with the insight that they are by no means immune to the processes of institutionalisation.

3

Psychology as a discipline has much to offer. Psychologists as a profession have a potentially pivotal role in effective implementation of psychological methods and models for working with prisoners. Yet a frequently neglected aspect of the application of psychology in prisons and indeed applied psychology in general is that it takes place in a social, economic and political context. Because psychology is generally portrayed as a 'scientific' endeavour, broader contextual understanding may be neglected or even worse ignored, often under the guise of misunderstood notions of 'objectivity'. This view often appears to adopt the misplaced notion that acting as if such factors are merely extraneous variables is, in some sense, part of attaining scientific 'objectivity'. It is evident that scientific approaches do not take place in such a vacuum. Social policy issues often impact directly and, far from being extraneous to understanding, are often fundamental to it.

In recent years, there has been some blurring of such traditional boundaries between notions of 'private' and 'public' sectors, 'markets' and 'politics'. Such distinctions, though, still serve a useful illustrative purpose. Early studies of interventions with offenders provide a relevant example, with often highly selective presentations of the evidence. Results from tentative and equivocal research went on to be presented as if they were exclusively supportive of a 'nothing works' viewpoint in criminal justice (Lipton, Martinson & Wilkes, 1975; Martinson, 1974). At best, this was an unfair representation of the evidence but one which fitted comfortably with emerging social policy trends on crime. Despite such examples of interactions between social policy and researcher, there has been a continuation of this process, with research treated as if it occurs in a political vacuum. Arguably, some of the current large-scale UK evaluation studies of interventions, subject to a similarly selective presentation, could be used to support a 'nothing works' literature. There is merit in a more balanced and measured approach mindful of the importance of issues of political receptivity to particular findings which often impact on how research is 'remembered'. A key theme in this text is concerned with the effects of an unreflective approach to evidence, leading not only to a highly selective understanding of 'the literature' but also risks of harm both to inappropriately assigned participants and subsequently to the rest of the public. A critical awareness of the impact of social policy is therefore fundamental to ethical and effective professional psychological practice.

New Public Management

The development of psychology in prisons has in recent years taken place in a social policy context of major shifts in the nature and organisation of public administration and public services. These are often captured under the political rubric of 'New Public Management' (NPM), or alternatively and more critically 'neo-Taylorism' (Carlisle & Loveday, 2007). These terms capture a series of fundamental changes including a focus on measurable standards of performance and 'pre-set output measures', division of budgetary control into 'cost centres', the introduction of competition and subcontracting and the 'disaggregation' of public services by increasing separation of roles into purchaser and provider (Dent, Chandler & Barry, 2004). The UK was an early advocate of this approach during the Conservative administration in the 1980s and 1990s. It has continued as the dominant approach to the reform of public services over the last 25 or so years, through successive UK government administrations (Faulkner, 2007). Managerialist methods were used, ostensibly from the world of 'business', to improve efficiency in what were sometimes viewed as state-based organisational monoliths, namely public services. Historically in terms of management theory, the Tayloristic principles of the early twentieth century were revived as an ideological tool to help implement the increasing marketisation of public services. The influence of management thinkers such as Drucker remains key to many of the mechanisms of market reforms in public services, for example, with the importance placed on 'management by objectives', 'target setting' and the ubiquitous 'key performance indicators'.

For a number of readers, these developments will have a real resonance in the politically receptive environment within which psychologically based 'programmes' were organised, and for a time have flourished, in terms of the increasing numbers of prisoners who have 'completed' them. These manualised approaches to the administration of cognitive behaviourally based, structured group-based interventions expanded throughout the late 1990s and a little beyond that, fitting well with notions of pre-set output targets. Part of the managerial or managerialist appeal to such organisational and 'delivery' arrangements was that such work was, in principle, easily broken down and measured. The notion of a 'completion' is measurable at a basic level in similar terms to the manufacture of an industrial product. It can be ascertained whether or not a prisoner has attended the relevant sessions of a particular intervention. This tells us nothing in itself about the suitability of the intervention for the prisoner or indeed about the impact of the intervention. The predictable problems associated with such an approach have become manifest. The unhelpful focus on numbers of 'completions' builds in a perverse incentive for staff selecting prisoners to allocate individuals to such interventions even if they are less than ideally suited candidates. It becomes crucial that facilitators keep the numbers attending the groups high once they have started, despite the fact that such organisational arrangements can be clearly counter-therapeutic. Empirically, if prisoners are inappropriately matched to the groups, then the prediction would be that they would not benefit from them. An ethical concern is that some prisoners may experience adverse or harmful effects either through their own inappropriate selection or indirectly through the selection of other participants who are unsuited to the intervention. Facilitators faced with management targets, though, are understandably reluctant to remove participants. The system problem here is that people are 'fitted' to interventions rather than the more ethically, empirically and clinically sound approach of fitting interventions to the needs of the person. This is not, however, an inevitable consequence of setting performance targets. An alternative approach might, for example, involve targets that assessed the proportion of participants who meet (or met) the criteria for inclusion and the proportion that were offered a place on a treatment intervention. This suggests that better quality measures, to replace crude measures of completions, are not difficult to devise.

Such organisational problems are further compounded by the extensive overuse of psychometric testing before and after interventions. Both prisoner and facilitator have an interest in meeting targets and in showing that 'progress' has been made. 'Progress' reported in this manner may or may not be related to the reality of any cognitive, affective or behavioural changes attributed to attendance at the intervention. It may alternatively simply represent evidence of response biases in the completion of highly structured assessments. The extent of use of such psychometric assessments has grown markedly in recent years to a professionally questionable level, sometimes evidently at the expense of cheaper and more clinically relevant measures. There is a need here for clarity about the precise purpose and resource costs of psychometric testing and tests. This suggests a compelling case for reviewing and reducing the resources invested in such indirect and potentially flawed psychometric measures in 'programmes'. This perhaps provides a salutary reminder of the importance of keeping an appropriately ethical and measured relationship with the growing psychometrics industry. There has arguably been an overreliance on psychometric testing as part of efforts to both allocate individuals to particular interventions and assess outcome effects. This has drawn much-needed resources away from frontline delivery of services. There is also a need for greater caution in using psychometrics to draw inferences about allocation and outcomes. On the whole, psychometric assessments do not provide a convincing substitute for behavioural measures.

At a general level, the division of public services into contractual or pseudo-contractual relationships appears essentially based on the notion that free markets provide a powerful method to drive upwards both the quality and quantity of work undertaken. The approach has been subject to a number of incisive criticisms both in terms of its effects on public policy and its economic underpinnings (Clarke & Newman, 1997; Dent, Chandler & Barry, 2004). It has been suggested that the approach leads to a decrease in the power of professions to regulate services in favour of the free market. In turn, this has been associated with a deskilling of the workforce, replacing highly skilled and expensive professions with lower-cost competence-based workers (Dent & Barry, 2004; Thomas-Peter, 2006a). Professionals have increasingly been channelled into the role of competitive subcontractors. As such, the economic pressures on them are essentially to minimise the requirements of contracts (quality) and maximise income streams. The efficacy of what is delivered essentially becomes a problem for the contractor and not for subcontractors here. It can be suggested that the influence of this change in philosophy has in a number of respects spread widely across professional groups and psychology has not been immune to these contextual changes (Faulkner, 2006a; Towl, 2006).[1]

The economic basis of NPM has been critiqued as being predicated on an unduly simplistic conception of economics theory. The notion that free markets are the best way in which to regulate the delivery of goods and services has a long history and perhaps a particular salience in the UK (Smith, 1905). Indeed, there remain a small number of economists deeply committed to such models, yet in practice efforts to introduce completely free markets have proved highly illusive. The economic and human costs of unfettered competition have often been unpalatable and the introduction of publicly owned services in the UK was largely designed to address the failings of such competitive and market-driven systems. Public water companies were created to ensure a supply of clean and affordable water to growing urban populations.[2] The creation of the National Health Service was to allow the population reasonable and affordable access to health care.[3]

NPM-based approaches to the organisation of services have arguably had some positive impacts, focusing often inefficient and complacent managers and staff of public services more clearly on their core functions. Evidence of this can be seen with the impacts of 'market-testing' in prisons which appear to have contributed to some service improvements. Much of the stress on the efficiency of private sector organisations, however, appears misplaced and many of the 'new' approaches adopted in the public sector could equally be helpfully applied within large sections of the private sector which have suffered from inefficiencies and ineffective services. Private rail companies in the UK perhaps provide an illustration of this, being subject to extensive criticism for increasing prices and deteriorating services to customers. An interesting effect of reactions against the effects of privatisation of public services in such areas has been that private sector companies taking on public sector services have moved to re-brand themselves as the 'independent sector' in bidding for contracts. This terminology appears more publicly and perhaps politically palatable, although it is unclear how such companies are in any meaningful sense 'independent' – 'for profit' is perhaps a more accurate descriptor.

One direct and clear impact of NPM in prisons has been in the receptivity of prison managers and many psychologists to the manualisation of much of professional practice. There have been some benefits to the introduction of such structure, especially perhaps for less experienced trainees who may enjoy training benefits from such approaches (Towl, 2004a). Misleading terms such as 'treatment integrity', though, are sometimes used to describe manual compliance. Integrity in this context is based on the elementary and sensible empirical premise that interventions should be largely replicable. Manual-based approaches provide one mechanism for this but can be criticised for missing the central point about what precisely needs to be 'replicated'. A more sophisticated understanding of consistency in practice can be achieved with a clearer focus on the theoretical approach adopted, a theoretically driven understanding of both the 'content' of the intervention and also the therapeutic style of the groupworkers. Mere compliance with a manual fails to capture this complexity and if on occasion inappropriately followed may result in unnecessary problems such as potential lack of 'fit' with particular needs at given points. 'Therapeutic integrity' is a more complex but also more valid approach to replication and recognises an important distinction. It captures not only the 'content' elements of manual-based approaches but also 'process' elements based on a more in-depth understanding of the 'therapeutic' elements of interventions. This has a number of significant implications for work in prisons. It suggests a need for a shift towards improved, higher level, training and support for those who facilitate such groups. The therapeutic approach needs to be 'replicated', maintaining its theoretical integrity, but facilitators need the ability and confidence to adapt psychological interventions to fit the needs of group members.

Specialisation versus a Unified Psychology

The term 'unified psychology' is not new and was coined to refer to multiparadigmatic, multidisciplinary and integrated approaches to psychology (Sternberg & Grigorenko, 2003). In looking at psychology, it was convincingly suggested that three negative characteristics typified recent development:

- an exclusive or almost exclusive reliance on a single methodology rather than using multiple convergent methodologies;
- the identification of psychology in terms of subdisciplines and sub-specialisms such as clinical psychology and clinical psychologists or social psychology and social psychologists, rather than specialisation in terms of studying phenomena of interest;
- an adherence to single underlying paradigms for investigating psychological phenomena, for example, cognitive psychology.

It has been suggested that there is an underlying crisis of disunity within psychology that has needed resolution for many years, requiring the development and application of inter-level and inter-field theories (Staats, 1991). Psychology, in contrast to many of the natural sciences, has generally been poor at developing such theories. It has also been criticised for more profound weaknesses in terms of attaching multiple concepts to single terms and for the poor and imprecise use of pseudoscientific language. Recent developments in the application of psychology within prisons provide a perhaps especially stark illustration of this. The development of psychology in prisons in recent years has largely focused on a single-paradigmatic approach, little informed by, or integrated with, other paradigms. It has been delivered largely by a single (forensic) sub-specialism within psychology and has arguably been professionally limiting for this part of the profession. There has been an increasingly narrow focus on pre-set output targets (completions), often at the expense of impacts for individuals or for broader outcomes with social utility.

Such narrow approaches within psychology have historically been subject to significant and persuasive criticism. Some have argued that conceptualising psychological development as a set of interlocking systems as the basis for studying such development based on micro-, meso- and exo-systems, representing the differing levels at which psychological processes develop, is more helpful than simple reliance on single-paradigm, largely proximal, attempts at explanation (Bronfenbrenner, 1979). The need for less fragmentation and greater unity across psychology, if improved understanding of complex processes is to be attained, is not a new argument (Royce, 1970). It has until recently, though, made little substantive progress in academic and applied settings.

Specialisation within psychology has also been criticised as leading to 'regressive fragmentation' and 'self-limiting specialisations', alienating

9

practitioners from the larger human concerns that should have been the focus of their attentions (Bevan, 1991; Bevan & Kessel, 1994). Such fragmentation has been described as chaos and as feeding into the notion that psychology is a pre-scientific rather than a scientific discipline (MacIntyre, 1985). There have of course been counter-views proposed which suggest that such fragmentation is a sign of the health and growth of the discipline (McNally, 1992). Alternatively it has been suggested that the nature and breadth of psychology may mean the subject is not now unifiable (Koch, 1981). The former notion seems largely implausible. The latter argument whilst more convincing is not primarily concerned with issues of unification: it might better be seen as a valid argument suggesting a need for greater circumspection in what psychologists seek to address.

In practice, knowledge is a seamless cloth and a pragmatic balance will always need to be struck between distinct areas that allow manageable fields of study and the development of an adequate understanding. Despite scientists' best efforts to 'carve nature at its joints', distinctions within and between subject areas are to an extent necessarily arbitrary. The process of striking such a balance within psychology can however be seen as needing improvement and, in turn, exacerbated by a sometimes narrow nomenclature within the discipline. The British Psychological Society (BPS), in supporting the development of applied psychology, has seen a proliferation of sub-specialist areas that have become routinely referred to as 'divisions'. Such terminology can be criticised as begetting differences rather than commonalties within psychology, let alone beyond it to other overlapping disciplines. Many of the arbitrary 'divisions' are of questionable utility in relation to fuller understanding. Ethical difficulties have often flowed from the structure of the profession being closely dictated by mode of employment rather than subject area, creating an artificially imposed lack of breadth and depth in issues of professional ethics. This is a real concern given the core underpinning concern and interest of applied psychologists in human rights and well-being. Current levels of fragmentation and the isolation of small artificially bounded areas of psychology seem both dysfunctional and also unsustainable if psychology is to deliver on its as yet unfulfilled promise in addressing broader social concerns. In the context of applied psychology in prison settings, the current dividing lines within psychology seem much too firmly drawn and indeed to be drawn often in the wrong places.

The most striking example of this is perhaps the break-up of applied psychology into ever-smaller sub-specialisms. In the United Kingdom, these have historically been largely dictated by the needs of employing organisations rather than any rational attempt to fit applied psychology to address broader social needs. The clinical sub-specialism, therefore, emerged out of the system of asylum-based mental health care, with associated patterns of training and practice. The forensic sub-specialism emerged largely from prisons, borstals and approved schools. The educational sub-specialism emerged largely to meet local authority needs to allocate children to special education. Patterns for other sub-specialisms emerged in a similar ways, with scant regard for overlapping concerns, or skills and the need to address social goals and concerns beyond employing organisations. The situation in the UK has arguably been further exacerbated by a lack of a sufficiently well developed interchange between applied psychology and its foundations in basic and applied research, primarily in the higher education sector.

What does this mean for psychological theory, policy and practice? Violence provides an especially vivid and socially important example here. It constitutes a public health problem of enormous proportions that can afflict people from the cradle to the grave. It is a complex phenomenon and one unlikely to be understood from any single perspective. Yet this is largely what has happened with psychologists in prisons focusing on single-paradigm approaches, whilst often neglecting evidence from social psychology on group processes, physiological psychology on the neurobiology of violence and developmental psychology on the ways violent behaviour emerges and is maintained. Researchers in parallel have often not engaged sufficiently with applied practice, influenced practitioners or undertaken research of practical value. This is a major and continuing problem within the wider fields of evidence-based policy and practice.

There are hopeful signs of change in the medium to long term, with moves towards the increasing integration of the initial future training of applied psychologists and specialisation only relatively late in training. At this time, though, the position remains one of firm employment-based boundaries across applied psychology and between the conceptually convenient but inadequate dichotomy between 'fundamental' and 'applied' psychology. Access to and across these 'divisions' is strictly controlled and 'protected'. This may be further exacerbated where training opportunities from single employers may be unduly restricted and psychologists may miss out on the potential for greater breadth and depth of understanding in practice and research. In training, psychologists based in prisons are often exposed to a single methodological approach. The current fashion is for cognitive behavioural group-based approaches. Having trained in a single approach, individuals will often have invested heavily, both intellectually and emotionally, in it. Understandably perhaps where limitations become evident, they may be sometimes resistant to change or to using alternative perspectives when they have no experience or skills in alternative methods and approaches.

Arguably, the two most important elements of recent BPS guidance on training in forensic psychology are the joint foci on the notion of 'competencies' and the requirement to have an experienced qualified supervisor (with at least two years' practice) responsible for training and supervision arrangements (British Psychological Society, 2007). The focus on competencies allows this to be demonstrated in a wide range of potential settings, involving many different types of work. This contrasts with past and to a large extent current practice. Historically. specific employers have tended to establish training arrangements and, as such, generally focused these on meeting organisational needs rather than having a primary focus on the needs of trainee psychologists in their development towards qualification. A practical consequence of the changes is that those training to become psychologists will be less characterised by their title and more by the fact that they are 'doing psychology' whilst being appropriately supervised by qualified and experienced practitioners. Such change is likely to impact on employment practices, with trainees becoming more focused on the settings that will enable them to develop a broader skills and knowledge base. Employers who wish to retain the best psychologists will need to significantly invest in breadth and depth of professional training, rather than simply relying on historic arbitrary 'divisions' within applied psychology restricting professional mobility. Some employers may, of course, be content to plan for a relatively high turnover of professional staff but in general such changes are bringing a range of exciting opportunities and also significant potential uncertainties for those who go on to train in applied psychology. However, from a professional perspective, such moves which help ensure a greater breadth of understanding and skills are to be very much welcomed as part of a move towards greater unification of psychology as a discipline. How effective these changes are will depend to a great extent on qualified psychologists in combination with their employing organisations and how they respond to change in their broader organisational contexts. In the context of prisons, this will be critical for both 'provider' organisations such as public sector prisons and those who commission and fund services such as the National Offender Management Service.

Evidence-Based Practice

Evidence-based practice (EBP) has achieved wide use in the mental health field but has until recently been rather less used in the criminal justice context. It refers to efforts to use scientific evidence to inform and direct professional practice. Its comparatively slow take-up in criminal justice is regrettable because evidence-based approaches to psychological interventions in prisons have the potential to yield significant gains. Instead, in the criminal justice field more restricted discussions, where indeed there has been any discussion, have taken place. These have revolved around the rather parochial and political term 'what works'. Within this frame of reference, narrow technical issues have been the primary focus, for example, the correct cut-off points on psychometric assessments, rather than matters of greater scientific substance and utility. Even within discussions of technical aspects such as these, some fundamental issues appear to be routinely avoided, such as the problem of high rates of false negatives and the lowering of diagnostic thresholds when administering psychometric assessments with offenders. The restriction of debate within much of applied psychology in prisons to such a conceptually narrow framework as 'what works' cuts against the foundations of psychology as an attempt to use scientific method and work with other disciplines to develop better quality explanations of social and behavioural phenomena.

What We Can Learn from Public Health

There is a great deal of potential learning for forensic practitioners in drawing from evidence-based public health models. These provide a powerful analogy to the development of criminal behaviour since they are concerned with problems that are, generally, multi-factorial. In addressing this challenge, public health researchers have developed powerful conceptual and analytical tools. They have also needed to address issues of the utility of a variety of potential interventions. In contrast, much of the psychological literature captured under the 'what works' heading, has continued to be overreliant on simplistic and mechanistically applied statistical models and methods.

Public health models suggest a number of practice considerations as well. Looking at criminal pathways and trajectories, it is evident that there is potential for multiple points of intervention (Farrington & Coid, 2003; Piquero, Farrington & Blumstein, 2007). Associated with this is the finding that prevention approaches are often more effective, both in clinical and cost terms, than treatment approaches. In turn, where treatment is necessary, the most clinically and cost-effective interventions will not always be those that are intuitively obvious.

The application of psychological interventions in prisons provides an illustration of failure to recognise and act on this type of complexity.

13

Intervention resources have traditionally been and are currently heavily and disproportionately concentrated in high security prisons in relation to prisoner needs and the evidence base. Comparatively little work has been directed at open prisons, young offender institutions (YOIs) and local prisons which hold prisoners for relatively short periods of time. This runs counter to what public health analyses would suggest, given the joint aims of protecting the public from harm and rehabilitating offenders. A public health analysis might suggest that early intervention would be better than later intervention, so that more resources should be directed to increasing desistance from crime at an early age. When considering adults, a focus of resources on those who will shortly return to the community is likely to reduce harm more effectively than interventions with prisoners who will spend years, in some cases decades, in high security prisons. Indeed, a public health model concerned with public protection would suggest a significant shift of resources to those who have the longest criminal careers ahead of them and who will have the greatest access to potential victims.

Regrettably, the late 1980s saw the closure of much of the system of 'approved schools' and secure children's homes in England and Wales as part of the increasing shift to community care in social services. Despite warnings and concerns expressed at the time, this resulted in a shift of resources away from such early intervention with troubled children, young people and families. This has only recently begun to be corrected with the advent of the Youth Justice Board (YJB) and direction of more resources to early interventions.

Public health approaches have in many areas also been characterised by the creation of an extensive and high quality evidence base. There is a need to be realistic about the evidence base for psychological interventions generally and those designed to reduce criminal behaviours in particular. This is generally of only moderate quality, with many studies rated poorly on standardised ratings of methodological quality (Lösel & Schmucker, 2005; Crighton & Towl, 2007). Progress in improving this parlous state has been slow, not aided by overblown claims about efficacy that have given little political incentive to fund appropriate methodologically rigorous research. There is a need for high quality studies of outcomes including, though not exclusively, randomised control trials (RCTs). Such studies allow the possibility of eliminating many of the threats to the validity of research. Large-scale RCTs also have the power to identify modest and transient effects, favourable and adverse, as well as differential effects across populations.

Within the forensic field over the last 10 to 15 years, a curious language has developed in relation to interventions designed to reduce the risk of reoffending. Widespread use of a pseudoscientific language, including terms such as 'criminogenic' primarily to describe correlates of crime and 'high dosage' to describe levels of psychotherapeutic contact, has become prevalent. Such terms provide a veneer of 'scientific' face validity, yet at best they add little to understanding. It is then not surprising that they have increasingly been criticised as little more than marketing devices (Faulkner, 2006a; Thomas-Peter, 2006a). Such criticism makes more than a linguistic point. It reflects a more substantive and regrettable failure to use the full range of potential benefits that the discipline of psychology has to offer (Needs & Towl, 2004).

Summary

- Recent years have seen something of a golden age for applied psychology with marked growth in funding and more widespread application of applied psychology. There have, however, been a significant number of constructive challenges to these developments in prisons, urging greater eclecticism, greater empirical rigour and clearer professional ethical values.
- The growth of psychological approaches has occurred with a context of rapid social policy change, often captured under the heading of New Public Management, an approach that has been called into question in recent years. It involves fundamental changes in public services, with a focus on such things as 'pre-set output measures', division of budgetary control, competition and subcontracting and the 'disaggregation' of public services with high value placed on learning from 'for-profit' organisations.
- In prisons, in social policy terms, a receptive environment existed for psychologically based 'programmes' using manualised approaches to cognitive behavioural group-based interventions. These expanded throughout the 1990s, dovetailing neatly with managerialist approaches.
- The term 'unified psychology' has been coined to refer to multiparadigmatic, multidisciplinary and integrated approaches. Unified psychology has been posited as a means of addressing an underlying crisis of theoretical and practice disunity within psychology.
- Applied psychology in the UK has historically been largely structured on the basis of the needs of employing organisations, rather than any rational attempt to fit applied psychology training and practice to address social needs. This has been exacerbated by a lack of sufficiently

developed interchange between applied psychology and fundamental and applied research.

- There are hopeful signs of change towards more unified psychology with increasing integration of applied psychology training arrangements and specialisation relatively late in training. An increasing focus on competency-based training suggest that psychologists will become less characterised by their title and more by the fact that they are 'doing psychology'. Employers wishing to retain the best practitioners will need to invest significantly in breadth and depth of professional training, rather than simply relying on historic arbitrary 'divisions' restricting professional mobility.

- Evidence-based practice (EBP) has achieved wide use in the mental health field but has until recently been little used in criminal justice. It refers to efforts to use scientific evidence to inform and direct professional practice. It provides a more persuasive and effective framework than restricted terms such as 'what works', providing firm scientific foundations and improved scope for multiparadigmatic and multidisciplinary working.

- There is a great deal of potential learning in forensic practice from evidence-based public health models. These models are concerned with multi-factorial and multidisciplinary areas. They suggest that prevention is often more effective than later treatment and that many effective treatments may not be intuitively obvious.

- Learning from public health contexts has not been integrated into criminal justice settings. Intervention resources have traditionally been heavily concentrated in areas such as high security prisons, where they are likely to have much lower impacts in terms of public protection and long-term outcomes. Comparatively few resources have been directed at young people, open and local prisons where the greatest impacts are likely.

- In relation to applied psychology, the evidence base in prisons is of moderate quality and has been slow to develop. Progress has not been helped by overblown claims about the efficacy of current intervention approaches that have given little incentive to fund appropriately rigorous research. There is a pressing need for high quality studies of outcomes, including randomised control trials and qualitative studies.

- In recent years, the use of jargon has been increasingly drawn on, developing a pseudoscientific language such as 'criminogenic' to describe correlates of crime, or 'high dosage' to describe levels of psychotherapeutic contact. Such terms add little to understanding and may have

16

simply served to obscure the full range of potential benefits that the discipline of psychology has to offer.

Notes

1 An example here might be the aggressive marketing of psychometric assessments. Many of these will have limited utility, yet use has grown. Whilst such methods are profitable for those who subcontract such services, their value in terms of meeting prisoner needs or improving public protection may often be marginal, at best.

2 Such public corporations replaced systems of private water vendors. They had major advantages over this system as they invested in improved capacity for water supply and, just as importantly, waste water removal. They also had little incentive to maintain shortages of supply. Changes of this type also had largely unforeseen positive effects in terms of public health.

3 Here the system of private medical care had failed to provide services to poorer areas or adequate access to hospital care, whilst services were highly concentrated amongst the most affluent groups. Areas such as health promotion had understandably suffered serious neglect.

Chapter 2

Psychological Services in Prisons

Introduction

The history of psychology in prisons parallels that of other areas of applied psychology dating back to the postwar period, about sixty years ago, when the then Prisons Commission began a policy of recruitment of psychologists to work in prisons, young offender institutions and Prison Commission Headquarters[1] (Towl, 2004a). In part, this reflected a need and desire to overcome the problem of attracting graduates to work in prisons (Faulkner, 2006a). Interestingly, much of the early work of psychologists was concerned with areas such as staff training and vocational assessments, what would now be seen as organisational psychology. From the late 1940s onwards, there was slow growth in the numbers of psychology staff employed but the main focus below is on the recent development of applied psychology services. The improvements in psychological services in recent years have been unprecedented with year-on-year growth in the recruitment of psychological staff in prisons (Needs & Towl, 2003; Towl, 2004a, 2004b). This chapter traces the development of services based around a number of key professional and organisational milestones, followed by a critique of contemporary developments.

In drawing conclusions from recent history, it is essential to develop a firm grasp of future challenges and opportunities, both in terms of a greater range of applied psychologist expertise and a greater range of prospective employers. Additionally, there is a need to organise and deliver psychological therapies in ways that work with, and make the best use of the skills of, staff other than psychologists.

Three key trends emerge from this analysis and these are considered in turn. First, the growth of forensic psychology as a professional specialism within psychology warrants detailed consideration with, by 2005, around 1000 psychological staff directly employed by public sector prisons in England and Wales (Crighton, 2005a). Secondly, there has been development of a greater range of applied psychology knowledge and skills being used to undertake work within prisons. There was growth in clinical, counselling, educational, health and occupational psychology work delivered in prisons (HM Prison Service & National Probation Service, 2003). Indeed the need for increased unification across applied psychology became increasingly widely acknowledged (Towl & Crighton, 2005). Thirdly, and linked to this, there was an increasing recognition of the need to address what the full range of psychological approaches have to offer in meeting prisoner needs. In order to gain maximum benefits from psychological interventions, it became evident that there needed to be a clear shift of focus from simply the work of psychologists to that of the best ways to develop and apply psychology to prisons.

Background

In considering the recent history of professional developments within applied psychological services in prisons, there are a number of key milestones, indicating influential changes.

The Development of Forensic Psychology in Prisons

The history of forensic psychology in the UK is comparatively short. The Division of Forensic Psychology (DFP) of the British Psychological Society (BPS) metamorphosed from the previous Division of Criminological and Legal Psychology (DCLP) by an overwhelming vote of the membership in favour of the change in 1999. A vigorous debate about the merits and demerits of a change of name of the Division had preceded this and much of this focused on the precise meaning of the term 'forensic' (Towl, 2004a). Some argued that the term did not fully capture the strands of both 'legal' and 'criminological' traditions within the discipline. Linked to these internal professional debates was a shifting picture in the use of professional designations to describe the various applied psychology specialisms. Curiously, prior to this the term 'prison psychologist' had been routinely used to describe the work of psychologists in prisons, largely irrespective of professional specialism. This was in marked contrast to the practice in other areas of the profession where terms such as 'hospital psychologist', or 'school psychologist', had passed into history, replaced by professional specialism designations. The predominant and indeed rapidly growing specialism in prisons was, and indeed remains, forensic psychology.

Some involved in the professional debate had sought to establish forensic psychology as a sub-specialist branch of clinical psychology. The formation of the DFP in 1999 was a clear statement of the distinctiveness of forensic psychology as a specialism within applied psychology and not a sub-branch of another specialism. This was a watershed moment in the development of professional forensic psychology in the UK and set the framework for the future development of forensic psychology in the twenty-first century.

The work of forensic psychologists in the prison service for England and Wales has in recent years received greater professional currency and recognition than at any time in its history. Application rates for posts in the prison service soared between 1999 and 2003. Future generations of forensic psychologists may indeed look back upon this period as a golden age for the recruitment of forensic psychological staff, with the field experiencing a boom period. One very influential attraction for the prison service in recruiting psychology graduates was that this served to build up very significantly the graduate staff capacity in the organisation. The prison service has traditionally struggled to recruit good quality graduates to work in management positions. Also, within the broader context of what may be termed the 'marketisation' of public services, the 'unit costs' of employing psychological staff was such that they represented good value in relation to the knowledge and skills they brought to the organisation. As such, the increased recruitment of psychologists in prisons fitted well with broader public sector reforms, which have been termed the 'New Public Management' (Hood, 1991; McLaughlin, Muncie & Hughes, 2001). Additionally during this period there was a growth in the advocacy for and use of manual-based groupwork-based interventions, designed to reduce the risk of reoffending for participants. Although these structured interventions were largely based on psychological models, there was no a priori evidence that they needed to be delivered by psychological staff. The impact of such conflated thinking was that this contributed to large cohorts of trainee psychologists being recruited, despite a stretched infrastructure, for providing the levels of supervision and professional support that they might reasonably expect. Unsurprisingly, this in turn appears to have led to some significant problems in staff retention levels particularly amongst trainees, with consequent difficulty in maintaining continuity in service delivery.

20

Professionally, these developments generated two key problems. Most importantly, they may well have compromised the quality of services because of insufficient levels of professional supervision. This in turn linked to high turnover rates for psychology staff in prisons at the end of the last century and at the beginning of the twenty-first century. To illustrate this, for 2000–2001 the rate of staff turnover amongst trainee psychologists was 24 per cent per year and for qualified staff it was 18 per cent (HM Prison Service and National Probation Service, 2003).

A second consequence of these recruitment practices, which remain very much with the prison service in England and Wales today, is the problem of a tension in expectations of trainee psychologists and prison managers. Prison managers have the expectation that the trainee psychologist will simply go on delivering a specified set of manual-based interventions. Trainees know that this is incompatible with getting qualified as forensic psychologists and with ongoing professional practice. Clearly, a much greater range of supervised and post-qualification experience is necessary. Some in the forensic field have become increasingly concerned by such 'dumbing down' of the training arrangements for trainee forensic psychologists (Thomas-Peter, 2006a; Towl, 2005a). This remains an issue that senior psychological staff in prisons need to address as an urgent strategic and professional priority. As the training routes and rules for qualifying in forensic psychology tighten, as they have consistently done over recent years, it will become increasingly challenging to ensure that trainees have a range and depth of supervised experiences compatible with their success-ful qualification and continuing practice. The other side to this equation is that, if the DFP becomes too demanding in its requirements for qualifica-tion, prospective employers are likely to reassess the extent of their invest-ment in the professional training of forensic psychological staff.

In summary, the key professional milestone of 1999 was the passing into history of the widespread use of the term 'prison psychologist' and the development of forensic psychology as a distinct branch of applied psychol-ogy. It also saw the coming of age of the work of a range of applied psy-chologists in prisons who in future would be more appropriately referred to, reflecting their professional specialism.

A Strategic Framework for Psychological Services

A second milestone, published four years after the creation of the DFP, was the first strategic framework document for psychological services in prisons and probation (HM Prison Service and National Probation Service, 2003). This was the product of an extensive consultation process, including a very wide range of stakeholders. Previously there had been a marked and potentially costly absence of a sense of strategy in the organisation of psychological services. The need for the production of a strategy document had become more pressing, partly as a function of the sheer increase in the number of psychological staff employed in prisons. Indeed, HM Prison Service has become the largest single employer of forensic psychologists in the UK (Towl, 2004a).

The strategy also served to highlight some of the many and significant improvements in psychological services during the period from 2000 to 2003. These included marked improvements in staff recruitment and retention. The retention of qualified psychologists had improved from 82 per cent in 2000–01 to 93 per cent by 2002–03. The improvements for trainees were even more pronounced, with retention for 2000–01 at 76 per cent, improving to 90 per cent by 2002–03 and 95 per cent by 2003–04. The strategic framework also, perhaps most importantly, acknowledged the need to have a clear and coherent approach to the further development of applied psychological services in prisons (HM Prison Service and National Probation Service, 2003).

Public Service Reforms

A key underpinning theme of the strategy was recognition of the contemporary context of the work of psychologists employed by the prison service as civil servants: namely, public service reform. This was not new; successive governments have called for a more efficient and effective civil service. For the first time, though, this was explicitly acknowledged, rather than working as if such matters had no direct impact on the work of psychologists.

Probably the most professionally important issue concerned training, supervision and continuing professional development (CPD). There was a very strong need to ensure and improve (in some cases markedly) this area. Historically, the focus had largely been on structures and systems to help trainee forensic psychologists become qualified as quickly as possible. Relatively, the area of CPD for qualified practitioners had been neglected. Despite a high degree of centralisation, issues of training and CPD were not in a good state. Improved quality in these areas was therefore at the core of the strategy, building from an existing low baseline.

The strategy also involved a clear focus on meeting organisational needs. The prison service faced and continues to face very considerable service delivery pressures. In the target-driven managerialism of the day, these were reflected in a number of key performance targets and indicators. Such targets and indicators continue to dominate many areas of work in the prison service and arguably there may have been some initial merit in this, with such targets serving to focus efforts to improve delivery. As in other areas of public service, however, they have had a distorting effect on the work of prisons. An example here is the targets for delivery of structured groupwork which produce an emphasis on completions rather than outcomes. The task for managers in prisons therefore becomes one of ensuring that a given number of prisoners attend a given number of group sessions and that manual-based approaches are mechanistically delivered. Issues of clinical impact and utility become, within this framework, largely irrelevant. Examples of the distorting effects of this abound with some offenders participating in the same intervention twice to be double-counted for the purpose of national targets. Such developments have been, in large part, a manifestation of broader public sector reform (McLaughlin, Muncie & Hughes, 2001).[2] As already noted, alternatives to crude measures such as number of completions are not difficult or costly to devise. For example, in the context of interventions in prisons, measures of the proportion of those suitable for a given intervention who receive it would provide a measure with significantly greater utility.

Key Strategic and Organisational Changes

Between 1999 and 2003, a degree of necessary change emerged as part of the process of developing a strategic approach to applied psychology. Four instances of such change perhaps stand out as particularly significant.

Bringing Prisons and Probation Closer Together

The creation of a new joint post of Professional Head of Psychology for the prison and probation services took place in 2000. The first postholder was jointly appointed shortly after, formally employed by HM Prison Service but with a remit for psychology in the probation service.

Pressing issues included low professional morale, high turnover of staff, inadequate professional training structures and wholly inadequate continuing professional development (CPD) arrangements. In turn, these were associated with significant disruptions to service delivery. In substantively addressing these emergent themes, a strategic approach was critical. Managerial 'quick fixes' were wholly inadequate to the challenges faced and would potentially store up additional problems for the future.[3]

23

Career Structure and Salaries

The need to make changes to the career and salary structure emerged clearly as a key issue. Significant overlap in the pay of trainees and qualified staff was inherited, with some qualified psychologists being paid less than some trainees. Generally, there were comparatively small pay differences between qualified and unqualified staff, due primarily to two factors. Historically, some individuals had been recruited significantly above the base of pay scales whilst others had not. Also, with the marked increase in recruitment, large numbers of qualified staff were recently qualified and thus towards the low end of the qualified psychologist pay bands, with slow progression across these scales. This mix resulted in a number of pay anomalies. Most importantly in terms of the implications for the organisation, these were completely inconsistent with the market for both qualified and unqualified staff. Those with the Graduate Basis for Registration (GBR), the necessary starting point for professional training, were applying in high numbers and those leaving rarely cited pay as the main issue, expressing instead concerns about lack of good quality training. In marked contrast, the market was much tighter for qualified staff and poor salary was often cited as a major reason for leaving. A cap to the starting and ceiling pay for unqualified staff was effectively introduced early on, in combination with a significantly increased minimum pay for qualified staff. Effective partnership working with the probation service was also developed and this served to address concerns about the potentially inappropriate creation of competition for scarce professional resources (Towl, 2006).

Area Psychologists

The prison service is managed through a number of predominantly geographical areas, some of which accord with the boundaries of the government offices of the regions. Each contains a range of prisons. The aim here was the introduction of a national network of senior and experienced practitioners to provide prisons with area-based professional leadership in the strategic organisation and delivery of psychological services within the developing national framework. This also helped with the introduction and augmentation of a number of subsequent national policies linked to the work of psychologists and the ongoing development of the five-year strategic plan. It proved important to have this additional layer of professional structure between national professional leadership and heads of applied psychology departments in prisons.

Area psychologists had a number of key roles, including that of ensuring appropriate use of psychology staff within their areas. The role also involved responsibility for succession planning for trainee and qualified staff. Ensuring appropriate supervision and CPD were pivotal to the role and remain so. An additional role made possible by these structural arrangements was the policy decision to use area psychologists to ensure the development of a continuously 'on call' service to prisons, in the event of serious incidents (primarily hostage incidents but also other prison disturbances). Each area psychologist was accountable for setting up area-based arrangements.

The creation of a professional area structure also allowed psychologists to contribute to other broader policy developments. These included the introduction of a national approach to the assessment of external research requests. This involved roles for both the area psychologist and many heads of applied psychology units in prisons, who became research contacts at establishment level. This enabled the prison service to tap into key areas of expertise amongst its professional staff and was also good for the profession, contributing to reinvigorating the knowledge and skills of psychologists in this important area as 'scientist practitioners'.

Flexible and Fair Career Structures

Prisons have traditionally employed psychological assistants with minimal entrance requirements on permanent contracts of employment. In contrast in the National Health Service (NHS), assistant psychologists are graduates in psychology, usually employed on fixed-term contracts. In practice, over 80 per cent of applicants for assistant posts in prisons were psychology graduates. Despite this, there was curiously no route of promotion to trainee psychologist.[4] The practical result of this was that an appropriately qualified assistant could not become a trainee unless securing appointment through an external recruitment process, having resigned from the prison service only to take up appointment again in a trainee post. This unhelpful practice had lasted for decades and presented a significant and unnecessary problem for professional staff, prison managers and service users.

Another concern was the problem of institutionalised racism within prisons and professional psychology (Narey, 2002). Psychological services in prisons were by no means free from the racism seen elsewhere. Black and minority ethnic groups were overrepresented in the psychological assistant grade and underrepresented at trainee psychologist grade and above. The opening of a promotion avenue from psychological assistant to trainee was one means of dismantling some of the inherited edifices of often unknowing discrimination.[5]

Applied Psychology – Unifying the Skills Base

The strategic plan set out in 2003 represented a marked change of professional direction. This change was intended to lay the foundations for unification across applied psychology. Services were dominated by a single-paradigm approach combined with a limited range of professional expertise. Indeed, in this respect psychology in prisons may be seen as having gone backwards, with progressive reduction of professional diversity during the 1980s and 1990s. Clear potential existed for improving services to prisoners, staff and the organisation by drawing on a more diverse range of paradigms, knowledge and professional skills. Such change offered the promise of a more unified applied psychology, more effectively addressing need (Crighton, 2006a; Towl, 2006).

The late 1990s onwards saw a marked growth across applied psychology in public sector settings. Within prisons, much of this growth was built on the development and delivery of manual-based groupwork interventions, termed 'accredited offending behaviour programmes'.[6] These were associated with a growing recognition of the work of psychologists in prisons. They were, though, experimental interventions and clearly remain so. Yet they have sometimes been promulgated as 'proven to work'. The approach taken to delivery of this type of intervention in prisons has tended to follow a very fixed pattern, involving high levels of centralised planning and prescription. Criticisms of this approach have concerned a number of issues, both managerial and clinical, suggesting that such efforts are likely to be counter-productive in terms of reforming the delivery of public services (Crighton, 2006b; Faulkner, 2006a; Thomas-Peter, 2006a; Towl, 2006).

One example of over-centralisation has been what might be termed the moral costs of strict compliance requirements in delivering manual-based sessions. Ethically, the key concern is the potential for over-compliance with the letter of a manual despite clinical inappropriateness to individual participants at a given point in time (Thomas-Peter, 2006a). Professional psychologists clearly have a personal duty not to engage in such practices and not to comply with the inappropriate application of any psychological intervention. Indeed, professional duty clearly goes beyond this, with a duty to challenge such inappropriate practices (British Psychological Society, 2006).

There are, of course, sound empirical and clinical justifications for reasonable consistency of delivery across psychology. Treatment protocols are extensively used across a range of interventions and serve a number of useful functions. They ensure that, in carrying out any intervention, practitioners do so in an ethical and competent manner. Effective protocols also ensure that evidence-based practice spreads more quickly and that practitioners do not have to 'reinvent the wheel' continuously. In prisons, however, manual-based interventions differ markedly from protocols seen elsewhere in practice and across the health field. Efforts to eliminate professional judgement and present behavioural compliance as equivalent to 'treatment integrity' may be misleading and potentially harmful.[7]

Ethically, there is a need to balance protection of the public and the needs of individual recipients of services. Both are crucial in effectively working in the context of prisons. Arguably, different areas of applied psychology may show differences in emphasis here. Drawing from a more unified psychology using the full range of professional perspectives might helpfully serve to provide better balances and checks in this area and, as such, richer ethical practice. There are potential risks of going down narrow single-paradigm paths, rather than adopting multiparadigmatic approaches drawing on a fuller and more unified range of psychological knowledge.

An additional ethical issue is linked to concepts of citizenship and membership of society. Prisoners are rarely explicitly seen as citizens, yet not to do so is nonsensical. Such misperceptions have potentially harmful effects. In seeking to rehabilitate prisoners, the aim is to help them to rejoin society without needing to again be excluded by prison custody. Issues of public protection are rightly and reasonably part of the core professional remit of applied psychology in prisons and risk assessment is part of the key skill sets that psychologists bring to working with prisoners. There are, however, real risks of this 'forensic' remit creating an artificial and damaging separation of 'public' and 'prisoner'. Logically, all prisoners are members of the public and a significant number of members of the public are at any one time prisoners. The adoption of the European Convention on Human Rights into legislation places an additional duty on professionals to strike an appropriate balance between the competing rights of different individuals, both in custody and in the community (Mason & Laurie, 2006; Towl, 2005a, 2005b).

Context, Knowledge and Skills

There are potential benefits to drawing from a diverse mix of multiple paradigms in applied psychology in working with prisoners, but there are also important practical considerations. Different areas of applied psychology have historically been linked to particular employment sectors and patterns of training. Clinical psychology evolved from work with patients in the NHS, primarily in mental health services. Modern forensic psychology developed largely from work with offenders, often in prison, probation or court contexts. Such divisions can be criticised on a number of grounds. Perhaps most seriously such divisions have tended to lead to narrow and non-unified approaches, often drawing on single paradigms. There are potential professional benefits in seeking to break down these artificial barriers within psychology and importing understanding, knowledge and skills on a more unified basis across psychology. Current moves to reform training in applied psychology appear helpful in this respect (Kinderman, 2005). Equally, efforts at public sector reform with the establishment of core sets of Professional Skills for Government (PSG) create the opportunity for psychologists to broaden their knowledge and skills and increase their contribution (Cabinet Office, 2005).

Contemporary Developments in Psychological Services in Prisons

In December 2003, the Carter Report was published which set out an agenda for change across prisons and probation (Carter, 2003). A key theme of the review was the further development of 'market forces' into the criminal justice sector. The review anticipated 'contestability' in the provision of services stimulating improvements in quality. A division between 'commissioners' and 'providers' was advocated. The government response to Carter set out bold plans for changes which were aimed at ensuring that prison and probation services were more 'offender-centred' (Home Office, 2004).

The implications of this for professional psychology have to date been relatively small. Longer-term effects, though, seem likely to be profound and far-reaching. The overwhelming majority of psychological staff employed by HM Prison Service remained within public sector prisons concerned with the direct delivery of services. National professional leadership, however, was subject to marked changes with policy, standards and practice in psychology across prisons and probation moved to be part of a joint Home Office and Department of Health Directorate (Health and Offender Partnerships) in 2004. In 2007, this psychology function moved to the newly formed Ministry of Justice with a modified remit to include the courts.

Two main themes informed these changes. First, given movement towards a split between commissioners and providers of services, it was thought important to ensure that high-level policy on psychology should inform intelligent commissioning of psychological services. Second, with the emergence of plans for the statutory regulation of psychology through the Health Professions Council (HPC), it seemed most appropriate to locate the group within the joint Health and Home Office Department.

The later move to the Ministry of Justice placed national psychology more closely at the centre of commissioning of psychologically based services.

Remarkable changes in the organisation of health care in prisons had pre-dated these changes. The NHS, through Primary Care Trusts (PCTs), had taken responsibility for the healthcare needs of prisoners, replacing a separate prison healthcare service (Department of Health, 2006). NHS psychological services were increasingly 'mainstreamed', predominantly in the form of clinical and counselling psychology delivered as part of health service in-reach teams (Cinamon & Bradshaw, 2005; Crighton, 2005a).[8]

Future Challenges and Opportunities

Psychology services in prisons have never been as healthy as they are now. The recent history of psychological services, however, suggests that there is no automatic right to such buoyancy. Planning and preserving a sense of a wider strategy, particularly at the national, area and head-of-department levels, combined with hard work amongst all psychological staff will be critical to sustained development.

Interventions will need to be evidence-based and one key consideration will be in relation to the availability and accessibility of psychological therapies for prisoners (Department of Health, 2004). How services are provided will largely be a matter for service providers. Further growth in the range of providers seems likely. If psychological services are to be provided on a scale that matches need, then current models of delivery are likely to be unsustainable. A wider range of practitioners with appropriate training will be needed to deliver psychological therapies. Downgrading the scientist-practitioner training favoured within applied psychology seems both inappropriate and unnecessary. From a commissioning perspective, the chief concern will be ensuring that prisoners and prisons derive maximum benefit from psychology as a body of knowledge. Graduate mental health workers[9] have the potential to play key roles in delivering psychological models, freeing up psychologists to develop multiparadigmatic approaches and work requiring broad-based knowledge and skills.

Statutory Regulation

The British Psychological Society has striven for the statutory regulation of psychologists for many years (Powell, 2005). It now appears that such a regulatory framework will be introduced, albeit through the HPC rather than BPS. This will bring the profession into line with longer established professions such as medicine and law. It is also likely to change markedly the work of psychologists in prisons. It will have significant impacts on training, supervision and CPD arrangements, as these become statutory requirements. This will increase professional leverage to ensure the adequacy of such arrangements. Another consequence will be to help drive up the overall quality of psychological services.

Such changes will also impose short-term and longer-term costs. Initially at least they are likely to push up 'unit costs'. In the medium to long term, this has the potential to be translated into savings, as professional practice becomes more focused and less vulnerable to litigation. Individual practitioners will become more personally and directly accountable for their actions. They will also face more severe sanctions for engaging in poor professional practices. Failure to adapt swiftly to the changes involved in statutory regulation would be very costly for individual practitioners, the profession and prisons.[10]

Evidence-Based Practice

One of the many potential benefits of having a more unified and multiparadigmatic approach to psychology is the scope to broaden the development of the evidence base for work with prisoners. Curiously, in the forensic field the term evidence-based practice has yet to gain widespread currency. Debates on evidence have tended to be restricted to a somewhat parochial and often superficial discussion of the so-called 'what works' debate.

Summary

- The relatively short history of psychology in prisons parallels that of other areas of applied psychology with recruitment dating from the post-Second World War period. In part, the development of psychological services was a reflection of a need and desire to overcome the problem of attracting graduates to work in prisons.
- The recent history of applied psychology in prisons has been dominated by the growth of forensic psychology. This followed a vigorous professional debate over whether forensic psychology should be a sub-specialist branch of clinical psychology or a branch of applied psychology in its own right. The formation of the Division of Forensic Psychology in 1999 signalled a clear statement of the distinctiveness of forensic psychology.
- A lot has changed in psychological services in prisons over its recent history. Most strikingly, perhaps, there has been a substantial

growth in talent within the provider organisations, with high potential to contribute to the further development of evidence-based practice. This has clear potential to yield significant social benefits.

- Recent development in prisons has been predicated on a narrow range of knowledge and skills and a lack of professional diversity. There is significant potential for further development in these areas, with an increase in diversity and the use of more unified multiparadigmatic approaches to the application of psychology. The increasing prominence of evidence-based practice as a key feature of psychological interventions and therapies will need to be central to the development of professional practice. It represents a marked break from the parochial and narrow reading of evidence often captured under political headings such as 'what works' and 'nothing works'.

- The development of the first strategic framework document for psychological services in prisons and probation took place between 2001 and 2003. Based on an extensive consultation process, this addressed the potentially costly previous absence of national strategy in the organisation and delivery of psychological services in prisons.

- The strategic plan represented a marked change of professional direction; addressing longstanding issues about career structures and laying the foundations for the use of a broader range of applied psychology knowledge and skills in the prison environment.

- The recent separation of commissioning and delivery of services for offenders is likely to have profound effects on professional psychology over the long term. Greater professional diversity will be needed to meet future challenges. Professional practice will need to draw from the full evidence base across applied psychology, with more multiparadigmatic and unified approaches to psychology being delivered from a range of providers.

- There has been in recent years a very marked growth in the scale and range of professional talent available within prisons. This creates significant opportunities to positively drive the development of evidence-based practice (EBP) with prisoners to the benefit of prisoners, the community and psychology.

Notes

1   The terminology for penal institutions has changed a number of times. Throughout this chapter the term 'prison' is used to include prisons,

young offender institutions and HQ roles, and to include historical terms such as youth custody centres and borstals.

2   With the benefit of hindsight, it could be suggested that the strategic frameworks could and should have said more about meeting the needs of prisoners and the professional approaches to this.

3   As with other professional groups, this required a balance to be struck between professional interests and public interests. Failure to do this would, it was felt, result in unsustainable changes. There have been a number of such failures resulting from efforts to reform public sector practice. Perhaps the most directly relevant one is the implementation of changes to NHS psychology services under the Agenda for Change (Department of Health, 2005, 2006) framework. Here the costs and grading of psychology posts has resulted in marked reductions in availability of psychology posts and training posts.

4   For historical reasons, the only available route for promotion was to the civil service grade of executive officer, a progression route that was of little interest to most psychological assistants.

5   Diversity issues have often been inadequately addressed in professional psychology in prisons. There has arguably been a high degree of denial that areas such as social class, race, gender and disability have impacted on professional progression. The evidence (with the exception of gender) has suggested the contrary. One area of significant progress has been in relation to gender, where women are currently appropriately represented in the most senior professional grades in prisons.

6   There was parallel growth in other areas of psychology. The development of services within the NHS is perhaps the most obvious, although here the growth in services was based on a very different model of delivery, largely on one-to-one interventions, with a shift towards intensive work that carried more complex problems (Department of Health, 1996, 2004).

7   A protocol is distinguished from a manual in a number of ways. The most important in this context is the degree of specification provided. A manual provides detailed specification of the exact actions and sequence of actions. A protocol specifies a number of steps involved in reaching a given outcome but requires a high degree of professional judgement at every stage (see, for example, Gospodarevskaya, Goergen, Harris *et al.*, 2006).

8   Mainstreaming of psychology services was also seen, on a more modest scale, in other areas, most notably in the development of educational psychology services to address the needs of prisoners with educational needs and specific learning difficulties.

9   Graduate mental health worker is a grade of staff developed in the NHS
    to undertake routine and protocol based work with patients. There is
    no reason why a parallel grade of Graduate Criminal Justice Worker
    should not be developed across the Ministry of Justice.

10 Historically, psychologists have been subject to voluntary registration
    and sanctions for malpractice have in practical terms been minimal.
    Psychologists working in the public sector have also benefited from
    effectively unlimited Crown protection. The situation under statutory
    regulation is likely to involve potentially severe sanctions, such as loss
    of entitlement to practice and criminal penalties, including imprison-
    ment. As such, it represents a completely new regime for psychology
    practitioners.

Chapter 3

Development and Criminal Behaviour

Introduction

Development can be defined as the process by which an organism grows and changes over the full course of its lifespan. As such, developmental psychology has been largely concerned with the earlier periods of human life, when the greatest degree of growth and change occurs. As a discipline, it overlaps significantly with many other areas of research and study but perhaps especially the areas of biology, sociology and anthropology.

Psychologists have taken a number of approaches to investigating human development. In outline, these have primarily included cross-sectional, longitudinal and cohort studies, along with mixed designs.

Cross-sectional studies are those that look at a number of age groups at the same time, for example looking at attachment in 3-, 5- and 7-year-old children. Longitudinal designs involve following a group of individuals over time and measuring change. For example, following a group of children and assessing levels of delinquent behaviour at age 5, 10 and 15. Cohort studies involve studying groups born in different years at the same age. Mixed designs involve combinations of these methods of study, for example cohort sequential designs involve following birth cohorts longitudinally over time.

A major distinction within the evidence base has been between observational and experimental approaches. Both methods have been extensively used within developmental psychology and both have a clear role in contributing to evidence-based practice. The key distinction here is in the extent of control and in turn the degree of confidence in the explanations attached to given outcomes. Observational studies tend, on the whole, to yield correlational findings which do not prove causation. Well-constructed experimental studies in contrast allow stronger inferences about causal mechanisms. Studies of development however cannot be separated from their ecological and ethical contexts and as such many areas are rightly not open to experimental study.

A further major distinction is between qualitative and quantitative methods. Both have made significant contributions to the understanding of development. Qualitative studies have generally used systematic methods to analyse information, such as discourse analysis and grounded theory approaches (Smith, Cowie & Blades, 2004). Quantitative approaches have been primarily concerned with the collection of data expressible in numeric forms.

Ecological and Stage Models of Development

It has been noted that development occurs within an ecological context (Bronfenbrenner, 1979). This is an observation that has often been neglected within psychological research but the model outlined by Bronfenbrenner provides a helpful framework when looking at development.

Four overlapping levels of ecological system were suggested: 'micro', 'meso', 'exo' and 'macro'. Microsystems refer to what has often been the core concern of developmental psychology, an individual's experiences within a given context, such as a child's interactions with their father in a given situation. Mesosystems refer to the links between the microsystems that an individual participates in, such as the links between boys' interactions with their fathers and with each other in school. Exosystems refer to the effects on individuals of systems they do not directly participate in, such as parents' employment. Finally, macrosystems refer to the broader patterns of ideology and organisation of social systems in the subculture that the individual lives in. A salient example of this might be the impact of high levels of unemployment in the UK on working-class children during the 1980s and 1990s.

Such ecological systems are likely to interact in complex and, to date, poorly understood ways. However, it has been suggested that there are a number of 'proximal' or basic processes involved within these systems which operate to allow the genetic potential of an individual to be realised (Bronfenbrenner & Ceci, 1994).

Biological Factors in Development

Each person develops from a single cell comprised of deoxyribonucleic acid (DNA) from both parents. It is this material which constitutes that person's genotype and sets the genetic limits on development. The processes involved in cell division are, however, open to errors that may modify these limits. An example here is Down's syndrome, which results from a genetic error[1] and has significant and variable effects on both physical and psychological development.

Twins have been of great interest to those concerned with researching the relative impacts of genetics on development. Twins are born where two types of event occur: in one case a single fertilised cell or zygote divides and then goes on to develop as two children with an identical genetic make-up (monozygotic twins). In the other case, two ova are fertilised more or less simultaneously and both develop to full term (dizygotic twins). In this case, the twins are no more genetically alike (or different) than siblings. This natural occurrence creates a powerful natural experiment which has been extensively used and indeed misused in the study of behavioural genetics.

The interaction between an individual's genetic potential and their environment begins from conception. Whilst in many respects the uterine environment is, in physiological terms, a highly protected one for the developing child, it can have a marked impact on development. It is clear that factors such as alcohol consumption, smoking, diet and drug use can all have powerful effects on the quality of the uterine environment (Barker, 2001).

Research in developmental psychology, physiology and biology demonstrates clear interactions between instinct, maturation and learning. In turn, these rest on the interface between genetic potential and environment. This has led to notions that key aspects of development may be strongly guided by genetic maturation or 'canalized', whilst others remain relatively changeable or 'plastic' (Hinde & Dennis, 1986; Hinde & Stevenson-Hinde, 1973). Building on cross-species research into areas such as imprinting, it has been suggested that there are 'sensitive periods' for some aspects of development (Lorenz, 1981). Where relevant experience or learning does not occur during these periods, it will be subsequently much more difficult or perhaps impossible to acquire. A very clear example of highly canalized learning with such a sensitive period is the acquisition of spoken language in children. Normally, between the ages of 12 and 24 months, children begin rapidly to acquire spoken language. By 4 or 5 years old, they are more or less fluent, although they still make a number of systematic errors. During this phase, children can learn any human language (and seemingly any number of languages to which they are exposed) and go on to become fluent speakers. Where learning does not take place within this window, it subsequently becomes much harder to learn, as anyone who has tried to learn a foreign language at a later age can attest.

Sociobiologists have sought to apply theories from evolutionary biology to the explanation of social behaviours and suggest that a number of aspects of human behaviour are the result of processes of natural selection. In essence, it is suggested that behaviours which increase the chances of the survival of offspring have been selected for. An example here might be aggression. Although in modern social contexts aggression is often seen as undesirable, it has clear survival value and as such would be expected to become highly canalized. In this way, sociobiological approaches can provide an explanation for a range of 'positive' and 'negative' behaviours (E.O. Wilson, 2000).

The approach, however, is open to a number of criticisms. Current estimates suggest that the evolution of modern people has largely taken place over the last 50,000 years. In biological terms, this is simply not long enough for genetic evolution to take place. Most of the changes seen in this timeframe must therefore be cultural rather than physiological (Eibl-Eibesfeldt, 1989).[2] It has been further suggested that people, as a result of the development of cultural transmission, have become largely or wholly 'decoupled' from genetics. What does seem clear from the evidence base is that cultural factors have a major impact on behaviour whilst some fundamental behaviour remains highly canalized.

Early Experience

Embryonic development is clearly strongly predetermined following a specific sequence. This is, however, subject to environmental effects such as genetic abnormalities and exposure to teratogens during pregnancy such as tobacco, alcohol and infection. It has also been suggested that maternal stress during pregnancy may have marked negative effects (Essex, Klein, Cho et al., 2002).

There is some evidence to support foetal learning during the last three months of pregnancy and possibly before, with the foetus evidently reacting to stimuli (Smith, Cowie & Blades, 2004). Human infants also face high risks during birth. Given the developmental needs of the human brain, it has been noted that the gestation period is short when compared to primates. The human birth canal is also relatively narrow, creating high risks for both the child and mother. It has been suggested that this has given rise to a need for assisted childbirth (Lovejoy, 1981). Certainly, it means that human infants are born in a highly dependent state, requiring high levels of care in the early years of life. Bonding between mothers and human newborns is generally seen within minutes of birth and for most signals the establishment of a powerful initial bond linked to feeding the child.

A full-term baby is generally defined as one born at 38 weeks or more and there is a clear association between earlier births and higher levels of mortality (Luo & Karlberg, 2001). The development of modern midwifery and neonatal medicine has seen an increase in the number of pre-term infants surviving. Whilst the pattern of deficits and functional recovery is a complex one, it does seem clear that those born before 32 weeks, described as very pre-term infants (VPI), show significantly increased risk of physical injury and ongoing neurological impairment (Luciana, 2003).

Low birth weight has also been shown to be associated with increased risk of physical and neurological impairment. Birth weights are normally categorised as normal (3000–4000 g), low (<2500 g), very low (<1500 g) and extremely low (<1000 g). Perinatal risk factors associated with birth weight include such things as breathing difficulties. Psychosocial risk factors relating to the care of the infant also have an evident impact, with moderate perinatal risk factors often outweighed by good psychosocial care. The evidence is less clear for severe perinatal risk factors, where such mitigation seems less effective. Gender also appears to be a significant factor with boys generally shown to be more susceptible to such risk factors (Laucht, Esser & Schmidt, 1997, 2001).

Deficits were seen in very premature and very low birth weight infants at 4½ years with perinatal risk factors decreasing in importance with age (Laucht, Esser & Schmidt, 2001). Such infants also showed higher levels of problems such as isolation, shyness and depression at 11 years (Tessier, Nadeau, Boivin et al., 1997). Overall, the picture is one where infants of 1500 g and above only showed slight deficits but infants born at lower weights tended to show more severe and prolonged deficits, with extremely low birth weight children faring worst (Taylor, McGue & Iacono, 2000; Wolke, 1998).

Early Social Interaction

Given the high level of dependency seen in human infants, it is critical for survival that the child establishes a strong attachment to the mother or another caregiver. Some of the behaviours involved in helping to achieve this appear to be largely instinctive and predetermined. Soon after birth, infants are able to orient to auditory stimuli. They show a number of important reflexes with clear survival value such as grasping, rooting and suckling. At another level, infants are able to cry and smile, behaviours that they gradually learn have social consequences.

Within a few days, infants can discriminate their mother's voice and from around two months begin to prefer pictures of faces to other stimuli. Learning about social turn-taking also begins around this time, with the ability to play simple turn-taking games. There is evidence that infants around this time begin to expect contingent responses from caregivers and become upset when these expectations are unmet. Imitation is a key aspect of learning throughout development and this is seen to develop from between 6 and 12 months.

Attachment

The role of attachment and bonding in development has long been recognised. Early bonding of mothers to their babies usually takes place within 6 to 12 hours post partum and seems largely achieved through physical contact. Recent research suggests though that infants and mothers are more robust in this respect than once thought, with only small adverse effects being observable where initial bonding is disrupted. Any critical period for establishing bonds seems to be significantly longer than the initial post-partum period (Smith, Cowie & Blades, 2004).

In an early pioneering study of attachment, four attachment phases were suggested, with a fifth phase extending the development of attachment from infancy into childhood and, more vaguely, throughout the lifespan (Bowlby, 1969; Svanberg, 1998). Aspects of this initial research have been subject to experimental study and further refinement. Initial stress placed on a single central attachment figure, primarily mothers, appears to have been misplaced. Young children seem well able to have multiple attachment figures. Indeed at 18 months old, 87 per cent of children show such multiple attachments. Around a third of the children studied showed strongest attachment to someone other than their mother, usually a father, grandparent or sibling (Schaffer & Emerson, 1964).

Individual differences in attachment relationships have been subject to extensive study, much of it drawing on observations of reactions to separation and return of attachment figures in strange settings, generally termed the 'strange situation' paradigm (Ainsworth, Blehar, Waters *et al.*, 1978). Ainsworth's original observations suggested three patterns of attachment:

* Type A – Avoidant
  'Avoidant' children tend to show conspicuous avoidance of their attachment figures when reunited with them. They may not appear distressed during separation although physiological evidence contradicts that appearance.

- Type B – Secure
  'Securely attached' children actively seek to maintain contact and prox- imity especially when reunited after a brief separation. Such children often show distress when separated and pleasure when reunited.
- Type C – Ambivalent
  'Ambivalently attached' children tend to show a pattern of mixed feel- ings, both seeking and resisting contact, for example wanting to be picked up, then pushing away the attachment figure.

Experimental studies have demonstrated that not all infants fit these three patterns and understanding of these cases has proceeded in two parallel directions. The better known of these, termed the 'ABCD' model, is based on Main and Solomon's description of behaviour that they considered 'dis- organised' in a sample of middle-class advantaged infants (Main & Solomon, 1986). In later work, this was associated with unresolved maternal loss, expressed to the infant as frightened or frightening maternal behaviour (Main & Hesse, 1990). The disorganised pattern has been called 'D/control- ling' for preschool-aged children and 'unresolved' for adults. Other tenets of the ABCD model are that the pattern of attachment is relatively stable from infancy forward and is transmitted across generations from mother to child.

The parallel approach, termed the Dynamic-Maturational Model (DMM), began as a doctoral thesis under Ainsworth's direction, using a sample of abused and neglected children (Crittenden, 1983, 1985). These children showed many of the same 'odd' behaviours that Main and Solomon had

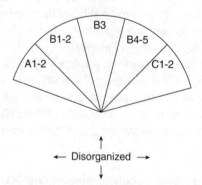

Figure 3.1 Dynamic-maturational
model of attachment behaviours
Source: (Crittenden, 1997)

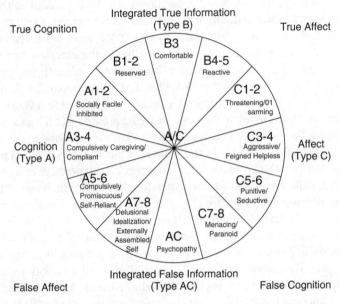

True Cognition — Integrated True Information (Type B) — True Affect

Cognition (Type A)

Affect (Type C)

False Affect — Integrated False Information (Type AC) — False Cognition

B3 Comfortable

B1-2 Reserved

B4-5 Reactive

A1-2 Socially Facile/ Inhibited

C1-2 Threatening/01 sarming

A3-4 Compulsively Caregiving/ Compliant

A/C

C3-4 Aggressive/ Feigned Helpless

A5-6 Compulsively Promiscuous/ Self-Reliant

C5-6 Punitive/ Seductive

A7-8 Delusional Idealization/ Externally Assembled Self

C7-8 Menacing/ Paranoid

AC Psychopathy

Figure 3.2 Dynamic-maturational model of attachment strategies
Source: (Crittenden, 1997)

listed. In this case, however, the behaviour was considered to constitute the child's use of both the avoidant and the ambivalent patterns. Over the next decade, research on older individuals produced an array of new DMM patterns at different ages (A3-8 and C3-8), each tied to children's neural maturation and exposure to danger (Crittenden, 1997). In contrast to the ABCD model, the DMM proposed that humans were exquisitely prepared to organise to protect themselves and their progeny from danger and that this had evolutionary significance. The DMM also proposed a dynamic and changing interaction of pattern of attachment with maturation and experience across the lifespan. Finally, the DMM proposed that mothers and infants could have different patterns, depending upon what strategy best promoted the infant's safety and comfort with the mother.

The two models, in other words, approached the expansion of Ainsworth's model in opposite ways, one from normality and safety with a discovery of disorganisation, and the other from abnormality and danger with a discovery of an age-related array of organised self-protective strategies.

Empirically, there are more data on the ABCD model than the DMM and even less comparing the models. The ABCD findings indicate that most individuals in clinical samples can be classified as 'disorganised', although a persistent subgroup of maltreated children and patients in psychotherapy are classified as 'secure'. The data on the DMM more consistently find maltreated children and patients to be classified in the new, less normative patterns, with more severe problems being associated with higher subscripts of A5-8 and C5-8 (Crittenden, Claussen & Kozlowska, 2007; Ringer & Crittenden, 2007). The comparative findings are limited to reviews of the literature and two empirical studies comparing preschool children's attachment using the two methods (Crittenden, Claussen, & Kozlowska, 2007; Spieker & Crittenden, 2007). Both the reviews and the empirical evaluation suggest that the DMM assessment is more precise and predictive, especially for at-risk children. A key question therefore becomes which model better fits the developmental pathways and psychotherapeutic treatment of individuals who have committed criminal offences.

Three characteristics of the DMM model are central to exploring the application to criminal offenders. First, the DMM patterns have associated models of information processing, especially of information regarding danger. Individuals using higher subscript patterns tend to transform recalled information in ways that increase their expectation of danger in the present (Gregory, 1998; Tversky & Kahneman, 1982), thus calling for deceptive and risk-taking self-protective strategies. Second, the information processing associated with each pattern is reduced to different forms of representation, each of which disposes behaviour differently (Damasio, 1994; Schacter & Tulving, 1994). It may be important to know how violent adults use information about past danger to organise their current behaviour. The DMM outlines the process developmentally in ways that are (a) open to empirical test (and revision of theory based on results), and (b) informative regarding opportune times to intervene preventively and ways to intervene correctively. Third, the DMM directly addresses sexuality and its integration into attachment relationships and self-protective strategies. Because both attachment and sexuality function to draw people together and do so with overlapping sets of behaviour (e.g., touching, holding, kissing, signalling) and compatible feelings of arousal/desire and comfort/satisfaction, understanding of sexual disorders may require an understanding of the interaction of attachment with sexuality.

Although much has been written about the effects of children's temperament on attachment (Chess & Thomas, 1996), there is little evidence that temperament alone has a direct effect. Three decades of research have revealed a complex picture, with differences resulting from dyadic characteristics between the child and their caregivers. Consequently, transactional models are currently favoured. For example, in a longitudinal study of 1000 children at age 3 years, 40 per cent were categorised as easy/well adjusted, 10 per cent as under-controlled or impulsive and 8 per cent as inhibited. On follow up at 18–21 years, small but significant differences between these groups were found in mental health, employment and quality of adult relationships (Caspi, 2000).

It is worth noting that children can and do show different patterns with different people and so, for example, might show an avoidant pattern with mother but a secure pattern with their father. Cross-cultural differences have also been described (Crittenden & Claussen, 2000). For example, research in Japan, where by cultural tradition infants are very rarely left alone before the age of 12 months, showed increased levels of type A attachment. Japanese mothers also tended to immediately pick up infants on return which tended to increase levels of type C behaviour at 12 months, something no longer evident at 24 months (Takahashi, 1990).

There are considerable methodological challenges in studying attachment in older children and adults but a number of attempts have been made to overcome these. The crucial component has been development of assessments of attachment to operationalise theory. The Strange Situation has become the accepted procedure for infancy and the preschool years. The school years and adolescence do not yet have generally accepted assessments. The Adult Attachment Interview (AAI) (George, Kaplan & Main, 1985) is the accepted procedure for adults. Most assessments can be interpreted through either the ABCD model or the DMM.

Research during the 1990s increasingly came to see attachment as a construct with application across people's whole life, rather than something limited to childhood. With increasing age, it seems likely that attachment becomes increasingly internalised in the form of mental models of attachment figures. Individuals with a history of secure attachment, it is suggested, will develop models based on trust and affection. Those with insecure attachments will develop models based on threat.

The original method of discourse analysis of the AAI (Main & Goldwyn, 1984) yields the four main patterns of attachment, with 'cannot classify' (Hesse, 1996) being a fifth pattern. Almost all clinical cases are classified as 'cannot classify'.

The newer DMM method identifies a wider array of patterns in Figure 3.2 and, for each pattern, the possibility of unresolved loss, trauma, depression, disorientation or intrusions (Crittenden, 1999). Although there are fewer publications using the DMM method, the findings indicate that the patterns at the top of the circle most frequently fit normative individuals, those in the middle fit individuals in treatment, and those at the bottom fit individuals in mental hospitals and prisons. The latter two groups are also

Table 3.1 Normative data for the AAI based on 33 studies

	Dismissive (%)	Autonomous (%)	Enmeshed (%)
Mothers	24	58	18
Fathers	22	62	16
Adolescents	27	56	17
Lower SES	33	48	18
Clinical patients	41	13	46

Source: Crittenden, 1997

marked by greater unresolved trauma and loss, as well as depression and intrusions (Ringer & Crittenden, 2007).

Many studies have been undertaken to look at the degree of continuity in attachment over time. There is a substantial evidence base suggesting a high degree of continuity through life for securely attached individuals. Marked discontinuities are more common in the anxious patterns, especially when combined with other sorts of risk (Vaughan, Egeland, Sroufe *et al.*, 1979). In the ABCD model, the greatest switching is between secure and disorganised (NICHD, 2001); in the DMM, the changes are in both directions, toward 'earned' security and to higher subscript patterns in cases of ongoing risk.

In one study, 100 mothers and 100 fathers were followed up longitudinally to look at the extent to which disruption and deprivation in childhood impacted on their parenting behaviour (Fonagy, Steele, Steele *et al.*, 1994). Although there was evidence for ongoing effects, they were mediated by the way in which these negative experiences had been dealt with psychologically. The researchers noted that both 'earned' and 'continuous' secure groups had more experiences of positive parenting. That is, in spite of sometimes poor parenting and exposure to danger, the parents of 'earned' secures had promoted their children's being able to reflect on their difficulties. Of course, not all troubled children have this advantage.

Styles of Parenting

Variations in approaches to parenting have been extensively studied, yielding a number of typologies or dimensional approaches. One example of a popular typological approach divides parenting styles into authoritarian, authoritative and permissive (Baumrind, 1980). An alternative example of a dimensional approach divided styles into two dimensions demanding/undemanding and responsive/unresponsive (Maccoby & Martin, 1983).

In a longitudinal study of 6400 adolescents aged between 14 and 18 years, authoritative parenting was associated with improved school performance, although this was mediated by the degree of parental involvement. Authoritarian approaches were associated with better school performance but in this case it was not mediated by level of parental involvement. Authoritative parents were characterised as showing three main characteristics: acceptance and warmth, behavioural supervision and strictness and granting psychological autonomy (Steinberg, Lambourn, Dornbusch et al., 1992).

There is also a substantial evidence base on the effects of disrupted family relationships. In a study of 144 children, half from divorced families and half not, a number of negative effects were observed amongst the former group. After one year, most children in this group experienced emotional distress and showed behavioural problems associated with disrupted family functioning. By two years of age, these problems were much reduced but with some exceptions, the main one being ongoing poor relationships between some boys and mothers who had custody of them, with increased levels of antisocial and defiant behaviours (Hetherington, Cox & Cox, 1982; Hetherington, 1989). In a six-year follow-up, it was found that children in divorced families had experienced more independence and power in decision-making at an earlier age. The nature of relationships between mothers and daughters was similar for both groups. Mother–son relationships often continued to be tense where mothers had not remarried. These findings are however significantly moderated by the family situation prior to divorce, with divorce clearly making matters worse for already troubled families. It has been noted that there is a need to direct at least as much research effort towards the dynamics of troubled intact families (Cherlin, Furstenberg, Chase-Lonsdale et al., 1991).

The area of step-parenting and stepfamilies has received relatively little attention. A study of 907 children in New Zealand entering stepfamilies provides significant insights. Children entering stepfamilies between the ages of 6 and 16 years were at increased risk of drug abuse, juvenile crime and poor school achievement. However, this effect largely disappeared when prior family disruption, socio-economic status and parent characteristics were corrected for. In essence, it seems that children already experiencing difficult family situations were also more likely to have step-parents and stepfamilies (Nicholson, Fergusson & Horwood, 1999). The role of parenting, though, is contentious and some researchers have suggested a greater role for genetics, arguing children are highly robust. Provided that parents provide a warm, supportive and nurturing environment, it is suggested that behavioural genetics can do the rest (Scarr, 1992). Whether this contentious view is accepted or not, it is clear that many children experience families that are not warm, supportive or nurturing.

Child Abuse and Physical Punishment

Survey data suggests that a majority of parents in the UK smack or hit their children at some point, with mothers and fathers showing similar levels but fathers using more severe punishments and higher levels of physical restraint. A number of studies have also reported a correlation between levels of physical punishment and misbehaviour and aggression in children (Smith, Cowie & Blades, 2004).

It is difficult to know precisely how many children are killed and seriously non-accidentally injured. In a study covering England and Wales between 1985 and 1995, an average of 335 children and teenagers died as a result of homicide, suicide and injuries of undetermined intent per annum (Roberts, Li & Barker, 1998). Earlier estimates had suggested that around 200 children are killed annually (Creighton & Noyes, 1989). Except for suicide, steep social class gradients for each category of intentional injury and homicide are evident. The rates for children in social class V are reported to be seventeen times greater than for children in social class I. Taking all intentional injury, homicide, suicide and injuries of undetermined intent, the relative risk of death for manual versus non-manual occupational groups was higher for the four-year period 1992–1995 than in the four-year period 1980–1983. This is suggestive of increasing social class differences (Roberts, Li & Barker, 1998).

A recent study in Wales suggests that severe abuse is six times more common in babies (54/100,000/year, 95% CI +/− 17.2) compared to children from 1 year to 4 years of age (9.2/100,000/year, 95% CI +/− 3.6). It is around 120 times more common than in 5- to 13-year-olds (0.47/100,000/year, 95% CI +/− 0.47). The researchers found this was mainly associated with two types of serious abuse (brain injury, including subdural haemorrhage, and fractures) more commonly seen in babies under the age of 1 year than in older children.[3] Overall, they suggested that this equated to 1 baby in 880 being abused in the first year of life. Risk was significantly greater in urban areas and boys were consistently at greater risk than girls ($p <$ .025) (Sibert, Payne, Kemp et al., 2002). The extent of unreported abuse has been the subject of concern and remains difficult to ascertain. It seems probable that there is a significant pool of unreported physical and sexual abuse of older children, the true nature and extent of which is unclear (Crighton, 2006c; Towl & Crighton, 1996). Similar patterns have been noted in the United States, with the number of deaths peaking on the first day of life (infanticide), in the early years of childhood (child abuse), and at the end of adolescence for boys (Crittenden & Craig, 1990). Boys are at greater risk of physical abuse than girls, with girls being at greater risk of sexual abuse. Mothers and fathers seem to be equally likely to perpetrate serious physical abuse but 95 per cent of convicted sexual abusers are men.[4] The risk of abuse by step-parents also seems to be markedly increased.

Links between attachment and abuse have been researched. Abusing parents are more likely to show insecure attachment patterns than non-abusing parents. In a study of 124 mothers in the United States, attachment was assessed using the Separation Anxiety Test (SAT). Adequate mothers in the study generally showed warm and supportive relationships with their children. In contrast, abusing mothers often conceptualised their relationship with their children in terms of power struggles and neglectful mothers tended to see the relationship as emotionally empty (Crittenden, 1998).

Abuse of children has been demonstrated to have potentially wide-ranging and long-lasting effects. A review of childhood physical abuse found links with adolescent criminal behaviour, adult familial violence and non-familial violence (Malinoski-Rummel & Hansen, 1993). Childhood sexual abuse has also been identified as being associated with long-term mental health problems. In both cases, though, such negative effects could be moderated by positive factors such as good availability of support and the use of effective ways to appraise, understand and deal with such experiences.

Peer Groups

Children are interested in peers from an early age, initially in the form of low level social behaviours such as looking, smiling, sharing toys and so on. Later interactions with peers become more complex as the ability to socially interact develops. There is a clear pattern of development for peer interactions beginning in the preschool years. Here children will engage in solitary play for much of the time. However, they will also engage in parallel play, where they play similar 'games' alongside other children, without socially interacting. Group play begins in the form of relatively simple games, with levels of group play increasing during free play outdoors and decreasing for indoor structured activities.

From around six years of age, the most striking characteristic of peer interactions is gender separation. From this age until puberty, boys tend to interact with boys and girls with girls. Marked differences in the types of peer activity also emerge. Boys tend to focus on group games, often competitive and often involving structured rules. They tend to play in larger groups, with wider age ranges. Girls in contrast tend to focus more on exclusive friendships and play in smaller groups, with greater emphasis on intimacy (Maccoby, 1998).

Adolescence again sees a marked change, with large same-sex groupings being common. This period of development also sees the re-emergence of social relationships between the genders, with sexual relationships increasingly important towards later adolescence. Initiation of contact with the opposite sex tends to be by the most mature or high status within social groupings.

It has been noted that a number of children tend to be left out of social groupings either because they are rejected or neglected. There are a variety of reasons for this but some key factors have been identified. The largest proportion is rejected because of high levels of aggressive behaviour, with such children also tending to be dishonest, impulsive and non-cooperative with their peers. This is also the most stable group in terms of ongoing rejection by peers and shows associated problems in terms of poor academic performance. A smaller group of children appear to be rejected by peers for being too submissive but the rejection of this group is less stable and tends not to be associated with academic problems. It is also clear that children can 'escape' from being rejected by peers. A key factor here appears to be the child's own perception of their social status, having an internal locus of control and high levels of parental monitoring. Participation in extra curricula activities was also associated with leaving rejected status behind. Interestingly, in the case of older boys, aggression could also be useful in not continuing to be rejected. This appears to be a way in which older boys can assert higher social status and so join in peer activities (Sandstrom & Coie, 1999).

A number of children are popular within peer groups and these children tend to have good social skills, not being withdrawn or showing high levels of aggression. Perceived physical attractiveness also seems to play a part in girls but not boys. The relationship between aggression and popularity seems complex and varies as a function of age. In young children, aggressive peers were markedly unpopular. For adolescents, in contrast, aggression could act to increase popularity and could be used by socially skilled children to gain standing amongst peers. Neglected children seem quite different from unpopular children, tending to be pro-social and compliant. As such they tended to be liked by teachers but ignored by peers, linked to low levels of sociability and increased levels of social withdrawal (Newcombe, Bukowski & Patee, 1993).

A longitudinal study in New Zealand found that problem relationships with peers at age 9 years predicted educational underachievement and unemployment at age 18. On further analysis, it was clear that adverse family situations, socio-economic factors and low IQ explained some of this observed association, but that problems with peer relationships did link directly with a number of later interpersonal problems not accounted for by such factors (Woodward & Fergusson, 2000).

Aggressive Behaviour

A small number of children show high levels of aggression outside the normal bounds and this has been shown to be associated with later delinquent and criminal behaviour (Farrington, 1995; Loeber & Farrington, 1999; Piquero, Farrington & Blumstein, 2007). A number of explanations for this have been suggested and it seems likely that there is a limited genetic contribution to such variation. An association between high levels of aggression and low self-esteem has not been supported by research. There is however considerable evidence of correlation between poor home circumstances and aggression. In particular, high levels of aggression in children have been associated with a lack of parental warmth, poor parental monitoring of activities and ineffective discipline at home (Patterson & Bank, 1989).

High levels of aggression also appear to be linked to academic failure and peer rejection, although during adolescence antisocial peer groups may play an important role. Such children tend to form antisocial peer groups, which may result in escalation of behaviour (Berndt & Keefe, 1995).

Pro-social Behaviour

Pro-social behaviours are seen early in some children at around 2 years old, with simple behaviours such as comforting another child who is upset, or sharing toys. Before this age, children may become upset when another child does, but little or no comforting behaviours are seen. The appearance of such behaviours in some children seems to be linked to the development of sympathy and empathy.

This process has been studied experimentally using a variety of paradigms. Attempts have been made to experimentally increase the level of pro-social behaviours by either having an adult model generosity to others, or using a teaching group where children are encouraged to be generous. The results suggested that modelling has a marked effect on behaviours in the teaching group but only a small effect on subsequent behaviour outside the group. On follow-up three weeks later, little observable effect is present

(Grusec, Saas-Kortsaak & Simutis, 1978). Such studies have been criticised on a number of grounds, including the suggestion that they are measuring social compliance rather than pro-social behaviour. Yet the broad finding from such studies, that the ability to take the perspective of others is a key factor in emotional responsiveness to others, does seem to be well founded (Grusec, Davidoff & Lundell, 2002).

A number of elements seem central to development of this ability and early family environment seems especially important. There is a positive correlation between children's behaviours and their mothers assessed empathy, scores on perspective-taking assessments and ability to respond sensitively to their children. Interactions with siblings are also likely to be important, with pro-social behaviours developing early and showing high levels of consistency. This is not simply a process of unfolding cognitive abilities, rather self-concern and affective experiences play key developmental roles here (Dunn, 1992; Dunn & Kendrick, 1982).

A number of gender differences have been noted in such behaviours, with girls generally being better at peaceful conflict resolution, with boys more likely to use physical aggression. Girls have, however, been reported to use more indirect or 'relational' aggression, such as social exclusion (Björkvist, Österman & Kaukiainen, 2000). Boys are less likely to use such indirect aggression or indeed to be motivated to intervene to prevent such behaviour.

There appears to be a generally straightforward pattern of development over time in girls with the ability to empathise increasing, along with the ability to intervene to reduce distress. For boys, a similar pattern is seen as for girls in distress but at older ages the likelihood of intervention for a boy in distress begins to reduce. It has been suggested that this may be linked to notions of masculinity and to boys wishing to retain status amongst male peers as they get older (Olweus & Endresen, 1998). Later research has cast doubt on this simplistic analysis, noting that girls are in fact no more likely than boys to provide comfort and help. Girls are however more likely to act pro-socially when the person in need is an adult rather than a child and they are more likely to self-report pro-social behaviours (Grusec, Davidoff & Lundell, 2002).

There is evidence of some cultural differences in such behaviours as reported in a study that looked at four countries – Finland, Poland, Israel and Italy. In this study, Finnish and Israeli children tended to use more constructive approaches to resolving conflicts. Finnish children also tended to withdraw earliest from conflicts, whilst Polish children used the least conflict resolution. Girls were observed to use more conflict resolution approaches than boys and to more frequently seek third-party

Table 3.2 Piaget and Kohlberg's stage models of moral development

Piagetian stage	Characteristics	Kohlberg stage	Characteristics
1. Pre-moral	Where the moral rules are not understood	1. Punishment and obedience orientation	Moral rules are understood in terms of punishment by those with superior power. Obedience is valued for its own sake.
2. Moral realism	Where moral rules are seen as coming from a higher authority	2. Individualism (instrumental purpose and exchange)	Moral rules are understood in terms of immediate self-interest. What is good is what brings pleasant results.
3. Moral Subjectivism	Rules are seen as mutually agreed	3. Mutual interpersonal expectations, relationships and conformity	Moral actions are understood in terms of the expectations of family or other significant groups. 'Being good' becomes important for its own sake.
		4. Social systems and conscience	Moral actions come to be defined by larger groups or by society as a whole. Laws and rules should be upheld except in extreme cases.
		5. Social contract and individual rights	Moral actions come to be understood in terms of their utility, achieving the greatest good for the greatest number.
		6. Universal ethical principles	Moral actions come to be understood in terms of self-chosen ethical principles. These are part of an integrated, reasoned and consistently followed pattern of actions.

interventions. Girls were also more likely to use indirect approaches to escalate conflicts (Österman, Björkvist, Lagerspetz *et al.*, 1997).

Moral Reasoning

Early psychological research on the role of moral reasoning can be traced back to the work of Jean Piaget (Piaget, 1977[1932]). In this, a three-stage pattern of development was suggested:

1. Pre-moral   where the moral rules are not understood;
2. Moral realism   where moral rules are seen as coming from a higher authority;
3. Moral subjectivism where rules are seen as mutually agreed.

In a later longitudinal study in the United States, a six-stage model of moral reasoning was suggested (Kohlberg, 1969). This research has been subject to a number of criticisms and subsequent refinements, but five of the six stages have been consistently identified across cultures and for men and women.

Later approaches to moral development have suggested that children's thinking is organised from an early age into 'domains' of 'morality' and 'social convention'. The former tends to be seen by children as unchangeable but the latter is changeable by authority figures, or by mutual agreement. This complex distinction has been reported as evident as early as 4 years of age (Turiel, 1998).

Adolescence

Adolescence can be defined as the transition period from childhood to adulthood, with the physiological changes at this time often referred to as puberty. The age of transition varies between individuals and tends to be later for boys than for girls. For girls, the full range of physical changes usually ends at around 17 years and for boys around 21 years, with the end of skeletal growth. The most marked changes are related to the achievement of reproductive maturity and an associated growth spurt. Children at this time also experience very marked endocrine changes.

There is evidence to suggest a genetic component to the onset of puberty but it is also subject to strong environmental influences. Undernourished children tend to experience delayed onset. Likewise, poorer children tend to show later onset of puberty except for the most developed industrial nations where this trend is less evident.

A number of clear psychological effects have been observed during this developmental phase. Levels of parent–child contact tend to reduce, with increased peer-group contact. Levels of risk-taking behaviour also increase (Arnett, 1999). A number of theorists have stressed the importance of sociocultural factors in mediating the nature of development at this stage of life. Indeed, many traditional cultures have formal ceremonies to mark this transition (Erikson, 1968).

Adolescence is also the time when levels of antisocial, delinquent and criminal behaviours increase rapidly and reach a peak. Longitudinal studies suggest a number of predictors associated with such behaviours. At age 8, the best predictors of subsequent offending are hyperactivity, impulsivity, attention deficits, marital discord between the child's parents, harsh or erratic parenting and socio-economic deprivation (Farrington & West, 1990; Farrington, Loeber & Van Kammen, 1990; Shepherd & Farrington, 1995). Separation from a parent for reasons other than death or illness has also been shown to be significant (Farrington, Loeber & Van Kammen, 1990). Evidence from studies on vulnerability and resilience suggests that such factors can act cumulatively and may act synergistically (Farrington, 1994; Piquero, Farrington & Blumstein, 2007). The provision of family support and training for parents, along with good quality preschool education, have been shown in randomised studies to produce long-term benefits when effectively targeted (Farrington, 1994).

Family Relationships

Adolescence is often portrayed as a time of increased family conflict and disturbed family relationships. Recent evidence suggests that this may have been overstated for the majority of children. In a study of 3000 young people aged 13–19 years, evidence of disturbances to sleep patterns was found. Those studied tended to go to bed late and rise late but overall got less sleep than younger children. Some evidence of negative and depressed mood was reported but this seemed largely associated with a lack of sleep (Wolfson & Carskadon, 1998).

A study of 483 10–14-year-olds reported significantly more negative affect amongst the 12–14-year-olds than for the younger children. This was partly accounted for by negative life events connected with family, school and peers (Larson & Ham, 1993). A large-scale study in the UK of 2303 children aged 14–15 years assessed two sub-samples of 200 and 304 in more depth. Here, one in six parents reported altercations or arguments with their children, although they did report higher rates of disapproval of relatively minor issues such as clothing and hairstyles. Interestingly a slightly higher proportion of children reported such disagreements and one in three made detailed criticism of their parents. Perhaps against expectations, though, the vast majority of parents reported approving of their children's friends.

Overall the researchers' findings did not confirm the notion of adolescence as generally a time of great conflict between parents and children for most families. They did though identify a small subgroup that was characterised by high levels of conflict and in some cases outright rejection of their parents. This pattern was much more common in children with prior histories of behavioural or psychiatric problems (Rutter, Graham & Chadwick et al., 1976).

The increased importance of peer groups during this time has been largely supported by research. Adolescents spent more time with their peers than younger children and conformity with peers peaks during this time. This appears especially marked for antisocial behaviours and the effect may well be stronger in boys than girls (Coleman, 1980).

Summary

- Development can be defined as a lifelong process, although to date most research has focused on childhood and adolescence, largely on the basis that this is the period of most rapid change.
- Historically, research in developmental psychology has perhaps been overly focused on dyadic relationships between child and primary caregiver. Recent research has increasingly focused on more family systems-based approaches.
- Development occurs within an ecological context which involves complex interactions at individual, group, intergroup and social and economic levels. An adequate understanding of development needs to take such levels into account.
- The role of attachment and bonding in development has been long recognised. Early bonding of mothers to their babies usually takes place within 6 to 12 hours post partum. Recent research suggests, though, that infants and mothers are more robust in forming attachments than once thought, with only small adverse effects being observable where initial bonding is disrupted. Young children also seem well able to have multiple attachment figures, showing different patterns of attachment with different people.
- Individual differences in attachment relationships have been subject to extensive study and two major explanatory models of attachment

behaviour have developed: the 'ABCD' model and the parallel Dynamic-Maturational Model (DMM). These approach attachment from differing directions, one from studies of normal attachment and safety with a discovery of disorganisation, the other from abnormality and danger with a discovery of an age-related array of organised self-protective strategies.

- Although much has been written about the effects of children's temperament on attachment, there is little evidence that this alone has a direct effect. Three decades of research have revealed a complex picture, with differences resulting from dyadic characteristics between the child and its caregivers. As a consequence of these findings, transactional models of parent–child interaction are currently favoured.

- Research during the 1990s increasingly came to see attachment as a construct with application across people's whole life, rather than just childhood. With increasing age, it seems likely that attachment becomes increasingly internalised in the form of mental models of attachment figures. Individuals with a history of secure attachment seem likely to develop models based on trust and affection. Those with insecure attachments may develop models based on threat.

- Survey data suggests that a majority of parents in the UK smack or hit their children at some point, with mothers and fathers showing similar levels but fathers using more severe physical punishment. A number of studies have also reported a correlation between levels of physical punishment and misbehaviour and aggression in children. It seems reasonable to conclude that physical punishment of children is at best generally ineffective.

- It is difficult to know precisely how many children are killed and seriously non-accidentally injured. Studies in the UK suggest around 300 children and teenagers die as a result of homicide, suicide and injuries of undetermined intent per year. The death rates for children in social class V are reported to be 17 times greater than for children in social class I.

- Abuse of children has been demonstrated to have potentially wide-ranging and long-lasting effects, with links between childhood physical abuse and adolescent criminal behaviour, adult familial violence and non-familial violence. Childhood sexual abuse has also been identified as being associated with long-term mental health problems. In both, negative effects may be moderated by positive factors such as good availability of support and the use of effective ways to appraise, understand and deal with such experiences.

- Peer group influences are of marked and increasing importance through-out childhood. Acceptance tends to be associated with the ability to use a range of pro-social behaviours in interacting with peers. Socially with-drawn or aggressive children tend to be neglected or rejected more frequently than pro-social peers.
- Adolescence is the time when antisocial, delinquent and criminal behaviour peaks. Longitudinal studies suggest that the extent of disturbed behaviour in most families is moderate. For those with histories of problem behaviours or mental health difficulties, however, it may represent a time of marked escalation. A number of predictors of such outcomes have been identified, suggesting a number of potential early interventions to address antisocial, delinquent and criminal behaviour.

Notes

1 Down's syndrome results from the presence, due to various causes, of all or part of an extra 21st chromosome (21 trisomy).

2 Sociobiological explanations are also criticised, often inaccurately, on the basis that they are not testable in the way that scientific hypotheses should be. As such, it has been at times unfairly suggested that they are often 'just so' stories (Holcombe, 1996).

3 One major factor in this is likely to concern rates of detection. Assaults on infants are likely to result in life-threatening and obvious injury requiring urgent medical intervention. In older children, similar assaults may be more likely to go undetected.

4 An important caveat here is that much of what we know about sexual offenders is based on the small minority who are successfully prosecuted through the criminal justice system (Crighton, 2005b; Towl, 2006).

Chapter 4

Prisoner Needs

Introduction

It is difficult to overemphasise the importance of ensuring that services, whether psychological or otherwise, are based on needs. With around 1000 directly employed psychological staff[1] and additional contracted staff, engaged in work across 140 prisons, psychology has the potential to make a key and growing contribution to ensuring increasingly needs-driven services.

There have been numerous and wide-ranging contributions over the past century to a psychological conceptualisation of human needs. The starting point for much of this work has been an understanding of the individual (Adler, 1992; Harre, 1984). Others have been more focused on what might be construed as adaptation to social contexts, developing hierarchical models of what might broadly be seen as mental health (Vaillant, 1998) and needs (Maslow, 1970).

Much of the work of psychologists in prisons has historically been undertaken with the express intention of assessing the risk of reoffending and this continues to be a major focus. Unsurprisingly perhaps, forensic psychologists have undertaken the majority of this, sometimes working with prisoners to reduce risk of reoffending. This has clear importance for criminal-justice-based practitioners, feeding into the core objectives of public protection and helping prisoners lead law-abiding and useful lives.

It is perhaps helpful at this point to put prisoner needs into context. In a survey study of prisoners conducted in the late 1990s for the Department of Health, it was reported that high levels of mental health problems were present. The rates of prisoners with depression in the prior twelve-month period ranged from 39 per cent for sentenced men up to 75 per cent for women on remand; 10 per cent of men and 14 per cent of women on remand have a history of psychosis. More than two thirds of men and women have a history of abusing illicit drugs (Singleton, Meltzer, Gatward *et al.*, 1998). Similar findings were reported in a study by the Social Exclusion Unit (2002) which found that 70 per cent of prisoners reported a wide range of needs and high levels of mental health problems.

In line with the view that prisoners present with complex multifaceted needs, it has been argued that work with prisoners will need to be multimodal, with a focus on those prisoners with the greatest needs (Harper & Chitty, 2005). Within such an approach it seems essential that issues of risk, need and what might broadly be termed 'readiness to change' are all taken into account, yet it has been noted that this latter area has been largely neglected in favour of a simple risk–needs model. This suggests that it is sufficient to rely on an analysis of risk and needs, followed by allocation to predetermined interventions (Hollin, 2002; Latissa, Cullen & Gendreau, 2002). A number of commentators have expressed concerns about this unduly simplistic approach on a number of grounds. These have included serious concerns that such an analysis neglects key aspects of the readiness for and response to interventions (Hodge & Renwick, 2002; Howells & Day, 2003; Howells, Day, Bubner *et al.*, 2002; Thomas-Peter, 2006b; Towl, 2004a, 2004b). In turn, it has been noted that attempts to intervene with offenders regardless of their readiness to change may yield undesirable effects (Hodge & Renwick, 2002; Howells & Day, 2003; Thomas-Peter, 2006b). In support of these views, there is evidence suggesting that those who fail in treatment do worse in terms of subsequent risk, although the precise reasons for this remain unclear (Crighton & Towl, 2007; Lösel & Schmucker, 2005).

Such mechanistic psychological models based on such simplistic 'risk–needs' analysis seem clear since they tend to lead to simple mechanistic responses. These in turn dovetail neatly with managerialist approaches. They are easy to explain and market, promising straightforward solutions to complex problems, easily broken down into 'pre-measured outputs'. Such promise is, however, misleading and such models run the risk of being, at best, ineffective and at worst leading to adverse outcomes and poorer public protection.

If the needs of prisoners are to be effectively addressed, an alternative and more conceptually coherent approach is needed, with a broader-based understanding of needs (Crighton, 2005a; Harper & Chitty, 2005; Hayles, 2006; Hedderman, 2007; Thomas-Peter, 2006b; Towl, 2004a). An important starting point is recognising that many prisoner needs may not be primarily psychological. The framework suggested by Maslow makes this clear, with more 'basic' physical needs at the base of the hierarchy. Of course such needs may impact psychologically and relationships between needs and outcomes will often interact. In some, depression may be associated with substance abuse and, in turn, accommodation difficulties. In others, homelessness, poor education and low income may be risk factors for depression. Needs are often associated in complex and interactive ways. As a result simple, risk–needs psychological models may have marginal utility. Attempts to separate 'psychological needs' from other 'needs' in this way run the risk of being misleading, misplaced and potentially harmful.

The fundamental human needs of prisoners are no different from those of everyone else and can be seen in similarly hierarchical terms, with issues like housing at the base of the hierarchy, work and education in the middle layers and areas such as attitudes to offending at the apex. Recently much of the work of psychologists in prisons can be convincingly criticised for an undue focus on the apex of this hierarchy of need and, indeed, narrow areas within this apex. However, there is in fact little convincing evidence to suggest that simply changing attitudes will produce changes in behaviour. Indeed, much of the evidence base in psychology suggests that attitudes often follow behaviour (Festinger, 1957). In practice, any benefits of work at the apex of such a model are unlikely to be realised in the absence of prior effective work being undertaken and consolidated at the other levels of need in the framework. As such, a diverse range of interventions is needed to address each of these,[2] starting with the foundations needed for long-term change; what might be termed as 'readiness' to change (Crighton, 2005a; Towl, 2005a).

Prisoner Needs

Prisoner needs might usefully be described under three main headings: physical health needs, mental health needs and social needs. This is heuristically helpful but should not diminish the significance of the interaction and overlap of such needs. The use of largely arbitrary separation of needs does, hopefully, serve the useful function of making presentation of this complexity clearer.

Physical Health Needs

The prison population tends to be relatively young and, as such, could be expected to show relatively good levels of physical health. Behind this generalisation, though, the evidence suggests that prisoners engage in a range of behaviours likely to have negative impacts on physical health. In particular, elevated levels of smoking, alcohol and other substance misuse are evident (Marshall, Simpson & Stevens, 2000).

Over the years, psychologists working in prisons have not tended to focus on such physical health needs. There are nonetheless some examples of engagement with these needs, with psychological studies in the area of Acquired Immunodeficiency Viruses and the Human Immunodeficiency Virus (HIV) (Curran, McHugh & Nooney, 1989).

In the early 1990s, 'The Health of the Nation', a policy document on the development of health services, was published (Department of Health, 1992). It included a focus on five key aspects of health-related behaviours: smoking, drinking, drug use, physical activity levels and diet. This was subsequently built upon in the context of prisons, with the commission of a national survey of physical health in male prisoners (Bridgwood & Malbon, 1995). This survey sampled 992 sentenced male prisoners and revealed a great deal about their health. The study comprised three parts: a prisoner record search to establish the length of sentence; a 25- to 35-minute interview covering health and health-related behaviours; and a longer assessment conducted by a nurse where a number of physical measurements were taken.

The sample covered 32 of 139 prisons in England and Wales, with 85 per cent of prisoners approached agreeing to take part. The study noted that the prison population is on average markedly younger than the general population. This suggests the need for considerable caution when drawing comparisons with the general population in the absence of efforts even to match for age.

Smoking was reported as commonplace in prisons, with prisoners aged 18–49 more than twice as likely to be smokers as the general population at 81 per cent. This was slightly more marked in the percentages reporting smoking amongst younger age groups (16 to 24 years). A later study reported levels of smoking in prisoners as a risk factor for cardiovascular disease. The results were striking, with only 15 per cent of male remand prisoners and 23 per cent of male sentenced prisoners reporting as non-smokers. For women, only 18 per cent of remand and sentenced prisoners reported being non-smokers (Singleton, Meltzer, Gatward et al., 1998). Of smokers in prison, around a quarter of men and a third of women prisoners were described as heavy smokers (Marshall, Simpson & Stevens, 2000).

Within the general population, smoking has been in decline and there has been an increasing level of restriction of smoking in public areas. The question of whether prisons should be smoke-free areas will undoubtedly arise again over the coming years. In 2006, exemption for prisons was granted on the basis that they are permanently or temporarily an individual's home rather than a public place. In practice, though, prisoners are often required to share cells and hence no guarantee can be given that non-smokers will have the choice of a smoke-free environment. Nonetheless, there has been significant movement within prisons towards becoming smoke-free environments.

Through direct work and the dissemination of psychological therapies, applied psychologists potentially have a great deal to contribute to support for prisoners to reduce or stop smoking (Marks & Sykes, 2002). Given the strong link between smoking and cardiovascular disease and the enormous human and economic costs, reducing the levels of smoking remains a long-standing public health goal. There is the opportunity here to work with 'high risk' groups in reducing smoking and the lack of such work to date is surprising. There is also considerable scope to advise prison managers on moves towards smoke-free environments at a more strategic level.

A second major area of concern is alcohol consumption. This is an area which again has received too little attention from psychological staff working with prisoners. Prisoners are at high risk of alcohol misuse. Such misuse is associated with negative criminal justice and public health outcomes, suggesting the potential to impact significantly on improving the health of prisoners and to reduce risk and levels of reoffending, with much violent youth crime being fuelled by alcohol (Morgan, 2005; Scottish Executive, 1999).

Amongst prisoners under 21, 82 per cent reported heavy drinking compared with 25 per cent of prisoners in the 45-and-over age group. A range of psychological treatments has been developed to help individuals reduce alcohol consumption and the health benefits from these are potentially great. Successful intervention here is also likely to impact in economic and human terms across the full range of healthcare services, from Ambulance and Paramedical Services through to hospital-based specialist liver services affected by the earlier onset of alcohol related cirrhosis of the liver (Department of Health, 2001).

There is surprisingly little firm data on the levels of physical activity in prisoners. Many younger prisoners tend to be physically active in custody as perhaps reflected in some physical measures. Prisoners tend to have lower Body Mass Index (BMI) scores than the general population (Bridgwood & Malbon, 1995). This perhaps reflects access for many to a better diet when in custody and also improved access to structured physical education, gymnasium facilities and also reduced access to television and video games.

Context

Diet is a key aspect of health; prisoners interviewed for the 1995 study reported eating less fruit and vegetables but also less fatty processed foods than prior to imprisonment. They reported eating less sweets, biscuits and cakes. Attitudes towards food have a potentially major impact on body weight and composition with obesity a growing cause of morbidity and mortality. Links between diet and behaviour have been less extensively researched but impacts seem likely. In this particular area, prisoners appear significantly healthier than similarly aged peers, with rates of obesity measured at 6 per cent of the prisoner population compared with 12 per cent of the general population. Similarly, systolic blood pressure of prisoners was significantly lower (Bridgwood & Malbon, 1995). Prisoners seem to make physical health gains whilst in custody, with improved diet, reduced alcohol and drug use and better access to health care all playing a part. It is, however, unclear to what extent such gains in prison are maintained on return to the community in the form of long-term changes in health behaviours. Overall, though, this picture suggests a positive basis on which to undertake psychological work with a view to improving long-term health outcomes and also in some areas to potentially reducing the risk of reoffending.

Mental Health Needs

Given the extent of mental health problems in prisoners, these have tended to be more to the fore in terms of policy and practice than physical health needs. In many areas of research and practice, however, the fields of physical and mental health are miscible. Drug misuse provides a clear example of this and may result in particular physical and mental health needs.

The evidence base in mental health is better developed than that for physical health but it does come with some major caveats. One of these is that a number of the observations about mental health can be criticised as somewhat tautological. This can be a more general problem with categorical approaches where the categorisation is mistakenly used to both describe and account for particular behaviour or outcomes, something that may be amplified in prisons. Perhaps the most marked example of such a tautological error in the context of prisons is the use of the notion of 'antisocial personality disorder'. Individuals are categorised as such, largely on the basis of antisocial behaviours. The notion is then sometimes used, with circularity, to describe the prison population and account for their antisocial behaviour.

A further necessary caveat is that methodologically there is a clear potential for some response bias. In seeking to address areas of mental

62

health, such as intentional self-injury, researchers have often been keen to stress anticipation of high levels of positive responding. Questions on such areas have therefore tended to be positively framed, and skewed in the direction of the 'normalisation' of such acts, in an effort to avoid negative-response bias with prisoners underreporting such difficulties. This in turn creates a risk that interviewees will take this as a steer to report such feelings, whether or not they have them. Prisoners are by definition often in a vulnerable situation and will generally be rewarded for compliance. This may in turn generate positive-response bias with prisoners keen to give what they perceive to be the 'right' answer.

The most detailed study of the prevalence of mental disorder amongst prisoners to date was undertaken in 1997 with the explicit aim of the collection of baseline data on the mental health of male and female prisoners across age groups (Singleton, Meltzer, Gatward *et al.*, 1998). The study involved a large sample of prisoners (n = 3563), of whom 88 per cent (n = 3142) were interviewed by researchers. It is a detailed study with a rich data-set that was intended to inform policy and it has made a significant contribution to our understanding of this challenging area.

The study used fixed sample fractions to identify 1 in 34 sentenced men, 1 in 8 men on remand and 1 in 3 women prisoners both sentenced and remanded. The study involved interviews with prisoners by both lay and health professionals. Significantly, the study used an explicit methodology with defined operational terms, making the study highly replicable. Ethnic- and gender-based differences in diagnostic categories were covered in the study; an important contrast with earlier research.

The majority of findings were reported in three sub-samples: male remand prisoners, male sentenced prisoners and female remand and sentenced prisoners as one group. Strikingly, over half the male-remand sub-sample had no educational qualifications at all and just over a third indicated they had been in legal work prior to imprisonment. The prevalence rates for mental disorders in the sub-samples were high, with diagnosis of personality disorder being very common indeed. Using the Diagnostic and Statistical Manual IV (DSM IV) categories, 78 per cent of male remand prisoners, 64 per cent of male sentenced prisoners and 31 per cent of female prisoners were deemed to have 'personality disorders'. Antisocial personality disorder was reported to be the most common, with 63 per cent (male remand), 49 per cent (male sentenced) and 31 per cent (female remand and sentenced) meeting the criteria for this category. Interestingly, all the women deemed to be experiencing personality disorders appear to have fallen under the antisocial personality disorder category. For men, a broader range of reported personality disorders was noted.

There were some differences in the identification of psychotic experiences between the clinical and lay interviewers. In general, rates ranged between 4 per cent and 21 per cent overall, with a tendency towards the lower end of these figures for sentenced male prisoners. The reported rates for women on remand were about twice those for men. It should be noted that these figures covered psychotic experiences for up to a year before the interviews took place, so many of the psychotic experiences may have pre-dated imprisonment.

Coverage of 'self-harm' within this study used a broad definition that included suicidal ideation, suicide attempts and what the authors have referred to as 'parasuicide'. In terms of the reported results, 2 per cent of male remand prisoners reported attempting suicide in the previous week, with remand prisoners reporting slightly higher levels of suicidal ideation and attempts. In general, there appear to have been higher rates of broadly defined 'self-harm' for white prisoners than black prisoners, a finding consistent with large-scale empirical studies into prisoner suicides (Crighton, 2000b; Towl & Crighton, 1998).

Alcohol and drug misuse illustrates well the interaction between areas of need affecting both physical and mental health. In this critical area, white prisoners were more likely to report problems and the rate of misuse for white remand prisoners was just under double that for black remand prisoners. White prisoners were also more likely to report misuse of opiates and stimulants. Women prisoners held on remand showed higher reported levels of injecting drug, 28 per cent having injected drugs in the month before their imprisonment and 40 per cent injecting drugs at some time. Overall, just under half of prisoners reported a measure of dependence on drugs in the year before imprisonment. It is perhaps worth noting that there were some marked age-related differences in reported drug misuse showing a strong inverse association between dependence on drugs in the year prior to imprisonment and age.

In summary, prisoners categorised as personality disordered tended to be younger and were more frequently unmarried, white and charged with acquisitive offences. Those with significant alcohol problems tended to be more likely to be aged 16 to 24, unmarried, white and held for violence. About half of the women studied were on prescribed drugs and about a fifth of men, commonly being prescribed hypnotics, anxiolytics and antipsychotic drugs. Unsurprisingly, perhaps, reported levels of multiple problems were common. A finding of particular concern was that healthcare staff had often appeared not to help prisoners with drug misuse problems. The proportion that reported being declined help since coming into prison was almost double that of those who had had requests declined before their imprisonment. It seems likely that this will have changed significantly since the research was undertaken as a result of significant investment in drugs interventions for prisoners in recent years (Towl, 2006).

The public discourse on prisoners is often conducted as if they are not members of the public themselves, yet evidently they are (Faulkner, 2006a, 2006b; Towl, 2005b). Evidence shows that, as members of the public, they have not always been protected as effectively as many others. One in three women and one in ten men in prison report they have been victims of sexual abuse. Given the well-documented high levels of underreporting of sexual crimes, this may underestimate actual levels of sexual abuse. High numbers of women prisoners in particular also report having been victims of family violence. This combination of being victims of crime with the manifestation of behaviours associated with mental disorders results in a group of people with potentially very high levels of mental health needs. This problem is exacerbated by what appears to be a mainstream professional reluctance to work with this group of people with high levels of need.

Recent efforts have been made to address these concerns effectively with moves to 'mainstream' services to prisoners to bring their care and support into line with that in the community. Although affected by marked regional and local variations in health provision, this has often included the provision of multidisciplinary 'in-reach' teams to work in prison settings in a similar way to that of community mental health teams for adults and children. In many respects, this has involved an important shift in philosophy and policy, away from interventions provided largely through forensic services and towards services provided through mainstream NHS services (Cinamon & Bradshaw, 2005; Lane-Morton, 2005; Towl & Crighton, 2006). This shift has a number of advantages. Many of the problems faced by prisoners are not specifically 'forensic' so the previous practice of referring all prisoners through forensic services has had a number of undesirable consequences. Unnecessary processes have been built into the system resulting in delays in access to appropriate services or indeed non-access. Related to this, prisoners have sometimes fallen through gaps created between organisations, with specialist forensic services feeling that problems could be best addressed by general service practitioners and general service practitioners denying access on the basis of the person having a sometimes relatively minor criminal background. Such systems have led to wasted time and effort, poor use of scarce highly skilled resources within forensic services, and also a loss of skills and expertise within general mental health services in working with many of those in greatest need.

There is considerable future potential for psychology to contribute to meeting the pressing mental health needs that face prisons. General mental health services will need to provide interventions that address the needs of socially excluded groups such as prisoners. Applied psychologists and psychology has scope to offer a great deal in this context. Indeed, it has been suggested that such work should become fundamental to the training of applied psychologists, both as a means of improving service delivery and also as a counter to the development of professional isolationism (Crighton, 2005b).

Social Needs

A Social Exclusion Unit report entitled 'Reducing Re-offending by Ex-Prisoners' provided wide-ranging coverage of factors linked to the risk of reoffending amongst prisoners (Social Exclusion Unit, 2002). In the years immediately preceding this report, there had been an increasingly narrow focus on a small part of the evidence base into reducing reoffending. The report signalled a marked reinvigoration of policy in this area, looking at preventing crime and also addressing the broad-based causes of crime.

The report began by describing the scope of some of the challenges ahead, perhaps most starkly noting that, amongst 18–20-year-old prisoners, 72 per cent are reconvicted within two years of their release from prison and nearly half (47 per cent) are back in prison. Many of the costs of crime such as pain, suffering and the fear of crime are not readily quantifiable in economic terms, although the overall economic costs of crime are salutary enough on their own. Recorded crime by ex-prisoners was estimated to cost about £11 billion[3] a year (Social Exclusion Unit, 2002). To put that figure in some context, it represents just under one third of the cost of the entire National Health Service.

The financial costs of keeping prisoners in custody, although very variable across the prison estate, amount to an average of over £37,500 annually per prisoner (Social Exclusion Unit, 2002). Given that recorded crime broadly is thought to account for between a quarter and a tenth of all crime (depending on the type of crime and method of estimation), this suggests that estimates of the financial cost of crimes may be multiplied accordingly. When additional health costs associated with the poorer physical health of prisoners are added to this, it is clear that there are compelling economic reasons, in addition to obvious moral and social reasons, why improvement of the outlook for prisoners on their release is urgently needed.

The Social Exclusion Unit review highlighted nine factors linked to crime: education, employment, drug and alcohol misuse, mental and physical health, attitudes and self-control, institutionalisation and life skills, housing, financial support and debt and finally family networks. Employment and accommodation provide helpful illustrative examples of these effects. Simply by being in employment, an ex-prisoner's level of risk of reoffending is reduced by between a third and a half. Having stable accommodation reduces the risk by about one fifth (Social Exclusion Unit, 2002).

Prisoners have a number of profound social disadvantages. To illustrate this more specifically, prisoners are 13 times more likely than the general population to have been in local authority care as a child and also about 13 times as likely as the general population to be unemployed. Levels of educational skills amongst prisoners are typically poor, with low levels of literacy and numeracy, ruling them out of much of the employment market. There is a very significant risk that the act of imprisonment itself may serve to increase the risk of reoffending, removing potentially protective factors. Of those prisoners who have been in employment immediately prior to imprisonment, two thirds lost their jobs and one third lost their accommodation whilst in prison.

Applied psychologists working with prisoners need to be acutely mindful of the social disadvantages that prisoners have and the impacts of these. This need is perhaps most marked in key areas of professional psychological practice in prisons such as 'risk assessment'. In recent years, there has been a preoccupation with 'new generation'-structured risk assessment tools, at times to the detriment of an understanding of social and contextual factors. There has been considerable professional enthusiasm for efficient – or short cuts to – accurate risk assessment. Yet there is a need for caution as these generally involve simple models based on relatively weak correlational data. It has been suggested that enthusiasm for such approaches is frequently misplaced and is at times responsible for fundamental misunderstanding about the processes of risk assessment (Crighton, 2005a; Wald & Woolverton, 1990).

Terms such as 'resettlement' are something of a misnomer for many prisoners who may never really have been 'settled' in the first place. Often it is settlement that we are seeking to achieve, rather than an imagined process of 'resettlement' (Hedderman, 2007; Social Exclusion Report, 2002). This is a significantly more difficult challenge, although nationally there are some excellent examples of prison staff making real progress in this, where there is improved partnership working with, amongst others, job centres and housing associations.[4] Such work is by its nature multidisciplinary and regrettably in recent years the involvement of psychologists has become comparatively rare, this despite the potential impact of settlement work in terms of reducing the risk of reoffending.

The Politics of Prisoner Needs

As discussed above all prisoners are members of the public and some members of the public are prisoners (Towl, 2005b). Prisoners are a relatively powerless group within society, tending overwhelmingly to come from the poorer and more socially excluded sections. It is important that applied psychologists working with prisoners understand and acknowledge this if they are to work effectively. The social and cultural environment that prisoners are released, and hopefully settled, into will be the context in which they need to apply any new knowledge, skills and attitudinal changes that they may have benefited from whilst undertaking psychological interventions in prison. It therefore becomes essential that psychologists (and those involved in the delivery of psychological therapies) have a good understanding of the importance of a range of interventions. These need to include interventions that may assist prisoners in getting a job, finding stable accommodation, addressing their drug and alcohol problems and benefiting from improved levels of educational attainment.

Summary

- Psychology has provided numerous and wide-ranging contributions over the past century to the conceptualisation of human needs. A variety of frameworks have been suggested that may be usefully applied to considerations of the nature and structure of services in prisons.
- Much of the work of psychologists in prisons has historically involved assessing risk of reoffending and often working to reduce risk. This has clear importance for criminal-justice-based practitioners, feeding into the core objectives of public protection and helping prisoners lead law-abiding and useful lives. Such work with prisoners over the last decade has, however, been increasingly based on unduly simplistic risk–needs models. This has led to the neglect of factors that do not easily fit this framework and interactions between such factors.
- The prison population tends to be relatively young and may be expected to show relatively good levels of physical health. However, prisoners show high rates of tobacco smoking, heavy alcohol use, illicit drug use, sexually transmitted infections and poor diet. These are associated with poorer long-term health. Applied psychology has the potential to

contribute to change health-related behaviour but, in prisons, relatively little work has been done in this area.

- Many younger prisoners tend to be physically active in custody. Prisoners tend to have lower Body Mass Index (BMI) scores, better diet when in custody and undertake more structured physical activity. For many, being in prison is associated with improvement to health.
- The evidence base on mental health in prisoners is better developed than that for physical health. Detailed studies suggest very high prevalence of mental disorder amongst prisoners Based on DSM IV categories, 78 per cent of male remand prisoners, 64 per cent of male sentenced prisoners and 31 per cent of female prisoners have been identified as having 'personality disorders', with antisocial personality disorder being most common. Rates of depression and intentional self-injury are similarly high.
- Notions of personality disorder have been used to describe and categorise behaviour. They have also been used in a largely circular manner to suggest explanations for observed behaviour.
- Recent progress has been made in 'mainstreaming' services to prisoners, bringing their care and support into line with that found in the community. This has included the provision of multidisciplinary 'in-reach' teams to work in prison settings and shifts in philosophy and policy. There remains considerable potential for further development of applied psychology to contribute to meeting the pressing mental health needs that face prisoners.
- The costs of keeping prisoners in custody are substantial. The human, social and economic costs of criminal reoffending are enormous. There are compelling reasons to improve the outlook for prisoners on their release. Broad-based interventions that address mental and physical health, attitudes and self-control, institutionalisation, life skills, housing, financial support and debt and finally family networks and employment are likely to be most beneficial as part of an integrated programme of care and support.
- Prisoners as a group are drawn from significantly socially disadvantaged groups and applied psychologists need to be acutely mindful of the impacts of this. The social and cultural environment that prisoners are released and hopefully settled into will be the context in which they need to apply any new knowledge, skills and attitudes that they may have benefited from in prison. A good understanding of the importance of the community context is therefore essential to effective practice.

Notes

1   Based on 2004 figures.
2   One example here is the fact that a large proportion of prisoners have been the victims of sexual abuse, yet in recent years this has received little attention (Crighton, 2005c; Lane-Morton, 2005).
3   This equates to approximately $20 billion.
4   An example here is the Canterbury Project, a multidisciplinary approach adopted at a local prison (HMP Canterbury). This local initiative brought together a range of service providers such as housing associations, health and social services, police and probation to work alongside other stakeholders, including potential private sector employers and education providers (Galbally, personal communication, 2001). Such an approach seems to fit well with efforts to address a hierarchy of needs but is less suited to managerialist approaches with 'predetermined outputs'.

Chapter 5

Psychological Assessment

Introduction

In looking at the assessment of prisoners, it is important to start with an understanding of the contextual factors that may have an impact and to ensure that these are taken adequately into account in decision-making. Taking account of the ecological context in this way reflects good professional practice and, with assessment, will lead to more accurate and useful findings.

Prisons are the result of a particular social history within a particular social policy context. A full understanding of this goes well beyond the province of psychology but it is nevertheless important that psychologists working in such institutions have a grasp of this context. Prisons in England and Wales developed primarily from a patchwork of often privately run local and county jails. These tended to hold prisoners for relatively short periods of time, often while awaiting execution and frequently in appalling conditions. Prisons have developed over at least three centuries into a highly centralised prison service under central government control. This service is managed by public sector prisons and also a number of private contractors. It is perhaps worth reflecting on the fact that much of the positive change in prisons in the UK resulted from pressure by external reformers, rather than internally driven moves for reform. John Howard (1726–90) is generally seen as the founding father of prison reform, with Elizabeth Fry (1780–1845) perhaps being the most widely known reformer. Along with others, they began the long process of making prisons more humane and effective institutions (Bardens, 2004).

Prisons are also fundamentally coercive institutions (Towl, 2005a). Unlike many public institutions, prisoners are there because they are directed to be, not because they have exercised any meaningful agency in the process. Of course prisons are not unique in this and other public bodies such as schools are also coercive in the case of children between the ages of 5 and 15 years.[1] Prisons differ, however, in the extent of coercion that may, with legitimacy conferred by the state, be used. Force similar to that of the police or military services can be used within the confines of prisons. Prisons also differ from other public institutions in that they are intentionally and explicitly punitive in nature. They exist, at least in part, to punish by depriving of their liberty those citizens who have been judged to have seriously transgressed society's rules. This has an impact on the character of prisons and presents a number of complex cultural and management challenges. Prisoners themselves also can and do present an array of challenges (Murtagh, 2007).

In common with a number of other institutions, prisons are closed communities and, in this respect, in England and Wales perhaps most closely resemble the asylums built mainly during the eighteenth and nineteenth centuries to house the mentally disordered. Only a comparatively small minority of citizens will ever set foot inside a prison and there is a widespread lack of knowledge about the nature of prisons and prisoners. Like other closed communities, prisons have suffered from the twin problems of isolationism and parochialism. They have tended to develop their own idiosyncratic systems of working and also to be resistant to change, often justified by the very curious appeal to notions such as 'If it isn't broken, don't fix it.' This is an approach that presumably teaches us it is always a bad idea to service an aircraft prior to boarding.

Examples of the isolation of prisons are found graphically in the development, until 2000, of a healthcare system separate from the National Health Service (NHS) and also the development of a psychology service largely outside the mainstream of professional frameworks and standards. In both these examples, very significant progress has been made in recent years to mainstream both services and standards (Cinamon & Bradshaw, 2005; Crighton, 2005a; HM Prison Service & National Probation Service, 2003; Lane-Morton, 2005; Towl, 2004a).

Nonetheless, isolationism remains in the management structures within prisons, those who can manage prisons being limited to a small pool of those already doing so. Curiously, those with managerial experience outside prisons, or designated as 'specialists' within prisons, are in practice largely excluded from such managerial roles. Thus, a lack of diversity is institutionalised and perpetuated. This approach is odd, given the marked similarities between managing prisons and managing any large complex organisation or process (Podmore, 2004; Towl, 2004b).

A further curiosity is the division within prisons between uniformed staff and non-uniformed staff. Essentially for historical reasons, prison officers wear uniforms similar to those of the police and fire services while prison managers and most specialist staff do not wear uniforms.[2] Such practices serve to create and maintain artificial barriers between staff engaged in a similar endeavour. The use of surnames and prison numbers by some staff to address prisoners is another example of institutional practices which serve to create unnecessary barriers and undermine more positive relationships.

Finally, it is important to note that prisons in democratic systems exist in a complex social policy environment. Within England and Wales, they are part of a National Offender Management Service, itself part of the Ministry of Justice and the broader criminal justice system. Prisons are accountable to government and ultimately to the public via their elected representatives. Prisons are also subject to bureaucratic pressures, alongside pressures from media and public opinion. In order to function effectively in the complex environment of prisons, psychologists need to have an awareness of the complexity and challenges presented in their broadest sense.

Psychological Models of Assessment

Scientist-Practitioner Model

The scientist-practitioner model emerged as the preferred approach to the training of clinical psychologists at a conference in Boulder in 1949, often being called the Boulder model as a result. The model was formally adopted by the American Psychological Association (APA) and its use was subsequently adopted in the UK and across other branches of applied psychology. The model stresses the role of scientific approaches to gathering, developing and assessing the evidence base and using this to formulate hypotheses for interventions (Barlow, Hayes & Nelson, 1984; Hecker & Thorpe, 2003).

This model has been subject to ongoing discussion and debate and it is not the only model that has been suggested or indeed that is in use. The scientist-practitioner model has been criticised from two contrasting directions. It has been suggested that the model unduly stresses skills in developing and gathering evidence. Such ostensible research skills are, it is argued, often not used and indeed are largely unnecessary for those engaged in day-to-day practice work. As an alternative, a scholar-practitioner model is advocated. This is concerned with training practitioners to deliver psychological interventions drawing on the existing knowledge base, rather than contributing to developing the knowledge base. Contrastingly, a clinical-scientist model has been suggested and this places greater emphasis on research skills in developing the research base, with more limited coverage of applications of psychology. Moves toward the scholar-practitioner model raise concerns on the basis that they represent a significant potential 'dumbing down' of professional psychology that serves to potentially undermine key aspects of evidence-based practice (EBP) (Thomas-Peter, 2006a; Towl, 2005a, 2005b). Moves towards clinical-scientist models can be criticised on the grounds that they tend to develop researchers with very limited practice skills who, as such, are little different from those who follow traditional research training routes. The scientist-practitioner model continues to represent a working compromise between these alternative approaches and remains the predominant approach within applied psychology, albeit a compromise that is subject to inherent tensions. It is also an approach which, by setting the level of academic and professional skills at a high level, serves to limit the numbers of psychologists involved in directly delivering psychological assessments and interventions, often placing psychologists in consultancy and management roles (Crighton, 2005c).

Organising Data

Assessment data can be broadly divided into categorisation and description, both of which in the context of health care are often termed diagnostic. Taking each of these in turn, categorisation is essentially concerned with allocating individuals into meaningful groups. To be useful, such groups need to have one or more similar characteristics which will generally have some predictive utility either in terms of intervention needs or outcomes (Summerfledt & Antony, 2002). Categorical approaches have served a range of sciences, especially biological sciences, well and resulted in a number of positive technologies, examples of which would include the range of healthcare technologies. Here practitioners are often concerned to assess and allocate people to groups with common properties (diagnose them), identify interventions likely to be effective (treat them) and estimate the likelihood of a range of outcomes (give a prognosis).

This approach has been applied to psychological disorders, with perhaps the best known example being the American Psychiatric Association's Diagnostic and Statistical Manual (DSM), currently in its fourth revision (DSM IV) (American Psychiatric Association, 1994).[3] This framework is somewhat misleadingly described as multi-axial since it fundamentally adopts a categorical approach to abnormal psychological states. It is designed to do this on five 'axes':

- clinical syndromes (for example, schizophrenia);
- personality and developmental disorders;
- physical conditions;
- severity of psychosocial stressors; and
- the highest level of adaptive function in recent years.

This approach has been subject to a number of criticisms on both theoretical and pragmatic grounds. First, as noted, the description of it as an axial approach is somewhat of a misnomer since the approach is concerned primarily with categorisation, taking into account other factors. It might therefore be more accurate in this respect for DSM IV, and indeed similar frameworks, to be described as operationalised categorical frameworks, which explicitly acknowledges the importance of other factors. In this sense, the approach is similar to that used in the biological sciences in general and physical medicine in particular, where a person may be placed in a particular category but other factors, often of a dimensional nature, will influence the choice of interventions and likely outcomes. Such approaches have often been referred to, misleadingly, as the 'medical model', presumably on the basis that many areas of medical technology and practice use the categorical approach and this provides the basis for key parts of the training within medicine. The approach, however, is grounded in the biological sciences and might more accurately be described as a 'biological categorisation' model.

Purposes of Psychological Assessment

A generally helpful exercise is perhaps to look at the functions of assessment in its fundamental terms. Any assessment should be concerned with finding the answers to one or more questions.

Fundamental to any psychological assessment should be clarity of purpose. At a basic ethical level, the general expectation would be that this also needs to be disclosed to the person or people being assessed. Psychologists within prisons, as elsewhere, are charged with a need to make defensible professional judgements about how appropriate such an assessment is, and whether or not it is appropriate for them to undertake it. Such issues often take on particular salience within the coercive environment of prisons and within the context of criminal justice, where multiple stakeholders may be concerned with the outcomes of assessments. For example, in some circumstances it may be argued that it is useful to undertake an assessment to discriminate a particular problem by placing an individual within a particular 'diagnostic' category or at a particular point on a descriptive dimension. This may serve a function in terms of determining the best approach to care or intervention. In other cases, such descriptive or categorical placement may have little utility and, as such, run the risk of being inappropriate and indeed unethical. In yet other cases, such assessment may have little immediate significance for the person being assessed but might have research value. Such research can be important, or indeed central, to progress in building the evidence base but, as with other areas of scientific and technical research, ethical practice requires that participants, and indeed other stakeholders, are informed about and consent to participation (Crighton, 2006a; Towl, 2006). Issues of professional ethics need to be seen as both inherent and fundamental to the assessment process, with an ongoing awareness and consideration of such issues throughout. The initial consideration of whether a request to undertake an assessment is justified is nonetheless a key and fundamental starting point.

Practice within psychology also stresses the need to think carefully and on an ongoing basis about professional practices. Consideration needs to be given to what professional practices are being followed, what is being done and why, on an individual professional level. Fundamentally there is a requirement to look at each person being assessed as an individual and to tailor any assessment to individual needs (Lezak, 2004).

In global terms, psychological assessments can be conceptualised as a process of generating, testing, rejecting and reformulating hypotheses to answer specific questions. Essentially this is an application of the scientific method to the difficulties faced by individuals (Shapiro, 1961). As such, it is a naturally iterative process, where successive 'factors' are considered and eliminated or considered further until probable conclusions are reached. Ethical considerations have sometimes been construed or presented in overly simplistic terms within this process, compliance with professional standards being checked against some form of listing involving issues such as consent, confidentiality, competence and so on. Yet only where this is part of a more systemic consideration does it act to ensure appropriate professional standards are adhered to (Towl, 2005a).

76

Assessment Information

In applying scientific methodologies to answer specific questions about individuals, it is necessary to begin with a theoretical basis. This provides the logical starting point for generating hypotheses and gathering data to test these.

Such data will in general be drawn from one or more of four sources:

- self-report data;
- data from others;
- direct observation data; and
- indirect measures data.

Psychological assessment is at its heart a fundamentally collaborative process in which the assessor and the person they are assessing try to work together to reach a shared understanding of what is being assessed. This can and does present particular challenges in the context of prisons and other forensic settings where there are almost invariably multiple stakeholders. Whilst presenting significant challenges, it remains the case that an effective and ethical assessment will require:

- a clear formulation of problems and difficulties developed in consultation with the person being assessed;
- adequately detailed information about the factors thought to be maintaining the problems and difficulties; and
- efforts to introduce the person being assessed to the collaborative nature of psychological approaches.

The reasons for this are relatively clear. Most psychological assessments depend on a high degree of self-report and, even where efforts are made to rely on other forms of measure, it is very rare that self-report information will not be important. This in turn derives from the subject matter of psychology and the nature of much of the data that can be gathered. Much of what psychological assessment in prisons is concerned with simply cannot be directly observed and needs to be inferred (Miller, 1967).

Characteristics of Data Collection

In considering psychological assessment data, a number of technical considerations are important. The most central of these are notions of reliability and validity.

Reliability

Reliability essentially refers to how replicable and stable a particular assessment is. If the same process was followed repeatedly, would it yield the same results and would it continue to yield the same results over time if there were no change in the characteristic being assessed? Perfect reliability is a theoretical rather than an attainable notion and a degree of unreliability will be present in any measure. Some of this will be due to real differences and some will be due to various forms of error (Popper, 2004). Despite this, low levels of reliability in the data gathered will always be problematic for a number of reasons. These include the possibility that any observed data or changes to that data are simply a result of using inherently unreliable measures. A part of any psychological assessment is therefore the attempt to find reliable measures that are not unduly susceptible to random variation.

Statistical methods are used in an attempt to address the issue of reliability and the primary assessment measures used are inter-rater and test–retest reliability. Inter-rater reliability is concerned with the degree of agreement, as measured by a correlation coefficient, for different observers. Test–retest reliability is concerned with the extent to which the same observers will get the same result using the same assessment at a later time.[4] Subjects are most commonly assessed using Cohen's Kappa, a coefficient of correlation that exists in a variety of forms. This statistic is used in preference to measures such as percentage of agreement because it corrects for the level of agreement by random chance (Lezak, 2004).[5]

Validity

Validity is a central concept in relation to any assessment and, as such, warrants detailed consideration. It should be routinely considered in relation to the various parts of psychological assessments, for example the use of psychological tests. It also needs to be considered more broadly in relation to the overall assessment process. Validity essentially refers to the extent that an assessment measures what it claims to measure. It does not, in itself, suggest that what is being measured has any utility. Validity is also an abstract and difficult concept to pin down. In this respect it is quite different to estimating reliability which is essentially a straightforward technical matter (Kline, 2000).

Face validity Validity can be subdivided into a number of distinct forms. One of these is face validity, which is often seen as a relatively trivial, although intuitively appealing, form of validity. It refers to the extent to which a test or assessment appears to be measuring the correct attribute. In fact, it has no logical relationship with other forms of validity (whether the assessment actually measures what it claims). Indeed, although there may be a correlation between face and other forms of validity, in some cases high levels of face validity are likely to be a disadvantage and can potentially serve to reduce other forms of validity (Cattell & Warburton, 1967). Specifically where face validity is too high, it is likely that those completing assessments will simply be able to guess accurately exactly what is being looked for. This may in turn yield misleading results due to, for example, response biases. A few of what have been termed 'new generation' risk assessments clearly have the potential to suffer significantly from such biases, as a result of high face validity.[6]

Face validity can, though, have important effects, especially in relation to motivation. Where face validity is too low and assessments appear irrelevant or even absurd, then the levels of motivation in those completing the assessment are likely to be lower. In turn, this may adversely impact on the validity of the assessment (Kline, 2000).

Concurrent validity Concurrent validity refers to the extent that an assessment can be shown to correlate with other measures that are thought to be similar where the measures are taken at the same time. The level of inter-correlation needed to support this form of validity will depend on the quality of the criterion against which the assessment is being compared. As a general rule, a correlation of $>=0.75$ has been suggested as good support where benchmark criterion tests exist (Kline, 2000). Unfortunately, for most areas of psychology such benchmarks do not exist.

Indeed, even where benchmarks exist, primarily in the area of intelligence assessment, a number of difficulties arise. Taking this example, two clear benchmark tests have emerged: the Wechsler Adult Intelligence Scale (WAIS) currently in its third revision (with standardisation work for the fourth version currently ongoing) (Wechsler, 1997) and the Stanford-Binet, currently in its fifth edition (Roid, 2003). Yet notwithstanding the revisions made, both these tests were fundamentally developed from conceptions of intelligence that were dominant in the early decades of the twentieth century. Neither test fits easily with much of the current evidence and conceptions of intelligence that have emerged from cognitive psychology. Outside this circumscribed area, the situation is in even more of a state of flux and such tests and assessments need to be used with considerable circumspection and also with a clear understanding of the commercial imperatives under which test publishers work.[7] It has been often noted that most psychological assessments are of moderate reliability and low validity

(Buros, 1978; Plake & Spies, 2005). Elaborating on this, it has been noted that 'in attempting to establish the concurrent validity of a test, in most normal practice we have to correlate the experimental tests with one or more measures of dubious validity, a situation far different from that envisaged in most theoretical accounts of validity' (Kline, 2000). It can be argued that much of the incentive for cross-validating tests in this manner is largely commercial rather than scientific. Clearly, such development is less expensive both in terms of time to bring products to the market and of development costs. Yet this is a poor rationale for such professional practices and need not be the case. It is possible to develop assessments with good psychometric properties and utility in addressing specific questions without engaging in these practices (Sternberg & Wagner, 1994; Sternberg, Wagner & Okagaki, 1993; Sternberg, Wagner, Williams *et al.*, 1995).

Predictive validity Predictive validity refers to the extent to which an assessment predicts a given outcome. This is a common form of validation within much of psychology. Prediction is also an important part of the scientific method. It is also frequently confused with understanding and it is perhaps worth making the explicit point that the ability to predict something empirically is not necessarily associated with any additional understanding. An illustrative example often used in science is that of sunrise and sunset. It is possible to empirically predict both, with very high levels of accuracy, without any understanding of why the sun rises and sets.

Attempts at prediction involve the problem of finding clear criteria. Taking again the well established area of intelligence assessment, IQ tests were correlated with academic success. This relies on the assumption that academic performance depends, at least in part, on intelligence. This is a not unreasonable assumption as far as it goes. Yet it is also clear that many other factors impact on academic success, including such things as social class, income, social compliance within school, the quality of schools, motivation, family support, peer attitudes and so on. Indeed, such factors are likely to interact in complex and potentially synergistic ways that mean that such criteria need to be assessed carefully (Bowles & Gintis, 1976, 2001).

Another issue in relation to predictive validity is that of sample homogeneity, which is perhaps of particular relevance to prisons. More homogeneous samples on any given criteria will generally serve to attenuate correlations. This is simply because much of the variance, which would improve the predictive power, has been removed. For this reason the use of, for example, intelligence measures in a sample of postgraduates is likely to have relatively poor predictive power. Likewise, assessments of antisocial behaviour in prison populations are likely to have lower predictive power because of more restricted variance within prisons. Such effects can be corrected for statistically but interpretation then becomes significantly more difficult and needs to be done with great care. Specifically, it is worth noting that such correlations may be better explained by other, overarching, factors (Howe, 1988; Kline, 2000).

Content validity This form of validity has a specific and narrow application in a small number of assessments where the range of items is especially clear-cut. It normally applies to assessments of attainment or ability in particular areas. The issue here becomes whether the assessment reasonably measures the correct range of attainment as assessed, for example, by a group with particular expertise. It is more than an elaboration on face validity, since it is measuring actual skills and behaviours, rather than self-report data. An exemplar here might be assessment of levels of skills performance on an occupational training course.

Incremental and differential validity Incremental and differential validity are both highly specialised forms of validity (Vernon, 1961). Incremental validity applies where a number of assessment approaches are used (an assessment battery) where one part of the battery only correlates moderately with the criteria being assessed. Where such an assessment does not correlate with other parts of the battery it may increase, incrementally, the overall validity of the assessment. It does this by measuring something that other parts of the battery are not serving to assess.

Differential validity refers to cases where a particular factor has validity depending on other factors. As an example, IQ tests might correlate to some degree with academic performance at university. An interest in science, though, is unlikely to correlate with performance in some subjects (English literature, perhaps) but is likely to correlate with performance in other subjects (chemistry, perhaps) (Kline, 2000).

Construct validity This is perhaps the most complex form of validity to conceptualise and measure. It refers essentially to the validity of the concept being assessed (Cronbach & Meehl, 1955). For example, where an assessment is concerned with trying to allocate individuals to a 'diagnostic' category, its validity will be bound to the validity of that category.

Unfortunately, there is generally no ideal standard to evaluate categories against. This has led to a variety of suggestions for improving the validity of assessments, for example, the 'Longitudinal observation by Experts using All available Data' (LEAD) model or what has sometimes been described as the 'best estimate' diagnosis (Spitzer, 1983). Such models are designed to increase the levels of intersubjective agreement between assessors at a conceptual level and so provide a base against which to assess the validity of any assessment measures.

The relationship between reliability and validity It is important to consider this key relationship within psychological assessments. *A priori*, it is unlikely that a test that is unreliable will be valid. However, high levels of reliability in an assessment do not ensure that it is valid. The danger of conflating these two distinct concepts needs to be clearly understood by psychologists.

Variance seen in assessments can be divided into error variance and reliable variance. A perfectly valid assessment would contain no error variance and would only contain reliable variance. Even this does not guarantee utility since this variance needs to relate to the criterion of concern and not some other criterion. An example here might be an assessment that has high levels of reliable variance which is due to individuals consistently responding on the basis of the 'social desirability' of their responses. Variance is also open to the additional effects of information variance, essentially the use of different information to reach conclusions. The second is criterion variance, where the same information is assembled in different ways or is assessed against different standards (Beck, Ward, Mendelson *et al.*, 1962).

Specificity and sensitivity The terms specificity and sensitivity are sometimes used in relation to assessment methods and are important measures to consider within any assessment process. Sensitivity refers to the proportion of cases of an event that are correctly identified or are 'true positives'. Specificity refers to the proportion of non-cases correctly identified, 'true negatives'. It is important that these measures are considered together, because it is, for example, relatively easy to develop assessments with high specificity but low sensitivity, or vice versa. Indeed these two measures are closely related (Gigerenzer, 2002). In looking at any assessment, it is therefore critically important to look at the relationship between specificity and sensitivity and interpret assessment results in the light of the balance that has been decided on between these.

Self-report Information

Self-report information can be divided initially into interview data and questionnaire data. Interviews are perhaps the best known and most frequently used assessment method. They are generally used to gather

Table 5.1 Test result outcomes

Test Result	Disorder	
	Yes	No
Positive	(a) True positive rate	(a) False negative rate
Negative	(b) False positive rate	(d) True negative rate
	Sensitivity	Specificity

background information that may improve understanding of the area being assessed. Whatever the theoretical basis being used, the evidence seems clear that effective interviews include some key elements. They will include the establishment of a positive rapport with the person being assessed, a generally non-judgemental approach to what is being said and the assessor taking an educational and explanatory approach to interviewing (Crighton & Towl, 2005; Hawton, Salkovskis, Kirk *et al.*, 1989; Towl & Crighton, 1996).

Interviews in turn can be subdivided into those with varying degrees of predetermined structure. In practice, competent psychological assessments are unlikely to include interviews with low levels of structure. This is because a theory- driven approach tends to structure what will be asked and to some extent how topics will be addressed. Interviews that are structured by individual practitioners in this way are potentially the most flexible approach to gathering relevant data. This approach also involves a number of methodological challenges. The evidence in this area, which seems clear and well established, is that interview approaches with low levels of structure will tend to show poor levels of reliability (Beck, Ward, Mendelson *et al.*, 1962; Meehl, 1973). The use of higher levels of predetermined structure for interviews has developed in an effort to address such concerns about poor reliability. Again it seems clear that this approach can act to significantly improve the reliability of assessments (Spitzer, 1983).

The other main vehicle for self-report data in psychological assessments is the questionnaire. Such an approach involves the reporting of information in a systematic way, for example, in the form of numerical ratings. Here, an individual might be asked to rate how depressed they feel on a scale of 1 to 10. Substantively this differs little from asking the same question in interview and, certainly, there is a marked area of overlap between structured interviews and other forms of self-report measure. There are two potential advantages in obtaining self-report in this form. The first is that this allows some, albeit limited, mathematical manipulation of the data – such as the plotting of scores over time. Secondly, it allows for the comparison of an individual's score with scores at population levels. An example here might be a comparison of the self-reported levels of depression in one person with a sample of the general population.

There are clear potential advantages in being able to track self-report data over time and compare data across populations in this way. There are also difficulties associated with this. Research in this area suggests that these types of self-ratings are subject to systematic attenuation. It has been observed that people assessed in terms of symptoms will tend to increase the level of negative responding in the absence of any change, so attenuating scores (Lucas, Fisher, Piacentini et al., 1999). On a more prosaic level, the conversion of scores into numeric form may also tend to give the impression that such scores are more than an alternative form of self-report data. Clearly the role of individual scientist practitioners is to distinguish between scientifically meaningful data and numeric data that have the form, but not the substance, of science.

Information from Others

Another form of data commonly used in psychological assessments is that elicited from others. Again this can be done in a number of ways. One of the most common is probably the use of interviews or discussions, again with varying degrees of structure, generally conducted with people who will have had significant contact with the person being assessed. Information from others can also be elicited in other ways, for instance through the use of questionnaires. It can also be obtained from indirect sources such as previously written reports, or through discussions at case conference meetings. Data like this are frequently used in producing assessments but are not without problems. The most striking is that it is in effect a somewhat degraded form of data, in the sense that it has been gathered by others and will be selectively reported. Human cognition is demonstrably subject to a number of heuristics and biases and, in using data from others as part of a further assessment, there is potential to repeat or indeed increase such effects (Connolly, Arkes & Hammond, 2000). In using such data, there is a need to be especially sensitive to this. Whilst such caveats are important, it would be potentially foolish to ignore data that may have significant value if used correctly.

Direct Observation

Direct observation is one of the most useful forms of data that can be gathered. Observation of *in vivo* behaviours can yield accurate and detailed descriptive data. Examples here would be observation of the early stages of an anxiety attack in someone with a specific phobia or the behaviour of a depressed prisoner on a residential wing.

However, direct observation presents significant challenges. It is frequently a difficult approach to use. It also raises ethical issues. Some behaviours, certainly many of those of concern in prisons, cannot ethically be used for assessment observations. Stringent efforts to prevent incidents of violence to others or to prisoners themselves are, quite rightly, advocated in prisons. In an attempt to circumvent this problem, efforts to use observation of 'analogue' behaviours have been suggested (Jones, 2004). These have been criticised as being largely unconvincing, with the associations between 'analogue' behaviours and the behaviours of real interest at best unclear (Towl & Crighton, 1996).

Physiological Measurement

In many respects, this can be seen as a subset of direct observation and is concerned with making direct physical measures as analogues of psychological states. An example here might be the measurement of penile response as an analogue of sexual arousal (Marshall, Laws & Barbaree, 1990).

Again, though, the use of such analogue data is problematic. The extent and robustness of the hypothesised relationship between criterion behaviours and physiological measures are unclear. In the example above the physical measure taken tells us little about the extent of control, or indeed the use of countermeasures to prevent negative results (Towl & Crighton, 1996). Another example is the use of the polygraph to assess the veracity of answers given by an individual. This assessment is based on the assumption that untrue answers will be evidenced by increases in psychophysiological arousal. A number of reviews of this assessment approach have been undertaken with generally disappointing results. From these it seems that such assessments have not been subject to adequate scientific evaluation, that relatively poor psychometric properties are generally evident, with high levels of identification of deceit often being at the expense of high rates of false positives. The method also suffers from the relative ease with which countermeasures can be identified and deployed resulting in false negatives and, in the context of studies of sexual offenders, possible false admissions conceivably intended to satisfy those conducting assessments (British Psychological Society, 2004; Office of Technology Assessment, 1983).

Functional Analysis

The terms behavioural or functional analysis are often used to describe the structured way in which data can be gathered and evaluated. Behavioural analysis is one form of multi-method, multi-trait approach to assessment. In this case, the theoretical basis is derived primarily from social learning theory and cognitive theories (Hawton, Salkovskis, Kirk *et al.*, 1989; Shapiro, 1961).

Assessors need to analyse the antecedents, behaviour and consequences surrounding an event or events. In simpler terms, they gather data about the period before, during and after an event (O'Leary & Wilson, 1975; Towl & Crighton, 1996). In turn, these phases can be broken down, for the purposes of assessment, into a number of pragmatic divisions, for example cognitive, behavioural, affective, situational and physiological aspects (Hawton, Salkovskis, Kirk *et al.*, 1989). Such information can be broken down and collected in a wide variety of ways but the essential point is that, in gathering detailed information across categories and temporally, a more

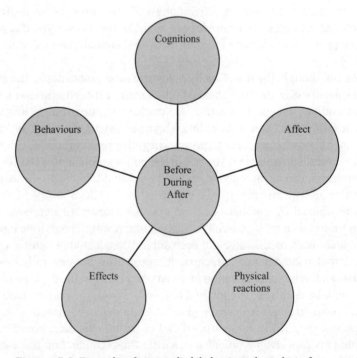

Figure 5.1 Example of an applied behavioural analysis framework

detailed and useful assessment of events can potentially be interpolated and extrapolated.

A potential drawback to such an approach is that making sense of an often large and complex set of data is itself a difficult process. The evidence base here is severely limited but it seems likely that this process will be subject to heuristics and biases common to human decision-making (Connolly, Arkes & Hammond, 2000; Gigerenzer, 2002).

Iterative Assessment Approaches

A number of commentators have suggested that much of what constitutes psychological assessment is, at best, misguided (Meehl, 1973). In assessing complex data, it has been widely suggested that experts are generally little better than non-experts. Experts often evince the view that they are engaged in a process of integrating and interpreting data in very complex ways. Research, on the other hand, suggests that in making unstructured judgements experts generally rely on a small number of variables analysed using relatively simple algorithms (Monahan & Steadman, 1994; Monahan, Steadman, Silver et al., 2001). However, this conclusion hides additional complexity with a range of performance seen amongst assessors (Connolly, Arkes & Hammond, 2000). This is important, given the sometimes glib and dismissive attitude to clinical risk assessment in comparison to actuarial approaches.

Those assessors who perform well appear to be able to effectively structure their assessments in a number of important respects. First, they are able to collect data effectively, secondly, they are able to integrate this data and, thirdly, they seem able to take account of statistical base rates (Connolly, Arkes & Hammond, 2000; Crighton, 2004; Towl, 2005b). A number of models can be used to structure approaches to overall process of assessing risk in a manner that helps to achieve this. An example of a public domain framework for structuring assessments, widely used within prisons, is the Cambridge Model for Risk Assessment (CAMRA) (Crighton, 2005a; Towl & Crighton, 1996).

A method commonly used in a number of areas of science and technology is the 'classification tree' approach. In essence, this involves collecting data to answer carefully specified questions and using evidence to attempt to address these. This is done by means of a series of systematic assessments. One example of this approach is seen in physical medicine where classification tree (CT) approaches can be used to improve diagnostic accuracy, improve prediction of outcomes and direct intervention

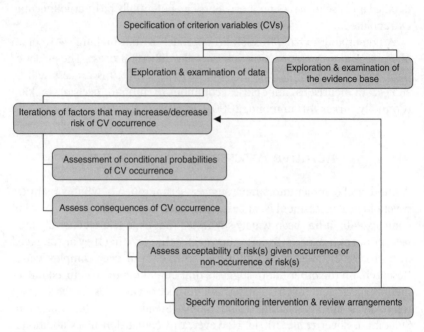

Figure 5.2 Cambridge Model for Risk Assessment
Source: (Modified from Crighton, 2006c)

approaches. The method has been used to positive effect in a wide range of fields including medicine, surgery, engineering and meteorology. An example of the application of this approach with offenders is given in the MacArthur Risk Assessment study, a large-scale study of the risk of violence amongst mentally disordered offenders in the United States (Monahan, Steadman, Robbins *et al.*, 2005; Monahan, Steadman, Silver *et al.*, 2001).

Much of the writing on CT approaches has focused on the process of classification and the development and application of the evidence base to support this process (see Figure 5.3). Within applied sciences such as engineering, the careful definition of questions to be empirically addressed has been the foundation for progress. Engineers are used to beginning with narrowly specified and temporally circumscribed questions and building from these.[8] Yet within applied psychology and much of forensic practice, it remains common to see poorly defined questions without explicit temporal parameters (Towl, 2005b). Essentially unanswerable questions are set, such as whether a person is 'dangerous', whether they are 'treatable', or if they are a 'suicide risk' – similar fundamentally flawed examples abound.

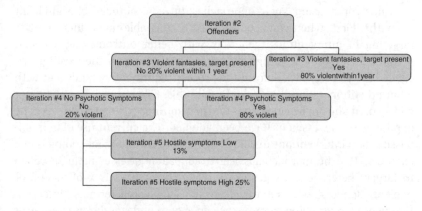

Figure 5.3 A simplified example of an iterative classification tree approach
Source: (Modified from Monahan *et al.*, 2001)

Attempting to supply answers to such questions is largely futile. If such questions are to be meaningfully addressed, then they need to be framed more precisely and any assessment time limited.[9] In short, specific temporal parameters are fundamental to accurate risk assessment.

Such approaches are potentially powerful in yielding more accurate assessments, based on the identification of meaningful differences between individuals. In turn this allows interventions to be more closely specified to meet individual needs. Such approaches have tended to be used in the context of areas of safety critical technologies. Current evidence-based practice requires assessments to a level that enables specification of the most effective evidence-based interventions. Providing interventions on the basis of broad divisions is not only likely to be less effective but in many cases may in fact be ineffective, as differentially diagnostic data are discarded or never gathered. An example might serve to illustrate here. A physician faced with a series of patients with pyrexia (a rise in core body temperature beyond normal limits) could intervene with all those assessed by administering aspirin. In some cases, this would be effective in reducing the body temperature but in others it would be ineffective. In cases where the underlying cause of the rise in temperature was pneumonia, the intervention would at best be largely ineffective and at worst fatal. In fact, no competent physician would adopt such a 'one size fits all' model to assessment and intervention. They would go through further levels of classification, making additional assessments and tailoring their further assessment in light of the emerging data (Crighton, 2006a, 2006b; Crighton & Bailey, 2006; Towl, 2005b, 2006).

Frameworks using such approaches have a number of significant strengths. First, when competently used they enable much more precise targeting of interventions, generally with better outcomes as a result. Secondly, they provide a logical framework that allows the existing evidence base to be used to inform the process. Thirdly, they tend to fit with what practitioners intuitively do. Despite this, CT approaches are still not widely used and applied in prisons and in some areas diametrically opposite approaches to assessment have been adopted. The current use of manual-based group interventions to address the risk of criminal reoffending is one example. Here the approach has been to adopt a single assessment approach to largely heterogeneous groups of offenders such as 'sex offenders' or 'violent offenders', which in turn leads to a single predetermined intervention approach, drawing from the evidence base and standardised as far as possible.

Such an approach has some strengths. It is, in managerial terms, convenient. It is possible to manage and 'process engineer' such an approach relatively straightforwardly. It is also an approach that can be developed using a narrow and relatively low-level skill base, reducing costs. There are, though, a number of disadvantages. The most pressing of these is that it is in many respects equivalent to the example of treating all cases of pyrexia with aspirin and is, in turn, likely to be largely ineffective for similar logical reasons. Given the range of difficulties being addressed with single manual-based assessments and interventions, it is perhaps not surprising that the evaluation data for prisons in England and Wales have not shown the hoped-for positive treatment effects (Falshaw, Friendship & Bates, 2003; Falshaw, Friendship, Travers *et al.*, 2004).

Summary

- Prisons are coercive institutions influenced by a range of historical factors. Assessments by applied psychologists take place within this context and it is important that practitioners have an understanding of the broad historical and social policy context in which they work.
- The scientist-practitioner model is the key underlying approach across applied psychology. It represents a compromise between research and practice skills and is an approach that specifies a very high level of skills and knowledge. It is concerned with developing practitioners who can contribute to the development of the evidence base and who can also draw effectively from it. The model is largely based on assumptions that much psychological intervention work will be undertaken by

staff other than psychologists and that psychologists will often undertake consultancy and managerial roles.

- Assessment is fundamentally concerned with gathering data to answer
  one or more carefully specified questions. Psychological assessment data
  is drawn from one or more of self-report data, reports from others, direct
  observation and indirect measures.
- Any form of data can be characterised in terms of its reliability,
  validity and utility. Reliability refers to how replicable and stable a particular assessment is over time. Validity refers to the extent to which
  an assessment measures what it claims to measure. Utility refers to
  the extent to which an assessment measures something that is of use,
  for example in estimating the prognosis for a person with a particular
  illness.
- Assessments in prisons are often primarily concerned with categorisation and risk assessment. The former is concerned with grouping individuals on the basis of common characteristics with likely predictive
  value. The latter is concerned with attempts to estimate the probability
  of specific, generally negative, outcomes.
- A number of frameworks exist to improve the quality of risk assessments
  undertaken by practitioners. One such framework, widely drawn on by
  psychologists in prisons, is the Cambridge Model for Risk Assessment
  (CAMRA). This specifies a number of logical stages necessary in undertaking risk assessment. The model supports the assessment of risk as an
  iterative and ongoing process.
- Classification tree (CT) approaches have been extensively used in
  medicine, engineering and a range of disciplines concerned with categorisation and risk assessment. This approach has the advantages of
  producing more finely graded and potentially more accurate prognosis
  and risk assessments. It also has the advantage of fitting with what
  practitioners intuitively seek to do in completing sound and thorough
  assessments.

Notes

1   The same is arguably true of hospitals where patients do not choose to
    be ill and have little real choice. The key distinction here is largely
    theoretical in that patients can discharge themselves from hospital,
    with the exception of psychiatric hospitals under some circumstances.
2   Prisons run by private contractors differ somewhat in this respect as in
    many cases all staff wear corporate dress.

3 In fact, a temporary revision of DSM IV was produced in 2000 and termed DSM IV-TR, pending the arrival of DSM V planned for 2001 or later.

4 An example here is the ASSET assessment used nationally in England and Wales by Youth Offending teams. A major issue in relation to this assessment are the poor levels of inter-rater reliability (Youth Justice Board, 2007). This means that different assessors may reach very different conclusions ostensibly based on the results of the same assessment 'tool'; in turn drawing into question the utility of such assessments. Emerging evidence on the Offender Assessment System (OASys) suggests similar difficulties of poor inter-rater reliability.

5 Such correction is especially important where base rates can make descriptive statistics, such as the percentage agreement, misleading. In the case of low frequency events such as suicide, two assessors could obtain very good inter-rater reliability by always opting for an assessment that the person will not go on to complete suicide.

6 An example here might be assessments that ask sexual offenders about how many sexual partners they have had. Here the question has high face validity, which also gives the person being assessed obvious guidance on what might be a 'good' answer in terms of making a more positive presentation. One obvious strategy here is likely to be reporting some median estimate for the population that the person making the assessment comes from, rather than an accurate figure.

7 This in turn raises issues of ethical practice with the routine overuse of such tests and assessment within applied psychology.

8 An example here might be whether the fuselage of an aircraft will fracture after 5000 cycles of pressurisation to X Kilograms per square metre, over a period of 2400 hours. Here the nature of the question and the criteria for assessment are made clear, as are the time limits of the prediction.

9 At best, such questions might serve as a first step in a classificatory process as in physical medicine. Here the question 'is this person sick?' would, at best, provide an initial step to narrowing down, step by step, exactly what the problems are and what meaning these data have before going on to develop strategies to address them.

Chapter 6

Groupwork within Prisons

Introduction

People are characterised by high levels of cognitive complexity set in the context of a range of emotional and social needs. A capacity, and indeed need, for social interaction appears to be evident at a neurobiological level and seems 'hard wired' into us. The study of social processes has been fundamental to much of experimental and applied psychology (Aronson, 2003). An understanding of the human need for interaction has the potential to inform practice in therapeutic groupwork. A great deal has been written on groupwork in prisons, much of which has recently come to be referred to as 'offending behaviour programmes' (Towl, 1995). The focus here is primarily on a psychological understanding of groupwork with the aim of covering the practice and research skills in this area of forensic practice.

At particular points in their lives, individuals may be more or less receptive to specific changes. Interventions conducted in groups have the potential to impact powerfully to produce change, both therapeutic and counter-therapeutic. This mode of intervention has become popular, indeed predominant, within prisons. It is therefore appropriate to focus in some detail on this method of delivering interventions. In seeking to do this, a number of key themes emerge as central to understanding group-based work. First amongst these is the social psychological context. Groups involve and indeed rely on such processes as part of the means of achieving change in individuals. Psychological interventions are also heavily dependent on process. An understanding of these broadly defined 'process issues' is therefore essential. Finally, in the context of prisons and elsewhere, group-based interventions raise a number of more practical challenges.

The Psychology of Groups

There is an extensive evidence base relating directly and indirectly to the effects of groups. For applied psychologists, an understanding of this evidence base is fundamental to informing good psychological practice and also to the development of practice. The body of potentially relevant research is vast so the focus below is on three major areas of the evidence base. These areas are used for illustrative purposes because they highlight especially well, or clearly, key areas of groupwork. The areas chosen are cognitive dissonance, non-verbal communication and attribution theory. These serve to illustrate the role of aspects of everyday psychological functioning and the potential of these to impact when conducting interventions with groups rather than individuals. They also relate well to some broader observations made in the area of groupwork practice (Brown, 1994; Preston-Shoot, 1987; Yalom, 1985), highlighting the way the dynamics and processes involved in such activities often parallel broader psychological, social and political processes.

Cognitive Dissonance

Cognitive dissonance is a term coined to describe the common experience where individuals hold conflicting and competing views on something (Festinger, 1957; Festinger & Carlsmith, 1959). Cognitive dissonance theory postulates that there is a tendency for people to try to achieve cognitive consistency among their beliefs and attitudes. Inconsistency between a belief and behaviour will therefore result in 'dissonance', a form of psychological discomfort. People are generally motivated to reduce such discomfort. In the case of a discrepancy between beliefs and behaviour, however, it is most likely that the attitude will change to accommodate the behaviour.

Two factors are suggested as central to the strength of the dissonance experienced: the number of dissonant beliefs involved and the importance the individual attaches to each belief. Where there are few dissonant beliefs or the belief is not of much importance to the individual, then little dissonance will be generated. In turn, three ways of reducing such dissonance are sometimes suggested: reducing the importance of the dissonant beliefs, adding more consonant beliefs that outweigh the dissonant beliefs and changing the dissonant beliefs so that they are no longer inconsistent. Cognitive dissonance occurs most often in situations where an individual must choose between clearly incompatible beliefs and behaviours and may be most pronounced when the two behavioural alternatives are equally attractive (Festinger, 1957). Somewhat counterintuitively, the theory suggests that attitude change is most likely to progress in the direction of less incentive since this tends to result in lower dissonance.[1] In this respect, dissonance theory contradicted behavioural theories that predicted greater attitude change with increased incentive.

Dissonance appears to be widely applicable to a range of situations involving attitude formation and change. It is especially relevant to areas such as decision-making and problem solving. Here, to a large degree, it is relevant to problem-solving and decision-making in groupwork settings. To take a generic example, someone may purchase an expensive car but discover that it is not comfortable on long journeys. This may create dissonance along the lines that it is a good car and a good car should be comfortable. Such dissonance could be eliminated by deciding that it does not matter since the car is mainly used for short trips (reducing the importance of the dissonant belief) or focusing on the car's strengths such as safety, appearance and handling, thereby adding more consonant beliefs. The dissonance could also be eliminated by admitting that an error in judgement had been made and changing the car.

There are multiple examples where dissonance may be important in group-based interventions with prisoners. An individual may experience anxiety at the thought of returning to prison and experience positive thoughts about enjoying stealing and driving cars at high speed, creating dissonance. It is common in group- based interventions for participants to experience dissonant feelings. The key point here is that such processes are, from a practice perspective, not intrinsically 'good' or 'bad'. Rather, they may have potentially negative or positive consequences for change. These will depend in large part on the linkages the individual makes between cognitive processes and behaviour. An understanding of such basic psychological processes may help to enable improved understanding in the context of group-based interventions.

Non-verbal Communication (NVC)

Non-verbal communication is a powerful means of communicating with others. Such patterns of communication remain fundamentally important, despite the development of relatively high-level verbal skills that develop from around the age of 12 months. Yet this means of communication is often poorly attended to or misinterpreted (Argyle, 1994).

Facilitators of groups and prisoners participating in groups are generally under a high degree of scrutiny. Facilitators need to be aware of the potential impact of NVC on group members. This is also a potentially important area of observation of prisoners. NVC may act as a powerful means of reinforcing behaviour. For example, this can be the case if the NVC of facilitators is consistent with showing an interest in what a prisoner has to say. Such interactions may be further reinforced with verbal behaviours, too. A basic congruence between verbal and non-verbal communications is important if a group facilitator is to retain credibility. The constant monitoring (and, where appropriate, adjusting) of facilitator NVC adds to the demands of group-based intervention as a therapeutic method. The NVC of prisoners in a group situation can also be a rich source of additional information for gauging the response of the group and individuals within it.

Attribution

Attribution theory is essentially concerned with how individuals interpret events and how this links with their thinking and behaviour. Useful psychological theories of attribution have been extensively developed since the 1950s and it is not possible to do these full justice here (Baron & Hartnagel, 1997; Heider, 1958; Jones, Kannouse, Kelley et al., 1972; Weiner, 1974, 1980, 1986). In brief, attribution theory assumes people will generally be motivated to explain why people do things; in other words, they will seek to attribute causes to behaviour. Attribution theory identifies three stages. First, the person must perceive or observe the behaviour of another. Second, they must believe that the behaviour was intentional and, third, the person must determine if they believe the other person was forced to perform the behaviour (in which case the cause is attributed to the situation) or not (in which case the cause is attributed to the other person).

Attribution theory focused on achievement and identified ability, effort, task difficulty, and luck as the most important factors affecting attributions for behaviour (Weiner, 1974, 1980, 1986). Using this approach, attributions are classified along three causal dimensions: locus of control, stability, and controllability. The locus of control dimension has two poles: internal versus external locus of control. The stability dimension captures whether 'causes or does not cause' changes over time. A number of key practical issues in groupwork interventions emerge from attempts to apply this theoretical model. It is a well-replicated observation within the evidence base that people tend to make 'dispositional' attributions about the behaviour of others; they also make stronger attributions where the outcomes are negative. With regard to themselves, they have a greater tendency to focus on situational attributions, potentially in relation to negative events or behaviours, not least perhaps because they have greater insight into these (Jones, Kannouse, Kelley et al., 1972).[2]

Group-based Interventions in Prisons

Over the past decade or so, the term 'groupwork' has gone out of fashion to some degree in prisons with the active promotion of the use of the term 'programme' instead. In fact, in the UK the term 'programme' has been used very much as a synonym for groupwork. Such usage is something of a misnomer and is arguably misleading. The term 'programme' is perhaps most helpfully reserved for integrated sets of interventions, which address a broad-based range of needs and may (or may not) include groupwork.

The core of groupwork delivered in prisons is currently manual-based and draws heavily from a cognitive behavioural perspective. Such manualised cognitive behavioural approaches enjoy a number of merits (Free, 2002). The manualisation of such work helps to improve the consistency and comprehensiveness of what is covered during sessions. Another potential benefit is ensuring that only evidence-based approaches are used. A number of important practical and research benefits also emerge. These include the potential to conduct large-scale evaluations across multiple sites, involving large numbers of psychological therapists (Free, 2002). A further strength has been the opportunity to develop highly structured approaches to the training of staff involved in delivering psychological interventions, and particularly inexperienced trainee applied psychologists. Inexperienced staff may professionally benefit disproportionately from highly structured prescriptive approaches to working with offenders (Towl, 2006). The approach, though, is not without problems. It may be unduly and inappropriately restrictive, especially in terms of allowing practitioners to respond to emerging needs. Experienced practitioners in particular may feel, and indeed be, constrained from adopting effective approaches relevant to particular points in the therapeutic process or responding to individual emerging needs appropriately (Towl, 2004a, 2004b; Towl & Crighton, 2007).

Recent historical developments in groupwork in prisons are particularly informative here. Up until the early 1990s, much of the groupwork undertaken in prisons was led and facilitated by probation officers. Indeed, much of the historical experience and practice base of groupwork in prisons rested with probation service staff and was professionally based in social work,[3] with multidisciplinary teams sometimes including psychologists. A significant weakness was that there was little in the way of effective routine evaluation of the extensive work being undertaken (Towl, 1995). Where evaluation studies were initiated, these tended to be of the most basic kind. Much of the groupwork previously carried out in prisons ceased with the advent of what became referred to as 'accredited offending behaviour programmes'. The argument was that only rigorous evidence-based interventions should be undertaken with prisoners; however a narrow research base was drawn upon and assumed to generalise to UK prison populations.[4] Some have suggested that this approach was built on sand (Mair, 2004). Others have raised concern that the use of manual-based approaches has contributed to a deskilling and 'dumbing down' of the training of forensic psychological staff. The implementation of manual-based approaches often resulted in an uncritical acceptance of the efficacy of the approach, despite a less than compelling evidence base (Crighton, 2006a; Towl, 2004a). The impression given has sometimes been one of what has been referred to as a 'programme fetishism' whereby there has been and, it appears, remains an intolerance of alternative and sometimes more effective approaches (HM Inspectorate of Probation, 2002). Indeed, as has been noted elsewhere, subsequent UK evidence testing the efficacy of accredited offending behaviour programmes has been disappointing. Perhaps equally disappointing have been the missed opportunities to conduct sufficiently rigorous evaluations and to take a more eclectic and integrative approach to interventions with prisoners. In effect, practice has swung from extremes of unlimited discretion to centralised prescription. Neither is likely to be very effective for prisoners or, ultimately, for the protection of the broader public.

It is important not to restrict discussion of groupwork in prisons exclusively to that aimed directly at reducing the risk of reoffending. Particularly with the advent of improved health services for prisoners, which sees responsibility for their care moving to the National Health Service from the directorate of the Prison Service, there is the opportunity for a fuller range of groupwork-based interventions. Indeed, the need for an increase in the availability of psychological therapies is a key tenet of current government policy. Increasingly, the lack of interchange between clinical psychology in the health service and forensic psychology in the prison service is being successfully challenged with a focus on competence and relevant professional skills. This implies that health and prison services may, potentially, benefit from a wider range of applied psychology expertise across professional applied psychology. It is also important not to confuse psychological models of therapy (such as cognitive-behavioural approaches) with a requirement that psychologists directly deliver such services. Such errors, it can be argued, have contributed to significant failures to deliver services to prisoners. Psychology and its applications are not and indeed never have been the exclusive preserve of psychologists. Indeed, a fundamental aspect of the scientist-practitioner model of applied psychology is recognition that, if psychological approaches are to have their full potential impact, it is important that a broader range of practitioners uses them. Other professional and para-professional groups may often be better placed to make such approaches more effective.[5]

Group-based Interventions as a Method of Psychological Therapy

Group-based interventions have a number of advantages and disadvantages when compared to individual interventions. Within a group situation, there are potentially more psychological resources to draw from across the whole group. Where this is working well, there can be a range of professional expertise and also participant expertise. This can be a potent mix in which individuals potentially gain more than could be offered in one-to-one work with a professional or peer. Groupwork, though, may not be suited to all prisoners or indeed to all types of offence and considerable caution is needed in tailoring the method of delivery to the needs of the individual. There is also no simple dichotomy between individual and group-based interventions. A judicious mix of the two approaches may be the most effective in terms of delivering positive outcomes as part of an integrated programme of change.

Group-based work may allow a broader range of therapeutic techniques to be drawn upon. This increases the chances of engaging and working more effectively with individuals. Structured exercises within groups may be used effectively to work with prisoners enhancing intra-group communications, self-reflection and enabling an environment of mutual respect. There are a number of further therapeutic opportunities that present themselves in groupwork methods. One commonly referred to phenomenon in the literature is the principle of universality, whereby there is therapeutic advantage in prisoners being exposed to the reality that others are often in similar, sometimes challenging, situations to themselves and experience common worries and concerns. There is the potential in groups for mutual support, shared learning, optimism, humour and the opportunity to help others (Sharry, 2006; Yalom, 1985).

Some of the potential advantages and disadvantages of groupwork methods may be associated with different types of group in content, purpose or theoretical perspective. One potentially helpful approach, which has gained popularity in the therapeutic literature recently, has been that of 'solution-focused brief therapies'. As the name suggests, such interventions tend to be short-term and focus primarily upon 'solutions' rather than examining the problems or the past of participants in too much detail. There are parallels with self-help groups in that the participants are explicitly drawn on as a key shared resource for group members (Sharry, 2006).

Another potential advantage of groupwork approaches is the capacity to leave more potential power with participants, in comparison with the unequal power relationships that tend to characterise one-to-one work with professionals. This may have particular resonance and importance in the context of prisons. Group-based approaches may also be less intense than individual work from the perspective of participants. At a fundamental level, there is the potential for change through social interaction, role modelling and the reinforcement afforded by positive social contacts (Brown, 1994). The notion of redressing power relationships within the coercive environments of prisons is potentially contentious; however, it can have potentially positive therapeutic outcomes. Sometimes the challenges laid down by peers can be far more powerful and influential than that made by a group facilitator or therapist. The extent of such influences may be mediated by factors such as age and the extent to which participants have similar backgrounds and experiences.

There are a number of potential disadvantages to groupwork, too. Not least of these is the difficulty in maintaining appropriate levels of confidentiality. Although group members may initially agree to keep discussions confidential, some may not ultimately adhere to such agreements. Sometimes it can be necessary for facilitators to protect individual group members to ensure that they do not over-disclose in ways that may be harmful to themselves or others. Group membership may also, on occasion, increase labelling and stigma (Towl & Bailey, 1995). Other difficulties with groupwork include the practical complexities of planning, organisation and implementation. Groups require significant additional resources such as physical space to accommodate group members and also to ensure appropriate levels of privacy. For some potential participants, groupwork may even be damaging (Brown, 1994). Some group members may not be comfortable sharing their problems in a group situation and may prefer a one-to-one setting before they feel able to share what is sometimes personal information, thoughts and feelings. Although groups in one sense may be less intense experiences, for many this may not always be the case. Facilitators have less time to spend helping individuals in groupwork. The bigger the group, the more opportunity there is to psychologically 'hide' within the group. Arguably the single most problematic aspect of groupwork methods, though, is a tendency to rely on one common denominator for membership, resulting in differences in the degree of 'fit' for each member of the group.

One argument in support of group-based interventions is the potential for cost and efficiency savings. Group approaches, particularly those narrowly specified and circumscribed, have a clear managerialist appeal. Notions of financial and efficiency savings are easily overstated in this context. First, there is the issue of whether the intervention works more or less effectively in a group format. There is to date little good quality evidence for this but it seems highly unlikely that groupwork will be the most effective and least harmful mode of intervention for all prisoners. Groupwork also involves a number of additional activities that surround such work. Perhaps most saliently, they involve time spent on planning, organising and implementing groupwork. This will include ongoing joint meetings between groupwork sessions for facilitators, involving significant time commitments. Furthermore, where facilitators are trainee psychologists, additional professional supervision sessions may be necessary. Finally, the number of participants in a group will be important and is likely to be relatively low, when account is taken of attrition rates, for effective group-based interventions.

Group Facilitation Skills

With directive leadership, the group leader assumes responsibility for setting the agenda for the group and for ensuring that appropriate ground is covered. Permissive leadership styles tend to be characterised by a non-directive approach, other than indicating the general purpose of the group. Effective facilitators tend to fall somewhere between these approaches, giving structure and order but psychological space too. Such flexible styles of leadership tend to be characterised by movement along such a permissive–directive continuum as the situation or group warrants it (Benson, 2001). In undertaking groupwork, it is generally important to have an awareness of issues of power inequalities, difference and diversity. Such matters, which touch on a number of fundamental ethical issues, are brought into especially sharp focus in prisons because of their coercive nature (Towl, 1993; Towl, 1995; Towl & Dexter, 1994).

Applied psychologists in prisons tend to be predominantly white, middle-class and relatively affluent women. By contrast, prisoners tend to be men from lower socio-economic classes and are relatively poor, with black and minority ethnic (BME) groups overrepresented (Towl, 2006). As such, the concerns and everyday lifestyles of those undertaking groupwork as participants and facilitators are generally markedly different. This can result in communication and credibility problems for facilitators. Such differences may be addressed, and perhaps the first step in this process is an acknowledgement of the potential problems. Curiously, this is comparatively rarely acknowledged or may even be denied or minimised. Groupwork facilitators may well experience such denial and minimisation, perhaps especially in relation to aspects of their practice that might be seen to compromise their effectiveness. An example here might be the presence of social class differences between facilitators and group members. Prisoners come, on the whole, from the most socially and economically deprived parts of the community; whereas psychologists come, by and large, from the most socially and economically privileged groups. The idea that such differences may impair the effectiveness of groupwork is likely to be uncomfortable for practitioners and, as such, may engender feelings of 'dissonance'. This often involves practitioners having to choose between incompatible beliefs; one way to achieve this is to reduce or deny the importance of these, for example, by denying the relevance of a belief. Another is to add more consonant beliefs, accepting that dissonance exists but reducing its impact, for example, by stressing positive motivations for working with groups that are often socially and economically very different from their facilitators. Thus both prisoners and facilitators may experience dissonance, or make attribution errors.

It is perhaps worth mentioning that prisons are also predominantly masculine environments. The majority of the population (both staff and prisoners) are white adult men and prison norms tend to be based on this. Since prisons are based on authoritarian models of discipline and management, some therapists may understandably wish to call into question whether or not they are an appropriate environment for group-based therapy at all. Whilst the environment is a particularly demanding one, in this respect there are a number of compelling reasons to support the continued use of groupwork interventions. Not least of these are the very high levels of need for help and support in behavioural change seen in prisons, the access to offenders at times when they can be engaged in positive work and the costs of not providing effective interventions. Prisons are also not unique in having different levels of power relationships with such differences being common to settings such as hospitals and schools.

Groups may take much out of participants and facilitators alike. Running groups can be both an emotionally and intellectually demanding activity. It is important that there are appropriate support structures in place. Professional supervision is essential for facilitators. This can take a number of forms, including group supervision sessions (for group facilitators), individual face-to-face supervision and telephone and e-mail support and advice. The training and development of facilitators is central to constantly improving the quality of services received by prisoners. One key character-istic of good quality supervision arrangements is the accessibility of the supervisor. It is important that such relationships are effective and that both parties are aware of their rights and responsibilities towards each other.

Finally, it is important to note that all interventions are likely to have multiple effects and these will not simply be in one direction. Facilitators need to have a developing awareness of the effects of groupwork interven-tions on them, as well as of impacts on participants. This has been a little studied area within the evidence base, although there are isolated examples of good quality research into process issues (Houston, Wrench & Hosking, 1995). Effects on facilitators and participants in groupwork can be positive or present a range of possible adverse effects. It is important that facilitators have a good awareness of these, along with strategies to try to address such effects. As part of the therapeutic groupwork process, it is worth being mindful of this in order to help maximise the benefits and minimise the costs of such work for all concerned.

Group-based Interventions

Planning

Thorough planning is essential if a success is to be made of groupwork in prisons. There are perhaps three aspects of planning groupwork which need to be carefully considered: first, establishing what the levels and types of prisoner needs are; second, ensuring appropriate resource allocation; third, ensuring that there is an evidence-based approach which may address the identified needs using groupwork methods. Groupwork should be aimed at meeting clearly specified needs as part of a broader consideration of poten-tial interventions. Prisoners have many multifaceted needs; hence there will be a range of areas of groupwork that potentially could be helpfully undertaken. However, it has sometimes been a problem in prisons to find sufficient prisoners to undertake particular types of groupwork. This is often due to unrealistic planning and inappropriate target-setting that provide salutary learning for future work.

It is necessary to assess the amount of resources available, or potentially available, for undertaking groupwork. There are a number of aspects to consider. Appropriate levels of financial support are essential. In practice, there is more money than ever being spent on groupwork in prisons. But it is important to ensure that managers are willing and able to allocate the necessary budgets for the groupwork to be undertaken. Another aspect of resources is the securing of the physical space to undertake groupwork. Identifying staff for the planning, implementation and evaluation of group-work is also important. At the planning stage, it is always important to build in contingency plans in case of foreseen and unforeseen problems in imple-mentation. It is imperative that full management support is secured for the delivery of the most effective groupwork because this helps secure the rel-evant resources and enable concrete support if and when organisational difficulties are encountered. In recent years, much of the implementation of groupwork has been based on a process of bidding. These processes were designed to ensure that money was effectively spent but they have, in some cases, had unintended effects. One of these was the implementation of a number of overambitious bids, leading to sometimes under-resourced interventions.

There is also a range of significant organisational challenges in addition to resourcing. Issues warranting consideration include the prison culture and the suitability of prison as a place to undertake intervention work. This is especially important where the planned groupwork is reliant on prisoners being enabled and supported in practising newly acquired and acquiring skills in the environment of the wing. An example of this would be that of anger management interventions whereby assertion skills may be tested in the wing environment (Towl, 1995). Prison staff, however, will not habitu-ally be warmly receptive to assertive behaviours from prisoners, especially if the skills are initially clumsily demonstrated, although of course this is common in any new skill acquisition activity. This serves to illustrate the importance of cooperating to ensure that staff to whose wings prisoners return are aware of what is being attempted and also of their role in sup-porting any new learning and behavioural changes. This is where middle- and line-management support, professionalism and commitment is most needed but regrettably is sometimes most lacking.

Intervention

Ensuring an appropriate evidence base can be one of the most challenging aspects of groupwork in prisons. Although there have been elaborate struc-tures set up over the past decade with regard to groupwork aimed at reduc-ing the risk of reoffending, desistence from future crime is not the only basis on which groupwork may be constructively planned. In addition, group-work has tended to be predominantly cognitive-behavioural in its orienta-tion, with perhaps insufficient regard for alternative approaches. Some of the restrictions imposed have clearly been useful in eliminating the worst examples of poorly thought out or ineffectual interventions. In other respects, though, the restriction of practice may have been unhelpful or potentially damaging by putting an end to promising alternative approaches. What has undoubtedly been achieved is a historically high level of cognitive-behavioural manual-based approaches to working with offenders. Manual-based approaches have been strongly marketed within prison settings. The approach has also provided a major stimulus to the for-profit sector involved in psychometric testing despite generally weak evidence of links between test results and behaviour change. The planning of groupwork in prisons needs an awareness of such factors. Consideration of who a particular intervention is for is central. In practice, there will invariably be multiple stakeholders, including not only prisoners but members of the public.

Most of the groupwork that can be effectively undertaken in prisons will not be about evidence-based approaches to directly reducing the risk of reoffending. Rather, it is likely to be in two related and largely neglected areas of practice: interventions which may indirectly impact upon offending; and those which would not be expected to impact on offending but may impact on areas such as mental health. In terms of the involvement of psychologists doing groupwork in recent years, the work has increasingly tended to be skewed towards attempts to directly reduce the risk of reoffending (Towl & Crighton, 2007; Towl, 2005a).

Clear accountability is essential for effective groupwork implementation, based on thorough and detailed planning as outlined above. One important distinction is that between management responsibilities and supervisory responsibilities. These accountabilities and responsibilities need to be clear from the start. As we have seen above, establishing management commitment and support for the work is fundamental to underpinning and securing the groupwork. When there are problems such as staffing or logistical issues, managers can help resolve any such difficulties. The roles of the supervisor and supervisee are rather different, although both have a responsibility to bring organisational problems to the attention of managers. Undertaking groupwork in prisons is likely to be emotionally, intellectually and professionally demanding work. It is a considerable tribute to the diligence of prison staff that currently so many prisoners undertake group-based treatments.

Summary

- People show high levels of cognitive complexity set in the context of a range of emotional and social needs. Each of us has a capacity for social interaction that appears to be embedded at a neurobiological level.

- An understanding of issues of diversity in terms of such things as social class, culture and ethnicity are of particular importance when undertaking groupwork in terms of maximising potential benefits and minimising potential adverse effects.
- The study of social processes has been a major focus of both experimental and applied psychology. The broad range of research within this area is of relevance to group-based work. Three areas provide illustrative examples of this in the context of group-based interventions: cognitive dissonance, non-verbal communication and attribution theory.
- Early development of group-based interventions in prisons was driven primarily by staff other than psychologists. The majority of groupwork was developed and undertaken by probation officers, teachers within prison education departments and prison workshop staff. This resulted in a very wide range of pioneering and positive work. It also led to problems often associated with too much discretion in approach and content and a lack of emphasis on adequate evaluation.
- Over the past decade, efforts have been made to restrict the range of group-based interventions in order to raise the quality and effectiveness of what is being delivered with the aim of reducing criminal reoffending. It seems clear that this has served to eliminate some examples of poorly thought out and inadequately delivered interventions. It can also be convincingly argued that it served to contribute to prematurely closing down much innovative and potentially effective groupwork.
- There is a case now for broadening the range of groupwork undertaken in prisons and ensuring improved matching of prisoners to such interventions.
- Much of the groupwork which goes on in prisons is only indirectly related to reducing reoffending and is, for example, concerned with addressing mental health or physical health problems. Such work is increasingly being subject to various processes of 'accreditation' and it will be important to ensure that decisions are made on the basis of evidence rather than fashion.

Notes

1 In essence, what appears to happen here is that individuals seek to reduce the dissonance they experience and ascribe reasons to the change. Where they have a clear incentive, they tend to ascribe at least part of the change to the incentive. Where there is no incentive, they

appear to ascribe this to a greater genuine change in the dissonant beliefs (Davis & Jones, 1960).

2   Various paradigms were used to study this phenomenon and they suggest a level of complexity that goes beyond the scope of this chapter. A number of early studies looked at such things as hypothetical auto-motive accidents. Where these involved strangers, dispositional attribu-tions were common (e.g., they were an incompetent driver) but, where they focused on themselves, situational attributions were common (e. g., the road was poorly lit).

3   Probation officers were employed directly by local probation boards: most were trained in social work, for example having completed the Certificate of Qualification in Social Work (CQSW) or equivalent. Changes in the 1990s altered the training of probation staff, implement-ing a diploma training route for England and Wales, intended to have a greater stress on training specifically for criminal justice settings.

4   The notion that only evidence-based interventions should be used with prisoners is a reasonable one. However, the lack of evaluation of exist-ing groupwork interventions in the UK meant that there was effectively a very limited evidence base to draw from. It seems likely that in dispens-ing with the vast majority of these interventions, much poor practice was removed along with many examples of innovation and excellence – here the baby may have been thrown out with the bath water. The interventions which replaced the groupwork of the 1990s tended to be drawn from a narrow part of the evidence base and were largely imported from Canada. In many respects, policy changes may have been based on a limited presentation of a relatively weak and incomplete evidence base of questionable generalisability.

5   A curiously neglected area, outside of the area of interventions to reduce suicides, intentional self-injury and drug misuse, is the involvement of former prisoners in delivering psychological interventions as part of multidisciplinary teams. Whilst recognising the practical difficulties involved here, such approaches may have significant potential.

Chapter 7

Principles of Risk Assessment

Introduction

Effective risk assessment is first and foremost a logical process that seeks to estimate the likelihood of future events. It can be operationally defined as 'a combination of an estimate of the probability of a target behaviour occurring with a consideration of the consequences of such occurrences' (Towl & Crighton, 1996). This definition still serves in what is an increasingly technical area, heavily dependent on the use of scientific and technical methods. Sometimes indeed the 'technologies' involved have served to somewhat obscure the 'science', to the detriment of effective and evidence-based work.

Risk assessment is not exclusive to psychology nor indeed to behavioural and health sciences. Sophisticated approaches to risk assessment are seen across many branches of science and technology. Until comparatively recently, however, the degree to which multidisciplinary and multiparadigmatic approaches have informed practice within psychology has been relatively circumscribed.

In looking at risk assessment within the context of prisons in England and Wales, the example chosen – for illustrative purposes – is violence. This is perhaps often the most salient example and one where psychologists are frequently called on for expert comment. It is also an area of serious concern as a criminal justice and public health issue. Yet it is important to clarify that it is only an example. Risk assessment can be applied to a vast number of areas and potential outcomes, although in practice the focus tends, quite understandably, to be on behaviours with serious outcomes either for the individual or for others.

The Logical Basis of Risk Assessment

A key logical issue is the specification of the risk that is being assessed, what is sometimes termed the 'criterion variable'. This is not simply a moot point as, particularly in the behavioural sciences, risk assessment often appears to involve poorly specified or even unspecified criteria (Garb, 1998; Meehl, 1954). It is important to understand this as an essential first stage in the logical process of risk assessment, as well as to appreciate the potential interactions between and synergies of multiple risks.

The Cambridge Model of Risk Assessment (CAMRA) is a public domain model of risk assessment designed to assist practitioners in structuring and undertaking risk assessments[1] (Towl & Crighton, 1996, 1997; Crighton, 2006a; Crighton & Bailey, 2006). The model is predicated on the notion that risk assessment can be usefully divided into separable but interacting stages. It is also based on the assumption that classification tree approaches have greater clinical utility than simple main effects approaches, particularly where it is possible to apply these iteratively, as this will lead to more accurate specification of levels of risk, as well as risk management needs.

Ethical Issues

A seminal paper on risk assessment in the area of child protection high-lighted a number of key ethical, legal and practice issues and these remain as salient as ever (Wald & Woolverton, 1990). This review highlighted the importance of not seeking to apply inadequate, simplistic and untried methods in haste and often for profit. The criticisms raised have had a marked impact within the field of child protection but to date have had limited impact in other criminal justice contexts. Indeed, in much of the forensic literature there continues to be little consideration of such issues.

The use of appropriate and clear language to describe areas of risk and the criteria against which they are measured underpins effective risk assessment, yet is often poorly addressed. Similarly, defined temporal and ecological parameters are critical. The notion that a risk assessment will provide an accurate estimate over an unlimited time frame and across an unspecified range of environments seems logically implausible. Yet this is often what is asked of practitioners and implied in, or inferred from, risk assessments (Monahan & Steadman, 1996). Practitioners therefore have a professional responsibility to make such limitations explicit.

109

The onus is also on individual practitioners to ensure that they act in professionally ethical ways, going beyond 'checklist' approaches. Issues such as informed consent and confidentiality are of clear importance in assessing risk. So also is the need to consider structural inequalities and power relationships. With the advent of the statutory registration of psychologists, the need to ensure effective consideration of these issues will become more pressing, with potentially severe professional penalties for individuals who fail to do so. In this respect, assessment of risk needs to be understood as the dynamic process it is, influenced by factors such as social class, race and gender, all of which need to be considered in reaching determinations about risk. Recognition of such factors, though, has the potential to improve significantly both the quality and justice of such assessments (Crighton, 2000a; 2005a; 2005c; Towl, 2005b).

Evidence-Based Practice (EBP)

There is a substantial body of research that suggests the marked superiority of 'empirical' approaches to risk assessment compared to unsupported 'clinical' assessments (Meehl, 1954; Swets, Dawes & Monahan, 2000). From research that looks at purely empirical approaches, it is clear that the combination of a relatively small number of variables can yield relatively good predictors of future outcomes on a group basis (Klassen & O'Connor, 1988). This has been employed by a number of researchers to develop what have come to be termed, rather curiously, risk assessment 'tools'.[2] In the context of interpersonal violence, there are numerous examples of this approach to risk assessment. The Violence Risk Assessment Guide (VRAG) is based on twelve predictor variables, shown to correlate with violent behaviour. The Historical and Clinical Risk 20 (HCR-20), using a similar approach, is based on twenty risk factors. Both these assessments and many others yield results that are better than those achieved by chance. For example, when data from the VRAG was dichotomised into high and low risk groups, it was found that 55 per cent of the high risk group went on to behave violently compared to 18 per cent of the low risk group (Harris, Rice & Quinsey, 1993). A two-year follow-up study using the HCR-20 looked at patients who scored above the median, who were significantly more likely to be violent than patients scoring below the median (Douglas, Ogloff, Nichols et al., 1999). Such findings compare favourably with studies of unstructured 'clinical' assessments that suggest poorer levels of performance. In one study of defendants in court, 39 per cent of those rated as 'medium' or 'high' risk went on to commit a violent act within two years, compared to 26 per cent of those

110

rated as 'low' risk (Sepejak, Menzies, Webster *et al.*, 1983). In another study with acute psychiatric patients, 53 per cent of those who aroused professional concern committed a violent act within six months compared to 36 per cent amongst those who did not elicit concern (Lidz, Mulvey & Gardner, 1993). Whilst such results are statistically significant, they are not particularly clinically useful and their utility is clearly limited when applied to individual cases. They also hide additional complexity in that data collected on 'clinical' assessments in this manner serve to pool the performance of assessors. In reality, some assessors appear to perform relatively well, some do little better than chance and some make predictions that are negatively correlated with outcomes (Connolly, Arkes & Hammond, 2000).

Actuarial approaches raise a number of significant issues. Many of the assessments used draw on a constricted range of risk factors. This is not wholly surprising given that theoretical understanding of violence remains relatively weak, yet this in turn is likely to limit accuracy. Another feature has been the use of weak criterion measures. In the context of violence, re-arrest rates have frequently been used, despite it being well-known that detection and conviction rates for violence are low. In addition, actuarial approaches have often involved narrow sampling, raising questions over the extent to which findings may be generalised. These aspects are important but perhaps more important than these is the lack of knowledge about base rates. Few actuarial risk assessment 'tools' have included the consideration of this fundamental aspect of risk assessment and the likely accruing effects.

The importance of base rate information is vividly illustrated in findings from the MacArthur risk assessment study (Monahan, Steadman, Silver *et al.*, 2001). Unusually and refreshingly, this study looked in detail at base rates and also the nature and context of the violence identified. Based on officially recorded incidents, the base rate for violent acts was reported to be 4.5 per cent of the patients studied: when multiple sources of information were used, this increased to 27.5 per cent (Monahan, Steadman, Silver *et al.*, 2001).[3] Clearly, the implications of these two figures are very different, yet many currently fashionable approaches to risk assessment have been using assumptions based on official rates of recorded violence or, less accurately still, official reconviction records. Such an approach seems, at best, to be inadequate.

Factors in the Risk of Violence

A recurrent theme in the area of risk assessment has been the attempt to identify the 'best' single predictor of 'risk'. This trend has perhaps been marked in the area of suicide, but has also been increasingly evident in the area of violence. This has led to a number of 'risk factors' being posited as in some sense 'key' to understanding risk of violence. Indeed, this has been a clinical challenge that the psychometric testing industry has readily sought to focus on and so achieve dominance, empirically and financially, of the risk assessment domain.

Mental Health Factors

Many of the factors proposed might be termed 'clinical' characteristics. Currently most fashionable is the notion of 'psychopathy', particularly as measured using a group of Psychopathy Checklists (including the PCL, PCL-R and PCL-SV) (Hart, Cox & Hare, 1995). This structured assessment schedule is normally scored to produce two factors which in turn this may be collapsed into a single score. It acts as both a categorical and dimensional assessment yielding a dimensional score with cut-off points suggested. A number of empirical studies suggest that this construct is a relatively strong predictor of general and violent recidivism (Serin & Amos, 1995). Using the screening version of the PCL, those scoring eight or more on this assessment were five times more likely to commit a violent act and fourteen times more likely to be arrested for a violent crime. There is an above-chance level of association between scores on the PCL and subsequent violence.

This assessment was considered in detail as part of the MacArthur study using Receiver Operating Characteristics (ROC) analysis.[4] It was found that this assessment predicted violence at significantly better-than-chance levels (ROC AUC 0.73), with a PCL-SV score of 8 achieving the best balance between sensitivity (AUC 0.72) and specificity (AUC 0.65). Indeed, the choice of cut-off point was quite crucial for this assessment. Using a cut-off of 4, sensitivity was high (AUC 0.91) but the specificity fell to (AUC 0.31): with a cut-off of 12, sensitivity dropped markedly (AUC 0.40) but with improve specificity (AUC 0.84) (Skeem & Mulvey, 2001).

It has been persuasively suggested that this assessment is not measuring an underlying 'personality disorder' as claimed but rather that it is simply grouping a number of risk factors together which correlate with future criminal behaviour (Toch, 1998). This notion was tested in a study that controlled for fifteen co-variate risk factors and suggested that these largely but not fully accounted for the predictive power of the PCL-SV. This study reported that those categorised as 'psychopathic' using this assessment were more likely to be black, male, from lower social classes, less well-educated and with lower verbal intelligence. The researchers reported that

112

the extent of these differences was not large, though, and that they did not fully account for the differences seen (Skeem & Mulvey, 2001). The clinical implications of this finding are open to a degree of interpretation. It has been argued that in a small percentage of cases there is some utility in using such assessments. Alternatively, it has been suggested that better assessments can be achieved using classification tree approaches, drawing on more easily available data which is also likely to lead to more individualised, targeted and focused risk management (Crighton, 2004).

The latter view receives some support from analysis of the two-factor solution for the PCL. Factor 1 relates to hypothesised personality elements but adds little to the predictive power of the assessment. This derives primarily from Factor 2, which relates primarily to measures of antisocial behaviour. Indeed, scores on this element of the PCL-SV were as predictive as the score on the full assessment (AUC 0.74 compared to AUC 0.73), suggesting a high degree of redundancy, with little impact from the hypothesised emotional and personality characteristics (Douglass, Ogloff, Nichols, *et al.*, 1999; Salekin, Rogers & Sewell, 1996). Such findings give support to the idea that the PCL (and many similar assessments) simply represent a pooling of risk factors, primarily those concerned with previous antisocial behaviours (Toch, 1998). This also tallies with findings from developmental psychology that suggest the relatively good predictive power of prior behaviour over time (Piquero, Farrington & Blumstein, 2007). Considerable caution is therefore appropriate in the application of this assessment as a risk indicator. In addition, sub-threshold scores require specific interpretation, taking into account the factor scores and the potential implications of these (Blackburn, 1988; Gunn, 1998; Lösel, 1998).

The evidence base in relation to delusions and hallucinations has received much less attention than that for 'psychopathy'. The view has consistently been that both may be implicated in violence, although interestingly the MacArthur study found no direct effect of delusional beliefs on violence in a sample of community psychiatric patients up to 20 weeks post discharge. In fact, a slight negative relationship over one year was found. They reported no effect on the violent content of delusions or of the duration of individuals' delusional beliefs. However, the combined presence of delusions and hallucinations was associated with an increase in violence over one year ($\chi^2 = 5.52$ df = 1 p = 0.019) (Monahan, Steadman, Silver *et al.*, 2001).

The evidence in relation to hallucinations was similarly complex. In general, no relationship between hallucinations and subsequent violence was found. The exception to this was the presence of command hallucinations directing the individual to be violent towards others. Here there was a significant increase in violence at 20 weeks and one year (χ^2 = 3.84 df = 1 p < 0.05 and χ^2 = 10.23 df = 1 p < 0.001) (Monahan, Steadman, Silver *et al.*, 2001).

Childhood Experiences

There is strong evidence of a relationship between dysfunctional family environments and later violent and criminal behaviour (Piquero, Farrington & Blumstein, 2007; Welsh & Farrington, 2007). This relationship appears to hold equally true for those with mental health problems (Yesavage, Becker, Werner *et al.*, 1983). Parental loss through death, divorce or absence and particular attachment patterns have been shown to be associated with increased levels of subsequent violence (Crittenden, 2000; Klassen & O'Connor, 1990). In addition, injury from an adult prior to the age of 15 years is associated with later violent behaviour in adult men with and without schizophrenia (Klassen & O'Connor, 1988).

Anger

There is an established theoretical association between anger and aggression with good evidence of a reciprocal relationship (Novaco, 1994). The relationship between anger, aggression and violence though is not simple. It is evident that aggression and violence can serve to reduce feelings of anger and also that aggression and violence can occur in the absence of anger. Any model therefore needs to be able to account of such findings.

The presence of violent thoughts and fantasies are often posited as significant risk factors for subsequent violence. The baseline for such thoughts appears, from the limited evidence available, to be high. Over one year, for example, 57 per cent of a community sample of psychiatric patients in the MacArthur study reported violent thoughts and fantasies (Monahan, Steadman, Silver *et al.*, 2001). Amongst this sample, the presence of these was associated with the occurrence of violence, although the difference was perhaps not as marked as may have been anticipated. Over a year, 36 per cent of those who reported such thoughts went on to be violent compared to 24 per cent of those who did not.

Social Context

There has been a recent and somewhat belated increase of interest in the effects of environmental or neighbourhood effects on the risk of violent behaviour (Sampson, Raudenbusch & Earls, 1997). Socially disadvantaged

114

and socially excluded areas show significantly higher levels of interpersonal violence than more socially privileged and socially included areas (Anderson, 1990; Miethe & McDowell, 1993). Yet, disappointingly, risk assessment studies have focused primarily on aspects of individuals, rather neglecting social contexts (Applebaum, Clark Robbins & Monahan, 2000; Monahan, Steadman, Applebaum et al., 2000; Monahan, Steadman, Clark Robbins et al., 2005). This is a potentially important weakness in such approaches.

The impact of social and economic environment on risk of violence is somewhat contentious. It has been suggested that such findings are an artefact due, in this study, to patients being discharged selectively to poorer areas. A similar argument might apply to more violent prisoners who may be selectively discharged to economically and socially deprived areas. This hypothesis, though, is not supported by the finding that the socio-economic status of patients was less predictive of violence than the socio-economic status of the area they were discharged to (Monahan, Steadman, Silver et al., 2001).

Models of Risk Assessments

The recently favoured approach to risk assessment has involved the use of groups of potential risk factors selected on the basis of likely association with the criterion variable. These variables are then subject to statistical analysis that identifies the combination of factors most closely correlated with the criterion. This is also known as a standard main effect approach and it has a number of significant and often unacknowledged weaknesses. These include the fact that the selection of risk factors underpinning such methods is often not drawn from any convincing theoretical base. In other words, what are produced are a series of inter-correlations with limited explanatory power. In turn, many potential risk factors may be discarded from initial sample data on empirical grounds. The approach also requires that every individual be assessed on every risk factor included in the 'tool', even though for a number some risk factors will not be relevant. This is somewhat counterintuitive for many clinicians. Advocates of this type of approach are unmoved by such objections, suggesting that main effects actuarial approaches are the single best method for predicting violence. Indeed, many advocate their use to completely replace clinical assessment, arguing that objections to this are at best unconvincing: 'The objections are akin to rejecting actuarial methods for predicting tornadoes next summer because it was developed on the tornadoes of last summer (after all, it could be that the two populations of tornadoes differ in some way), and then using

115

a Ouija board instead' (Quinsey, Harris, Rice *et al.*, 1998). Advocates of such approaches risk significantly overstating their case. It is, for example, entirely appropriate to question the utility of even a good empirical model of tornado formation and action developed in Florida, when efforts are made to apply it to Asia or Europe.

It is also unclear that simple main effect approaches have good utility. Certainly, in areas such as meteorology, far more sophisticated and theory-based models are used (Nolan, Amgren & Bell, 2000). Alternative approaches used extensively in biological sciences and engineering, such as classification and iterative classification tree methods, have existed for many years but have received relatively little attention until recently. This is perhaps linked to the fact that such models are less easily marketed in the form of standardised assessments, suitable for administration by less professionally skilled staff. Such approaches seek to classify individuals into subgroups as the risk assessment progresses and the next area addressed is contingent on the assessment of the previous area (Crighton, 2006b; Crighton & Bailey, 2006). Such methods are widely used in medicine and surgery where, for example, a clinician would be likely to identify high blood pressure and then conduct further assessments related to this but would generally not conduct these same assessments for someone with normal or low blood pressure. This has the intuitive appeal that it is more in line with what experienced and competent clinicians routinely seek to do.

There has been recent development of interest in such classification tree approaches in psychology (Applebaum, Clark Robbins & Monahan, 2000; Crighton, 2005c). ROC analyses of simple classification tree approaches have been conducted in relation to a large sample of civil psychiatric patients discharged into the community but have yielded disappointing results. Performance was at a slightly poorer level than a logistic regression approach with the classification tree approach achieving (ROC AUC 0.79, $p < 0.001$) and logistic regression (ROC AUC 0.81, $p < 0.001$).

In seeking to improve on this level of performance, the curious but common approach of categorising risk using a single cut-off point (violent versus non-violent) was looked at afresh (Monahan, Steadman, Silver *et al.*, 2001). An approach using two cut-off points was tested. This created three groups, one where the level of risk appears indistinguishable from the population base rate on the basis of the available risk factors, one where it is lower and one higher (Applebaum, Clark Robbins, Monahan *et al.*, 2000; Monahan, Steadman, Silver *et al.*, 2001; Shah, 1978; Steadman and Silver, 2000). It was hypothesised that, by focusing on the two extreme ends of the distribution, the accuracy of estimates of risk may be improved (Menzies & Webster, 1995; McNeil, 1998).

Drawing on the base rates for violence in their sample, high risk was defined operationally as twice the base rate (>37% over 12 months) and low risk as half the base rate (<9% over 12 months).[5] They found that, using these cut-off points, 42.9 per cent of the sample was unclassified using the logistic regression main effects approach and 49.2 per cent using the simple classification tree approach (Monahan Steadman, Silver et al., 2001). In practice, this highlights a major weakness of such models of risk assessment. Even with the addition of a low risk cut-off point, this approach was successful in identifying only slightly over half of those assessed as high or low risk. The remainder of those assessed were not differentiated from the base rate for violence group, providing little in the way of added utility from the risk assessment.

Disappointed with current models, the researchers went on to look at the use of repeated iterations within a classification tree approach (an iterative classification tree (ICT) model). In essence, this involved conducting repeated iterative analyses on the large 'unclassified' group which had not, on first analysis, been distinguished from the base rate population. A second iteration allocated 119 of these individuals to either high or low risk groups; a third iteration 63 and a fourth iteration 60, at which point the researchers stopped. Using this form of recursive partitioning, the researchers found that 77 per cent of the sample could be allocated to high or low risk groups, representing a significant improvement. As a result of the analysis they had identified six low risk subgroups (49%), 4 high risk subgroups (27%) and two average risk subgroups (23%).[6] The area under the ROC curve was AUC 0.82, suggesting comparable accuracy with non-recursive models but with the ability to classify a significantly greater proportion of cases into high and low risk groups.[7] The authors went on to test the model statistically using a technique called 'bootstrapping'. This involves mathematically increasing the sample size by randomly duplicating cases. This larger hypothetical 'sample' is then randomly sampled and tested to see how effectively repeated samples fit the new model (Mooney & Duval, 1993). Here the results suggested that the model continued to work effectively.

Of the risk factors included in this analysis, the single factor which performed best was the PCL-SV (Odds Ratio (OR) 2.40), followed by grandiose delusions (OR 2.28), fathers' drug use (OR 2.18) and drug abuse diagnosis (OR 1.58). The researchers noted that a number of the risk factors included in the initial analysis raised both clinical and economic issues. The use of psychological assessments such as the PCL is labour-intensive and expensive; raising the question of whether they have additional utility and, if so, whether this is cost effective. The researcher went on to omit the PCL-SV as an item noting that cost-benefit analyses are crucial in considering effective risk assessment and management policy and practice (Monahan Steadman, Silver *et al.*, 2001). This was tested by re-conducting the analysis, removing the 28 risk factors that would be most difficult to obtain in a civil mental health context. Detailed psychological assessments such as the PCL and details of criminal history were included. The model was then tested using the remaining 106 risk factors that were relatively easy for clinicians to obtain. This analysis achieved three iterations allocating 72.6 per cent of individuals to high or low risk subgroups and yielding 4 low risk subgroups (51%), 3 high risk subgroups (22%) and 4 average risk groups (27%). The average ROC AUC was reported to be 0.80 (p < 0.001) (Monahan, Steadman, Silver *et al.*, 2001).

This analysis suggested that the performance of the ICT model was comparable in terms of efficacy using 106 risk factors or using 134.[8] The use of expensive assessments, such as the PCL, appeared to have at best marginal utility. Equally good accuracy in risk assessment was achieved using relatively straightforwardly obtained clinical risk factors when analysed appropriately (Applebaum, Clark Robbins and Monahan *et al.*, 2000; Monahan, Steadman, Silver *et al.*, 2001; Monahan, Steadman, Clark Robbins *et al.*, 2005; Towl, 2005b; Towl & Crighton, 1997; Crighton, 2006b).

Whilst this model achieved comparable levels of accuracy, it did result in a degree of differential allocation, with 57 per cent of cases being similarly allocated under both approaches (r 0.52 p < 0.001). This is of course a general characteristic of any actuarial risk assessment where approaches will generally be imperfectly correlated with each other. In order to address this issue, an analysis was conducted repeating the ICT approach and combining two models giving an ROC of AUC 0.83. Interestingly, of those classified as low risk in both models, 3 per cent were violent during the 20-week follow-up period, of those classified as high risk by both models 64 per cent were violent during the 20-week follow-up period (Monahan Steadman, Silver *et al.*, 2001).

Building on this, the researchers used different risk factors as the starting point for each of ten analyses, using 106 factors. The ROC for these analyses varied (from AUC 0.73 to AUC 0.81) and the percentage of cases classed as high and low risk ranged from 55 per cent to 73 per cent. When the ten models were integrated, the ROC increased (AUC 0.88), with only five of the models achieving a good fit (chi square = 300 df = 5 p < 0.0001 C = 0.878 Pseudo R^2 = 0.44) (Monahan, Steadman, Silver *et al.*, 2001).

From the emerging evidence base, it can be argued that risk assessment 'tools' based on logistic regression models have some significant limitations and should now be replaced by more scientifically sophisticated models and levels of analysis. There are a number of significant potential advantages in

118

doing this. The use of repeated ICT models of risk enables greater confidence that the allocation of individuals to groups is accurate. It does this by giving repeated opportunities for an individual to be allocated to high or low risk groups. In turn, it can be suggested that the identification of groups at the extreme ends of the continuum lend themselves better to risk- management decisions (Crighton, 2005c; Monahan Steadman, Silver *et al.*, 2001; Towl, 2005b). The approach also has additional advantages. Allocating individuals effectively to subgroups helps clinicians empirically with what they seek to do naturally. Competent clinicians endeavour to do this largely as a guide to intervention and iterative classification achieves a similar systematic outcome. As such, the approach is likely to have greater utility as a means of identifying needs and directing individually tailored interventions to more effectively manage risk (Crighton, 1997a, 2000a, 2004; Crighton & Towl, 2005; Towl & Crighton, 1997).

Managing Risk

As noted above, the use of repeated ICT models to the assessment of risk can result in both a more accurate assessment of overall levels of risk and a more precise allocation to what might be termed subgroups. This implies that individuals may be allocated to a similar level of risk on the basis of entirely different risk factors or partially overlapping risk factors. This in turn provides much clearer guidance to risk management than simpler models that identify a relatively modest proportion of a group as simply being 'high risk'. The potential of greater accuracy and precision for improving public protection seems largely self-evident.

The relationship between 'actuarial' and 'clinical' risk assessment remains a challenging one. In particular, the extent to which one approach should take precedence has been the subject of extensive and sometimes

Table 7.1 Iterative risk classification and violence and repeated violence

Risk class	% of cases	Violent acts	Repeated violence
1	36.5	1.1	0.0
2	26.4	7.9	1.6
3	19.5	23.7	9.7
4	10.9	33.8	21.6
5	6.7	33.5	36.5

Source: Data from Monahan, Steadman, Silver *et al.*, 2001

119

polarised debate. In the context of the VRAG, it was initially (some would say arbitrarily) suggested that scores on this could be modified by up to 10 per cent by clinical judgement. The authors of this assessment have subsequently modified their view, suggesting that modification of actuarial assessment in this way is inappropriate (Quinsey, Harris, Rice *et al.*, 1998). Others firmly take the view on scientific and ethical grounds that actuarial assessment should inform clinical judgements rather than direct them (Crighton, 1997a, 2000a, 2004; Hanson, 1998; Towl, 2005b; Towl & Crighton, 1996, 1997).

There are a number of reasons for not uncritically accepting evaluations based on specific existing risk assessment 'tools' or indeed accepting 'actuarial' assessments per se for individual patients or prisoners. As noted above, current off-the-shelf risk assessment 'tools' tend to be based on relatively simple models of risk and, in interpreting the meaning of these, it is important to fully understand the extent of their limitations. Indeed, there is a compelling case for moving on from unduly simplistic statistical models of risk and replacing these with more sophisticated and theoretically grounded models as a more appropriate basis for informing accurate and effective clinical judgements.[9,10]

Even in the case of well-developed and effective actuarial models, other practice issues inevitably arise. The most striking is the issue of how far actuarial assessments may generalise. Such assessments must, of necessity, be based on a sample of a given population. In the MacArthur study, for example, the analysis was based on civil psychiatric patients in three United States cities. It is open to question how far such results might extend to other American cities, other industrialised nations with lower crime rates, developing nations or forensic populations. In addition, empirical models are developed at a given point in time and the relevance to future cohorts is unclear, with changing cultural and social circumstances. Of course such questions are open to empirical test but it is a practical impossibility to test models on every possible population over time. As such, judgements are necessary to decide the applicability of a given empirical model. This is also important in terms of appropriate professional accountabilities.

Another issue relates to the occurrence of rare risk or protective factors. Often empirical models will be poor at picking up statistically rare events, something that has been increasingly widely recognised (Grove & Meehl, 1996; Hanson, 1998). This has been illustrated with reference to a model designed to predict cinema-going. A highly accurate model of this could be rendered inaccurate for those with a broken leg (a low frequency but high impact event). It is quite straightforward to see parallels in the context of prisons. It is difficult in professional terms to see practitioners in this context not changing their assessment of risk, whatever the actuarial assessment, when told by a prisoner that they intend to kill a named person on release (a low frequency but high impact event). Failure to react to such events within the context of risk assessment would be unethical and unprofessional, leading in turn quite rightly to professional and legal sanctions.

There are in fact good positive reasons for retaining an element of clinical judgement in risk assessment and management. The analogy of weather forecasting has been used to highlight this (Monahan & Steadman, 1996). Here, actuarial models have been developed by meteorologists to a very high degree of sophistication, with variables measured using a degree of accuracy as yet far beyond those seen in most of the biological and social sciences. Even here, though, the addition of expert judgement leads to improved predictive accuracy when compared to purely actuarial models (Carter & Polger, 1986). This view echoes that of others who have advocated that actuarial approaches are best seen in support of clinical judgement. The greatest utility from risk assessment in turn is likely to derive from the accurate targeting of interventions to manage identified levels and types of 'risk' (Grisso & Applebaum, 1998).

In terms of what those interventions might be, the use of more sophisticated analysis is likely to imply much more closely targeted risk factors, in turn proposing more closely targeted interventions, rather than the 'one size fits all' approach inherent in simpler methods. Bivariate analysis of the data in the MacArthur risk assessment study suggests some promising avenues for addressing risk of violence. Most striking is the importance of a range of risk factors, including substance abuse, anger, the reporting of violent fantasies, being unemployed and physical abuse in childhood. From a public health perspective, this is encouraging as it suggests a number of points of prevention and intervention to manage and reduce risk. It is also noteworthy that public health approaches suggest it is often sufficient when managing risk to reduce one or more areas to sub-threshold levels, rather than trying to achieve complete elimination, something which gives hope for improved outcomes in future (Rothman & Greenland, 1998).

Summary

- Risk assessment is first and foremost a logical process that seeks to estimate the likelihood of future events. Sophisticated approaches to risk assessment are seen across many branches of science and technology. Until recently, the degree to which multidisciplinary and multiparadigmatic approaches have informed practice within psychology has been relatively circumscribed.

- The illustrative example chosen to explore risk assessment is violence as this is perhaps the most salient example in prisons and one where psychologists are often called on for expert comment. It is also an area of serious concern as a major public health issue.
- In conducting risk assessments, a clear logical framework is essential and here the Cambridge Model of Risk Assessment (CAMRA) has been used for illustrative purposes. This model is concerned with the process of assessing risk, beginning with definition of the risk or risks being assessed, the very important setting of temporal parameters and the stage of data collection, analysis and decision- making. The model also outlines risk management as an additional and iterative stage in the risk assessment process.
- At a basic level, there is a substantial body of research to suggest marked superiority for 'empirical' approaches to risk assessment compared to unsupported 'clinical' assessments. In the field of violence, this has led to numerous examples of structured risk-assessment approaches being aggressively marketed. These may improve on unstructured 'clinical' assessment, although even this conclusion obscures additional complexity. However, these approaches draw on simple models and constricted ranges of risk factors, often measured against weak criteria. Few of these assessment approaches have adequately addressed issues of base rates and generalisation across populations.
- The importance of base rate information has been vividly illustrated by the findings from the seminal MacArthur risk assessment study. Officially recorded incidents suggested a base rate for violent acts in the community of 4.5 per cent compared to 27.5 per cent using multiple sources. This finding alone has important implications for psychologists working in prison settings.
- A recurrent theme in the area of risk assessment has been the attempt to identify single best predictors of 'risk'. This trend has perhaps been most marked in the area of suicide but has also been increasingly evident in the area of violence to others. This has led to a number of 'risk' factors being posited as in some sense 'key' to unlocking the complexities of assessing the risk of violence. These have included clinical constructs such as 'psychopathy', specific mental health symptoms (such as hallucinations and delusions) and family and social environments. In reality, risk of violence is a complex and dynamic process with multiple pathways to a common outcome, it is unlikely to be 'explained' by any single factor. Effective risk assessment needs to take this adequately into account.

- The recently favoured approach to risk assessment has involved identification of groups of potential risk factors selected on the basis of likely association with the criterion variable. These variables are then subject to analysis in order to identify the combination of factors most closely correlated with the criterion. This is also known as a standard main effect approach and it has limitations.
- Alternative approaches such as classification tree methods have been proposed to address these. Such methods are widely used in medicine, surgery and engineering. There has been a recent development of interest in classification tree approaches in psychology using multiple cut-off points, repeated iterations and combination of multiple ICT risk models. The performance of such methods, using relatively easily available risk factors, is promising in terms of improved levels of accuracy and much better differential allocation to risk groups. It also provides a more effective means of identifying needs and directing possible interventions, with individuals allocated to a similar level of risk on the basis of entirely different risk factors or partially overlapping risk factors.
- The issue of whether actuarial assessments should inform or direct clinical assessments is contentious. Yet there are a number of reasons for opting for the former approach. One issue is how far actuarial assessments may generalise across populations and time. A second is the occurrence of rare risk or protective factors which are poorly addressed in exclusively empirical models. Thirdly, it has been noted that even in well-developed areas in the physical sciences such as meteorology expert judgement leads to improved predictive accuracy when compared to purely actuarial models. Such decision-making is not a purely empirical matter. It involves judgements about, for example, the acceptable levels of 'risk'. Related to this are the ethical issues which underpin such judgements. The current evidence base therefore supports the notion that empirical assessments should be used to inform clinical judgement rather than replace it.
- It is also noteworthy that public health approaches suggest that it may often be sufficient to reduce one or more areas of risk to sub-threshold levels, rather than trying to achieve complete elimination of risk factors.

Notes

1   The title is slightly misleading in the sense that the framework also addresses issues of risk monitoring and management. Whilst these processes are logically separable, in practice this seems both

undesirable and unhelpful, given that the overall aim is to reduce risk. Separation of risk assessment and monitoring and management would perhaps be akin to estimating the risks of failures in an engineering context such as aviation but then not acting to replace worn components on an aeroplane when they are likely to fail (Towl & Crighton, 1997).

2   A variety of terms have been used to describe these actuarial approaches such as 'second generation', 'third generation' and 'new generation' risk assessments. The utility of such terminology appears to be greatest in terms of marketing, since in reality they represent efforts to develop more precise revisions using a common methodology. For this reason, these terms have not been used throughout this chapter where the focus has been on substantive differences in logic and methodology.

3   The study concerned drew on official records, self-reported violent and aggressive behaviour and collateral reports from family members. The study was designed to maximise willingness to report violence, with no penalties for disclosure. It seems unlikely that such high levels of self-report would be achieved in criminal justice settings where there are powerful disincentives for honest accounts of such behaviour.

4   Receiver Operating Characteristics (ROC) area under the curve (AUC) analysis is a measure of efficacy of risk assessment that is independent of base rates. The area under the curve here corresponds to the probability that a randomly selected individual will have been identified as higher risk than a randomly selected non-violent individual. This may range from 0.5 to 1.0. A figure of 0.5 represents performance in line with chance, whilst a score of 1.0 represents perfect predictive performance (Swets, 1988; Swets, Dawes & Monahan, 2000).

5   Here the definition of 'high' and 'low' risk groups is, as with main effects approaches, arbitrary. The inclusion of base rate data does though make the basis for the assumptions clear. Unfortunately, in a number of areas of risk assessment such clear base rate data are largely missing and the definition of concepts such as high and low risk becomes less clear as a result.

6   The percentages here have been rounded so do not total to 100.

7   The researchers also conducted this iterative analysis for a logistic regression model. This proved significantly less effective, allocating 62.3 per cent of cases to high or low risk groups.

8   This performance is all the more impressive because of the elimination of criminal history factors.

9   One of the barriers to this is likely to be one of health economics in that there has been considerable investment in assessments that are simple

to develop and administer based on logistic regression analyses, often incorporating expensive psychometric assessments of marginal utility. Such assessments have been aggressively marketed. In contrast, recursive partitioning of classification tree models is more concerned with detailed analysis of often easily available data and as such is less suited to this form of health products marketing.

10 Paradoxically, the technology for such detailed analysis of easily available risk factors existed within public sector prisons in the form of the Profiling Behaviour (PROBE) IT system. The data concerned were never capitalised on in this manner and the system, with the exception of a reduced infrastructure in high security prisons, was discontinued. The Offender Assessment System (OASys) provides a much less sophisticated and limited IT system but still provides scope for the development of repeated ICT approaches for use by clinicians based on easily available data.

Part II

Evidence-Based Practice

Chapter 8

Mental Disorder

Introduction

There are many possible ways of addressing the area of mental health. One is to provide brief coverage of a large number of forms of mental disorder. Such an approach, though, would necessarily be superficial and, as such, would miss many of the key themes pervading the area of mental health. An alternative approach and the one adopted here is to look at a specific, relatively narrow, area, using this as an exemplar for exploration of some key themes.

The area of mental health chosen for discussion below is depression. This is chosen for a number of reasons. First, it is an area where a high quality evidence base has developed over many decades. This means that it is possible to draw out themes based on good quality evidence. The notion of depression also graphically illustrates some of the key challenges inherent in the area of mental health. Furthermore, depression is a pervasive problem within prisons. The level of mental health difficulties in prison is markedly higher than that seen in the general population and prisons contain people with many of the risk factors associated with depression. This can be seen indirectly in the high rates of suicide and intentional self-injury amongst those in custody. Finally, depression is chosen because of its links to subsequent risk of reoffending. Depression appears correlated to a range of social disadvantages and problem behaviours, including criminal behaviour, from childhood onwards.

In looking at depression, the approach adopted below is one that draws on developmental psychopathology. This is multidisciplinary and multiparadigmatic in nature, involving a range of disciplines such as epidemiology, genetics, psychiatry, psychology, neuroscience and sociology (Rutter & Sroufe, 2000). This illustrates a fundamental aspect of mental disorders, namely that they cannot be convincingly accounted for, or addressed by, single disciplines. Developmental psychopathology approaches are also underpinned by a number of useful key themes. These include the notion that the aim is to understand emerging patterns of development, that the focus should be on understanding causal processes in development and that links need to be made between normal and pathological development.

Depression as a Concept

Depression is a relatively recent term used to describe a range of human experiences evident throughout recorded history. The term was probably initially coined very much in its modern form during the seventeenth century, where it was used to describe a lowering of spirits and severe unhappiness (Burton, 2001). The term 'melancholia' was in more common use at this time and was recorded through subsequent centuries as a relatively unusual illness, probably analogous to severe depression and seen primarily in asylums. The nineteenth century saw a steady growth in the medical diagnosis of 'dysphoria', deriving from the Greek meaning unpleasant mood and including unhappiness but also irritability and anxiety. From the 1860s onwards, the term 'depression' was seen increasingly in medical dictionaries.[1] The use of the term 'depression', in an ever broader construction, has since followed (Shorter, 2001). Indeed, it has been observed that 'Depression has passed from being a rather obscure illness called "melancholia" mainly seen in asylums, to the number one source of clinical disability in the world. This is a familiar trajectory for a psychiatric illness: from obscurity to epidemic status . . .' (Shorter, 2001). It has been convincingly suggested that one of the key drivers for this growth has been the increased availability of treatments. One of the first drug treatments for depression was opium, which became progressively available after the 1840s. This treatment was popularised by a family of psychiatrists (the Engelken family) and was extensively used to treat depression (Shorter, 2001).[2] The next major development in treatment for depression was the discovery of electroconvulsive therapy (ECT) at the University of Rome by Cerletti in the late 1930s (Cerletti, 1940). This approach was based to a large extent on the earlier work of the Austrian physician Julius Wagner-Jauregg. ECT quickly gained popularity, being used for an increasingly wide range of mental disorders throughout the 1940s, 1950s and into the 1960s.

The development of diagnostic frameworks was followed by the development of the first version of the Diagnostic and Statistical Manual (DSM I) (American Psychiatric Association, 1952). This established a pattern, used in successive revisions, of defining categories on the basis of current opinion. As such, DSM I suggested that depressive reactions were a symptom of underlying efforts to deal with anxiety. The DSM framework has been subject to progressive revisions and by the 1980s DSM III offered multiple diagnostic categories of depression. Indeed, DSM III provided 608 potential diagnostic categories for depression and subsequent revisions have contained similar numbers (American Psychiatric Association, 1980, 1987, 1994; Ban, 2000).

The introduction of new antidepressant drugs began in the 1950s and has continued since. The newest family of drugs to be used to treat depression is the selective serotonin reuptake inhibitors (SSRIs). Such developments gave a major boost to the diagnosis of depression, so that by 1985 it represented 29.5 per cent of all diagnoses by American psychiatrists. In 1995, this had reached 46.8 per cent (Olfson, Marcus & Pincus, 1999). It has also been argued that the decision to make SSRIs prescription-only drugs was a major contributory factor in this, with restricted sales to a 'disease' market leading to an apparent increase in the burden of disease in the community (Healy, 1997).

In reviewing the area of depression in its current usage, it seems likely that there is need for caution in the application of categorical disease models. There is self-evidently an enormous worldwide burden of unhappiness. Some of this unhappiness will be due to mental disorder and, in turn, part of this will be due to depression. This is essentially suggesting a continuum of human experience of unhappiness, with 'clinical depression' at the far end of this. Such a formulation, it is argued, serves an important function in helping to prevent psychiatric imperialism: the conversion of all human problems into 'illness'. It also gives a rationale for holding the psychopharmacological industry at arm's length (Shorter, 2001).[3]

Diagnosing Depression

Diagnosing depression involves allocating people to pre-defined categories that describe mental disorder. This methodology enjoys considerable popularity, drawing as it does extensively on developments in the biological sciences from the seventeenth century onwards. The usefulness of such methods depends on very precise and detailed observation and recording. Indeed, this characterised the work of early pioneers of classification in psychiatry and psychology, such as Pinel and Pussin in France (Pinel & Maudsley, 1977).[4]

The use of categorical approaches is not without difficulty, though, not least of which has been the changing structure of categories over time. A number of possible reasons for this suggest themselves. The classification of depression is similar in form to biological models used very successfully in surgery and physical medicine. The expressed overall aim has been to develop a classificatory system of categories that individuals can be allocated to (case identification). This allows the study of the epidemiology (case distribution), in turn providing a powerful conceptual tool for identifying causal factors, course, outcome (prognosis) and pathology of a disorder, as well as helping guide interventions.

An effort to apply such a model to depression presents considerable challenges. Psychiatric classification systems such as that of the American Psychiatric Association have undergone repeated revisions since inception and are currently in a fourth revised version, DSM IV-TR, with version five in development (American Psychiatric Association, 2000). Within DSM IV-TR, depression is divided into multiple sub-categories. Notions of comorbidity and dual diagnoses have also been added to account for features that do not appear readily to fit the model. This increases the number of potential sub-categories of depression very markedly. Such categorisation poses significant problems for both researchers and practitioners in terms of the reliability, validity and the utility of the sub-categories. Some of these appear not to be substantively different from others whilst overall it is not possible to identify so many subgroups reliably (Dawson & Tylee, 2001).

Additional difficulties with the use of categorical models to describe depression include the fact that signs and symptoms[5] often coexist across different categories. Depressed mood is not exclusive to depression and is seen in a number of other mental disorders described within existing diagnostic frameworks. Linked to this, different signs and symptoms may carry different weight within different categories. An optimally effective categorical system needs to achieve mutually exclusive and jointly exhaustive categories; for psychiatric diagnoses, this ideal has so far proved elusive (Bebbington, 2004). As a result, a diagnosis of depression is polythetic and two individuals may be placed in the same category on the basis of different patterns of signs and symptoms. Consequently, this reduces the scientific validity of such categories.[6] Categorical approaches to depression are also problematic because the symptoms in such systems are not reflexively related. Common symptoms such as depressed mood do not predict rare symptoms such as delusional beliefs: rare symptoms, though, are often predictive of more common symptoms. A suggested explanation of this is that rarer symptoms are in some sense more 'powerful' and in fact indicate greater severity of depression (Bebbington, 2004).

Classification also raises issues in terms of developing cumulative understanding of depression. Recent developments of categorisation, it has been suggested, have strayed a long way from scientific method. The most striking illustration of this historically has been the resistance to changing or discarding concepts not supported by the emerging scientific evidence base and the creation of overlapping categories of questionable utility. Operational criteria may, relatively straightforwardly, be used to improve the reliability of category identification. This in turn allows comparisons between categories. Issues of validity and utility, however, are not so easily dealt with. Within current frameworks, it is clearly possible for a person diagnosed with one syndrome to meet the criteria for one or more other syndromes. Notions of 'dual-diagnosis' and 'comorbidity' have been developed to explain such findings. Attempts to justify these have focused on analogies to physiology. One view is that such comorbidity and dual diagnoses reflect important relationships between clearly defined separate disorders. The logical proposition here is that there is no reason why a person with 'illness A' cannot also develop 'illness B'. Indeed, there may well be relationships between illnesses A and B, whether these are well understood or not.

An alternative hypothesis is that the growth of such notions simply reflects a conceptually flawed system of classification. In essence, it is suggested, the approach has developed reliable categories with little validity. Such invalid categories work poorly since they are not based on underlying pathology, in turn requiring the addition of other categorical concepts to account for inconsistent findings (British Psychological Society, 2000).

These differences of view are clearly amenable to scientific test. What is evident is that models of categorisation of depression have become the dominant paradigm in research and practice. These models tend to be much less specific than the detailed sub-categories suggested in diagnostic frameworks. However, this fact needs to be logically separated from issues of scientific validity and indeed utility. It is possible and even likely that current categories may prove to be inappropriate in the long term, either because further evidence suggests different, more valid, categories: or alternatively that the use of categorical approaches per se proves misplaced. In everyday psychological practice, it is the often uncritical, and indeed at times unreflective, use of categorical approaches, in spite of their scientific limitations, that is of most concern both empirically and ethically.

Thresholds for Categorisation

In using even simpler categorical approaches, judgements need to be made about whether or not an individual fits a particular category based on their signs and symptoms. For depression, this involves imposing a 'cut-off' point on an apparent continuum. The validity of this depends largely on the presence of meaningful discontinuities. A useful analogy here might be blood glucose levels in diabetes. Normal levels of blood glucose are generally given as between 4 and 8 mmol per litre of blood (Henry, 2001).[7] Levels outside this range are associated with adverse physiological effects. Yet in the case of depression, research from the British National Survey suggests a distribution best described by a smooth, exponential curve (Meltzer, Tom, Brugha et al., 2002). The absence of visible discontinuities raises interesting questions, indicating that decisions based on clinical severity may potentially be more valid and have better utility. Indeed, as noted above, this is what appears in much of the evidence base where description and analysis is often focused on notions of mild, moderate, severe and very severe depression (National Institute for Health and Clinical Excellence, 2007a).

In relation to this, it has been suggested that in many circumstances health professionals are inclined to lower the thresholds for the detection of disorder (Double, 2002). There are contrasting explanations for this observation. One positive interpretation is that such trends are connected to a desire, where possible, to try to provide help and assistance to those experiencing distress. Less positive explanations include economic and historical analyses which see this as in large part reflecting efforts to expand the market for health services whilst limiting the individuals who can provide these. This trend may equally result from a mix of motives.

Epidemiology of Depression

The basis of epidemiology is case identification and, as noted above, this presents marked challenges. Most good quality studies of depression have tended for this reason to focus on depression at the further end of the spectrum and have often used standardised measures of mood to facilitate comparisons.

In a comparison across nations, it has been suggested by some that there is little variation in rates of depression by place, intimating a stronger biological basis to depression (Weissman, Bland, Canino et al., 1996). This study reported prevalence rates at a given time (point prevalence rates)

134

ranging from 0.8 per cent to 5.8 per cent and lifetime prevalence rates ranging from 1.5 per cent to 16.4 per cent. The conclusions reached on the basis of the data in this study were surprising and an alternative and, for many, more plausible explanation of these data would be that there was indeed significant variation in depression by place. In the UK, there have been two recent major epidemiological studies of depression which looked at one-week point prevalence rates. These studies reported similar rates of 2.3 per cent (Jenkins, Bebbington, Brugha *et al.*, 1997) and 2.6 per cent (Singleton, Bumpstead, O'Brien *et al.*, 2001).

A number of factors have consistently been shown to correlate with depression. Women are more prone to be diagnosed with depression with ratios ranging from 1.6:1 through to 3:1 (Weissman, Bland, Canino *et al.*, 1996). A large-scale study across Europe reported an overall ratio of 1.7:1 (Angst, Gamma, Gatspar *et al.*, 2002). There is to date no clear explanation of why this should be the case, with a number of biological, social and economic factors being suggested as possibilities.

There are a number of clear associations between childhood experiences and later appearance of depression. The presence of 'neuroticism', anxiety, depression and reduced cognitive ability in childhood are associated with depression in adulthood (van Os, Jones, Lewis *et al.*, 1997). A variety of traumatic experiences in childhood, including physical and sexual abuse, have also been reported to be associated with adult depression (DeMarco, 2000). This association is even more marked in the case of the most severe forms of abuse (Romans, Martin & Mullen, 1996). It has been noted that such abuse often occurs in the context of a range of other problems which, in turn, suggests complex causation and the need for interventions which recognise and address this (Finkelhor, Hotaling, Lewis *et al.*, 1990).

Developmental Perspectives

The recognition that depression may be seen in children and young people in similar form to depression in adults is a surprisingly recent one (Pearce, 1978). This is perhaps related to the less developed verbal and intellectual skills that children and young people have, making identification and categorisation more difficult. Even so, there is developing evidence to suggest emergent patterns of depression and links between normal and pathological development in this area (Kovacs, 1986).

There is evidence to suggest high rates of recurrence and persistence of depression in children who experience an episode of depression. A prospective study of recurrence of major depression in children found that after 12 months 26 per cent had experienced recurrence, by 2 years this was 40 per cent and at 3 years 72 per cent (Kovacs, Feinberg, Crouse-Novak et al., 1984). Evidence of significant continuity in depression has also been found in cross-cultural studies including New Zealand (Newman, Moffitt, Caspi et al., 1996), the United States (Lewinsohn, Rohde, Klein and Seeley, 1999) and the UK (van Os, Jones, Lewis et al., 1997).

Experience of depression in childhood is also associated with a number of subsequent social impairments including social withdrawal, irritability, decreased concentration and psychomotor retardation (Harrington, Fudge, Rutter et al., 1991). Social withdrawal and irritability in turn may lead to impairment of social relationships, itself a risk factor for subsequent depression. Impaired concentration and psychomotor retardation are likely to have links to specific learning deficits and poorer school performance. In turn, it has been noted that adolescent ratings of 'dysphoria' (marked unhappiness or sub-clinical depression depending on your viewpoint) correlate with heavy tobacco use, delinquent activities and impaired intimate adult relationships (Kandel & Davies, 1986). These 'comorbid' problems are, in turn, more predictive of later social functioning than depression itself (Harrington, Fudge, Rutter et al., 1991).

Findings of marked continuity of depressed mood from childhood onwards have become a focus for research. There are a number of potential explanations for this. The most obvious of these is perhaps the notion that depression simply persists but falls below the threshold for categorisation. This direct persistence hypothesis is given support from the findings of a 12-year prospective study of childhood depression. This reported rates of persistence of depression of 15 per cent but also found that 43 per cent showed sub-threshold levels of depressed mood (Judd, Akiskal, Maser et al., 1998).

Another potential explanation is that the experience of depression in early life leads to some form of psychological 'scarring' which is associated with greater vulnerability to later difficulties. Such effects have been suggested from neurobiological perspectives (Post, 1992) and psychosocial perspectives (Rohde, Lewinsohn & Seely, 1990). This notion gains support from findings that suggest second and subsequent episodes of depression are less clearly associated with environmental stress (Post, Weiss, Leverich et al., 1996; Kendler, Thornton & Gardner, 2000).

A number of factors have been shown to be associated with increased risk of depression in early life. These include specific learning deficits, low intelligence, patterns of negative attributions, family discord, early deprivation and adverse social and economic conditions. This has led to suggestions that vulnerability to depression is mediated through social disadvantage (Fergusson, Horwood & Lynskey, 1995; Lorant, Croux, Weich et al., 2007).

This hypothesis is supported by the finding that maternal depression is only associated with depression in their children where it results in social disadvantage. Of course, depression in parents is often associated with such disadvantages being correlated with impaired child management, insecure parent–child attachment patterns, poor marital functioning and hostility towards children (Crittenden, 2000; Cummings & Davies, 1994). Family dysfunction and a lack of confiding relationships are also correlated with persisting difficulties in depressed individuals (Goodyer, Herbert, Tamplin et al., 1997).

There is a suggestion that such risk factors may act in a cyclical (or possibly synergistic) manner in depression. Women who experienced a lack of care during their own childhood are at increased risk of depression in response to negative life events. They are also at greater risk of experiencing such negative events with higher rates of early pregnancy and familial abuse and violence (Brown, Harris & Bifulco, 1986). In a later study, patterns of personality functioning in older adolescents were seen to be linked to chronic levels of interpersonal stress, which in turn were linked to increased risk of depression (Daley, Hammen, Davila et al., 1998). A study of families of depressed girls also found their families to be more prone to negative life events as a result of parental psychopathology (Goodyer & Altman, 1991). There is substantial evidence relating to early risk and protective factors in depression. There is also good evidence of a high degree of continuity in depression. In contrast, there is surprisingly little research and evidence looking at discontinuity in this area. This is perhaps a surprising oversight that opens up a number of key questions, for example, whether making environmental change to reduce adversity would lead to discontinuities in depression and the adverse effects associated with it.

Overall, the evidence base from developmental psychopathology suggests difficulties with categorical models of depression, with the issue of defining meaningful boundaries between normality and pathology being a pervasive problem (Geddes, personal communication, 2007; Rutter, Graham, Chadwick et al., 1976). Epidemiological studies though suggest that even mild depression is associated with social deficits (Pickles, Rowe, Simonoff et al., 2001).

Life Events and Depression

Stressful life events have for centuries been recognised as playing an important role in depression and unhappiness, dating back to the work of

Pinel and Pussin in the eighteenth century. Yet for long periods what might generally be termed social factors were largely neglected in favour of a search for a genetic or physiological cause. Only in the twentieth century did such notions come back to centre stage with recognition and efforts to measure stressful or negative life events (Holmes & Rahe, 1967).

In the context of depression, the work of Brown and Harris (1978) represented a step change in bringing stressful life events back to the heart of the scientific study of depression. There is good evidence to suggest links between adverse life events and the onset of mental and indeed physical health difficulties (Creed, 1981). An excess of negative life events has been noted in the three months prior to first episodes of depression. It has also been observed that the risk of depression increases around sixfold in the six months after experiencing markedly threatening life events. This effect is similarly pronounced where events are those outside individual control, suggesting that the effect is largely independent of individual characteristics (Brown & Harris, 1978).

Based on their analysis of a large group of women in London, Brown and Harris (1978) divided life events that might increase vulnerability to depression into two major groups: long-term and vulnerability factors. Long-term factors included such things as longstanding difficulties in relationships or economic hardship. Vulnerability factors included such things as having three children under the age of 14 years, not working outside the home, lacking a close and confiding relationship and loss of mother by death or separation before the age of 11 years. It was suggested that vulnerability factors might serve to exacerbate depression but were not causal (Brown & Harris, 1978).

This research paradigm has been greatly extended across depression and to other areas such as physical illness, leading to progressive refinements of the model (Creed, 1985). In studying Scottish island communities, for example, Prudo, Brown, Harris et al. noted a number of differences in findings compared to their initial sample from inner-city London. Here, issues such as group cohesion and conformity to social norms proved to be more important protective factors than in London (Prudo, Brown, Harris et al. 1981; Brown, Bifulco & Harris, 1987; Brown, Harris & Bifulco, 1986).

Overall, the life events hypothesis and the research paradigms that have built on it have yielded a number of significant insights into the development of depression. It seems clear that negative life events play a significant role in vulnerability to depression and the occurrence of early depressive episodes. In the case of subsequent episodes of depression, however, the role of life events appears less clear-cut, leading to suggestions that the first episode of depression, once triggered, has a 'kindling' effect for subsequent relapses (Kendler, Thornton & Gardner, 2000).

Neurobiology of Depression

There has been a significant amount of research looking at the neurobiological bases of depression. It seems clear from the evidence that there is a genetic component for predisposition to depression but the means by which this is expressed is poorly understood. It is evident that simple Mendelean inheritance does not explain the occurrence of depression and that whatever genetic vulnerability is involved is transmitted in a more complex manner. It also seems likely that there are a number of complex mediators of such risk (Kendler & Prescott, 1999).

Attempts have been made to look at polymorphic variation in gene alleles that may be linked to depression. There is some evidence to suggest that affective disorders may be more broadly associated with polymorphism of 5 hydroxytryptamine (5 HT or serotonin) receptors in the brain and of the 5 HT transport system (Cravchick & Goldman, 2000). There is, however, little evidence that genetic loading or the associated neuropsychological differences leave the person needing less environmental 'stress' to become depressed (Hirschfield & Weissman, 2002).

Hypothalamic-pituitary-adrenal
Axis (HPA) Hypotheses

A number of explanatory models of the neurobiological basis of depression have been suggested. These have largely focused on two major systems within the central nervous system, generally thought to be associated with emotion. These are the hypothalamic-pituitary-adrenal axis (HPA) and the hypothalamic-pituitary-thyroid (HPT) axis. These systems are anatomically and physiologically complex and involve a number of neurotransmitters, which have also been the focus of study.

The hypothalamic-pituitary-adrenal axis (HPA axis) refers to a complex set of actions and interactions between the hypothalamus, the pituitary gland and the adrenal glands. This axis is a major part of the neuroendocrine system controlling reactions to stress and regulating various body processes including digestion, the immune system, mood, sexual behaviour and energy use. Around 50 per cent of those identified as having depression show elevated levels of cortisol within this system, with slightly higher rates amongst those identified as 'melancholic'

(Cleare, 2002). Studies of cortisol are, however, complicated by the nature of this hormone which is pulsatile as well as being subject to diurnal variations.

There is some evidence that lowering the level of cortisol can help to reduce depression (Murphy, 1997). High levels of cortisol are also associated with changes to the 5HT system and hypocampal atrophy. There is, in turn, some evidence of such changes in some of those with depression (Sheline & Minyun, 2002). Experience of childhood abuse has also been shown to be associated with similar long-term changes in the stress response (Heim, Newport, Heit et al., 2000).

Changes to the HPA axis have also been shown to correlate with treatment outcomes. The ability of the body to suppress dexamethasone (Dexamethasone Suppression Test or DST) is an indirect indicator of levels of cortisol. Depressed individuals who fail to suppress this, suggesting elevated levels of cortisol, show a weaker placebo response and poorer response to cognitive behavioural interventions to address depression. Curiously, response to antidepressants is no different (Thase, Dube, Bowler et al., 1996). Clinical response to this test also suggests some interesting findings, with non-suppression associated with a fourfold increase in the risk of short-term relapse or suicide attempts. Non-suppression has also been reported as a predictor of suicide risk (Coryell & Sehlesser, 2001).

Recent interest has focused on the steroid hormone dehydroepiandrosterone (DHEA). In many respects this hormone has an effect that counters those of cortisol. The ratio of cortisol to DHEA in depressed individuals has therefore been studied, with some suggestion that this ratio may be higher in those identified as depressed (Young, Gallagher & Porter, 2002). Levels of this hormone also appear to be inversely correlated with estimates of depressed mood using standardised tests (Barrett-Conner, von Muhlen, Laughlin et al., 1999).

Hypothalamo-pituitary-thyroid (HPT) Axis

This system came to be of interest following observations that disorders of the thyroid may be associated with mood disorders. Findings in this area, though, have been less consistent than those for the HPA axis. There is some evidence of a blunting of the response of thyroid stimulating hormone (TSH) in response to the trypotophan-releasing hormone (TRH) in around 30 per cent of those identified as depressed. There is also evidence of increased levels of antithyroid antibodies in a minority (9–20 per cent) (Cleare, 2002). A recent review of six randomised studies also suggested that thyroid hormone may help to potentiate the effects of antidepressants in some individuals (Altshukler, Bauer, Frye et al., 2001).

Evidence-Based Interventions

Evidence-based interventions for depression can be divided into two broad categories: neurobiological and psychosocial. The former includes a range of drug interventions as well as other physical interventions such as the use of electroconvulsive therapies (ECT) and neurosurgery. The latter category includes a variety of psychosocial therapies.

Psychosocial Interventions

Cognitive Behaviour Therapy

There is strong evidence of improvement following the use of cognitive behaviour therapy (CBT) compared to control individuals from waiting lists in terms of improved mood as measured by scores on the Beck Depression Inventory (BDI) (Beck, Ward & Mendelson, 1961) (WMD = −8.30 95% CI −13.14 to −3.47). There is some evidence for remission as measured using the Hamilton Rating Scale for Depression (HRSD) (Hamilton, 1960) (RR = 0.45 95% CI 0.23 to 0.91) but this was not seen on the BDI. Some studies, however, have provided evidence to suggest that CBT does not outperform placebo medication or normal primary care support (Freeman, Arikian & Lenox-Smith, 2000; Scott & Freeman, 1992; Scott, Moon, Blacker et al., 1994).

No clinically significant differences were found in trials comparing CBT to antidepressants in terms of remission and symptoms in moderate, severe and very severe depression (Elkin, Shea, Watkins et al., 1989; Keller et al., 2000; Thompson, Kinmonth, Stevens et al., 2000). However, one year post treatment, CBT appeared to be better at maintaining a reduction in symptoms (HRSD WMD = −4.06 95% CI −6.60 to −1.40: BDI WMD = −5.21 95% CI −9.37 to −1.04). CBT also seemed to be better tolerated by individuals with a clinically significant difference suggested (RR = 0.82 95% CI 0.67 to 1.00). This finding may, however, be due to more of those with severe depression leaving CBT treatment early (National Institute for Health and Clinical Excellence, 2007a).

The combination of CBT with antidepressant medication appears to, at least initially, improve the efficacy of the antidepressants (HRSD SMD =

141

−0.46 95% CI −0.61 to −0.31), although it is not clear whether this small effect is maintained. There is stronger evidence suggesting improved remission in moderate and severe depression as measured using the HRSD (RR = 0.71 95% CI 0.62 to 0.82). In a comparison between CBT plus antidepressants compared to CBT alone, a clinically significant difference was not found (National Institute for Health and Clinical Excellence, 2007a).[8]

Short-term interventions of between 6 and 12 sessions appear to perform comparably with long-term CBT interventions in the reduction of depressive symptoms. There is also good evidence that short-term interventions perform better than placebo in achieving remission when measured using the BDI (BDI WMD = −7.41 95CI −11.96 to −2.85), although this effect is not seen using the HRSD.

Couple-focused therapy (CFT) was assessed by the National Institute for Health and Clinical Excellence (NICE). It primarily consisted of modifications of CBT that took into account close family relationships with partners, although some forms were based on interpersonal therapy (IPT) approaches. A reduction in depressed mood compared to waiting list controls was found at the end of treatment, as measured using the BDI (WMD = −11.64 95% CI −16.12 to −7.16). However, there was no evidence of better efficacy than antidepressants and insufficient evidence of improvement compared to CBT or IPT at end of treatment (Leff, Vearnals, Brewin *et al.*, 2000; National Institute for Clinical Excellence, 2007a).

Interpersonal Therapy (IPT)

There is evidence to suggest that IPT is more effective in the treatment of depression than placebo combined with normal clinical care (National Institute for Health and Clinical Excellence, 2007a). A reduction in depressive symptoms was noted using the HRSD (HRSD WMD = −3.40 95% CI −6.17 to −0.63), along with improved rates of remission (RR = 0.73 95% CI 0.56 to 0.93). The approach performed better than normal primary health care in terms of scores on the BDI (WMD = −9.23 95% CI −15.45 to −3.01) and HRSD (WMD = −3.09 95% CI −5.59 to −0.59). The approach also outperformed placebo in relation to the rates for leaving treatment early (RR = 0.57 95% CI 0.33 to 0.99).

Comparison between IPT and antidepressants suggested no difference as measured using the HRSD (WMD = 0.64 95% CI −1.32 to 2.59). The use of IPT was better than 'treatment as usual' as a follow-up treatment in terms of remission (HRSD RR= 0.66 95% CI 0.52 to 0.82) and depressive symptoms (HRSD WMD = −3.80 95% CI −6.29 to −1.31) (National Institute for Health and Clinical Excellence, 2007a).

Problem-Solving Therapy (PST)

The evidence base in relation to PST is more limited than that for CBT and IPT, with only three random allocation studies that met the criteria for inclusion in the NICE review (National Institute for Health and Clinical Excellence, 2007a). These studies provide limited evidence of greater efficacy in reducing depressed mood than placebo (HRSD WMD = −4.70 95% CI −8.42 to −0.98: BDI WMD = −7.80 95% CI −13.78 to −1.82). At 6 and 12-month follow-up, however, there was insufficient evidence to suggest a continuing effect in terms of a diagnosis of depression. There was also insufficient evidence when comparing the approach with antidepressants.

Counselling

The term 'counselling' covers a very wide range of psychosocial interventions, making evaluation of this area problematic. There is, however, some evidence favouring counselling over normal primary health care in terms of ratings on the BDI (BDI WMD = −5.40 95% CI −9.11 to −1.69). There is insufficient evidence to suggest that this effect is maintained at follow-up after 12 months. Antidepressants appear to be more effective than counselling to a clinically significant degree in achieving remission, as measured using Research Diagnostic Criteria (RDC) (RR = 1.41 95% CI 1.08 to 1.83).

Adverse Effects

There is little evidence of adverse effects associated with psychosocial therapies. Indeed, there is a general failing in the evidence base to consider such issues, or to report statistical data that may give clues to treatment impacts, such as number needed to harm (NNH) and number needed to treat (NNT).[9] This is curious and in marked contrast to the evidence base for neurobiological interventions. Yet it seems probable that such effects will be present with some people being helped by such interventions and some harmed. The most obvious area for consideration is perhaps the effect of such therapy, particularly in the early stages, on suicidal ideation, suicide risk and intentional self-injury and poisoning (Crighton, 2002b; 2006c; Towl & Crighton, 1998).[10]

Neurobiological Treatments

Selective Serotonin Reuptake Inhibitors (SSRIs)

There is strong evidence of better efficacy of SSRI drugs compared to placebo (HRSD RR 0.73 95% CI 0.69 to 0.78). This effect seems more marked for those with more severe levels of depression and also for studies conducted over longer periods of time. However, there was also strong evidence favouring placebo in relation to treatment dropouts (RR = 1.19 95% CI 1.13 to 1.25) (National Institute for Health and Clinical Excellence, 2007a).

Overall, there is strong evidence to support the use of SSRIs in the treatment of depression with a 50 per cent reduction in depressive symptoms reported by those with severe and very severe depression. There is some evidence of a positive effect in cases of moderate depression, although this may largely be related to publication bias. SSRI side effects, however, were evidently a factor in leaving treatment early due to problems tolerating the intervention (Geddes, Freemantle, Mason *et al.*, 2002; Geddes, Carney, Davies *et al.*, 2003).

Tricyclic Antidepressants (TCAs)

Tricyclic antidepressants pre-date SSRIs and remain in wide use for intervention in depression. The NICE review identified a similar number of randomised studies as for SSRIs with a similar pattern of findings. TCAs were found to be more effective than placebo, particularly in more severe cases of depression. However, these drugs were less well tolerated than SSRIs, with higher levels of side effects and greater rates of treatment dropouts (National Institute for Health and Clinical Excellence, 2007a).

St John's Wort

St John's Wort is a traditional plant-based treatment for depression and has been subject to a small number of randomised trials. These have been complicated by variations in the level of active ingredients used but some broad conclusions have emerged. There is good evidence of greater efficacy than placebo in reducing the symptoms of moderate to severe depression. St John's Wort does not appear markedly different from SSRIs and TCAs except for findings that it appears to produce better response in cases of moderate depression and weaker response in severe depression (National Institute for Health and Clinical Excellence, 2007a).

144

Antipsychotics

This group of drugs is frequently used where there is evidence of psychosis along with depression. This is a relatively common occurrence in identified cases of depression with the Epidemiological Catchment Study (ECA) in North America reporting evidence of psychosis in 14.7 per cent of cases of major depression (Johnson, Howarth and Weissman, 1991).

Surprisingly, the evidence from randomised studies is inadequate to support such use. Such studies do though present particular problems since those who show psychotic features of depression tend to have very severe depression, and so are arguably less suited for inclusion in randomised trials.

Electroconvulsive Therapies

As noted above, ECT was initially adopted in a largely uncritical way with efforts to apply the technique to a very wide range of mental health problems. Use in relation to depression has also declined but ECT remains in common use as an intervention, normally to address very severe depression. There is good evidence that the method is effective in reducing depression (Geddes, Carney & Cowen et al., 2003). There is also evidence to suggest that unilateral ECT (administration to one hemisphere of the brain) gives equivalent in response rates to that of bilateral ECT. There is also some evidence of greater efficacy where the electrical current administered is markedly higher than the threshold to induce seizures, though the mechanism of operation is poorly understood (Geddes, Carney, Cowen et al., 2003; Sackeim, Prudic, Devanand et al., 2000).

Adverse Effects

There is a consistent and well-demonstrated relationship between antidepressant drugs and cardiovascular morbidity and mortality (Glassman & Shapiro, 1998). This relationship is not straightforward, though. Depression is a significant independent risk factor for both myocardial infarction and cardiovascular mortality (adjusted relative risk 1.5 to 2.0; Ford, Mead, Chang et al., 1998). For those with ischaemic heart disease, this rises to 3.0 to 4.0 (Carney, Freedland, Sheline et al., 1997). The prevalence of depression in those with coronary heart disease is estimated to be around 20 per cent (Glassman, O'Connor, Califf et al., 2002). There is mixed evidence on whether interventions to reduce depression serve to reduce the risk of heart disease (Avery & Winokur, 1976; Pratt, Ford, Crum et al., 1996).

Two large-scale studies have shown increased rates of myocardial infarction in those taking antidepressants with an odds ratio of around 5 : 8. Yet both studies did not distinguish between the increased risk associated with depression and that associated with the intervention (Thorogood, Cowen, Mann *et al.*, 1992). There is at least one study which suggests an increase in suicidal thoughts in the early stages of antidepressant treatment (Jick, Kaye & Jick, 2004).

A number of adverse effects are associated with the use of ECT. There is good and longstanding evidence of retrograde amnesia following ECT, with such deficits persisting after completion of the intervention. Such deficits appear greatest among those who have received bilateral administration of ECT and least for those who received unilateral administration to the right hemisphere. There is also a relatively high relapse rate associated with ECT, and this tends to be higher in those with more severe depression (Sackeim, Prudic, Devanand *et al.*, 2000; Squire, Chace & Slater, 1976).

Summary

- Depression provides a very good illustrative exemplar of efforts to understand and address mental health problems. It highlights a number of key themes that cut across this area of research and practice. It also provides a high-quality evidence base. In looking at depression, the approach adopted here can be characterised as 'developmental psychopathology'. This is a multidisciplinary and multiparadigmatic approach to mental health founded in the links between normal and pathological development.
- Depression is a relatively recent term used to describe a range of human experiences evident throughout recorded history. The use of the term 'depression' has become broader in its construction at the same time that new neurobiological and psychosocial treatments have become available and public knowledge of the concept has grown.
- The classification or diagnosis of depression draws on categorical models used successfully in surgery and physical medicine. The scientific aim here is to develop mutually exclusive and jointly exhaustive categories. For depression this has, so far, proved elusive. More successful have been approaches that have defined depression in terms of broad categories based on severity.
- Reported prevalence rates for depression depend heavily on the definitions used. Studies based on the more severe forms suggest that it is not

an uncommon problem with point prevalence ranging from 0.8 per cent to 5.8 per cent and lifetime prevalence rates from 1.5 per cent to 16.4 per cent.

- A number of factors have consistently been shown to correlate with depression. Women are more likely to be identified as having depression, with ratios ranging from 1.6:1 through to 3:1. It seems likely that multiple causes are interacting in respect to gender differences in epidemiology.
- There are a number of clear associations between childhood experiences and later appearance of depression. These include 'neuroticism', anxiety, depression, reduced cognitive ability in childhood, specific attachment patterns and traumatic experiences including physical and sexual abuse.
- There is evidence to suggest high rates of recurrence and persistence of depression that is associated with a range of psychological and social deficits.
- There is good evidence to suggest links between adverse life events and the onset of depression. An excess of such negative life events has been noted in the three months prior to first episodes of depression. Risk of depression also increases around sixfold in the six months after experiencing markedly threatening life events.
- There has been a significant amount of research looking at the neurobiological bases of depression. It seems clear that there is a genetic component for predisposition to depression but the basis of this and the means of expression are complex and poorly understood.
- A number of explanatory models of the neurobiological basis of depression have been suggested. These have largely focused on two major systems within the central nervous system, generally thought to be associated with emotion. These are the hypothalamic-pituitary-adrenalin axis (HPA) and the hypothalamic-pituitary-thyroid (HPT) axis. These systems are anatomically and physiologically complex and involve a number of interacting neurotransmitter systems.
- A number of psychosocial interventions have shown significant effects in addressing depression. These include cognitive behavioural therapy (CBT), family-based therapeutic approaches and interpersonal psychotherapy (IPT). Such interventions appear to be effective alone and in combination with antidepressant drugs. As with other areas of psychotherapy, the specific approach seems less predictive than other factors and short-term interventions appear as effective as longer interventions. Perhaps surprisingly there has been little research into potential adverse effects from psychosocial interventions.

- A number of neurobiological interventions have been shown to be effective in reducing depression. These include a range of drug-based and electroconvulsive treatments. A number of adverse effects are associated with these interventions. There is a consistent but complex interacting relationship between antidepressant drugs and cardiovascular morbidity and mortality. The use of induced convulsive therapies is associated with retrograde amnesia.

Notes

1 The nineteenth century saw a very marked growth in the medical treatment of mental disorder. Dysphoria appears to have been a very broad category, encompassing varying degrees of unhappiness, anxiety and irritability of mood. Other very broad categories were developed such as the diagnostic category of 'neurasthenia' (Beard, 1869). This concept had remarkable breadth, covering everything from loss of sleep, anxiety and traumatic responses through to psychoses. The concept appears to have been replaced with psychological explanations (Taylor, 2001). The concept perhaps has modern parallels in categories such as chronic fatigue syndrome.

2 Opium, its later derivative diamorphine (heroin) and cocaine were mainstays of nineteenth-century medicine. These drugs were used to treat a range of physical and psychological disorders, often administered in solution with alcohol.

3 In making this point, Shorter specifically addresses psychiatry as the predominant mental health profession but the analysis seems equally applicable to other mental health professions. Psychologists have often been keen to extend the use of categorical approaches. Examples here might include the definition of antisocial and violent behaviour as forms of 'personality disorder', which can in turn be defined as 'illness'. Similar caution is perhaps needed here with a view to avoiding, in this case, psychological imperialism and keeping the psychometrics industry at arm's length.

4 In August 1793, Pinel was appointed as a physician at Bicêtre Hospital in Paris which housed approximately four thousand imprisoned men including criminals, petty offenders, syphilitics, pensioners and about two hundred mental patients. Soon after his appointment, he became interested in the 200 mentally ill men housed there, having gained previous experience working in a sanatorium. Having asked for a report on these inmates, he received a table with comments from the

'Governor' Jean-Baptiste Pussin (1745–1811). In the 1770s, Pussin had been successfully treated for scrofula (tuberculosis of the neck or more precisely cervical tuberculous lymphadenopathy) at Bicêtre. Following a familiar pattern, he was recruited, along with his wife, Marguerite Jubline, onto the staff of the hospice. Pinel, clearly appreciating Pussin's outstanding talent in working with the mentally ill, essentially apprenticed himself to Pussin. What he observed was a strict non-violent, non-medical management of mental patients, which was translated into English as moral treatment. A more accurate translation of the original French 'moral' would probably have been 'psychological'. Pinel clearly gave Pussin the credit he deserved. However, the legend grew about Pinel single-handedly liberating the insane from their chains.

5   Throughout this chapter, a simplified working definition of the terms sign and symptom will serve. Symptom is used to refer to the subjective experiences reported by the individual (e.g., unhappiness) and sign is taken to refer to observable factors (e.g., weight loss).

6   This is a point of fundamental scientific importance. The use of inadequate or inappropriate categories significantly reduces the power of this method to develop scientific understanding since efforts to test hypotheses will be impaired. To illustrate this with a simplified example, biologists could have decided to categorise all flying creatures within a single category, on the basis of observed behaviour. This would have resulted in heterogeneous categories that included both mammals (bats) and birds. In turn, this would have made understanding the common basis within groups significantly more difficult.

7   This is of course an oversimplification of reality and the normal range will vary according to a number of factors. The normal range in North America for example will differ from that in Europe, Asia and Africa. Individuals will also vary. Time of day and diet will have marked effects and so on. Such parameters therefore act as a guide to inform clinical judgements.

8   Two studies of behaviour therapy were included in the NICE (2007a) review. They are not included for discussion here as the review did not describe evidence of efficacy and purely behavioural approaches to treatment are little seen in current practice.

9   Number needed to harm (NNH) is a measure of how many people need to be exposed to a risk factor to cause harm in one patient who would not otherwise have been harmed. It is similar to number needed to treat (NNT) except that NNT normally refers to an intervention and NNH to a detrimental effect or risk factor. Both are calculated with

149

respect to 'exposure' and 'non-exposure'. Both are important measures in evidence-based practice, helping to decide on interventions in the light of potential outcomes.

10   This is not a failing exclusive to this area but one that affects research on psychological interventions more widely. It seems likely that this is, at least in part, linked to failings in methodology such as the continued dependence on Null Hypothesis Significance Testing (NHST) and a failure to take up multidisciplinary and multiparadigmatic approaches.

Chapter 9

Problem Drug Use

Introduction

In looking at work with problem drug users within prisons, it is important to have an understanding of the broader contextual issues involved. These include the issue of how drugs are defined, the distinction between licit and illicit use of drugs and the complex area of how problem use is defined.

A drug can be defined as:

• noun 1 a medicine or other substance which has a marked effect when taken into the body. 2 a substance with narcotic or stimulant effects. • verb (drugged, drugging) make (someone) unconscious or stupefied by administering a drug. – ORIGIN Old French drogue, perhaps from Dutch *droge vate* 'dry vats'. (Online Oxford English Dictionary, 2007)

From this definition, it can be seen that substances such as food are excluded, although these clearly have a physiological action on the body. However, the term still incorporates a very wide range of substances, many of which have very positive uses. For example, antibiotics are drugs that fall into this category.

A possible further subdivision of drugs is into those that are psychoactive and those that are not. A psychoactive drug would be any substance that directly influences an individual's psychological functioning. There are a number of clear divisions within the broad group of psychoactive drugs. These divisions tend to be based primarily on the nature of the effects. For the purposes of this chapter we have used the broad divisions outlined in Table 9.1 below.

Table 9.1 Major groups of psychoactive substances

Examples	Major effects
Diamorphine, heroin, morphine, alcohol, cannabis	Euphoria, disinhibition, initially elevated mood
Cocaine, caffeine, nicotine	Elevated mood, increased risk taking, poor judgement
LSD, MDMA	Perceptual changes, mood changes
Imipramine	Elevated mood
Largactil	Reduction of psychotic symptoms
Testosterone	Increased drive, increased aggression

Some psychoactive drugs may have clear positive effects. Antidepressant and antipsychotic drugs are evidently psychoactive but, when used appropriately, have been demonstrated to have positive effects. Such drugs also have a range of potentially adverse effects even where appropriately used, often described as side effects.

Drugs may also be considered in terms of legal status. Licit drugs are those which are not proscribed by law. Such drugs may be restricted by law but can be relatively easily obtained through approved channels. Alcohol is perhaps the best known and most widely available legal drug. It may be relatively freely made, distributed and sold through state licensed outlets in the UK. Likewise tobacco is a licit drug that may be legally manufactured, bought and sold through restricted channels. The drug caffeine is an example of a drug that is freely available with no restrictions on its manufacture, sale or supply.

A wide range of drugs are available legally only when prescribed by an appropriately qualified healthcare practitioner. This list includes a wide range of psychoactive substances, many of which are otherwise proscribed. An example here is morphine and its related compounds which may be prescribed by medical practitioners, primarily for use in relieving and managing pain.

Illicit drugs are those proscribed by law and not legally obtained. Such drugs may not be freely made, distributed and obtained and are subject to a range of controls. Within the UK, drugs are classified hierarchically according to different levels of control, as outlined in Table 9.2, with opiates for example being subject to very strict controls.[1] This hierarchical framework emerged in a somewhat piecemeal manner and has been subject to considerable criticism, with the suggestion that it lacks a logical foundation

Table 9.2 Classification and legal penalties for controlled drugs

		Legal penalties for possession	Legal penalties for distribution
Class A	Ecstasy, LSD, heroin, cocaine, crack, mushrooms, magic amphetamines (if prepared for injection).	Up to seven years in prison or an unlimited fine or both.	Up to life in prison or an unlimited fine or both.
Class B	Amphetamines, methylphenidate (Ritalin), pholcodine.	Up to five years in prison or an unlimited fine or both.	Up to 14 years in prison or an unlimited fine or both.
Class C	Cannabis, tranquillisers, some painkillers, gamma hydroxybutyrate (GHB), ketamine.	Up to two years in prison or an unlimited fine or both.	Up to 14 years in prison or an unlimited fine or both.

in the extent of harm caused by specific drugs (House of Commons Science and Technology Committee, 2006).

Defining the problem use of drugs is complex. At one level it can be argued that even relatively low levels of use of some drugs can be problematic and may interfere with an individuals social, psychological and physical functioning. Alternatively, moderate drug use may have positively beneficial psychological and physical effects on individuals. What is perhaps most noteworthy is the ubiquity of psychoactive drug use. There is no society where such drugs are not and have not been used. In addition, there appears to be a general link between ease of availability and the numbers of people who go on to misuse drugs (Jones-Webb, Toomey, Short et al., 1997). It is also the case that the use of drugs can lead to a range of problems. Misuse of drugs is associated with serious difficulties in terms of work, family and social life, as well as physical and mental health.

The majority of problem drug users seen in prison are there as a result of Category A or B drugs and alcohol. Some of those sentenced in relation to drug offences are not users but rather are involved in the production and distribution of controlled drugs. However, a large proportion of those in prisons are users of drugs and many will have been convicted of offences directly or indirectly related to their problem drug use (Lee & George, 2005).

Preventing High Risk and Problem Drug Use

There have been a number of attempts to look at the costs associated with high risk and problem drug use. In one recent study of this area, it was estimated that 16 per cent of associated negative impacts were on the workplace, 22 per cent were in the home, 13 per cent were linked to crime, 7 per cent to road accidents and 4 per cent to healthcare costs (Collins & Lapsley, 2002). In a study of young people using drug services in a northern UK city, a cycle of adverse experiences was noted. Those studied had tended to come from disproportionately socially excluded areas and troubled families: 28 per cent had been in local authority care, 36 per cent had left school early through suspension or exclusion and 60 per cent had a history of criminal offending. On average, this group had begun smoking tobacco at 11, drinking alcohol at 12 and taking illicit drugs at 13 years old (Beckett, Heap, McArdle *et al.*, 2004).

A study conducted in Australia looked at the levels of harms associated with various drugs. This suggested that there were five priority areas of problem drug use from a largely public health perspective:

- the long-term and dependent use of tobacco;
- short-term heavy alcohol abuse;
- long-term alcohol use above low risk levels of consumption;
- use of illicit drugs by injection; and
- risk patterns of legal drug use during adolescence. (Stockwell, Gruenewald, Toumbourou *et al.*, 2005)

Perhaps the most surprising finding here was the level to which legal drugs generate the majority of serious concerns.

The area of problem drug use has drawn extensively on public health models in both seeking to explain and address drug misuse. A number of reviews have been conducted looking at risk and protective factors and a number of consistent patterns have emerged. It has been suggested that such factors may usefully be divided into individual characteristics, social bonding, health beliefs and clear standards for behaviour (Hawkins, Catalano & Miller, 1992). Whilst such divisions may be helpful in focusing attention on specific factors, there is little empirical evidence to support one framework over another.

A broad view of prevention is therefore helpful when looking at problem drug use. Approaches need to extend from efforts to reduce the level of harm caused by drug use, as well as efforts to achieve abstinence in some users.

Examples of harm reduction strategies would include the provision of needle exchanges for those who inject drugs. Such interventions serve two main purposes. First, they can help in reducing the spread of blood-borne viruses such as hepatitis and HIV. Secondly, they provide an opportunity to engage those who are using drugs in this way with relevant services that can provide information, education and other interventions as appropriate. Such 'harm reduction' approaches need not of course detract from other interventions with problem drug users.

Risk and Protective Factors

There is a developing evidence base which suggests a number of common risk and protective factors for problem drug use, criminal behaviour and mental health problems (Loxley, Toumbourou, Stockwell et al., 2004; Williams & Chang, 2000). A number of pre-birth factors have been shown to correlate with later problem drug use. These include extreme family economic deprivation, coming from a sole parent household, having a father with a history of alcohol abuse and maternal drug use during pregnancy. In infancy and early childhood, these risk factors can be added to by child neglect and abuse and also the presence of environmental tobacco smoke. One suggested protective factor at this stage appears to be the child's temperament, with children showing an 'easy' temperament[2] being somewhat protected from later problem drug use (Stockwell, Gruenewald, Toumbourou et al., 2005). It seems, though, more likely that such differences may in fact reflect more positive interactions and attachments between parent and child during development (Crittenden, 2000).

Between the ages of 4 and 11 years, main risk factors have been reported as being early school failure, conduct disorder and aggression. Protective factors at this age include the child being temperamentally shy or cautious. Children with high levels of social and emotional competence also seem to be protected from drug misuse to some extent (Teeson, Degenhardt, Hall et al., 2005). From the ages of 12 to 17, problem drug use increases markedly and a number of associated factors have been noted here. Risk factors appear to include having a low level of involvement in activities with adults, high perceived levels of community drug use, living in disadvantaged communities, availability of drugs, positive models of drug use in the media, conflict with parents and favourable parental attitudes to drug use. Protective factors include having a firm family attachment, low levels of parental conflict, having good communications with parents and involvement with organised religion (Teeson, Degenhardt, Hall *et al.*, 2005). It seems probable that these factors are related and interact in complex and possible synergistic ways that are, as yet, poorly understood. By young adulthood (18–24 years), the main risk factors appear to be frequent drug use and also poly-drug use. This refers to where individuals show problematic patterns of use for two or more drugs. Protective factors here appear to include living in a well-managed community environment and getting married in early adulthood.

Correlations such as this do not, however, provide an understanding of the process which leads to problem drug use. Knowledge of this is generally poor but the emerging evidence suggests that causation is complex, with risk factors acting cumulatively over time. Because of this, an adequate understanding of problem drug use involves drawing from the evidence base from a number of disciplines, an approach which has been referred to as developmental psychopathology (Rutter & Sroufe, 2000). This in turn requires a broad view of the evidence base. In common with other areas of practice in prisons, addressing problem drug use requires expertise from a very broad range of practitioners if an adequate understanding of the area and effective interventions are to be delivered.

Evidence-Based Interventions – Illicit Drugs

A wide range of interventions has been attempted with problem drug users. Initially these tended to focus on those with established patterns of problem drug use but, increasingly, efforts at intervention have been attempted earlier than this. Interventions based on what may have seemed 'common sense' ideas, for example seeking to cut off drug supply, have proven relatively ineffective in reducing problem drug use. Indeed, in some cases such approaches have had unforeseen negative effects such as increasing the transmission of blood-borne viruses. It seems clear that interventions to reduce problem drug use need to be firmly evidence-based (Brettle, Davidson, Davidson *et al.*, 1986).

Interventions prior to birth have focused on preventing or delaying pregnancy in high-risk mothers and on providing greater support to them. There is little evidence to support the effectiveness of the former approach. Providing greater support to high-risk mothers has yielded more promising results. Increasing support from health visitors to these mothers was assessed in a twin-site random allocation study and was shown to reduce foetal exposure to harmful drug use. Increased health visitor support was maintained in place up to two years after birth, so this study mixed pre- and postnatal interventions. On follow-up, the results for the intervention group were encouraging, with fewer instances of running away from home, fewer convictions or probation violations, fewer sexual partners, fewer cigarettes smoked per day and fewer days consuming alcohol (Olds, Henderson, Kitzman *et al.*, 1999).

A number of studies have been undertaken looking at postnatal parental education as an intervention. The focus for many of these studies have been efforts to foster strong attachment bonds between parents and children, with a view to better meeting the child's development needs. Most of these interventions have been based on cognitive-behavioural approaches drawing on social learning theories, although some have been based more closely on attachment theory. To date, evaluations in this area have tended to be based on small-scale trials and limited follow-up periods (Loxley, Toumbourou, Stockwell *et al.*, 2004). However, a number of systematic reviews of this area have suggested positive effects of moderate size. Improvements have been reported for two thirds of participants on short-term follow-up but with this improvement deteriorating over time (Mitchell, Spooner, Copeland *et al.*, 2001).

Interventions designed to prepare children for school have been more extensively studied. Although not initially intended as interventions to address problem drug use, these have yielded interesting results in this area. Several of the preschool interventions conducted in the United States have shown positive effects at follow up. In some studies follow-up has, to date, extended up to 27 years post intervention. An example here is the Perry Preschool intervention. This has shown moderate positive effects in reducing drug use, teenage pregnancy rates, high school dropout rates, unemployment, welfare claims, mental health problems in women and arrest rates in men (Schweinhart & Weikart, 1997). The positive effects of such interventions have been assessed in economic terms and such analyses have been suggested economic returns of $2 saved for every $1 spent (Mitchell, Spooner, Copeland *et al.*, 2001).

Preschool interventions though have also been contentious in some respects, particularly in the United States. A number of approaches have yielded less promising results than the Perry intervention, resulting in loss of funding. Approaches that did not attract the family to more systemic methods have often been reported to yield generally short-term gains that deteriorated over time. Such approaches have also become involved in debates about the ethics of helping high-risk families rather than taking whole community approaches with all children in the same equally impoverished communities (Beelmann, Pfingsten & Lösel, 1994; Svanberg, 1998).

157

A number of interventions have been tried with school-age children. These have included family-based interventions, parent education interventions and drug education during early school years. Early school-based education addressing knowledge, attitudes and values appear to be of limited value in reducing problem drug use (Godfrey, Toumbourou, Rowland *et al.*, 2002). The results from parent education interventions have been more promising, with some studies suggesting modest positive effects at follow-up 1–2 years later (Sanders, Turner & Markie-Dadds, 2002). It should, however, be noted that such findings have generally been based on small sample studies. Most promising have been the family-based interventions with emerging evidence of cost effective impacts (Toumbourou, Williams, Waters *et al.*, 2005).

A number of school-based studies have also been undertaken in North America, looking at interventions to improve the quality of interaction between students and teachers and reduce negative peer group interactions. Such studies are largely based on the notion that intervention in this way may act to reduce the chances of early developmental risk progressing to become social exclusion. Results from such studies are in an early stage of development but suggest a promising avenue for effective intervention work (Conduct Problems Prevention Research Group, 2002).

Interventions with adolescents are generally at an earlier stage of development than those with younger children. There are a number of promising avenues of research but, to date, there is limited hard data to support the efficacy of interventions at this point. One exception was a study conducted in Australia covering 14 schools, with a sample of 600 parents of children in their early high school years that underwent a parent-education intervention. They were followed up after 12 weeks and a number of positive effects were noted which included a reduction in family conflict, a reduction in problem drug use and a reduction in delinquent behaviour (Toumbouro & Gregg, 2002). Such a follow-up period is, though, relatively short and it remains to be seen whether such effects are maintained over a longer period of time.

A variety of systemic family interventions have also been tried. An example of such an approach was the use of multisystemic interventions with young people reaching the courts. Families were engaged in a system of preventive case management which sought to address a range of problems. This intervention produced promising results with modest reductions in criminal and delinquent behaviour, along with reductions in problem drug use. These effects were found to be maintained at 12 month and 24 month follow-up (Cunningham & Henggler, 1999). An economic analysis of this intervention was also conducted and suggested an economic benefit of $5 for each $1 spent (Aos, Barnowski & Lee, 1998).

In contrast, the evidence on the efficacy of social marketing campaigns and school drug-based education for older groups has been unclear and generally disappointing. There has been some evidence of short-term effects but these have generally not been shown to persist. The application of such interventions in terms of behaviour change is also unclear.

The use of legal regulation of drug use has been extensive and has also been widely studied, primarily in relation to the problem use of alcohol and tobacco. High levels of regulation enforcement concerning these drugs is linked to lower levels of use in under-age groups (Toumbourou, Williams, Waters *et al.*, 2005). The situation with reference to illicit drugs is harder to study by the very nature of the legal prohibition of these drugs.

Attempts to mobilise community resources to address problem drug use have also been made, in an attempt to alter community norms concerning drugs. These approaches have generally combined school, parental and community interventions and include both licit and illicit drugs. The results have been mixed but generally suggestive of only short-term positive effects (Holder, 1997).

Interventions in Prisons

Prisons contain a relatively high proportion of problem drug users. Indeed, it has been noted that prisons have the greatest concentration of problem drug users in one place (Lee & George, 2005). Prisons in England and Wales have a throughput of approximately 136,000 offenders in a year and of these around 80 per cent report some history of problem drug use, with 55 per cent reporting severe difficulties with drugs. Based only on severe drug use problems, this means that more than 70,000 problem users will pass through prisons per year. This provides a clear opportunity to engage and work with these individuals and address the needs of this otherwise difficult-to-access group. There are therefore sound reasons for a broad-based and coordinated approach to needs.

Practice within prisons is developing and has to a large extent been informed by the emerging evidence base. An initial strategy was introduced in 1998 and was subject to extensive review and updating in 2002 and indeed continues to be refined and developed. This strategy has subsequently been merged with the broader National Offender Management Service (NOMS) strategy which addresses work with offenders in the community as well as those in prison custody.

The strategic approach has three central elements:

159

- the reduction of availability of drugs in prisons through a range of measures designed to cut supply;
- the delivery of effective interventions to encourage long-term abstinence amongst problem drug users in prison; and
- the development of effective throughcare arrangements with community-based services.

Supply reduction Prisons have adopted a range of measures designed to reduce the supply of illicit drugs and alcohol. Such measures are designed to reduce ease of access to these substances rather than completely exclude the possibility of access and use. Whilst the latter approach is a theoretical possibility, the costs would be prohibitive in human and economic[3] costs. Within these constraints, however, prisons have invested considerably in improved methods to reduce drug supply.

In addition, prisons have introduced mandatory drug testing (MDT) of a random sample of 5–10 per cent of prisoners each month to monitor levels of drug use and act as a deterrent. Those failing a mandatory drug test face prison disciplinary procedures that may lead to days being added to the sentence. The MDT process can also provide a useful means of identifying prisoners who need to be referred for assessment and intervention work. Voluntary drug testing (VDT) and drug-free wings for prisoners who wish to remain abstinent are also in place. For many, prison provides a chance to address their problem drug use in a supportive and controlled environment. This contrasts markedly with the communities in which many problem drug users live where use may be prevalent. VDT offers prisoners access to support and the opportunity to demonstrate that they are not abusing illicit drugs.

Additional efforts to control supply within prisons includes the systematic use of intelligence to target those thought to be supplying and misusing drugs. This involves joint work with police forces to help reduce supply from outside the prison. Controls in prison visits areas have also been increased with the use of closed circuit television (CCTV) surveillance in all closed prisons. Visits areas have also incorporated special furniture designed to make it more difficult to pass drugs undetected. Improved searching of visitors and the use of other high profile measures such as drug detection dogs have also been put in place. A range of sanctions may be imposed on visitors attempting or suspected of smuggling drugs, including the use of closed visits, removal of rights to visit and criminal prosecutions.

The other main routes for drugs to enter prisons are via breaches of perimeter security and via corrupt prison staff. Efforts have been made to enhance perimeter security significantly. A Professional Standards Unit has also been established to identify staff who may be involved in, or at increased risk of, corruption.

Harm reduction Another central and somewhat controversial approach to working with problem drug users in prisons has seen efforts to reduce the range of physical and psychological harm caused by drug use. As problem drug use tends to be a chronic and relapsing condition, the majority of problem drug users will at some point relapse into problem use. Initially, prison managers are concerned with the safe and effective detoxification of those coming into custody, with such services increasingly delivered by mainstream National Health Service providers, using similar standards to those that apply to problem drug users in the community.

Harm reduction is concerned with minimising adverse outcomes from problem drug use. In seeking to do this, the prisons have in place advice services which address areas such as the risk of overdose, the risk of blood-borne viruses and other high-risk activities such as unprotected sex or tattooing. In prisons, disinfection methods are being gradually introduced to allow illicit needles to be disinfected before they are shared. A hepatitis B vaccination programme is also being delivered. Prisoners are also being made aware of community-based needle-exchange provision. However, prisons in the UK have not introduced needle exchange within prisons (Towl & Crighton, in press).

Prisoners who are released back into the community also have access to counselling about the risks of overdose following incarceration. It is well established that prisoners on release are at high risk of overdose (Singleton, Pendry, Taylor *et al.*, 2003). For most prisoners, this appears to be linked to the relative lack of access to drugs within prison, where they may have abstained or, if they have continued to use, where they may have received a much reduced quantity and purity of drugs. On release, prisoners may relapse into use based on the dose of drug which they were taking before imprisonment, making no allowance for decreases in tolerance.

Evidence-Based Interventions – Alcohol

The approaches to those who abuse alcohol are in many respects similar. Individuals are identified and referred to treatment services within prisons. Interventions in this area are designed to meet individual needs and motivation and increasingly involve support for the families of alcohol misusers.

Intervention work has been developed in relation both to illicit drugs and to alcohol, a drug that is legal outside prison but illegal in prison. Initial health screening on entry to custody is used to try to identify those with the most marked problem levels of alcohol use. Such prisoners would then be assessed more thoroughly to identify those in immediate need of the management of symptoms of alcohol withdrawal. Detoxification from alcohol requires effective supervision during withdrawal and is associated with a range of serious and potentially life-threatening complications. Such detoxification is therefore generally undertaken in a healthcare setting with the support of a primary care medical practitioner, nurse practitioner or alcohol treatment worker. Initial detoxification can then be followed by structured counselling, addressing issues of motivation to change, social and interpersonal skills, behavioural self-control training, systemic therapy and relapse prevention. Where appropriate, prisoners can also be referred to specialist residential interventions (National Offender Management Service, 2005).

Where individuals may benefit from a short intervention, especially where problems are not yet too severe, they may be referred to self-help interventions such as Alcoholics Anonymous (AA). Those assessed as requiring specialised treatment for physical health problems, such as liver disease, are referred to the local specialist services (National Offender Management Service, 2005).

The broad range of services available to adult problem drug users who use illicit drugs fall under a scheme called CARATS (Counselling, Assessment, Referral, Advice and Throughcare Services).[4] Within this approach, prison-based staff initially assess the need of prisoners, feeding these into systematic care plans. As part of this, they may refer prisoners to short-term counselling or groupwork interventions within prison.

Prisoners may be referred to a short duration or an intensive drug rehabilitation intervention, dependent on needs. At this point, they may also be offered systematic advice on harm minimisation. Efforts will also be made to ensure that prisoners are effectively linked into mainstream community addiction services to try to ensure continuity of effective care on release. CARATS is delivered by teams of specialist drug workers contracted to provide services to prisons and part of such contracts has been a stress on effective liaison with mainstream community-based services when preparing a prisoner for release. Where possible, such prisoners are located close to their home area in preparation for this. This serves a number of key functions. It is for example more likely that the prisoner will be able to return to fixed accommodation, stable family relationships and access timely community drug services where this is done. This in turn seems to contribute to lower rates of relapse and reoffending.

All local and remand prisons are now equipped to offer a range of clinical services to problem drug users. As with alcohol, initial detoxification services have been put in place (Lee & George, 2005). A limited range of maintenance-prescribing interventions has also been made available as a basis for prisoners to undertake broader-based drug treatment interventions. A number of prisons run '12-Step' interventions, based on the approach to addiction developed by AA. These interventions are designed to achieve complete abstinence. As outlined above, the evidence for the impact of such interventions is limited.

A short-duration intervention for problem drug users has also been developed for those serving relatively short sentences who would be unlikely to be able to engage in longer-term intervention work. This is founded on cognitive behavioural approaches and is designed to give prisoners a better understanding of the patterns of drug use and to develop skills that would enable them to abstain from, or reduce, their use.

In parallel to this, the Youth Justice Board (YJB) has also developed a service designed to help young people in custody address a broad range of substance-misuse needs. The intervention addresses alcohol, solvents and illicit drugs. In contrast to interventions with adult prisoners, it also addresses tobacco use as part of a wider process of addressing needs (Riala, Alaraisanen, Taanila et al., 2007; Youth Justice Board, 2003). As with adults, the transition from custody to community is seen as critical and resettlement and after-care provision (RAP) is being piloted in 17 Young Offending Team (YOT) areas which cover 15 drug interventions in high-crime areas. This new initiative is designed to engage young people in custody and provide high levels of support in the community. The core RAP provision will involve up to 25 hours of planned support and activities each week with access to substance-misuse and mental health treatment, support to access accommodation, education training and employment, positive use of leisure time, and peer and family support work.

The CJIP (Criminal Justice Intervention Programme) is a large-scale intervention which was established in April 2003 as a central plank of the updating of the strategy to address problem drug use. Its principal aim is the reduction of crime linked to problem drug use. This aim is to be addressed by moving problem drug users in custodial and community settings into appropriate interventions and post-intervention support. The intention here is to break the cycle of drug misuse, offending and custodial sentences by intervening at every stage of the Criminal Justice System to engage offenders in drug treatment. This approach is built on available interventions, such as arrest referral schemes. Drug testing for those charged with selected crimes was also introduced. Such interventions now exist at arrest, in court, during community and custodial sentences and for those finishing sentences or leaving treatment in the community (Home Office, 2003). Interventions are designed to provide rapid access to prescribing services, referral assessment and a tier 2 treatment service (including counselling, harm reduction, motivation and preparation for referral). Schemes also provide a single point of contact on a 24-hour basis by phone, particularly for those leaving custodial establishments and/or treatment. In parallel, they provide a single point of contact for referrals from practitioners including those in criminal justice agencies, CARAT teams and treatment agencies. A case management approach is used to ensure continuity of care.

Summary

- In looking at work with problem drug users within prisons, it is important to have an understanding of the broader contextual issues involved. These include definitional issues, the distinction between licit and illicit use of drugs, how problem use is defined and the social context of drug use.
- Drugs may be considered in terms of legal status. Illicit drugs are those proscribed by law and not legally obtained. Such drugs may not be freely made, distributed and obtained and are subject to a range of controls. Within the UK, such drugs are classified hierarchically as class A, B or C.
- Defining the problem use of drugs is complex and relatively low levels of use of some drugs can be problematic for some. It is clear that the use of drugs is ubiquitous across societies and has costs and benefits. Misuse of drugs, however, is frequently associated with serious difficulties in terms of work, family and social life as well as physical and mental health.
- The area of problem drug use has drawn extensively on public health models in both seeking to explain and address drug misuse. A broad view of prevention is essential when looking at problem drug use. Approaches need to extend from efforts to reduce the level of harm caused by drug use, as well as efforts to achieve abstinence in some users.
- There is a developing evidence base that suggests a number of common risk and protective factors for problem drug use, criminal behaviour and mental health problems. These include a number of factors linked with economic and social exclusion.
- A wide range of interventions has been attempted with problem drug users. Interventions based on simply seeking to cut off drug supply have

proven relatively ineffective in reducing problem drug use, with unforeseen adverse effects such as increasing the transmission of blood-borne viruses.

- Interventions providing support to high-risk mothers via healthcare staff have yielded promising results. Follow-up data suggests that children of these mothers have better long-term outcomes.
- Several of the preschool interventions conducted in the United States have shown positive effects. They have shown moderate and cost-effective positive effects in reducing drug use, teenage pregnancy rates, high school dropout rates, unemployment, welfare claims, mental health problems in women and arrest rates in men.
- Interventions with adolescents are generally at an earlier stage of development. There are a number of promising avenues of research but limited data to support the efficacy of interventions. Multisystemic interventions have, though, produced promising results with modest cost-effective reductions in criminal and delinquent behaviour, along with reductions in problem drug use maintained at 12-month and 24-month follow-up.
- Prisons contain the greatest concentration of problem drug users in one place. This provides a clear opportunity to engage and work with these individuals and address the needs of this otherwise difficult-to-access group.
- The strategic approach in prisons has three central elements: supply reduction, effective interventions to encourage long-term abstinence amongst problem drug users and development of effective throughcare arrangements with community-based services.
- The approaches to those who abuse alcohol are similar with prisoners identified and referred to treatment services within prisons. Interventions in this area are designed to meet individual needs and motivation and increasingly involve support for the families of alcohol misusers.
- The broad range of services available to adult problem drug users who use illicit drugs fall under a scheme called CARATS (Counselling, Assessment, Referral, Advice and Throughcare Services). Within this approach, prison-based staff initially assess the need of prisoners, feeding these into systematic care plans.
- The CJIP (Criminal Justice Intervention Programme) is a large-scale intervention established in 2003 as a central plank of the updating of the strategy to address problem drug use. Its principal aim is the reduction of crime linked to problem drug use. This aim is to be addressed by moving problem drug users into appropriate interventions and post-intervention support in custodial and community settings.

165

Notes

1 A review of the history of drug use is outside the scope of this chapter. However, it is worth noting that attitudes to currently proscribed drugs have changed over time. In the nineteenth and early twentieth century, opiates such as morphine were widely available, often in the form of 'tonics'. Likewise food products often contained drugs that are now proscribed. The effects of the widespread use of such drugs led to increasingly strict controls in the UK for drugs such as opiates and alcohol.

2 For a fuller discussion of early temperament in children, see Chapter 3.

3 In order to achieve such complete exclusion, all prisoners would need, for example, to be subject to closed visits which prevented any possibility of contact with their families and friends. Such an approach would raise a number of issues relating to fairness, human rights and conflicts with other prison aims such as improved integration of offenders back into the community.

4 The term 'throughcare' is one used in prisons but little used outside. It largely equates to treatment.

Chapter 10

Post-Traumatic Stress

Introduction

A medical dictionary definition of trauma defines the concept in very broad terms:

> '1 a: an injury (as a wound) to living tissue caused by an extrinsic agent ⟨surgical trauma⟩ ⟨the intra-abdominal organs at greatest risk to athletic trauma are the spleen, pancreas, and kidney – M. R. Eichelberger⟩ b: a disordered psychic or behavioral state resulting from mental or emotional stress or physical injury
> 2: an agent, force, or mechanism that causes trauma' (Merriam-Webster's Medical Dictionary, 2002)

Such breadth suggests wide-ranging impacts associated with trauma, making it difficult to do full justice to the area. Research and practice has therefore tended to focus on particular aspects of trauma. In recent years, a major focus in the field of trauma, and one of particular salience in prisons, has been on the notion of post-traumatic stress disorder (PTSD), a term which refers to disordered behavioural and psychological states associated with severely traumatic events. This is the focus of the discussion here as, in the context of prisons PTSD has been and remains an important construct. Within prisons, there is a high proportion of individuals who have had such experiences, often in the form of physical abuse but also as a result of sexual assaults and other forms of potentially traumatic events (PTEs). Prisons are also places where such experiences are more likely to occur in a number of ways. This may include PTEs in prison, occurring both legitimately and illegitimately. In addition, justice settings such as prisons are environments that by their nature present increased risks of trauma for both staff and visitors (King & Alexander, 2002; Stanko, 2001).

A range of dysfunctional responses to coping with potentially traumatic events has long been observed. In recent history, some of the most striking descriptions derive from World War I with observation of 'shell shock'. Here, the introduction of film provided a means of accurately recording both modern mechanised warfare and the reactions to it. World War II and subsequent conflicts saw many cases of 'combat fatigue' with similar effects, although the differences in traumatic experiences seem to have led to differing presentations. More recently, following the Vietnam conflict, such reactions to trauma came to be described in terms of post-traumatic stress disorder (PTSD), a specific concept introduced in the third edition of the Diagnostic and Statistical Manual of Mental Disorders (DSM III). This construction recognised that it was not just in the context of war that such reactions were seen (American Psychiatric Association, 1980). Later revisions have modified the definition of the category PTSD, including the recognition that children may react to trauma in different ways to adults (American Psychiatric Association, 1987, 1994). DSM criteria for PTSD include a requirement for exposure to one or more potentially traumatic events where the person experiences events involving actual or threatened death or serious injury, or a threat to the physical integrity of themselves or others. It also specifies the type of response to this as one involving intense fear, helplessness or horror.[1] Additional criteria include the event being persistently re-experienced in a recurrent, intrusive and distressing way, either in feelings or dreams. Individuals also need to show intense psychological distress at exposure to internal or external cues resembling aspects of the traumatic event, with physiological reactivity, persistent avoidance of stimuli associated with the trauma and a numbing of general responsiveness not present before the trauma. In order to meet the DSM criteria for PTSD, the disturbance associated with the traumatic event needs to last more than one month and cause 'clinically significant distress or impairment' in social, occupational, or other important areas of functioning (American Psychiatric Association, 2000).

It has been suggested that this and earlier categorical models of dysfunctional responses to trauma were introduced as a means of enabling interventions with sufferers. In the context of notions such as 'shell shock' and 'combat fatigue', this is a largely persuasive argument. PTSD was also increasingly used as the term for trauma in soldiers following wartime experiences in Vietnam and was initially used in a similar manner to enable access to treatment. Since then, however, the threshold for identification of

PTSD appears to have progressively shifted to include less severe trauma and much less clearly dysfunctional responses to such experiences. This shift opens up often valid criticisms that PTSD has become an example of 'psychiatric imperialism', the conversion of all human problems into 'illnesses' (Shorter, 2001).

Unlike some earlier notions of trauma, PTSD is construed in terms of a diathesis stress model that assumes an underlying vulnerability or diathesis.[2] This in turn may be 'triggered' by exposure to traumatic events. The model seems largely predicated on the notion that stress or 'triggers' are by their nature state-dependent, whilst the diathesis is a trait-dependent characteristic (Flouri, 2005). This hypothesis raises a number of logical issues. Most notably, perhaps, it says little about the nature of the trait or traits involved in any diathesis. Indeed, descriptions of these may often be confused, the same or similar factors being described as outcomes as well as part of the diathesis. Mental health difficulties such as depression may thus be described in a circular manner as both a 'cause' and an 'effect'. Additionally, the model of PTSD has tended to focus on research for trait characteristics, often at the expense of environmental factors. The concept of PTSD can therefore, with some legitimacy, be criticised for neglecting the role of social, personal, familial and cultural factors in trauma and individual responses to it (Flouri, 2005).

PTSD as a categorical construct is used to describe a range of human experiences that are far from new. Relatively fixed patterns of both functional and dysfunctional responses to trauma have been well documented and described (Head, 1916; Macleod, 2004; Myers, 1940). It has, however, been suggested that shifting thresholds for categorisation mean that notions of PTSD have been increasingly applied to experiences that would, in the past, simply have been seen as fairly routine parts of life. This is not to reduce the importance of such experiences on an individual or indeed group level; it is rather to question the utility of defining such experiences as 'illness' or for that matter as 'dysfunction'.[3] It is alternatively possible to view many of the reactions seen to traumatic events as part of the normal psychosocial and neurobiological processes involved in dealing with threats. These can clearly break down in extreme situations, such as where social structures prevent otherwise adaptive responses taking place. Yet there are clear economic and social implications from increasing the breadth of application of psychopathological concepts beyond such extremes.

The construct of PTSD also raises some more pragmatic issues, using as it does a number of vague, poorly defined and highly subjective criteria in describing PTSD. The area has also become closely associated with a number of economic vested interests as the result of the commercialisation of therapeutic approaches. Professional opinion therefore remains somewhat divided about the degree to which PTSD has validity and utility as a scientific category or diagnosis. It does seem clear, though, that there are commercial incentives to lower thresholds for identification, in turn increasing the apparent burden of 'illness' (Mezey & Robbins, 2001; Shorter, 2001; Summerfield, 2001).[4]

As with other categorical constructs, the limitations inherent in the approach apply to PTSD and need to be adequately recognised. PTSD may serve a useful function in providing a shorthand description of a general group of responses to traumatic events. Perhaps largely for this reason, it has come to be widely used across the evidence base and indeed it is now difficult to sensibly discuss the field of trauma without reference to PTSD.

Phenomenology and Epidemiology of Trauma

Exposure to traumatic events theoretically places anyone at risk of developing the traumatic adjustment problems characterised as PTSD. Drawing on the diathesis stress model, it is in principle possible that any event could potentially be traumatic to someone. Initially, though, the focus has been on extreme forms of human experience, such as participation in war or major civil disturbances. The steadily broadened use of PTSD to include a wide range of events with which traumatic responses might be associated has significantly changed the construct and thus its epidemiology. The criteria defined with the various revisions of DSM have nonetheless continued to emphasise a number of common characteristics. These include aspects of the traumatic events, including their unpredictability, uncontrollability and the violation of individual beliefs and expectations about safety, physical integrity, trust and justice. As noted, this allows considerable and, arguably, undue and excessive scope to alter the thresholds for categorisation, affecting epidemiological estimates of prevalence and opening the category to significant inflation over time.

It seems both axiomatic and healthy that any person exposed to traumatic events will experience a reaction, generally involving strong psychological and physical responses. The acquisition of adaptive responses to stressors is a fundamental aspect of the development of each person. Indeed, neurobiological systems to achieve just this are well adapted in people. Thus many of the reactions seen, whilst perhaps not subjectively pleasant, are probably adaptive in the sense that they serve to put in place resources for the individual to try to deal with the event. At a basic level, reactions such as fear, withdrawal, depression and what has been termed the 'fight or flight reaction' in the face of a serious threat can all be seen as means of trying to deal effectively with danger. It is argued that traumatic stress reactions contrast with such responses in that they are prolonged and characterised by ongoing feelings of vulnerability, loss of control and depersonalisation and de-realisation (Herman, 1992). Those who experience such traumatic reactions also appear to have increased rates of various other mental health difficulties. The most frequently observed comorbid problems appear to be substance abuse, depression and violence (Mazza & Reynolds, 1999; Saladin, Brady, Dansky et al., 1995). The separation of PTSD from reactions such as fear and depressed affect can therefore seem confused and potentially flawed (Flouri, 2005). Indeed, it seems likely that mental health difficulties such as depression may, in some people, be closely linked to efforts to adapt to past traumas, often in childhood (DeMarco, 2000).

As with depression, it is only comparatively recently that traumatic experiences in children have been recognised and subject to systematic study. Those studies that have been undertaken have tended to conclude that little is known about this area, despite the suggested importance of developmental factors in adult PTSD. The importance of the developmental process involved in PTSD in children has recently been stressed as a key area for future research (Ruggiero, Morris & Scotti, 2001). There is perhaps also a need for better integration of the evidence base on PTSD and in related areas such as the role of trauma in the development and recurrence of depression (Crighton, 2006b).

Research that has been carried out in this area suggests a number of risk and protective factors associated with trauma in children. Many of these are factors implicated in others areas of mental health and also evident from the research into developmental factors in delinquency and criminal behaviour. Factors with particular significance include parental warmth, high intelligence, family support and low family conflict (Piquero, Farrington & Blumstein, 2007; Punamäki, Qouta & El-Sarraj, 2001). Quite how these factors act and interact in the development of what might generally be captured as mental health problems, however, remains poorly understood (Crittenden, 2000; McNally, 2003; Piquero, Farrington & Blumstein, 2007).

A range of factors have similarly been shown to correlate with poor responses to trauma in adults. Risk factors identified have included the quality of social support, a family history of suicide and self-injury, the presence of family and marital problems, disturbances in sexual functioning, poor quality of emotional relationships with significant others, poor quality of life, somatic complaints and poor physical health (Kilpatrick, Resnick, Freedy et al., 1998; van der Kolk, 1997). In a review of the epidemiological evidence in this area, it has been suggested that these might be captured under three more global factors with relatively uniform effects: pre-existing psychiatric disorders, a family history of such disorders, and trauma during childhood (Breslau, 2002).

Because of the complex and heterogeneous nature of the concept, epidemiological studies of PTSD pose a number of problems. As outlined, issues of definition and the changing thresholds for categorisation make comparisons across time difficult. The US National Comorbidity Survey, using the fairly low threshold based on DSM IV criteria, has suggested a lifetime prevalence of just fewer than 8 per cent. However, some groups within the population appeared at markedly increased risk and it seems likely that this distribution would be mirrored using higher thresholds. Groups such as combat soldiers, police officers, prison, fire and paramedical staff appear at increased risk of PTSD (Koren, Norman & Cohen, 2005; Wright, Borrill, Teers et al., 2006). A long-term follow-up study of soldiers who had served during the Vietnam War reported point prevalence rates of 15 per cent for men and 9 per cent for women and lifetime prevalence rates of 31 per cent and 27 per cent respectively (Kessler, Sonnega, Bromet et al., 1995).[5]

High lifetime estimates of levels of exposure to PTEs have been reported, with 60 per cent of women and 51 per cent of men recalling at least one experience meeting DSM criteria (Kessler, Sonnega, Bromet et al., 1995). This is even higher in areas with high levels of social and economic deprivation where research suggests rates of 89 per cent of the population (Breslau, Chilcoat, Kessler et al., 1999).[6]

Most people who have experienced a PTE report an initial and intense reaction to the event which serves to interrupt their normal psychological and physiological functioning for a short time. Typical reported reactions include initial feelings of being stunned, subjectively impaired memory and ability to think, emotional lability and sleep disturbance. When exposed to reminders of the event, individuals will also frequently report visceral re-experiencing, negative affect and avoidance behaviour. From a psychological perspective, this is perhaps unsurprising and there is a wealth of evidence to show that people will generally try to avoid aversive experiences on the basis of previous learning. In this sense, a PTE can be seen as an example of powerful one-trial learning. Cognitive responses, such as blocking events out, may also be seen as functional in that they serve to prevent repeating aversive and distressing memories, with depressed mood appearing to link to issues of safety and loss of control (Basoglu, Livanou, Crnobaric et al., 2005).

In large part, the manner in which an individual deals with this initial reaction appears to determine long-term adjustment and risk of experiencing serious ongoing adjustment difficulties. Significant individual differences in adjustment to such events also emerge from the evidence. Some appear to be particularly avoidant and fail to disclose the event or events to significant others, or indeed lack close and supportive relationships in which they may disclose such events. Others may be exposed to environments that are harsh, rejecting or over-demanding or, conversely, environments that are unduly demanding of disclosure. Such settings do not appear to support effective adaptation and recovery and seem to increase the risk of long-term difficulties (Litz, Orsillo, Kaloupek *et al.*, 2002).

A number of individual characteristics have been associated with poorer long-term outcomes in response to traumatic events. These include attempts to fully suppress thoughts and feelings about the trauma. Such efforts seem to drain resources and also increase rather than reduce levels of psychophysiological arousal (Gross & Levenson, 1993). Multiple traumas or the experience of trauma early in development have also been associated with poorer prognosis. Other indicators include problems with self-care, affect regulation and changes to perceptions of personal agency and control. There is some evidence to suggest that poor adjustment is associated with selective attention to threats, which serve to confirm the perception of danger within the environment, habitual avoidance behaviour and negative responses from others. The best predictor of post-traumatic stress response, however, is situation. The intensity and degree of threat to life experienced during the traumatic experience or experiences and the individual's peri-traumatic response to this appear most predictive of outcome, accounting for the largest part of the variance seen in outcomes (Najavits, Weiss & Shaw, 1997).

Models of Post-Traumatic Responses

Cognitive behavioural models of PTSD hypothesise that conditioned emotional responses to traumatic events have a primary role in the development of the syndrome (Bisson, Shepherd, Joy *et al.*, 2004). Following on from the peri-traumatic response, a wide range of cues may come to be associated with the event and, in turn, be capable of triggering a negative response. Where the traumatic event is a road traffic accident, cues such as police and ambulance sirens may come to be associated and generate a stress response. This can become further generalised to include all loud noises, flashing lights and so on. A wide variety of stimuli are thus conditioned to produce responses and these may become ever more easily accessible (sometimes termed hyper-accessibility) to memory. Emotional responses may be triggered by such memories and result in defensive behaviours. In PTSD, such defensive behaviours become routine and over-learned with two clear effects. One is that it becomes difficult for the person to show other behaviours and the second is that this prevents sustained emotional processing of the trauma-related memory (Elzinger & Bremner, 2002; Foa, Steketee & Rothbaum, 1989).

Psychological 'scarring' associated with some of the most severe trauma appears to make a return to previous or normal functioning impossible. Examples here might include some combat veterans, survivors of concentration camps or those who have experienced prolonged sexual or physical abuse. In such cases, it has been unconvincingly suggested that there is a need for a separate diagnostic category of 'complex PTSD' (Herman, 1992). Given the difficulties with the existing category, it is difficult to see the scientific utility in such a category, representing what seems likely to be the extreme continuum of psychological responses to trauma.

Information-processing models of PTSD differ theoretically from cognitive behavioural theories in a number of ways. They hypothesise that PTSD is closely related to other difficulties in managing anxiety. Such disorders are characterised by pathological information-processing biases developed early in life, with excessive focus on some forms of information such as threat cues. These biases, it is suggested, result in greater susceptibility to trauma in adulthood. This model provides a possible theoretical account of links between experiences of childhood trauma, such as sexual and physical abuse, and problems in later life in developing adaptive responses to stress (McNally, 2003). The theoretical basis of information-processing models, however, has received only limited support from the evidence base (Ost, 2005).

Evidence-Based Interventions

PTSD is defined with reference to a range of heterogeneous signs and symptoms[7] that significantly disrupt an individual's life. As noted, this raises issues of accurate identification. Given the nature of the construct of PTSD, 'diagnosis' needs to be approached with circumspection. This has been vividly illustrated in the evidence base, for example in a recent study of head-injury patients. Here, two questionnaire assessments were compared to an assessment by experienced clinicians. Using structured assessments, very high levels of over-diagnosis of PTSD were reported, with 44 per cent and 59 per cent being 'diagnosed' as having PTSD compared to 3 per cent when assessed by a clinician (Sumpter & McMillan, 2005).

A key step in the assessment process is the identification of the traumatic event or events involved. This involves recognising severe events that fall outside the realms of normal experience. The DSM approach stresses that such events generally involve the threat of death or serious injury to the person. This is also commonly associated with feelings of helplessness or lack of control over the situation. These criteria also suggest that experiences involving the death or serious injury of others may result in similar effects. A major weakness of this approach, however, is its failure to take into account the interaction between the individual and the event, the largely dimensional nature of such events and individual responses during and after events. It has been suggested that a hierarchical model, comprising re-experiencing, avoidance, numbing and hyperarousal, subsumed by a higher-order general factor, provides a better fit in the case of PTSD symptoms (Asmundson, Frombach, McQuaid et al., 2000).[8]

A number of additional correlates have been described that influence individual responses to trauma. These include the events surrounding the traumatic incident. Where there are other significant stresses in the individual's life, they tend to cope less effectively with the stress of a traumatic incident. Events before, during and after the trauma also appear to have a significant impact in terms of outcomes. For example, where the person believes that they responded positively by actively escaping the traumatic event, outcomes tend to be better. The responses of others around the event may also impact positively or negatively. Finally, it seems clear that a person's previous history of exposure to traumatic events contributes to the variance in outcomes, with those who have a history of negative experiences tending to fare worse (Breslau, Chilcoat, Kessler et al., 1999).

Interventions in this area can be broadly separated into psychosocial and neurobiological approaches. Within each of these, a wide range of interventions have been tried, with mixed results. There is, however, an emerging evidence base to guide practice in this area (National Institute for Clinical Excellence, 2005).

Psychosocial Interventions

Trauma-Focused Cognitive Behaviour Therapy (CBT)

As the name suggests, this is a modification of CBT approaches to address responses to trauma. There is evidence favouring such interventions when compared to waiting-list control groups in reducing the likelihood of a PTSD diagnosis post intervention (k = 14; n = 716; RR = 0.47, 95% CI 0.37 to

0.59). There is also some evidence favouring trauma-focused CBT over waiting-list controls in terms of reduced severity of self-reported PTSD symptoms (k = 8; n = 388; SMD = −1.7, 95% CI −2.21 to −1.18) (k = 3; n = 609; SMD = −1.36, 95% CI −1.88 to −0.84). There is some evidence to suggest that this form of CBT performs better than remaining on a waiting list in terms of reducing self-reported depression (k = 13; n = 585; SMD = −1.2, 95% CI −1.65 to −0.75) and anxiety (k = 10; n = 375; SMD = −0.94; 95% CI −1.16 to −0.72) (National Institute for Clinical Excellence, 2005).

Eye Movement Desensitisation and Reprocessing (EMDR)

Eye movement desensitisation and reprocessing (EMDR) is based on a theoretical information-processing model which postulates that dysfunctional intrusions, emotions and physical sensations experienced by trauma victims are due to the improper storage of the traumatic event in implicit memory. Intervention based on this model involves seeking to modify the way that individuals process information to help integrate the event adaptively within memory (Shapiro, 2001).

There is limited evidence favouring EMDR over waiting-list controls in terms of a lower likelihood of being diagnosed with PTSD post intervention (k = 5; n = 169; RR = 0.51; 95% CI 0.28 to 0.95). There is also limited evidence favouring EMDR over waiting list on reducing the severity of self-reported PTSD symptoms (self-report measures) (k = 4; n = 116; SMD = −1.1; 95% CI −2.42 to 0.23). EMDR may reduce severity of rated PTSD symptoms (k = 4; n = 122; SMD = −1.54, 95% CI, −1.96 to −1.12) and reduce depression (k = 4; n = 120; SMD = −1.67, 95% CI −2.1 to −1.25). Evidence favouring EMDR over waiting list on reducing anxiety symptoms is less clear (k = 4; n = 116; SMD = −1.18, 95% CI −1.58 to −0.78) (National Institute for Clinical Excellence, 2005; Shapiro, 2001). Overall, there are strongly contrasting reviews in relation to this intervention. The National Institute for Clinical Excellence (2005) review concluded that there was sufficient evidence to recommend continued use. Others have argued that the approach is weak in terms of its theoretical base and that the evidence base is inadequate to support such conclusions (Ost, 2005).

Stress Management Versus Waiting List

There is limited evidence favouring stress management approaches when compared to a waiting-list control group in terms of the reduced likelihood of being diagnosed with PTSD post intervention (k = 4; n = 121; RR = 0.64,

176

95% CI 0.47 to 0.87). The evidence available to the National Institute for Clinical Excellence (2005) review, however, did not suggest clinically significant improvement was achieved compared to waiting-list controls in severity of self-reported symptoms (k = 1; n = 24; SMD = 0.33, 95% CI –0.47 to 1.14).

Group CBT Versus Waiting List

There have been few studies concerned with group rather than individual CBT. Evidence comparing group CBT to waiting-list controls in terms of PTSD diagnosis and self-reported symptoms, nonetheless, do not appear encouraging (k = 1; n = 48; RR = 0.56, 95% CI 0.31 to 1.01) (k = 2; n = 71; SMD = –0.71, 95% CI –1.2 to –0.22) (National Institute for Clinical Excellence, 2005). This is a somewhat surprising finding, given that it is the mode of delivery, rather than the therapeutic approach, which differs from individual CBT.

Comparisons between Psychosocial Interventions

There have been relatively few studies comparing psychosocial interventions with other active interventions, rather than drawing comparisons with waiting-list controls. However, one such study, a comparison of EMDR and trauma-focused CBT, suggested that there was no clear difference in effectiveness measured in terms of reducing the likelihood of PTSD diagnosis post intervention (k = 6; n = 220; RR = 1.03, 95% CI 0.64 to 1.66). It is also unclear whether there is any clinically significant difference between these approaches in reducing the severity of self-reported PTSD symptoms (k = 6; n = 166; SMD = –0.31, 95% CI –0.62 to 0) or in leaving treatment early (k = 7; n = 240; RR = 0.83, 95% CI 0.54 to 1.27) (National Institute for Clinical Excellence, 2005).

Trauma-focused CBT and EMDR have been compared with some other therapeutic approaches. The limited evidence base available suggests that trauma-focused CBT and EMDR perform better at reducing the likelihood of PTSD diagnosis post intervention (TF-CBT k = 5; n = 286; RR = 0.71, 95% CI 0.56 to 0.89) (EMDR k = 3; n = 84; RR = 0.69, 95% CI 0.46 to 1.04). There is similarly limited evidence favouring trauma-focused CBT over some other approaches in reducing the severity of self-reported PTSD symptoms (k = 3; n = 176; SMD = –1.18, 95% CI –2.32 to –0.03), something not found for EMDR. It is unclear if there is any clinically important difference in relation to leaving treatment early (k = 5; n = 290; RR = 1.14, 95% CI 0.68 to 1.9).

177

Comparisons of trauma-focused-CBT and EMDR tended not to reveal any significant clinical advantages of one over the other in treatment outcomes or speed of improvement (Duffy, Gillespie & Clark, 2007; Taylor, Fedoroff, Koch *et al.*, 2001; Taylor, Thordarson, Maxfield *et al.*, 2003). Similarly, studies comparing different versions of trauma-focused CBT did not find clinically significant differences (Marks, Lovell, Noshirvani *et al.*, 1998; Resick, Nishith, Weaver *et al.*, 2002).

Adverse Effects

As with other psychosocial interventions, there has there has been surprisingly little consideration of adverse effects. There are some exceptions to this and these have tended to focus on negative effects of repeating exposure to the original trauma. A Cochrane review of psychological debriefing following serious incidents was undertaken in 2002. This suggested that the evidence base did not support the use of such interventions which may serve to interfere with normal adaptation (Rose, Bisson, Churchill *et al.*, 2002). In the case of long-term adjustment problems where normal recovery has not occurred, this is less evident and it seems likely that the benefits of intervention generally outweigh adverse effects (National Institute for Clinical Excellence, 2005; Taylor, Thordarson, Maxfield *et al.*, 2003).

Neurobiological Interventions

A number of drug and physical interventions have been tried in PTSD, most commonly selective serotonin reuptake inhibitors (SSRIs) and tricyclic antidepressants (TCAs). TCAs are no longer licensed for use in PTSD in the UK and so only SSRIs are discussed below (National Institute for Clinical Excellence, 2005).

Paroxetine

Evidence suggests there is unlikely to be a clinically important difference between paroxetine and placebo on reducing the severity of PTSD self-reported symptoms on the Davidson Trauma Scale (DTS k = 3; $n = 1065$; SMD = -0.37, 95% CI -0.49 to -0.24). The evidence is inconclusive and so it is not possible to determine if there is a clinically important difference between paroxetine and placebo on reducing the severity of PTSD symptoms as measured using a clinician-rating scale (the CAPS) (CAPS k = 3;

$n = 1070$; SMD $= -0.42$, 95% CI -0.55 to -0.3). The evidence is also inconclusive in relation to clinically important improvement using paroxetine in reducing symptoms of depression, measured using a clinician administered scale, the Montgomery–Åsberg Depression Rating Scale (MADRAS k = 3; $n = 1069$; SMD $= -0.34$, 95% CI -0.61 to -0.07). There also appears to be no difference between paroxetine and placebo in leaving treatment early (k = 3; $n = 1196$; RR $= 0.95$, 95% CI 0.79 to 1.15).

There is some evidence concerning issues of relapse concerning the use of paroxetine based on an unpublished trial but reported in the National Institute for Clinical Excellence (2005) review. This involved 12 weeks of single-blind acute phase treatment, followed by a further 24 weeks of double-blind administered treatment for those assessed as having responded to treatment. In the continuation phase, responders were allocated either to placebo or paroxetine (dose range 20–50 mg). The results of this study suggest no clinically important difference between paroxetine and placebo in reducing the severity of PTSD symptoms for continuation/relapse prevention treatments (DTS k = 1; $n = 127$; SMD $= 0.06$, 95% CI -0.28 to 0.41).

Paroxetine Versus Trauma-Focused CBT

One small-scale study compared 12 weeks of paroxetine (10–50 mg) with 12 weekly sessions of trauma-focused CBT (Frommberger, Stieglitz, Nyberg et al., 2004). In studies comprising both drug and psychological intervention treatment arms individuals are not masked to treatment allocation, and in this study neither were the rating assessors. Given the lack of placebo control in the study, it is also not possible to isolate specific effects. The measures used though provided limited evidence favouring CBT based on self-ratings. These positive effects were not replicated in the clinician ratings, which suggested no difference. Withdrawal rates were also based on very small sample sizes, suggesting a need for considerable caution in interpretation (Frommberger, Stieglitz, Nyberg et al., 2004).

Sertraline

The evidence base in relation to sertraline is in line with that for paroxetine, suggesting a lack of clinically important impact compared to placebo for diagnosis of PTSD (k = 2; $n = 747$; RR $= 0.91$, 95% CI 0.85 to 0.98). Similar results have been reported in terms of reducing the severity of self-reported PTSD symptoms (DTS k = 5; $n = 1091$; SMD $= -0.18$, 95% CI -0.41 to 0.06).

The reported evidence is inconclusive in terms of reducing the severity of PTSD symptoms as measured by clinicians (CAPS k = 6; n = 1123; SMD = −0.26, 95% CI −0.51 to 0.00). The evidence is also inconclusive in respect of differences between sertraline and placebo on leaving treatment early (k = 6; n = 1148; RR = 1.10, 95% CI 0.90 to 1.33) (National Institute for Clinical Excellence, 2005).

Fluoxetine

The evidence is inconclusive on whether there is a clinically important difference between fluoxetine and placebo on reducing the severity of self-reported PTSD symptoms (DTS k = 3; n = 363; SMD = −0.41, 95% CI −0.98 to 0.15). It is also not possible to determine if there is a clinically important difference between fluoxetine and placebo on reducing the severity of clinician rated PTSD symptoms (CAPS k = 1; n = 301; SMD = −0.28, 95% CI − 0.54 to −0.02). There is, though, some evidence suggesting no clinically important difference between fluoxetine and placebo on reducing the severity of PTSD symptoms as measured by the 8-item self-report Treatment Outcome Scale (TOP8) (TOP8 k = 1; n = 411, SMD = 0.02, 95% CI −0.21 to 0.26). There is limited evidence favouring fluoxetine over placebo on enhancing self-reported quality of life (k = 2; n = 61; SMD = −0.62, 95% CI −1.13 to −0.1), although the significance of this finding is unclear. Fluoxetine does appear to perform better than placebo in terms of the likelihood of leaving treatment early (k = 2; n = 66; RR = 0.6, 95% CI 0.28 to 1.3) (National Institute for Clinical Excellence, 2005).

Repetitive Transcranial Magnetic Stimulation

Repetitive transcranial magnetic stimulation (rTMS) is a new technique used in a range of areas including depression and stroke. It involves placing an electromagnetic coil on the scalp and rapidly turning on and off a high-intensity current through the discharge of a capacitor. The magnetic pulse induces electrical effects in the underlying brain cortex. If this stimulation occurs faster than once per second (1 Hz), it is defined as fast or high-frequency rTMS.

There is limited evidence favouring high-frequency rTMS over control in reducing clinician-rated severity of PTSD symptoms at 14-day follow-up (CAPS k = 1; n = 16; SMD = −0.72, 95% CI −1.77 to 0.33). There is also limited evidence favouring high-frequency rTMS over control on reducing the severity of self-reported PTSD symptoms at 14-day (PTSD Checklist k = 1; n = 16; SMD = −0.68, 95% CI −1.73 to 0.36). The evidence is inconclusive about whether there is a clinically important difference between high-frequency rTMS and controls in symptoms of depression at 14-day follow-up using the Hamilton Rating Scale for Depression (HDRS $k = 1$; $n = 16$; SMD $= -0.13$, 95% CI -1.14 to 0.89). There is some evidence suggesting reduced likelihood of leaving the study prior to 14-day follow-up ($k = 1$; $n = 19$; RR $= 0.36$, 95% CI 0.04 to 3.35) (National Institute for Clinical Excellence, 2005).

Adverse Effects

Adverse effects associated with neurobiological interventions have been extensively studied. There are a number of well-known adverse effects associated with SSRIs. Fluoxetine is also known to have a long half-life, meaning that it remains active in the body for an extended time (Haddad, 2001; Lejoyeux & Ades, 1997). SSRIs may also be associated with akathisia, suicidal ideation and increased anxiety and agitation. There is also a consistent if complex relationship between antidepressant drugs and cardiovascular morbidity and mortality (Glassman & Shapiro, 1998).

Summary

- Recently, notions of responses to traumatic events have been dominated by the categorical construct of post-traumatic stress disorder (PTSD). Trauma is an important construct within prisons. Prisons detain those with high levels of risk factors associated with poor traumatic responses from childhood onwards. As a group, prisoners also tend to have bene-fited from fewer protective factors that may serve to reduce the impacts of subsequent traumas. In combination, this suggests greater vulnera-bility to traumatic reactions. In addition, prisons by their very nature present a setting where both prisoners and staff are at increased risk of traumatic experiences.
- PTSD is generally construed in terms of a diathesis stress model, which assumes an underlying vulnerability to dysfunctional reactions to trauma. The model, though, is primarily descriptive and has tradition-ally lacked good theoretical foundations.
- The use of PTSD has also been subject to significant criticism, with concerns that the threshold for categorisation has been increasingly lowered as a result of commercial pressures and is being applied to

experiences that would, in the past, simply have been seen as part of life. This draws into question the value of defining such experiences as 'illness'.

- As with depression, it is only comparatively recently that traumatic experiences in children have been recognised and subject to systematic study. Those studies that have been undertaken have tended to conclude that little is known about this area, despite the suggested importance of developmental factors in adult PTSD. A number of factors have, however, been shown to moderate the effects of trauma in children similar to 'protective factors' seen in other areas of mental health and the development of criminal behaviour. These include parental warmth, high intelligence, family support and low family conflict.

- Estimating the prevalence of PTSD poses a number of problems. As outlined above, these are associated with issues of definition and the point at which thresholds for categorisation are set. Using a relatively low threshold, point prevalence estimates of 8 per cent have been suggested, with some subgroups within the population being at markedly increased risk.

- Lifetime levels of exposure to traumatic events are high, with 60 per cent of women and 51 per cent of men reporting at least one experience meeting DSM criteria for PTEs. Rates are even higher in areas with high levels of social and economic deprivation. Most who experienced such an event report an initial and intense reaction interrupting normal psychological and physiological functioning for a short time, followed by a period of adaptation and a return to normality. At least in part, the manner in which an individual deals with this initial reaction appears to determine long-term adjustment and risk of experiencing serious ongoing adjustment difficulties.

- Interventions in this area can be broadly separated into psychosocial and neurobiological approaches. Within each of these, a wide range of interventions has been tried with mixed results.

- There is evidence of adverse treatment effects associated with blanket interventions for those who have experienced traumatic incidents. Such interventions may interfere with normal processes of adaptation. For those who experience ongoing reactions, psychosocial interventions based on information processing and cognitive behavioural approaches appear to have some beneficial effects as does neuromagnetic stimulation. Drug-based interventions, primarily using SSRIs, are poorly supported by the evidence base.

Notes

1 The assessment criteria outlined in DSM have been subject to criticism and regular revisions, as a result of difficulties with the criteria used. Taking this one aspect for illustrative purposes, it suggests that someone who does not react with initial fear, panic or horror should not be diagnosed as suffering from PTSD. This is to some extent contradicted by cases of professional staff such as paramedics who may initially respond without such immediate reactions but nevertheless go on to develop severely dysfunctional reactions in the longer term. Similarly, the arbitrary requirement that these problems last one month, whilst having some pragmatic value, is not theoretically or clinically grounded.

2 Shell shock, by contrast, was thought to be the result of neurobiological damage to the brain as a result of the blast waves from artillery shells.

3 Interestingly, many of the negative effects of PTSD seen following military combat, such as feelings of guilt, are seen as positive and functional signs in criminal homicide offenders (Crighton & Bailey, 2006).

4 The approach adopted here is one that recognises the existence of a number of invariant patterns of dysfunctional response to severely traumatic incidents throughout life. Such reactions have come to be termed PTSD and, given the ubiquity of this term, it is used throughout. The logical basis to PTSD is, though, less convincing and the notion has undoubtedly spawned a commercial sector with vested interests in the concept and professionalisation of assessment and intervention.

5 The reasons for these gender differences were not the primary focus of this study. A number of key differences, however, did emerge. It seems likely that one of the major reasons for the difference was exposure to combat and life-threatening experiences. As a group, the men were exposed to more frequent and more intense combat than women. Where women took on such roles, the responses to trauma are likely to be similar.

6 In both studies, experience of childhood sexual abuse was included as a PTE. Throughout this chapter, such experiences have similarly been viewed as PTEs.

7 Throughout this chapter, a simplified working definition of the terms 'sign' and 'symptom' will serve. Symptom is used to refer to the subjective experiences reported by the individual (e.g., unhappiness) and sign is taken to refer to observable factors (e.g., weight loss).

8   For example, it seems evident that some individuals have a greater capacity to deal with traumatic events than others and that what is a traumatic event for one person may not be so for another. It also seems evident that there are ways of addressing even highly traumatic events that result in better long-term outcomes.

Chapter 11

Suicide, Attempted Suicide and Self-Injury

Introduction

At first glance, the definition of suicide appears to be straightforward. In reality, it is complicated by legal definitions of suicide and variations in these across jurisdictions. As recently as 1961, suicide was defined as a criminal offence in the UK. Although this was brought to an end by the Suicide Act of 1961, many of the legal requirements have gone unchanged and it remains the case that a verdict of suicide needs to be established in line with the criminal burden of proof: beyond all reasonable doubt. There is a clear legal presumption against suicide that has been regularly reinforced by the superior courts which have asserted that suicide must be strictly proved. This derives largely from the Christian tradition in the UK that prohibited suicide. Routine reference is therefore still made to people 'committing' suicide, relating to the previous criminal status of the act. More modern, compassionate and informed commentators prefer the term 'completed' suicide, as this clearly focuses on behaviour without reference to historic legal status and the stigma associated with suicide (Crighton, 2006b).

The presence of a suicide note in the absence of other evidence of suicidal intent may not be sufficient to meet the legal requirements of a suicide verdict. Similarly, where a self-inflicted death occurs when a person is intoxicated, a suicide verdict may not follow on the basis that the person may have been unable to form the necessary intent for a suicide verdict. The result of this legal framework is that a large number of self-inflicted deaths are recorded under other verdicts[1] and the likely true levels of suicide are underreported (Jenkins & Singh, 2000; Kelly & Bunting, 1998).

Epidemiological studies have, in recent years, sought to circumvent this by adopting operational definitions. These have drawn primarily on International Classification of Diseases (ICD) categories. Although these have changed over time, in the case of self-inflicted deaths they have provided a more consistent baseline. They have also allowed cross-national comparisons. An example here is the study by Kelly and Bunting (1998) which used ICD-9 categories covering suicide and undetermined deaths, including poisoning but excluded homicides. Throughout this chapter, the term 'suicide' is used to include this broader range of self-inflicted deaths that take place in prisons (Crighton, 2006b).

Definitions of self-injury are equally complex, although in law issues of self-injury tend to be addressed only tangentially as in the Mental Health Act (1983) or the Female Circumcision Act (1985). Historically, the term 'deliberate self-harm' (DSH) or DSH syndrome has been used in this area (Morgan, Burns, Pocock et al., 1975). This raises at least three significant problems. First, the notion of self-harm is very broad and covers a range of behaviours likely to be only weakly related, if at all. At its most literal, the term includes such things as excessive alcohol consumption, smoking, excessive eating, nail-biting and tattooing. In an effort to address this concern, a number of researchers have suggested a more circumscribed notion of DSH. Less severe forms of harm and areas such as substance misuse are excluded from such definitions (Pattison & Kahan, 1983). This in turn raises issues of differential use and comparability across studies. Thirdly, the use of the term deliberation is contentious. The extent to which many acts of self-harm can be said to involve carefully considered decision-making, as implied by the term 'deliberate', is questionable in what often appears to be quite impulsive and poorly considered behaviours (Towl & Crighton, 1997). There are clear difficulties caused by terminology and definitions that change over time. Most strikingly, this makes longitudinal epidemiological comparisons significantly more difficult. This needs to be offset against the need for useful operational definitions. Recent trends in this area include a clearer specification of behaviour with the separation of self-injury and self-poisoning. There have also been moves towards the term 'intentional' replacing 'deliberate' as a more accurate description of motivation (Crighton, 2006b; Towl, 2005b).

Epidemiology

There is a relatively lengthy history of research into the epidemiology of suicide in prisons. In recent years, though, there has been a marked qualitative change in such research as work within prisons has adopted methodologically sophisticated approaches developed in community-based research.

A study conducted in North America pooled data from a number of small-scale studies (Hankoff, 1980). Amongst those who killed themselves, high levels of mental health problems, substance abuse and social exclusion were reported. The pooling of data in this way needs some caution and raises questions of interpretation. The system of prisons in the United States involves wide variations across local, state and federal prisons, significantly complicating the use of pooled data and comparisons with less devolved systems. In a reported questionnaire study of a sample of 155 deaths that occurred in Australian prisons between 1980 and 1985, it was noted that 77 of these went on to be officially recorded as suicides (Hatty & Walker, 1986). The other deaths were recorded as misadventure,[2] accidental death and natural causes. Higher death rates for women in prison were reported at 1.7 per 1000 (170 per 100,000) against 1.2 per 1000 (120 per 100,000) for men. However, this finding was based on very small numbers of women, making it very tentative.[3] A pattern in relation to age was identified, showing an overrepresentation of both younger and older age groups. The older age groups included an increased number of deaths recorded as natural causes. Increased rates of suicide were reported for the 20–24 and 25–29 years age cohorts. The 15–19 years age cohort, perhaps surprisingly, did not appear at increased risk of suicide. As with the comparisons made between men and women, the researchers noted a need for caution here, due to the small numbers involved. Deaths amongst ethnic minority (aboriginal) Australians were 50 per cent higher in the under 35-year-old age group than for other Australians. This striking finding was not analysed further but was replicated in later research which showed continued higher rates of deaths in this group (Joudo, 2006).

A sample of deaths in Scottish prisons between 1976 and 1993 was analysed in the mid-1990s (Bogue & Power, 1995). In all, 83 deaths had been formally defined as suicide and only these were included in the study. Drawing on general prison files, data was divided into four-year spans to conduct an analysis of trends which suggested a steady rise in the rate of suicides in Scottish prisons. The study helpfully corrected what had become the dominant and misguided view that the period of remand *per se* was a time of particularly heightened risk. The authors noted that rates of deaths had generally been calculated on the basis of average daily population (ADP) in prison. One such flawed study in this respect was that of Dooley (1990). In fact, using this figure serves to distort the calculated rate for remand prisoners as they will generally form only a small proportion of the

ADP. ADP represents a snapshot of the large numbers of prisoners who are sent on remand to prison over a year. For remand prisoners, the number of annual receptions provides a better estimate of the rate since it more accurately reflects the number of people placed at risk in the prison environment. A similar analysis of this in England and Wales (Dexter & Towl, 1995) suggested that this effect was similarly striking. Rates recalculated on the basis of receptions do not support the assertion that remand prisoners were at increased risk (Crighton, 2000b, 2000c, 2000d). Such patterns are, of course, likely to change over time. The key point here is the methodological one about the calculation of rates and other descriptive statistics on suicide. It is essential that such comparisons not be made in unreflective and mechanistic ways such as using ADP rates in comparing two samples with very different characteristics. A very robust finding, however, is that the early stages of custody show the highest rates of self-inflicted deaths in prisons (Bogue & Power, 1995; Crighton, 2000b, 2006b; Crighton & Towl, 1997; National Confidential Enquiry, 2006; Topp, 1979; Towl & Crighton, 1998).

The mainstreaming of research in this area has involved the introduction of discourses from sociological and criminological traditions (Liebling, 1992; Liebling & Krarup, 1993; Tumim, 1990) and also the application of mainstream public health models and methods (Crighton, 1997b, 1999, 2000a, 2000b, 2000c; Towl, 2000). As a result, there has been a marked reduction in the isolation of this area of research with improved understanding and theoretical models of suicidal behaviour.

In a detailed study of staff and offenders in four Young Offender Institutions (YOIs), drawing on criminological and sociological theory, an attempt was made to explain the processes involved in suicide. This involved an analogue study of 100 young offenders who had a recent history on intentional self-injury and who had also come to the attention of primary healthcare services. The choice of self-injuring offenders as the focus for an analogue study was based on the notion that suicide and self-injury form a continuum of self-destructive behaviours (Liebling, 1992). Such views have a long history, traceable back to the work of Menninger (1938) and Durkheim (1952), among others.

In contrast to previous studies, a matched 'control' group of young offenders from the same institutions was identified. A number of statistically significant differences between the groups were suggested. Those who self-injured were on average serving longer sentences than the controls, had received fewer positive recommendations in reports from the probation service and showed a number of differences in social and family background. A surprising finding was that the control group reported more unstable family backgrounds, whereas the self-injuring group reported higher levels of placement in local authority care. Those in the self-injuring group also reported more contacts with mental health services, along with higher rates of suicide and self-injury within their families. A link between intentional self-injury and drug abuse[4] has been mooted by a number of researchers (Menninger, 1938). Young offenders in the experimental group were more likely to have 'major' alcohol abuse problems[5] than controls. The experimental group also showed higher levels of use of other substances with some evidence that such behaviour was consistent across custodial and community settings. The experimental group were also found to have different experiences of custody. Those young offenders who intentionally self-injured tended to be less active and reported disliking activities such as physical education. They tended to show a greater preference for cell sharing and to be more lacking in personal resources that would let them address feelings of boredom and isolation. The research went on to explain such differences in relation to a construct of 'coping' ability, devising a profile of those who were described using a potentially circular notion of 'poor copers'.

This work represented part of a move towards a more qualitative approach to research into suicides in custody. It was largely descriptive but did begin theory building and hypothesis testing in a way that had been absent from much of the preceding research. Of course, there were methodological limitations. As alluded to above, notions that suicide and intentional self-injury are part of a continuum is hypothetical. It has an intuitive appeal and, if correct, would mean that it is valid and useful to study intentional self-injury as a way to gain insights into suicide. If these behaviours are not part of a continuum, then intentional self-injury is less relevant as a means of studying suicide. It is noteworthy that a number of the young people in this study reported engaging in intentional self-injurious behaviours without any apparent intent to complete suicide. This sits uneasily with the notion of a simple continuum. Equally, it seems evident that there is a degree of overlap between suicide and self-injury. It might be argued that this suggests the need for a more complex explanatory model, such as a continuum with marked discontinuities. Alternatively, classification tree and multidimensional approaches may yield more valid typological models and insights into differences between subgroups of those who self-injure and complete suicide (Crighton, 2006b; Crighton & Towl, 2002; Snow, 2006).

The posited theoretical construct of 'coping ability' raises a number of significant issues. In this study, it was used largely to suggest a causal explanation of behaviour but other explanations may be equally plausible.

For example, the profiles of the intentionally self-injuring young offenders might alternatively suggest that they were trying to adapt to what, for many observers,[6] might appear to be more difficult circumstances. They tended to be facing longer sentences, with lower levels of family support, to have poor contact with friends and poorer levels of contact with professional support. There is a widely recognised bias within human cognition to make internal or dispositional attributions about behaviour rather than situational attributions (Connolly, Arkes & Hammond, 2000). It might be suggested that this is at least in part an example of such a bias. There is scope for further investigation here, for example, by replicating the study using groups more closely matched on such variables. There is also a danger that notions of 'poor copers' and 'good copers' are simply tautological (Crighton, 2000b, 2006b; Towl, 2000).

In a study conducted in prisons in England and Wales, a mixed range of negative emotional states including boredom, stress, anxiety, depression and loneliness was reported to be associated with intentional self-injury (Snow, 2006). It was noted that those who reported feeling depressed for much of the time were at higher risk of suicide and attempted suicide than those who reported infrequent depression (χ^2 (1, N = 105) = 10.33 p = 0.001) (Snow, 2006). Using multidimensional scaling techniques, the author went on to suggest two clear dimensions – 'active' and 'passive' – suggesting different presentation and responses to negative emotional states.

Psychosocial Models

Another approach to the study of suicide in prisons has built on public health models and methods (Charlton, 1995; Crighton, 2000b, 2000c; Crighton & Towl, 1997; National Confidential Enquiry, 2006; Shaw, 2007; Towl & Crighton, 1997, 1998). Public health approaches have generally begun by using operational definitions of suicide most often using International Classifications of Diseases (ICD) definitions[7] (World Health Organisation, 2007). This facilitates the comparison of research internationally across differing legal systems. It also allows for more accurate comparisons of death rates in custody with those in the community (Towl, Snow & McHugh, 2000).

The largest and most comprehensive analysis of suicides in prisons to date in UK prisons built substantially on this approach by analysing all the self-inflicted deaths in prisons[8] in England and Wales between 1988 and 1998, using epidemiological methods of analysis (Crighton, 2006b). The research involved the retrospective empirical and qualitative analysis of a sample of 525 deaths from a total of 600 deaths over the period. The analysis was based on written records produced as the result of investigation of the deaths undertaken via the Prison Service's Suicide Awareness Support Unit. A clear upward trend in the rate of suicides with a rate of 80 per 100,000 ADP in 1988 and over 120 per 100,000 ADP in 1998 was reported. When calculated on the basis of receptions into prisons, a similar upward trend was noted with the rate increasing from just over 20 per 100,000 receptions[9] in 1988 to around 40 per 100,000 receptions in 1998.

For the period 1988–98, the rate of suicide for men was 94 per 100,000 ADP compared to a rate for women of 74 per 100,000 ADP. To ensure that this was not largely a facet of the calculation being based on ADP, figures were also calculated based on annual receptions yielding rates of 30 per 100,000 receptions for men and 16 per 100,000 receptions for women. However, the data did suggest greater fluctuations in the rates for women and, as a result of this, the rates for women were higher for some years. A trend analysis was conducted which showed higher rates for men. A plausible explanation for the variations in the rates for women prisoners' data is one of random statistical fluctuation, given the relatively small numbers involved and the much smaller population of women in prison. This does not rule out the possibility of other explanations but remains a significant methodological challenge in studying gender differences in prisons.

Interestingly, the issue of ethnicity rarely appears to have featured as a focus for research in this area, despite expressed concerns about racism in prisons (Narey, 2001). The results of this extensive study showed lower rates of suicide amongst black prisoners. For white prisoners, the rate was 89 per 100,000 ADP, compared to 84 per 100,000 ADP for south Asian prisoners and 13 per 100,000 ADP for black prisoners. This suggested that black prisoners were at lower risk of suicide, a finding that echoes the lower rates found in community studies (Crighton, 2006b).

In analysing mental disorder, the levels of prescribed antipsychotic medication[10] were looked at, with around 6 per cent of the sample receiving such medication at the time of death, suggesting the presence of a diagnosed psychotic disorder. The rates of prescription of antidepressant medication were surprisingly low at 7 per cent, suggesting low levels of treatment for diagnosed depressive disorders. From this, it was tentatively concluded that the levels of mental disorder likely to fall within the terms of the Mental Health Acts in the UK were similar or lower than the rates in the prison population as a whole. The overall levels of such disorders amongst prisoners were nonetheless markedly higher than in the general community. The levels of more broadly defined mental disorders were found to be very high with a rate of more than 30 per cent for abuse of controlled drugs.

The study went on to draw on the very large sample of data to replicate a number of previous research findings. A link between longer sentences and suicide was noted, with the effect being most marked for those serving indeterminate sentences.[11] Those with index offences of violence, or drug-related index offences, also tended to be at increased risk of suicide. Of those studied, 45 per cent had a recorded history of previous intentional self-injury. This casts some doubt on notions that those who self-injure are at low risk of killing themselves. Indeed, it was a striking finding that 12 per cent of the sample had a recorded history of self-injury during the period in custody when they killed themselves. It was also reported that 51 per cent of those prisoners who killed themselves had expressed an intent to do so, which runs counter to the popular myth that those who talk about suicide are unlikely to kill themselves.

Earlier research in prisons had suggested that the early period of custody was a time of increased risk of suicide. The relative level of risk during the first 24 hours after reception is consistently reported to be exceptionally high. Extrapolating the rate of suicides over a year, the rate of self-inflicted deaths was reported to be around 9500: from day 2 to day 7, the level of risk remained very high, with an annualised rate declining from around 7000 to 1500. Days 8 to 30 saw a continued decrease in the level of risk from an annualised rate of around 1000 to a baseline level. Crucially, this broadly exponential decline in risk takes place over a relatively lengthy period with baseline levels reached at around two months after reception (Crighton, 2006b). It is worth noting that just under half of those who killed themselves within 24 hours of reception into a prison had been transferred from another establishment. Interestingly, a similar pattern of increased risk has been noted during the first week of psychiatric hospitalisation and the first week post discharge (Geddes & Juszczak, 1995; Geddes, Juszczak, O'Brien et al., 1997; Qin & Nordentoft, 2005; Roy, 1982). This might suggest that it was not just being new to custody that is relevant but also the change to a novel environment and consequent changes in social support networks that is associated with an increased risk of suicide (Crighton, 2000b, 2006c; Jenkins & Singh, 2000). The mechanisms for this warrant further research although the breaking of social support networks, both within and outside prison, seems intuitively a potential factor for testing in future research. It also seems evident that the initial period after release from prison is similarly one of markedly increased risk (Pratt, Piper, Appleby et al., 2006).

The study went on to look at the process of care management within prisons. At the time of the research, public sector prisons used an approach named the 'F2052SH' system[12] after the standard forms used. This system was designed to provide an administrative framework to support and manage those felt to be at increased risk, as well as providing a structured record of support and monitoring. Around a third of those who killed themselves had been identified as being at increased risk, a finding which replicated earlier small-scale studies (McHugh, 2000). In turn, 18 per cent of prisoners had been subject to such procedures at the time of their death. No level of supervision, including 'continuous watches' appeared to be foolproof in preventing suicide. Routine 15-minute watches had limited effect, possibly in part related to the predictability of checks. Quantitative and qualitative analyses suggested that the F2052 system was failing for a number of reasons. The system had been explicitly devised on the basis that suicide and self-injury were part of a continuum of behaviour that could be effectively managed using the same system. As noted above, this assumption is by no means widely accepted and does not account for the majority of prisoner suicides (Towl, Snow & McHugh, 2000). If the general notion of a continuum is accepted, it seems likely that behaviour at the extreme ends of the continuum will be quite distinct and that a range of responses will be necessary. Unfortunately, such subtleties were largely lost in the F2052 system which imposed a predominantly 'one size fits all' model of managing those at inflated risk of suicide or intentional self-injury.

Another identified weakness was the reliance placed on prison officers to be instrumental in ensuring the detection and monitoring of the suicidal. Previous approaches were criticised, often with good reason, for being unduly focused on primary care medical practitioners. With the benefit of hindsight, it can be seen there was perhaps undue concentration on prison officers and away from healthcare professionals as the key staff involved in trying to manage the risk of suicide and intentional self-injury, often with relatively low levels of support from healthcare colleagues. Indeed, during the 1990s applied psychologists, for example, increasingly moved away from this area of work in favour of work intended to reduce the risk of reoffending. This shift was largely at the expense of work in relation to health and welfare. The work of healthcare teams additionally tended to become increasingly focused on those with mental disorders that fell within the Mental Health Act (1983). This view was echoed in the response by the Royal College of Psychiatrists (2002) to the earlier thematic review of suicide by the Chief Inspector of Prisons (HM Inspectorate of Prisons, 1999). This argued for increases in primary and secondary healthcare support and was critical of misunderstandings over issues of professional confidentiality and the failings of professional staff to give appropriate support to prison officers in such complex and difficult areas of work.

Much of the research on suicide and intentional self-injury can be criticised for an unduly empirical emphasis at the expense of theoretical models and understanding. This is highlighted where an increasing empirical evidence base has developed. There have been some attempts to begin building more theoretical and testable models to account for prison suicide and self-injury (Crighton, 2006b; Snow, 2006). In seeking to explain suicide, public health models of multiple causation (Rothman & Greenland, 1998) and also primary research into the development of emotions and emotional regulation (Plutchik, 1980, 1997) have been drawn on extensively (Crighton, 2006b). Such models might provide a future framework for research, as well as a model to direct the work of practitioners trying to reduce suicide risk significantly. Causation within this model is brought into line with models used in the community which suggest it is unhelpful to look for a single exclusive and inclusive 'cause' of suicide. Each death is the result of a chain of events and interventions therefore need to be aimed at breaking a link or links within this chain. Interventions therefore have to address a broad range of factors that can be shown to be causally linked to suicide. In turn, the strength of such associations and their amenability to intervention will determine their public health importance. As this is established, researchers will be better placed to identify factors that appear to be frequently 'necessary' if not sufficient components of suicides.

The structural models of emotion proposed as part of this approach to suicide prevention provide a theoretical basis for generating testable hypotheses. The model sees emotions as having a genetic underlying basis that exists as a means of communication and a survival mechanism. Emotions can be represented as chains of events and feedback loops that are designed to achieve behavioural homeostasis.

Such models suggest that parts of the process are not open to conscious appraisal. As a result, individuals may have little insight into their physiological states or indeed the functions being served by their emotions. Suicidal behaviour here is seen as being based on aggressive impulses, deriving from the emotion of anger. Clearly anger and aggression have an evolutionary survival value. The way such impulses are dealt with by an individual varies significantly and these impulses might be amplified and attenuated.

Within this model, the emotional states, the interaction of individual and environmental factors and the way that individuals manage these are likely to be central to the identification of factors that might increase or decrease risk. Such factors are also likely to be key aspects of the later stages of seeking to intervene and the monitoring and feedback processes outlined.

One clear and testable hypothesis generated from this model is that those who show high levels of violence towards others will, when prevented from doing so, be more likely to be violent towards themselves than non-violent people. This is consistent with the finding that those convicted of violent offences tended to be at greater risk of suicide than those who were not (Crighton, 2006b; Shaw, 2007; Towl & Crighton, 1998, 2000).

There are a number of practical implications from this proposed theoretical model. It moves away from the largely atheoretical yet empirical approaches that have tended to characterise this area of research and which, perhaps, have run their course. In doing this, the model provides a source of testable hypotheses which will allow the theoretical model to be tested and refined, or replaced with a more powerful explanatory model. It thus allows the research base to move away from the use of essentially circular explanations, such as 'attention seeking' and the more liberal alternative of 'poor coping', replacing these with concepts derived from fundamental research into emotions. In linking suicide to anger and aggression, it also moves away from an unduly exclusive emphasis on depression (Plutchik, 1997).

The model also suggests that there are a number of points at which intervention might be effective within what may be termed a 'biopsychosocial' approach. These could include efforts to reduce initial anger and aggression by working to improve self-regulation. Equally, interventions might be made earlier in the process to reduce levels of perceived threat and unnecessary loss of control experienced in the environment.

Evidence-Based Interventions

There are a variety of systemic interventions to reduce the risk of suicide and intentional self-injury in prisons. These include efforts to reduce the risk presented within the environment, such as the removal of easily accessible ligature points or of sharp blades and materials. Such approaches, although apparently common sense, have rarely been adequately evaluated. Indeed, such studies would present quite intractable ethical problems. Likewise, systemic changes to prison regimes are likely in part to have impacts on suicide and intentional self-injury. Such interventions, however, have a range of other aims and impacts. Again, there has been little in the way of good quality evaluation of such interventions.

The evidence base on interventions with intentional self-injury is also made more difficult by the fact that the vast majority of research is concerned with notions of 'self-harm'. As such, studies often pool together incidents of intentional self-injury and intentional self-poisoning. It is unclear to what extent there are significant differences between these behaviours and this, in turn, complicates analysis of the evidence base in this area. It is also a possibility that this may serve to partially mask specific intervention effects.

In a systematic review of this area, a total of 23 studies were found of adequate methodological quality for inclusion (Hawton, Townsend, Arensman et al., 2007). Of these, 17 were rated as 'A' (clear and effective concealment of allocation), 3 as 'B' (unclear concealment) and 4 as 'C' (inadequate concealment). The studies included looked at both neurobiological and psychosocial interventions.

Psychosocial Interventions

A comparison of the effects of hospital admission compared to discharge found no advantage in inpatient admission in terms of repetition (OR 0.75 95% CI 1.16 to 3.60) (Waterhouse & Platt, 1990). It is noteworthy, though, that in this study only 15 per cent of referred patients were eligible for inclusion. All participants needed to be assessed as 'low risk' and without immediate medical or mental health needs and all were subject to a relatively short follow-up period.

Five studies comparing problem-solving interventions with standard care were identified (Evans, Tyrer, Catalan et al., 1999; Gibbons, Butler, Urwin et al., 1978; Hawton, McKeown, Day et al., 1987; McLeavey, Daly, Ludgate et al., 1994; Salkovskis, Atha Storer, 1990). All reported a reduction in levels of 'self-harm' but the summary odds ratio suggested no statistically significant effect (OR 0.70 95% CI 0.45 to 1.11). Excluding one study with relatively weak allocation, concealment again yielded a non-significant result. Examination of only studies that included just those who repeatedly 'harmed' themselves and only those studies with mixed allocation also proved negative (Hawton, Townsend, Arensman et al., 2007).

A number of studies have been reported that look at intensive intervention and outreach compared to standard care to reduce 'self-harm'. As with studies of problem-solving, the summary odds ratio suggested no significant positive effect (OR 0.84 95% CI 0.62 to 1.15) (Allard, Marshall & Plante, 1992; Chowdhury, Hicks & Kreitman, 1973; Hawton, Bancroft, Catalan et al., 1981; van der Sande, van Rooijen, Buskens et al., 1997; van Heeringen,

Jannes, Buylaert *et al.*, 1995; Welu, 1977). Inclusion of only those studies with the highest quality allocation and concealment made little difference to these results (Hawton, Townsend, Arensman *et al.*, 2007).

A study into the effects of therapist continuity on follow-up interestingly found that the repetition rate for those seeing the same therapist was significantly higher (OR 3.70 95% CI 1.13 to 12.09). The interpretation of this finding is not, however, straightforward. Despite random allocation, differences between the groups were noted prior to intervention, with the same therapist group showing higher levels of pre-existing risk factors. Those who saw the same therapist were also more effectively retained in treatment with 71 per cent attending at least one outpatient appointment compared to 47 per cent for the control group (OR 2.75 95% CI 1.37 to 5.52) (Torhorst, Moller, Schmid-Bode *et al.*, 1987).

Interventions to reduce suicide are necessarily focused on correlates of suicide, risk and protective factors. The area is ethically very difficult to study in a similar way to studies of self-injury and self-poisoning, although with the issues perhaps in even starker relief. There is an extensive evidence base for psychosocial interventions to address depression. These suggest that cognitive behavioural therapy (CBT) and interpersonal therapy (IPT) can be effective in reducing symptoms and achieving remission (National Institute of Clinical Excellence, 2007a, 2007b).

There is some evidence to suggest that dialectical behaviour therapy (DBT) is effective in reducing incidents of 'self-harm'. A small but significant difference in self-injury and suicide attempts at 6- and 12-month follow-up has been reported using DBT (n = 63, RR 0.81 95% CI 0.66 to 0.98 NNT 12 95% CI 7 to 108) but DBT has also been compared with a combination of Comprehensive Validation Therapy and a 12-step substance abuse intervention, with no significant difference reported (n = 23, RR 1.09 05% CI 0.64 to 1.87) (Hawton, Townsend, Arensman *et al.*, 2007). In a comparison of DBT and client-centred therapy, no statistical difference in admissions to hospital was found (n = 24, RR 0.33 95% CI 0.08 to 1.33). It was noted, however, that fewer of the DBT group intentionally self-injured or attempted suicide (n = 24, RR 0.13 95% CI 0.02 to 0.85 NNT 2 CI 2 to 11) (Hawton, Townsend, Arensman *et al.*, 2007). In a comparison of dialectical behaviour therapy (DBT) with standard aftercare, a significantly lower rate of repetition of 'self-harm' was found (OR 0.24 95% CI 0.06 to 0.93) (Linehan, Armstrong, Suarez *et al.*, 1991). In assessing this positive outcome, though, it is worth noting that the comparison here was based on a subgroup that was smaller than the number entering the trial, creating the risk of selection bias. It is also perhaps worth noting that DBT was delivered by a highly motivated and skilled group of practitioners and, as such, the extent to which these results might generalise would benefit from testing.

Overall, it is striking that the available evidence base in this area is of only moderate quality. The research that exists involves small sample sizes, increasing the risk of sampling biases and also reducing the power of studies to identify modest treatment effects. A great deal of the available data has also been lost through unclear reporting. The evidence is to an extent encouraging, nonetheless, and suggests that psychosocial interventions warrant further experimental investigation.

Neurobiological Interventions

Several studies have looked at the effects of drug-based interventions in reducing levels of self-injury. A comparison of flupenthixol (an antipsychotic drug with antidepressant properties) and placebo found a statistically significant reduction in the levels of repetition of 'self-harm' (OR 0.09 95% CI 0.02 to 0.50). The analysis was, however, based on a small number of individuals and included only those who repeatedly 'self-harmed'. As such, the clinical utility of flupenthixol and the extent to which this finding might be generalised is unclear (Montgomery, Montgomery, Jayanthi-Rani et al., 1979).

The use of antidepressant drugs has, perhaps unsurprisingly, been a focus of attention, largely on the basis of associations between depression, self-injury, self-poisoning and suicide (attempted and completed). A number of comparisons of antidepressant drugs with placebo have been reported, with disappointing results that suggest no significant positive effects. One study of paroxetine (a Selective Serotonin Reuptake Inhibitor) compared to placebo and using a subgroup analysis of 'minor repeaters' (less than five acts) and 'major repeaters' (five or more acts), reported a statistically significant reduction. This was reported for 'minor repeaters' but not for 'major repeaters'. The clinical significance and implications of this finding, though, remain unclear (Verkes, Van der Mast, Hengeveld et al., 1998).

Overall, the evidence base on neurobiological interventions is surprisingly limited when compared to related areas such as depression. There is good evidence of the efficacy of neurobiological interventions in treating risk factors for some incidents of self-injury, self-poisoning and suicide, most strikingly in the treatment of severe depression. The direct evidence, however, is limited and current studies suggest no reduction in repetition of intentional self-injury and self-poisoning. There have also been some suggestions that some forms of antidepressant drugs may serve to disinhibit aggression and increase the risk of intentional self-injury (Bregin, 2004). Given the current state of knowledge, neurobiological interventions are probably best considered, like psychosocial interventions, as experimental in nature.

Summary

- Suicide involves a complicated legal definition which varies across jurisdictions. As a result of this, a large number of self-inflicted deaths are not recorded as suicides. To address this, epidemiological studies have increasingly adopted operational definitions drawn primarily on International Classification of Diseases (ICD) categories.
- Definitions of self-injury are equally complex and in law issues of self-injury tend to be addressed only tangentially. There are clear difficulties with changing definitions over time. Recent trends in this area include a clearer specification of behaviour with the separation of self-injury and self-poisoning. There have also been suggestions that the term 'intentional' should deliberate as a more accurate description of self-injurious behaviours.
- Historically, a number of mythologies have developed in relation to suicide and self-injury in prisons, for example, notions that those who self-injure are not at risk of suicide and those on remand are at greater risk of suicide. Such myths have often arisen from poor quality or misinterpreted research. In recent years, very marked improvements in the quality of research in these areas have begun to produce a more useful evidence base.
- There has been a clear upward trend in the rate of suicides in prisons in England and Wales, which has only recently begun to flatten out. Some general demographic trends have emerged which show the difference in suicide rates between men and women reducing. White prisoners tend to be at higher risk. High rates of mental health problems are seen.
- The evidence relating to the early period after reception into a prison is striking. The robust and replicated finding is that the early stages of reception into an individual prison are a time of markedly increased risk. This gives rise to a number of practical implications. It suggests that increases in the movement of prisoners between establishments are likely to be associated with increased risk. It also suggests that interventions to mitigate the stress associated with the early days in a given prison may be particularly effective.
- The notion of a link between intentional self-injury and suicide needs to be considered carefully. For most prisoners most of the time, the notion

that suicide and self-injury are part of a simple continuum does not stand up to scrutiny.

- Research into intentional self-injury and suicide has been poorly integrated with other areas of the evidence base. Recent changes have begun to address this but there remains considerable scope for development.
- The evidence base on interventions to reduce intentional self-injury is complicated by the fact that the vast majority of research is concerned with the more generic construct of 'self-harm'. As such, studies often include intentional self-injury and intentional self-poisoning. This complicates any analysis of the evidence base in this area and may also serve to mask some intervention effects.
- The evidence base on interventions to reduce suicide is even more limited and tends to focus on a range of risk and protective factors thought to be associated with self-inflicted deaths. There are clear ethical problems in attempting to study interventions to reduce suicide and, as a result, research has focused largely on those who have completed suicide and on what are hypothesised to be analogue behaviours.
- Overall, the direct evidence base on neurobiological interventions is limited. Studies to date are primarily small-scale and suffer significantly from the risk of selection biases. Findings are not generally encouraging and at present such interventions may best be seen as largely experimental.
- The results from psychosocial interventions face similar methodological and ethical challenges. The results are somewhat mixed but suggest that psychosocial interventions may produce some reductions in the risk of repetition of self-injury and self-poisoning. The evidence base is, however, relatively poorly developed and psychosocial interventions in this area should also be seen as experimental in nature.

Notes

1   The implications of a suicide verdict can often be severe for the deceased and their family with, for example, life insurance policies often being void. The Courts have thus sought to err in favour of the deceased person, taking the view that where suicide is not proven beyond all reasonable doubt, the deceased and their family should not be disadvantaged.

2   The legal distinction between misadventure and accidental death is a complex one which goes beyond the scope of this chapter. In general terms, a misadventure verdict tends to be returned where the

individual's actions are thought to have played some significant role in their subsequent death.

3   This is a recurrent challenge in making gender comparisons with prison populations that are predominantly male. For example, in 2002 it was reported that 40 per cent of deaths in custody in the Australian state of Victoria were women: two women and three men died. For the whole of Australia the figures were 5 women and 63 men (McCall, 2004). This highlights the need for caution when calculating rates on the basis of such small numbers.

4   The term 'drug abuse' is used here to refer to the abuse of drugs, both licit and illicit. The term therefore includes the abuse of alcohol and prescribed medication, as well as the illegal use of controlled drugs such as heroin.

5   A major alcohol abuse problem was operationally defined as an average consumption of more than eight units of alcohol per day.

6   The data here might more accurately be described as having high levels of intersubjective agreement rather than objectivity.

7   ICD provides a system of coding all deaths and a number of these codes are for self-inflicted deaths. This is a much broader category than many legal definitions of suicide but more accurately reflects the rates at which people kill themselves than do officially recorded suicide statistics.

8   The term 'self-inflicted death' is used because the sample included cases where prisoners had killed themselves but formal verdicts of suicide had not been returned. The selection of cases for inclusion was based on ICD classification of deaths.

9   The receptions data was corrected for double-counting of re-receptions of prisoners released on bail and for other reasons.

10   Classification of prescribed medication was based on British National Formulary (BNF) categories.

11   This group included those sentenced to life, detention for life and detention at Her Majesty's Pleasure.

12   Contracted prisons did not generally use the F2052SH system but all had developed similar systems for care management of prisoners identified as being at increased risk of suicide. Due to the relatively small number of deaths in contracted prisons, no reference is made to the specific care management processes used.

Chapter 12

Violence

Introduction

Violence is a complex and multifaceted phenomena with high rates of prevalence in the UK, the rest of Europe and internationally. It results in largely unquantifiable amounts of human suffering and could legitimately be characterised as one of the most pressing public health issues facing the world. It seems probable that violence draws on fundamental biological characteristics that cut across species. For human beings, it seems likely that these drives have been evident across all forms of social organisation and pre-date recorded history.

Violence raises a number of definitional issues and challenges. The severity of violent behaviour can vary along a continuum but the transition points are unclear and often involve complex value judgements. War involves the state-sanctioned and supported use of extreme and systematic violence, with the behaviours involved often, though not always, being characterised as heroic.[1] The systematic use of violence to resist oppressive regimes may be similarly lauded. Sporting events such as football often involve a range of violent behaviours, often strongly supported and encouraged by observers. The examples could be multiplied but the essential point is that the notion of violence is a construct, with issues such as intent, consent and outcome being central to our conceptions of violence. Concepts of psychological violence also raise contentious definitional issues. Here the intent is to cause psychological distress rather than physical injury and it is unclear to what extent the processes involved differ.[2] Historically, there has perhaps been greater interest in such areas than presently (D'Cruze, 2000).

202

Within the context of criminal justice, much of the discourse on violence has focused on a narrow range of behaviour, generally defined by specific legal offence categories: typically, homicide, assaults, robbery and rape.[3] Most appear to have as their focus what might be termed 'interpersonal violence' or, as some have described it, 'everyday violence' (D'Cruze, 2000). The area has also suffered from significant confusion between notions of anger, aggression and violence, with these often being inadequately distinguished and sometimes used, quite inappropriately, as synonyms (Towl & Crighton, 1996).

Impersonal and indirect forms of violence are often not considered in the research base from applied psychology at all and, although extensively studied in social psychology, such research has often been poorly integrated into a broader understanding of violence.[4] The actions of transnational companies may bring whole communities in and out of poverty as the result of economic decisions made in boardrooms. Such actions may legitimately be seen as acts of corporate violence and, in terms of public health impacts, can have devastating outcomes. There is a need to also consider such acts in seeking to achieve a better scientific understanding of violence.

It is taken here as axiomatic that violence cannot be adequately understood by adopting single-paradigm approaches in isolation from the broader social and cultural context. Issues such as inequalities in the distribution of resources and power, linked to aspects of social structures such as class, ethnicity, gender, religion, beliefs, economic status and age, all impact on the type, experience and expression of violence. The importance of such considerations here lies additionally in what happens as the result of a violent act, specifically in terms of the application, or otherwise, of legal and moral sanctions (Stanko, 2000; Steinmetz, 1999).[5]

The psychological literature in this area is also curiously disjointed. In much discussion and debate about violence, there often appears to be an undue focus on criminal violence perpetrated by strangers in public places. This has tended to result in much of the everyday reality of violence being lost where it occurs in private (and public) settings between those who know each other well.[6]

Interpersonal Violence

Recognising the importance of these factors, the focus of much of this chapter is on direct and primarily physical interpersonal violence which attracts legal sanction. Although many of those who participate in such acts of violence will not come into contact with the criminal justice system, the majority of violent offenders in prison fall within this sub-category of violence. Survey studies, though, suggest that a large proportion of inter-personal violence goes unreported (Walker, Kershaw & Nicholas, 2006). As with other forms of offending, perhaps most strikingly sexual offending, this means that much of what is sometimes claimed authoritively to be 'known' about violent offenders is based on the small sub-sample who are detected and prosecuted. This raises the likelihood of sampling biases and the exis-tence of a substantial pool of undetected perpetrators, about whom we know little.

Within known violent offenders, age appears to be especially significant, with a relatively small number of young people being responsible for a dis-proportionately large numbers of violence acts. A fuller understanding of this is likely to involve both neurobiological factors and also the impact of the family and social environments in which such young people have devel-oped and live. Families have a central role in such development by shaping initial experiences and expressions of aggressive feelings and violent behav-iour. They are also a focus for comparatively high levels of violence them-selves. There is some persuasive empirical evidence that family experiences of violence have a powerful effect in the perpetuation of violence across generations and in providing many of the skills needed to control aggression in later life. This is an important area of consideration when looking at violence because it may contribute to our understanding not just of vio-lence *per se* but of ways of intervening to reduce violence too.

Family violence occurs in relative privacy, in the context of differential power relationships. In this sense, violence may be seen as one manifesta-tion of the abuse of power. The psychological and physical intimacies which characterise aspects of 'family life' arguably have trust at their core. It is important to be aware of the strong emotions associated with being part of a family and that such emotions may manifest themselves both functionally and dysfunctionally. In discussing this particular area, the term 'family violence' is used throughout. This is preferred to the more commonly used term 'domestic violence' because it seems likely that it is the intimacy of family relationships which often underpin such violence, rather than the location of events. This is a weakness of the term 'domestic violence', used extensively across some of the evidence base in this area, which stresses the setting rather than the relationships involved.

Violence in families directed against children has a long and often shame-ful history. Both mothers and fathers physically abuse children, with a study of prevalence in the UK suggesting that mothers were more likely to be responsible for physical abuse, being responsible for 49 per cent com-pared to 40 per cent for fathers. Violence was also reported to be perpetrated by stepmothers (3 per cent) or stepfathers (5 per cent), grandparents (3 per cent) and other relatives (1 per cent).These findings may at least in part relate to the amount of time children spend with different family members (Cawson, Wattam, Brooker et al., 2000).

There is some evidence that children living with both biological parents are more likely to be physically abused by their fathers than their mothers. For children living with both biological parents, mothers were implicated in 36 per cent of violent assaults compared to 61 per cent for fathers (Creighton & Noyes, 1989). There is also some evidence to suggest that men living with children are more likely to perpetrate severe physical abuse and particularly homicide (Ewing, 1997). Single parents, adolescent parents and step-parents (particularly males) have been found to be at higher risk of physically abusing children (Gelles, 1989).[7]

Child deaths from parental abuse are unique among homicides in involving a high proportion of women. Offenders are predominantly biological mothers, whereas male perpetrators are usually step-parents to the child victim (Alder & Polk, 2001). Step-parents have also been found to kill children in their care at a much greater rate than biological parents, with many more step-children killed by stepfathers than by stepmothers (Daly & Wilson, 1994; Strang, 1995). This effect seems likely to be to some extent related to the fact that most small children reside with their mothers rather than their fathers (Daly & Wilson, 1994).

Studies based on child homicide convictions have suggested that the majority of perpetrators are males (Lyman, McGwin, Malone et al., 2003). A significant number of deaths related to parental maltreatment may not meet the criminal definition of homicide, particularly deaths due to neglect, potentially distorting the picture of violence in families (Finkelhor, 1997). When neglect is included for analysis, almost 80 per cent of fatal maltreatment cases in the US were primarily attributable to women (Sedlak & Broadhurst, 1996). Evidence also suggests that mothers are predominantly responsible for neonaticides (death of children aged under 24 hours) (Creighton, 1995).

Men are more often responsible for child deaths that result from physical assault, with many of these cases being apparent attempts to punish or discipline the child for behaviours such as crying (Alder & Polk, 2001; Ewing, 1997). Estimates of the numbers of children subject to less severe physical abuse by their families in the USA in the 1990s ranged from 1.5 to 6.9 million, depending on the definitions used and data collection methods (Wilson, 2000). A significant part of the problem with family violence therefore is its very ubiquity. It provides a potentially powerful vehicle for the development of further violence in a cyclical form (Iadicola & Shupe, 2003). An example of this is perhaps the comparatively recent change in the UK that curtails schoolteacher powers to physically assault children and young people in their care.

Estimates of the rate of violence between spouses are again heavily dependent on the methodology and definitions used. It has nonetheless been estimated that violence occurs in nearly a third of marriages in the USA (Bricklin, Hersen, & Van Hasselt, 1999; Straus, Gelles & Steinmetz, 1980). Women are more likely to encounter violence in their homes than outside them, and are more likely to be injured by family members than strangers (Jones, 1990). Recent studies in the UK have yielded similarly high estimates of the rates of such violence. In a study of women attending primary care health centres in East London, 41 per cent (95% confidence interval 38% to 44%) reported experiencing physical violence from a partner or former partner and 17 per cent (95% CI 14% to 19%) reported violence within the past year. Pregnancy in the past year was associated with an increased risk of current violence (adjusted odds ratio 2.11, 95% CI 1.39 to 3.19). The rates of formal recording of such violence were however relatively low, being noted in the medical records of 17 per cent of women who reported it in the study (Richardson, Coid, Petruckevitch *et al.*, 2006).

The strongest predictor of future partner-on-partner violence is the previous behaviour of the perpetrator. Most violence is perpetrated by men and there is a high degree of overlap between men who are violent towards their partners and their children (Crisp & Stanko, 2001). It is estimated that about two women a week are killed by their partner or ex-partner in England and Wales, accounting for around half of all women murdered (Crisp & Stanko, 2001). Lifetime prevalence for experiencing serious physical violence in the family is reported at about 26 per cent in the British Crime Survey (BCS), with an estimated 835,000 such assaults in 1997 in England and Wales. Women under 25 were most likely to be violently assaulted with the rate of assault only significantly reducing for women beyond their mid-40s. Current estimates from the BCS suggest some reductions in the rate of family violence from this high baseline (Nicholas, Povey, Walker *et al.*, 2006).

Approximately one in five men report having been violent in an intimate relationship. Physically abusive relationships also appear to last, on average, for seven years. Up to one in ten women who are physically abused in their homes will be knocked unconscious at some point (Crisp & Stanko, 2001; Stanko, Crisp, Hale *et al.*, 1998), with pregnancy being a time of increased risk of violence, some assaults seemingly intended to induce miscarriage.

A number of researchers and commentators have highlighted the potential harmful effects on children of witnessing and also experiencing violence. In public health terms, there is a pressing need to reduce violence in families for a number of reasons. Chief amongst these is the need to protect women and children from such suffering. In broader public health terms, though, it seems likely that such violence is itself a causal factor in children subsequently growing up to commit acts of criminal violence.

Predictors of Violence

There is considerable emerging data on developmental factors associated with violence in children and adults. Consideration of this is complicated by variations in the definitions used and studies have clearly varied in terms of threshold levels and inclusion and exclusion criteria (Farrington & Loeber, 1998; Piquero, Farrington & Blumstein, 2007). A number of clear and consistent themes are revealed in the evidence base. There is a marked and empirically demonstrated continuity between levels of aggression and violence in early childhood and later criminal violence. There is also an association between levels of experiencing violence and levels of childhood aggression and violence.

The largest and most methodologically sophisticated longitudinal study of this area in the UK is the Cambridge Study in Delinquent Development (CSDD). The children in this study revealed high levels of self-reported violence. A clear statistically significant association between the age of onset of offending and subsequent violence was also noted (Piquero, Farrington & Blumstein, 2007). The peak age for violent offending appears to occur around the age of 16 years and then, for the majority, declines in the late teens and early twenties, although a significant minority will continue to show relatively high-frequency violent behaviour. Evidence suggests that between 20 and 45 per cent of serious violent offenders at 16 or 17 showed initial violence in childhood (D'Unger, Land, McCall *et al.*, 1998; Elliott, Huizinga & Morse, 1986; Nagin & Tremblay, 1999; Patterson & Yoerger, 1997; Stattin & Magnusson, 1996). This percentage is even higher for girls who commit serious violent offences by age 16 or 17 (45 to 69 per cent) (Elliott, Huizinga & Morse, 1986). This suggests that adolescence is in some sense a critical period for the development and control of violence. A subgroup of the most violent young people, however, continues to be violent into adulthood (Loeber, Farrington & Waschbusch, 1998; Moffitt, 1993; Tolan, 1987; Tolan & Gorman-Smith, 1998). Such evidence suggests that late-onset youth violence is the most common developmental pattern, suggesting that most serious violent offenders will not be identifiable in early childhood. In fact, the majority of young people who become violent are likely to show little or no evidence of childhood behavioural disorders.

For both boys and girls, levels of violence show a progressive decline with age as previously violent individuals desist. It seems clear that biological factors are important in terms of both frequency and severity of violence with late adolescence being especially problematic for boys and their victims. Social influences on such behaviours are also undoubtedly important in terms of the moderation and expression of neurobiologically mediated aggressive impulses.

Ethnicity has been noted as a potential predictor of the risk of violence, with most UK studies breaking ethnicity into three broad groups; black, Asian and white.[8] The black grouping is generally overrepresented in figures for violent crime and especially robbery. For example, the rates of arrest for robbery in London in 1998–99 were 8.07 per 1000 for black groupings, 1.41 for Asian groupings and 0.47 for white groupings. Arrest rates for the overall violence figures by way of legal categories were 17.42 per 1000 for black groupings, 6.48 for Asian groupings and 3.95 for white groupings (Farrington, 2001). Such findings have been replicated in related areas of research, for example, in violence amongst mentally disordered offenders (Monahan, Steadman, Silver et al., 2001). There are a number of reasons for such effects. One obvious factor is the clear social and economic differences that emerge. In one study, being black was initially found to be one of the best predictors of subsequent violence; on further iteration, seeking to correct the data for economic factors (essentially whether individuals lived in an economically deprived area), the effect disappeared. In this study it seems likely that ethnic grouping was acting, at least partially, as a proxy for living in deprived areas. There are of course a number of reasons why those living in poorer areas might be more inclined to use violence, not least the greater numbers of other people being violent (Monahan, Steadman, Clark Robbins et al., 2005).[9]

The factor most strongly associated with adult convictions in the CSDD was having a parent with one or more criminal convictions. Harsh parental discipline was also a good predictor of both official and self-reported violence (Farrington, 1998). Peer, socio-economic and neighbourhood factors also come into play. Having criminal or delinquent friends was identified as a risk factor as was low socio-economic status.

The CSDD also identified a number of factors identified at the ages of eight and ten which were associated with reconvictions. These included low family income, large family size, a convicted parent, low IQ and poor parental child-rearing behaviours. The percentage of boys convicted for violent offences between the ages of 10 and 20 differed markedly, depending on the presence of these. Boys who had none of these characteristics had a 3 per cent chance of having a violent conviction whereas those with four or five showed a 31 per cent risk of being convicted for a violent offence (Farrington, 1997).

Neurobiological Bases of Violence

The most striking biological difference in violence is gender. Boys show higher levels of direct aggression and violence from an early age. Gender differences in the expression of direct aggression develop early in life and are fully evident during puberty. Social and environmental factors certainly impact on this. There is, however, significant evidence to suggest a neurobiological basis for part of the difference.

Elevated circulating levels of testosterone may be associated with aggression in young men (Dabbs, Carr, Frady et al., 1995). It is, though, unclear if this a consequence or a causal factor in violence. A large number of neurotransmitters have also been implicated in violence with the current evidence suggesting a particular role for serotonin and the catecholamines.

Serotonin (5-hydroxytryptamine or 5-HT) is concerned, amongst other things, with exerting inhibitory control over behaviour. It has been a major focus of interest in relation to depression as well as aggression and violence (Cravchick & Goldman, 2000). Levels of serotonin are difficult to study directly so much of the evidence base relates to known metabolites, commonly 5-hydroxyindoleacetic acid (5-HIAA) which can be measured in cerebrospinal fluid (CSF).

It has been suggested that serotonin levels are implicated in both violent and suicidal behaviour. Low levels of CSF 5-HIAA have been reported in samples of people who have attempted suicide, especially using more violent methods (Åsberg, Traskman & Thoren, 1975) and in persons showing high levels of aggression (Brown, Goodwin, Ballenger et al., 1979).

Noradrenergic systems are also known to play a role in aggressive behaviour, although the evidence for this is indirect. For example, plasma levels of adrenaline and noradrenaline have been shown to correlate with experimentally induced hostility in normal subjects (Gerra, Zaimovic, Avanzinmi et al., 1997). The extent to which this relates to violent behaviour, however, remains unclear.

A number of structures within the brain are associated with aggression, although the links to violence are less clear. The prefrontal cortex is thought to be closely involved in controlling impulses and lesions to this area of the brain can result in disinhibition and aggressive behaviours, as well as in self-injurious behaviour in some. Dysfunction in parts of the limbic system, including the amygdala and hippocampus, two limbic structures in the temporal lobe, has also been put forward as important (Bear, 1991; Volavka, 1999).

Unsurprisingly perhaps, characteristics in children such as poor cognitive executive functioning are associated with later violence. Areas such as emotional control, impulsivity and attention are similarly linked. Much of the research base in this area has focused on broad typological categories: attention deficit hyperactivity disorder (ADHD) and conduct disorder (CD). The use of these broad categories has the strength that it partially allows for comparisons over time, although overall the value of such categories is unclear as they are not mutually exclusive and exhaustive. As with other categorical approaches in mental health, caution is needed when using categorical structures on apparently dimensional characteristics without clear empirical discontinuities, whatever threshold is used. It is unclear whether such categorisation adds substantively to simpler descriptions of attention difficulties, intellectual functioning, impulse control and activity levels.

A number of school-related risks have been identified and these are associated with achievement problems and poor school-leaving qualifications. It is possible to postulate a number of links between these and characteristics such as high impulsivity and poor attention. Such findings have been replicated and demonstrated to have short- and also medium-term associations with violence (Lösel & Bender, 2006). Further theoretical work has also begun to address the challenge of drawing together empirical observations within developmental psychology (Lösel & Bender, 2006).

Most male-on-male (young) adult violence occurs in pubs, the workplace and on streets, often at night, particularly when fuelled by alcohol consumption. Such predictability in terms of likely locations and times for such violent interaction does serve to give considerable potential scope for working with violent clients to effect change by relatively straightforward methods. Gang violence can also be similarly predictable in terms of its location and timing. Alcohol intoxication can frequently serve to increase the probability of violence in particular locations and at given times. So, longer-term influences include biological, individual and peer-related factors. Shorter-term influences may include boredom, anger and frustration. For violence to take place there needs to be an opportunity, that is a prospective victim and perpetrator. For the perpetrator, cognitive processes – including considerations of costs, benefits and beliefs – may all input to the probability of interpersonal violence, although such cognitive considerations may be overridden either by high levels of impulsivity or indeed often by alcohol intoxication or other drug misuses. The consequences of such behaviours will impact upon the future likelihood of its reoccurrence. For optimal impacts, it is important that both assessments and interventions focus upon 'deficits' and 'strengths' too (Loeber & Farrington, 1998).

Evidence-based Interventions

Although there is much information about factors linked to the risk of violent offending, the mechanisms of such 'risks' are comparatively poorly understood. This only serves to underline the importance of theory-driven models of practice both for assessments and interventions. It can be a salutary exercise for practitioners to reflect upon their practice in terms of the theoretical underpinnings of such work which may be explicit or implicit. In broad terms, psychological interventions which are cognitive-behavioural, social-therapeutic, multimodal and family-orientated each have a potential role to play in working with individuals in reducing their risk of violence (Lösel & Bender, 2006). A combination of strategies are needed and the quality of the therapeutic relationships, and indeed therapist characteristics, are often important too (McNeil, Batchelor, Burnett et al., 2005). At a fundamental level, it is invariably important to have and demonstrate an appropriately respectful approach to working with prisoners. Arguably, and from our extensive practice with this client group, young violent prisoners will be especially focused on the degree of respect with which they see themselves treated by staff. This is possibly because these young people have experiences of being treated poorly and in an often disrespectful way both by adults (often amongst those in 'authority' roles) and other young people. But also young people's accounts of their own violent behaviour may sometimes reflect a response to a perceived threat manifested in a lack of 'respect'. These two observations taken together are illustrative of the importance of therapist characteristics, especially perhaps for our purposes when working with children and young people.

In general, characteristics that have been shown to correlate with future violence of interest to the criminal justice system have been broadly divided into 'static' and 'dynamic'. The former refers to historical correlates, such as the age at which someone was convicted of a violent offence. 'Dynamic' correlates are aspects of the person or their life which are, in principle, amenable to change. An example here might be living in an economically deprived area. Such 'dynamic' and 'static' correlates can also be subdivided into environmental characteristics such as family, peer groups and schools and into individual characteristics such as self-esteem and impulse control. Multi-level approaches of this type are advocated as the most promising approach when addressing violence (Lösel & Bender, 2003).

One helpful approach with family violence can be seen in work undertaken in 27 projects (Hester & Westmarland, 2005) and also with children who have been subject to environments of family violence (Mullender, 2000, 2004). Drawing upon models of public health in practice, such work shows primary prevention is important; this may mean direct intervention in both primary and secondary schools is necessary to promote responsible citizenship. Training for health visitors and nurses in encouraging and dealing with disclosure in a supportive and constructive manner may also be crucial. According to the authors reviewing these projects, the police still have a long way to go in this difficult area of practice. There is also an identified need for the training of judges and magistrates. In addition to improving criminal justice processes, there is also important direct support that could be offered, for example, individual and groupwork-based approaches to improving self-esteem. Overwhelmingly, the evidence suggests a combination of strategies to tackle such family violence (Herman, 1992). Some victims benefit from the installation of home security, such as panic alarms and other related environmental measures.

The same principles of multimodal and multi-level interventions apply to work with children and young people too. As we have seen, such approaches have been imported into criminology from medicine in general and public health-based approaches in particular. As is the case with working effectively with perpetrators and victims of domestic violence, much of what may be needed goes beyond the traditional and sometimes arbitrary boundaries of psychology in the UK. But in research and practice terms, it is worth being aware of the wider social, cultural and political context of the application of psychologically based approaches. It is crucially important to appreciate that sometimes broader social and health policy changes are needed to prevent and reduce violence. Such factors go beyond the scope of this chapter where the focus is primarily on psychological approaches that may helpfully contribute to the understanding, prevention and reduction of interpersonal violence, given its sociopolitical context.

In terms of individual and family-based approaches, four types of intervention have shown significant promise: parent education, parent management training, child skills training and preschool intellectual enrichment interventions (Farrington & Welsh, 2003).

In one randomly allocated study, nurses visited (for about one and a quarter hours) and supported young mothers during pregnancy and some for two years after birth too. The results were compared with young mothers not receiving such support. Those with both pre-birth and post-birth support had the most successful outcomes. There was a decrease in recorded child abuse and neglect, especially by poor unmarried teenage mothers (Olds, Henderson, Cole *et al.*, 1998). These are important findings that have some clear policy and practice implications for UK policy for children (HM Treasury, 2003).

One key US study focused on school-based prevention in Seattle. This involved the application of a combination of parent management training, teacher training and child skills training (Lonczak, Abbott, Hawkins *et al.*, 2002). The specific intervention for children focused on the improvement of their attachment to their parents. This overall approach has received further support from cost-benefit analyses (Aos, Phipps, Barnoski *et al.*, 2001). School bullying, which can often involve interpersonal violence, has also been the subject of targeting, not only with regard to addressing the immediate problem but also with a view to future prevention. School bullying has been seen as a risk factor for future offending (Farrington, 1993). A number of school-based interventions have been successful in reducing bullying, although they have perhaps tended to be met with more success in primary schools than in secondary schools.

One of the most successful community-based interventions has been the use of multisystemic therapy (MST) which is individualised and operates at a number of levels, including the individual child, the parent or primary caregiver, and school. Such work has arguably been seen to be the most effective in terms of cost-benefit analyses, especially when chronically 'at-risk' children and young people are targeted.

In addition to individual and family-based approaches, in keeping with a multimodal approach, some readers may wish to look at the evidence in support of community-based environmental interventions, sometimes referred to as situational crime prevention programmes, for example, the introduction and improvement of street lighting. The results from such studies are of particular interest because the evidence would seem to indicate that there is a decrease in interpersonal violence in those areas targeted. Robberies, assaults, threats and pestering decreased by 41 per cent over one year after the introduction of improved lighting in one study (Painter & Farrington, 1999).

Some key approaches in terms of the prediction, prevention and reduction of future violence have been touched upon. In addition to providing such support at a range of levels for especially vulnerable communities, we need also to look at interventions for those with convictions for violence, subject to negative legal sanctions either through imprisonment or community-based punishments. It is important to ensure the availability of such interventions in both residential and community settings. Psychologists have significant potential contributions to make to this important area of forensic practice.

Summary

- Violence is a complex and multifaceted phenomenon drawing upon fundamental drives and with high rates of prevalence. It is one of the most pressing public health issues facing the world.
- Much of the discourse on violence with criminal justice has focused on a narrow range of behaviour, defined by legal categories. The evidence base in relation to this has been generally poor at integrating evidence from multiple paradigms and disciplines. It also contains inherent sampling biases due to the existence of a potentially large pool of undetected perpetrators.
- Amongst convicted offenders, age appears to be especially significant. A small number of young people are responsible for a disproportionately large amount of violent crime.
- Families also seem to have a central role in the development of violence, shaping initial controls and expressions of violence. The family is also a focus for comparatively high levels of violence.
- There is considerable emerging data on developmental factors associated with violence in children and adults. There is marked continuity between early levels of aggression and later violence, as well as a clear association between experiencing violence as a child and later violent crime.
- The most striking biological difference in violence is gender, with boys showing higher levels of direct aggression and violence from an early age. A number of neurobiological and psychosocial factors are likely to be implicated in this.
- Characteristics in children, such as poor cognitive executive functioning, poor emotional control, impulse control and attention deficits, are also linked to later violence.
- Social context and the use of alcohol are associated with increased violence, primarily in young people. The largely predictable patterns associated with this type of violence yield significant potential for systematic environmental interventions to reduce frequency and severity.
- Risk and protective factors associated with violence have been the subject of extensive study. As yet, though, the mechanisms by which these operate are comparatively poorly understood. This serves to under-

line the importance of theory-driven models to inform research and practice.

- Therapist characteristics have been shown to be a fundamental aspect of effective psychosocial interventions. In addressing issues of violence with children, young people and families, such characteristics may have even greater salience. The use of population and public health-based approaches are likely to have greater utility than efforts to intervene with adult criminal offenders.

- Four main types of intervention have shown significant promise in reducing violent offending: parent education, parent management training, child skills training and preschool intellectual enrichment interventions. Later interventions with adult offenders remain largely experimental, although the results of some of these to date have been generally encouraging.

Notes

1 Exceptions to this include war crimes, where the conduct of combatants is seen to have broken conventions generally relating to the treatment of non-combatants and prisoners. Many example of this exist but two recently studied examples are the Mai Lai massacre in Vietnam and massacres in the former state of Yugoslavia.

2 The role of what might be termed psychological violence can be as severe as interpersonal physical violence and, of course, may often occur in association with physical violence. It is a field in which psychology has contributed significantly to understanding (Tajfel, 1982; Zimbardo, 2003). It is also the case that some individuals may engage largely or exclusively in such violence, the most striking example here perhaps being a number of war criminals who engaged in what might be seen as systemic bureaucratic violence.

3 Rape is also considered within the field of sexual offending but its status as a sexually motivated offence has been challenged, with a number of researchers and practitioners suggesting that it is frequently a violent offence with sexual assault used primarily by men to exert power over women. A detailed discussion is provided by Darke (1990).

4 The position is even more marked in respect of other disciplines such as social policy and economics which have much to say about these areas.

5 Elizabeth Stanko makes the point (Stanko, 2000) that, although she has often been asked about her research into violence, she is generally not

asked about police brutality, suicides in custody or prison officer violence.

6　Indeed, this is an error we have made in previous work (Towl & Crighton, 1996).

7　Violence and neglect are frequently associated with each other, although the degree to which the two are related is contentious. Neglect of children is most often seen in economically disadvantaged families with low income, poor housing and living conditions (Nelson, Saunders & Landsman, 1993).

8　This approach to ethnicity is not without serious problems and can be criticised as being unduly broad. Within-group comparisons often yield as much ethnic diversity as across-group comparisons. The white group, for example, includes many of the most economically and socially advantaged groups in the world. Also within this are subgroups such as Romanies, travellers and ethnic European gypsies who are some of the most disadvantaged groups in the world. Asian and black broad groupings hide similar effects.

9　This finding in turn is likely to hide further complexity. For example, the reasons why such a high proportion of the black community lives in poorer areas are unclear. Racial discrimination is a likely factor here. However, Asian groups appear to have been more successful in terms of social mobility and it seems unlikely that they have suffered from less discrimination.

Chapter 13

Sex Offending

Introduction

Efforts to define sex offending present a number of challenges. The use of the term varies across jurisdictions and has also markedly varied over time. Age of consent to sexual behaviour varies and the range of proscribed sexual behaviour has also been subject to change. One example here would be homosexual acts between adult men, which were illegal in England and Wales until decriminalisation under the Sexual Offences Act 1967.[1] The current position in relation to homosexuality remains contentious with continuing areas of unequal treatment, for example, in the armed forces, where sexual activity remains an offence. Setting aside such areas, though, there is broad general agreement that a number of actions related to sexual behaviour should be criminal. Such acts fall into two broad categories: forcible sexual activity and sexual activity with those unable to give consent.

The majority of the evidence base relates to those who sexually offend against children or against adults. A variety of terms have been used to describe and distinguish these groupings.[2] Terms such as 'paedophile' and 'child molester' are widely used to describe those who offend against children. A number of concerns have arisen from the term 'paedophile' which in literal translation means 'lover of children'. The term 'child molester' has been suggested as an alternative which stresses the harmful effects of such offending: the term does nonetheless direct attention away from a range of harmful and sexually motivated offences that may not involve physical contact. The terms 'sexual offender against children' and 'sexual offender against adults' are used below as inclusive terms for both main groups of offenders.

Research into sex offending and interventions with sexual offenders pose significant methodological and ethical challenges. In the past, these have often not been adequately considered (Towl, 2005a). Most striking is the low level of reporting of sex offences, with studies of levels of victimisation suggesting high degrees of underreporting of sexual offences (Dodd, Nicholas, Povey *et al.*, 2004; Nicholas, Povey, Walker *et al.*, 2006; Hood, Shute, Feilzer *et al.*, 2002). In turn, the levels of conviction of sex offences tend to be low (Hood, Shute, Feilzer *et al.*, 2002). This means that it is likely that there is a large pool of sexual offenders who are undetected. Of those prosecuted, the majority are not convicted and are unlikely to be accessible to researchers (Towl, 2005a).

In practice, most of the evidence base is concerned with convicted sex offenders involved in intervention work. Studies of this sub-sample of sex offenders have in turn produced reports of high levels of undetected offences (Abel, Becker, Mittleman *et al.*, 1987). When offered high levels of confidentiality, this group report much higher levels of offending (Abel & Rouleau, 1990). Such studies tend to reinforce the notion of a pool of undetected sexual offenders and sexual offending (Abel & Rouleau, 1990; Hood, Shute, Feilzer *et al.*, 2002; Towl, 2005a). A number of significant implications follow from this. First, much of the research in this area has focused on easily accessible samples of offenders, rather than facing up to the significant practical and ethical challenges of research into undetected and unconvicted sex offenders[3] (Hood, Shute, Feilzer *et al.*, 2002; Crighton, 2006c; Crighton & Towl, 2007). The logical implication of this is that what is claimed to be known about sex offenders generally refers to two relatively accessible sub-samples of sex offenders: those who have sought treatment and those who have been detected, arrested, convicted and, generally, imprisoned. It seems likely that there will be some overlap between these sub-samples. It is unclear how similar they are likely to be compared to the broader pool of sex offenders with a significant likelihood of systematic differences (Crighton & Towl, 2007). A number of characteristics reported may simply be an artefact of the processes of detection, prosecution and conviction. An example here might be the finding that those with low levels of intellectual ability are overrepresented in samples of sex offenders (Hawk, Rosenfield & Warren, 1993). This may simply be a systematic bias resulting from those with learning disabilities offending in ways that are more likely to be detected. Alternatively, it may be that those of lower ability are less able to avoid prosecution (Day, 1994). The higher rate may also be due to higher rates of sex offending. What seems clear is that those convicted of criminal sex offences and those who seek out treatment may show significant differences compared to other sexual offenders. This strong caveat needs to be borne in mind when looking at the evidence base on treatment outcomes or evaluating commentary on what is purportedly known about sex offenders (Crighton & Towl, 2007).

Prevalence

There is a largely disparate literature on prevalence rates for sex offending which is faced with significant methodological challenges. However, there has been at least one good quality study attempting to review the existing evidence (White, Bradley, Ferriter *et al.*, 1998). In this review, the areas of sexual offending and sexual paraphilias were considered together. The evidence on general rates of sexual offending was more heterogeneous and suggested rates of sexual offending against women ranging from 12–28 per cent and for men from 3–8 per cent (Baker & Duncan, 1985; Finkelhor, 1979, 1984; Furby, Weintrott & Blackshaw, 1989; Mullen, Martin, Anderson *et al.*, 1994). The median age of those who are sexually assaulted has been reported as 13 years and the median age of those raped as 22 years (Bureau of Justice, 1998). However, the available research base is predominantly North American and the extent to which these findings may be applied cross-culturally is unclear.

Evidence-Based Interventions

The evidence base relating to interventions with sex offenders has grown steadily from the 1950s onwards, although the available evidence remains of only moderate quality. In a meta-analysis of randomised and non-randomised studies using the Maryland Scale (Sherman, Gottfredson, MacKenzie *et al.*, 1997) to assess quality, it was noted that only a handful of studies were rated at the highest level of 5 (Lösel & Schmucker, 2005).

The available evidence can be broadly divided into studies where allocation to treatment was randomly assigned and those where it was not. Randomisation is a powerful methodology widely used in the assessment of a range of interventions which serves to eliminate most likely systematic biases. It therefore tends to generate more scientifically powerful results than non-randomised experimental designs.

Randomised Studies

Randomised studies into the treatment of sex offenders have been subject to recent systematic reviews looking at psychosocial and neurobiological interventions (White, Bradley, Ferriter *et al.*, 1998). Neurobiological interventions were divided into four types: the use of sex hormones; the use of antipsychotic drugs; the use of bromide-related compounds; and surgical interventions (primarily, castration of male sex offenders). Psychosocial interventions were subdivided into behaviour therapy, relapse prevention approaches and a category of others that included behavioural approaches such as orgasmic reconditioning. Studies were included where they compared interventions either with placebo or with 'standard care', provided outcome measures including reconviction and reported the numbers 'lost to follow-up'. Where possible, a number of other 'secondary' outcome measures were also assessed and these included death rates, other forms of criminal offending, measures of mental state, patient satisfaction, penile plethysmograph assessment, measures of resource use or cost-benefit and side effects. Where the data were of adequate quality, they divided the follow-up periods into short-term follow-ups (0–6 months), medium-term (up to 5 years) and long-term (more than 5 years). Based on their review, the researchers argued that only studies with long-term follow-up provided adequate measures of the true re-arrest and reconviction rates, due to the low rates of detection and conviction of sexual offences. In support of this view, it has previously been reported that a significant number of rapists studied were not reconvicted until late into a very lengthy follow-up period (Soothill, 1976).

An extensive search of published research was conducted and rated studies into three bands (A, B or C) on the basis of their methodological adequacy (White, Bradley, Ferriter *et al.*, 1998). Where individuals were randomly assigned to intervention and control groups and the process of randomisation was described, the study would be rated as A. Where there was randomisation but the process for ensuring this in the study was not described, the study was rated B. Where no mention of randomisation was made, the study was rated C. All C-rated studies were excluded since, in the absence of any evidence of randomisation, these failed to meet the minimum standards of scientific quality set out by the authors in their review. The reviewers found no studies which they rated as A.

Studies where more than 50 per cent of participants were lost at follow-up were also excluded as these studies were at risk of an unacceptable level of selection bias. As a result of this, 58 of the identified studies were excluded. At this point, only three studies were identified as meeting the basic scientific standards set out by the researchers.

The evidence on the use of neurobiological interventions was very limited. A small-scale study of 31 sex offenders was identified. This compared the use of medroxyprogesterone (a hormone), imaginal desensitisation and the use of both combined (McConaghy, Armstrong & Blaszcynski,

1988). Conclusions based on this study are necessarily tentative, given the small sample size. The use of medroxyprogesterone combined with imaginal desensitisation, however, was found to be no better than imaginal desensitisation alone, suggesting that the use of this anti-libinal treatment did not have a positive effect.

A methodologically sound study with a 10-year follow-up of 231 sexual offenders was reported in the 1980s (Romero & Williams, 1983). This study compared group psychotherapy and intensive probation supervision with intensive probation supervision alone. Of the cohort, 11 per cent had been reconvicted within 10 years and group psychotherapy did not have a clear effect on this rate. Of those receiving intensive probation alone, 7 per cent were reconvicted within 10 years, compared to 14 per cent of the group that received group therapy and intensive probation (RR 1.87 95% CI 0.78 – 4.47). They stressed the importance of very long follow-up periods in assessing treatment effects with sexual offenders, due in large part to the relatively low detection and conviction rates for such offences.

A study of the use of cognitive behavioural groupwork intervention using a relapse prevention approach compared with a no-intervention group was reported by Marques, Day, Nelson et al. (1994). The mean duration of follow-up for this study was three years. No difference was found between the two groups in terms of rates of sexual offending (OR 0.76 95% CI 0.26–2.28). The treatment group did however show lower rates for non-sexual violent offences (OR 0.3 95% CI 0.1–0.89, NNT 10 CI 5–85). The treatment group also showed lower rates of reoffending when violent and sexual offences were combined (OR 0.14 95% CI 0.02–0.98 NNT 20 CI 10–437).

A systematic review of random allocation studies in this area undertaken in 2003 looked at randomised studies with or without blinding (Kenworthy, Adams, Bilby et al., 2003). The review included the full range of psychological interventions within the review search, although studies of those aged under 18 years were excluded. The review criteria were similar to those used by White, Bradley, Ferriter et al. (1998), although the search process was even more extensive. As a result, a small number of studies were identified as meeting the criteria for inclusion. These met basic scientific criteria, had follow-up periods ranging from 1 to 10 years and dropout rates of less than the relatively high rate of 50 per cent. Only two studies of adequate quality were identified with large samples (Romero & Williams, 1983; Marques, Day, Nelson et al., 1994). A number of smaller-scale studies were also identified.

A recent randomised study conducted by Marques, Wiederanders, Day et al. (2005) involved randomised assignment to groups and included three comparison groups: a relapse prevention (RP) group, a volunteer control (VC) group and a non-volunteer control (NVC) group. Selection took place in prisons in California between 1985 and 1994 and, for comparison purposes, the researchers matched pairs of volunteers on age (over and under 40), criminal history (prior felony convictions or not) and type of offender (rapist, child molester girls, child molester boys and child molester boys and girls). Individuals were then randomly assigned to the RP or VC groups. All those involved were adult male offenders aged between 18 and 60. Those who had committed offences in concert with others (e.g., group rape) and incest offenders were excluded. Those with more than two felony convictions were excluded as were those who had an IQ of less than 80, did not speak English, had evidence of psychotic or organic conditions or who had presented severe management problems in prison.

In earlier studies of interventions with sex offenders, the nature of the treatments used and the relevance of these to current practice have often been raised as an issue. In this study, the RP group was transferred from prison to a secure hospital setting and underwent two years of intensive treatment and one year of a Sex Offender Aftercare Programme (SOAP) in the community. The Sex Offender Treatment and Evaluation Project (SOTEP), used in California, was described as a comprehensive cognitive behavioural treatment based on Marlatt's relapse prevention model (Marques, Wiederanders, Day et al., 2005). It involved three 90-minute sessions per week over two years. Delivery was highly structured and manualised to ensure 'treatment fidelity'. Apart from some small groupwork pilots in California, the researchers report that there was no comparable intervention work at that time in Californian prisons, enabling a more effective comparison with the VC and NVC groups. Offenders were then followed up over a five-year period to assess rates of reoffending. The total sample studied was 704, of which 259 were in the treatment (RP) group, 225 were volunteer controls and 220 were non-volunteer controls. The groups were mixed in terms of ethnic background and offence types. The RP group differed from the controls in that a larger proportion had been committed for treatment under previous state legislation (12.8% vs. 6.4% $\chi2$ (1, N = 64) = 820 p = 0.004).

Of those allocated to treatment, there was significant attrition. Of the 259 assigned to treatment, 55 withdrew before transfer to hospital; of those who began treatment, 167 completed their sentence and the aftercare process. Completers and dropouts did not differ in terms of assessed levels of risk, treatment need or on most demographic variables. Non-completers did however tend to be younger (t (202) = 2.25 p = 0.025 (2 tailed)).

222

The researchers conducted an extensive analysis of the data, including comparisons of groups as assigned and also comparisons involving those who completed the treatment and those assessed by the tutors as having done well during the treatment. A comparison across all three groups revealed no significant effect for treatment, either in terms of reconvictions or recorded parole violations for sexual and non-sexual violent offences. The researchers also conducted a survival analysis to compare progress of the groups and reported a similar pattern across all three, with steady rates of reconvictions and violations for around three years, levelling off at five years and beyond. They also reported no significant differences for those who appeared to do well on treatment (Marques, Wiederanders, Day et al., 2005). Significant differences were reported in terms of responses to psychometric assessment using the Multiphasic Sex Inventory (Nicolas and Molinder, 1984) and phallometric assessment (the PPG) in relation to female children, male children and rape. These findings were sustained when correction was made for repeated comparisons (Marques, Wiederanders, Day et al., 2005).

A similar pattern was noted for those who successfully completed the intervention with early treatment dropouts showing poorer outcomes. For violent reconvictions, the researchers reported that this was even more pronounced ($\chi2$ (3, N = 649) = 8.76 p = 0.033). The researchers then went on to look at the issue of treatment interactions, noting that even in the absence of an overall treatment effect it is possible that a subset of offenders benefited from treatment. In order to test this, they conducted a logistic regression analysis. They reported that the only significant term was whether the offender was intoxicated at the time of the offence ($\chi2$ (1, N = 390) = 5.23, p = 0.022). Those members of the treatment group who were intoxicated at the time of the offence therefore had a lower rate of reconviction. However, this effect disappeared when statistical correction was made for the use of multiple comparisons (Marques, Wiederanders, Day et al., 2005).

The researchers did report some initially promising findings in terms of the RP group showing less severe forms of reconviction. Again, however, these effects proved to be non-significant when statistical correction for the use of multiple comparisons was made. The researchers then went on to retrospectively band offenders, based on actuarial measures of risk, into low-, medium- and high-risk groups. This is an approach that has been used by other researchers (Falshaw, Friendship & Bates, 2003). Using survival analysis, a statistical technique initially devised to look at survival times following medical interventions, they reported clear differences in the survival rates for high-, medium- and low-risk offenders ($\chi2$ (2, N = 635) =

54.9 p < 0.0001). When these levels of actuarial risk were controlled for, the researchers found that the RP group appeared to have the lowest reoffence rate but that this finding was not significant.

The results from randomised studies in this area provide a powerful methodology for assessing the impact of treatment work on sexual offenders and, as such, have been subject to detailed consideration (Kenworthy, Adams, Bilby et al., 2003). The randomised study by Romero and Williams (1983) showed no impact in terms of a reduction in sexual reoffending amongst those treated. The study also highlighted the importance of adequate follow-up periods in this area of research, suggesting that in many studies this may have been unduly short. The treatment approach used in the Romero and Williams (1983) study raises a number of issues. Whilst it represented good practice at the time, it is quite dissimilar from current interventions with sex offenders. This has led to concerns that the results from this study tell us little about the likely efficacy of current treatments.

There has generally been a very high level of use of self-report scales or psychometrics in the assessment of sex offender intervention work. These measures have been used to assess change resulting from the interventions used. However, this approach has been subject to extensive criticism on a number of grounds. Perhaps most strikingly, there is little evidence to support a link between self-report and subsequent sexual offending (Kenworthy, Adams, Bilby et al., 2003). In addition, the use of psychometric measures can be criticised on economic and ethical grounds in that they are expensive and time-consuming to administer with little evidence of benefit to the offender or to wider society (Stockton & Crighton, 2003; Towl, 2005a; Crighton & Towl, 2007). Such measures do have potential to generate research hypotheses though it has been suggested that they often have 'little clinical utility' and that binary outcomes in terms of improved/not improved, combined with more powerful research designs, are possible to collect and would be of greater utility (Kenworthy, Adams, Bilby et al., 2003; Crighton & Towl, 2007).

The randomised study by Marques, Wie234randers, Day et al. (2005) looked at the use of an intensive two-year cognitive behavioural group treatment intervention with adult sex offenders. This study is perhaps the best available random allocation study of current psychological approaches. The study found no significant effect of treatment in terms of reducing the level or severity of sex and/or violent reconviction. In an earlier study, a reduction in violent reconviction was noted but this was not replicated (Marques, Day, Nelson et al., 1994; Marques, Wiederanders, Day et al., 2005). The authors go on to draw the conclusion that how and when treatment works is still poorly understood. Kenworthy, Adams, Bilby et al.

(2003) in contrast conclude that, based on current randomised studies, psychological interventions with sexual offenders are largely unproven and therefore represent experimental interventions which may be helpful, neutral or indeed harmful.

Meta-Analyses

A recent meta-analysis by Lösel and Schmucker (2005) noted the methodological problems and varied results obtained from earlier analyses in this area (Furby, Weintrott & Blackshaw, 1989; Hanson, Gordon, Harris *et al.*, 2002). In reviewing 2039 citations, this analysis identified 66 studies that met basic scientific criteria for inclusion that allowed for 80 comparisons. Sample sizes varied from 15 to 2557 (median 118), with around a third of studies having samples of 50 or less. Of these, only seven studies used randomised designs, one of these being compromised in terms of design.

Overall, Lösel and Schmucker (2005) reported recidivism rates of 12 per cent for the treated group and 24 per cent for the comparison group. When the researchers calculated these as weighted means the difference disappeared and both groups showed 11 per cent recidivism rates. This was due to the marked differences in sample sizes for treatment and comparison groups in some studies. Calculation of individual effect sizes however showed an average difference in sexual recidivism of 6.4 per cent.

Physical treatments showed higher effects (OR 7.37 95% CI 4.11 – 13.11, $z = 6.80$ $p < 0.001$) (Lösel & Schmucker, 2005). This was due largely to a single study of organic methods that showed a large effect. Hormonal treatments also showed more marked positive effects than psychosocial interventions. These findings raise a number of issues of interpretation associated with the selection of offenders for physical treatments and whether as a group they are representative. Interestingly, there was no evidence to suggest that currently used interventions were more effective than those used in the past.

Non-Randomised Studies

Seven non-randomised studies reported a statistically significant effect on the treatment group (Aytes, Olsen, Zakrajsek *et al.*, 2001 ($\chi 2 = 25.12$, df = 3, $p < .01$); Berliner, Schram, Miller *et al.*, 1995 ($\chi 2 = 4.474$, $p < .05$); Henning & Freuh, 1996 ($\chi 2$ (1, N = 124) = 4.2, $p < .05$; Looman, Abracen & Nicholaichuk, 2000 ($\chi 2 = 14.7$, df = 1, $p < .001$); Nicholaichuk, Gordon, Gu *et al.*, 2000 (F (1,162) = 46.39, $p < 0.001$; Turner, Bingham & Andrasik, 2000 ($\chi 2 = 6.12$, $p < .05$); Watson & Stermac, 1994 (F (1,25) = 7.32, p <

0.02). Four studies (Fisher, 1995; McGuire, 2000; Meyer, Cole & Emroy, 1992; Shaw, Herkov & Greer, 1995) report data in ways that were not usable by the reviewers (Kenworthy, Adams, Bilby *et al.*, 2003). Ten studies reported that intervention had no statistically significant effect on the attitudes or behaviour of sexual offenders (Craissati & McClurg, 1997; DiFazio, Abracen & Looman, 2001; Hanson, Broom & Stephenson, 2004; Hanson, Steffy & Gauthier, 1993; Marshall, Eccles & Barbaree, 1991; Marshall, Jones, Ward *et al.*, 1991; McGrath, Cann & Konopasky, 1998; McGrath, Cumming, Livingstone *et al.*, 2003; Proctor, 1996; Rice, Quinsey & Harris, 1991).

A large-scale study in public sector prisons in England and Wales (Friendship, Mann & Beech, 2003) looked at a sample of 647 sexual offenders. All those studied had been volunteer participants between 1992 and 1994 in the Prison Service's manualised group work intervention involving between 80 and 170 hours of treatment. All had been discharged from prison and a minimum of two-year follow-up data was available on all. This group was compared with a matched control group of 1910 sexual offenders who had not gone through this treatment. All controls had been serving a prison sentence of four years or more and were matched with the treated group on the year of discharge from prison. Both groups were also rated and matched on an assessment schedule called the Static 99 (Hanson & Thornton, 2000) which, it was claimed, rated them in terms of 'risk'. All life sentence offenders were excluded from the study. The authors also note that the control group may have included a number of prisoners who had begun but failed to complete treatment, potentially introducing a potentially significant sampling bias.

The two-year sexual reconviction rates were calculated and compared using the $\chi2$ statistic for non-parametric data (Friendship, Mann & Beech, 2003). They reported no significant difference in reconvictions between the treated and untreated groups (treated 2.6% vs. untreated 2.8%). They did, though, find a statistically significant difference between the groups when violent and sexual offences were combined (treated 4.6% vs. untreated 8.1% $p < 0.01$). Finally, the authors looked at levels of 'global' reconviction where they found no significant difference between the treated and untreated groups (treated 13.3% vs. untreated 16.5% p n.s.). In summary, disappointingly, the study did not show significant reductions in the rates of sexual reconviction for participants.

Qualitative Studies

Three of these studies were process evaluations. One looked at two cognitive behavioural group interventions in local prisons in England and Wales

(Houston, Wrench & Hosking, 1995). This study was marked out by the use of a strong theoretical base that was made clear in the write-up of the study. The researchers looked at the emergent patterns of group behaviour and how these interacted to influence the intervention. The researchers observed that, as with other forms of psychological therapy, these interactions were complex. In the case of sexual offenders, they also noted as particularly important the complex interaction between the roles of victim and victimiser, noting that many group members had been both at differing times. The authors suggested that the use by tutors of constructive peer-challenging was an important part of addressing issues such as responsibility. The research did, however, have a number of weaknesses. Most importantly, no detail was given as to how the themes that were drawn out were identified by the researchers.

Another process study involved a sample of 20 male incest offenders (Scheela, 1992). Here the primary focus was on therapist experiences and perceptions of work with these offenders and how this interacted with therapeutic work. They noted a range of factors that seemed to be of marked importance. These included frustration amongst therapists at the perceived negative effects of mandatory requirements. Also noted were issues of desensitisation as a result of repeated exposure to the detail of sexual offending, issues of countertransference, the need to develop realistic expectations about interventions with sex offenders and the need to effectively separate the person from the offence as part of effective working.

The final study included in the review explored the view of staff undertaking psychological interventions with sexual offenders in the UK (Lea, Auburn & Kibblewhite, 1999). Here the researchers conducted semi-structured interviews with 23 practitioners and used a triangulation of data.

The researchers found that the use of reflective and self-critical practice tended to increase in relation to the experience and length of training of the practitioner. More surprisingly, perhaps, they also reported that 30 per cent of their sample defined sexual offenders in terms of some form of biological abnormality.

Summary

- Practice and research in the area of sex offending and interventions with sexual offenders pose significant methodological and ethical challenges. At times in the past, these have been inadequately considered.
- Convicted sexual offences are likely to represent only a small proportion of those who sexually assault others and there are likely to be high levels

of hidden victimisation. The evidence base on sexual offenders is, however, largely based on offenders detected and convicted through the criminal justice system and those who voluntarily seek help. Both groups may be subject to systemic biases and this possibility needs to be taken into account when considering the evidence base.

- The evidence base relating to interventions with sex offenders has grown steadily from the 1950s onwards. The available evidence, though, is of only moderate quality.
- The evidence base in relation to the treatment of sexual offenders suggests a clear need to take stock of the research and to take on board some recent findings. It also suggests the need to develop more high quality and effective research in this area, including the use of randomised studies.
- In recent years, a small number of randomised trials of acceptable standard have been undertaken and these have suggested that current treatment approaches are ineffective in reducing sexual offending. Recent high quality meta-analytic studies have yielded more encouraging results, suggesting small but positive effects from intervention. Early meta-analytic studies suffered from a number of methodological flaws, casting doubt on the quality of support for the conclusions reached.
- The results from meta-analytic studies have suggested a greater impact from neurobiological than psychosocial interventions.
- There has been relatively little research looking at process issues in interventions with sexual offenders. Those studies that have been undertaken suggest a number of significant process effects. These include desensitisation as a result of repeated exposure to the detail of sexual offending, issues of countertransference, the need to develop realistic expectations about interventions with sex offenders and the need to effectively separate the person from the offence as part of effective working.

Notes

1   This followed a report by Wolfenden Committee set up in the 1950s to look at homosexuality and prostitution which recommended decriminalisation of consenting homosexual acts in private. The 1967 Act decriminalised sexual acts between men in privacy when both were over the age of 21 years. Decriminalisation took place in Scotland in 1980 as a result of the Criminal Justice (Scotland) Act and in Northern Ireland following the Homosexual Offences (Northern

Ireland) Order 1982. Armed forces, however, remain largely exempt from these changes.

2 An implicit assumption in much of the evidence base is that these are mutually exclusive and inclusive categories. In fact, the reality seems more complex and the extent of group exclusivity and inclusivity is unclear.

3 Any research into this area needs to overcome the practical difficulties of engaging with sexual offenders who have either not been convicted of a sexual offence or who have been undetected. This in turn raises ethical issues such as those surrounding the identification of undetected offences and the non-disclosure of future risks.

Chapter 14

Evaluation

Introduction

At its best, psychology might be broadly characterised as an effort to apply scientific approaches to better the understanding of mental life. Applied psychology represents the efforts to apply such knowledge ethically across settings to address a range of practical needs and evaluate the outcomes of this. The opportunity to contribute to this is perhaps the key attraction of applied practice and prisons represent a particularly demanding environment in which to undertake such work (Towl & Crighton, 2007a, 2007b).

It is important to note that such scientific approaches are not inherently ethical in nature. Sadly, the twentieth century provides numerous examples of unethical practice (Crighton, 2006c). The track record of the UK in this respect is not an inspiring one and it is perhaps one of the major lessons of the last century that morality and ethics need to be at the heart of all professional training and practice (Crighton, 2006c; Towl, 2006).[1] Such issues go beyond systematised codes of conduct, requiring a more fundamental consideration of issues such as power differentials and fairness (British Psychological Society, 2006). These form an essential basis for scientific evaluation and need to inform initial ideas, planning, execution and reporting arising throughout the process.

Scientific approaches are fundamentally characterised by a commitment to rational thinking in the development of knowledge. This includes notions that explanation should be parsimonious, replicable and subject to testing. In addition, precision and caution in thinking and the use of language are general characteristics of science (Kazdin, 2003). Scientific approaches seek to reason from the available data to explanations and

230

general theories or, in plain language, beliefs. Such beliefs are not dichotomous (true of false) but are rather based on estimations of likelihood. In respect of some of these fundamental aspects of the scientific approach, it has been convincingly suggested that psychologists have gone astray and that they often continue to do so (Fidler, 2006; Harlow, 1997; Hogben, 1957; Meehl, 1967; Rozeboom, 1960; Towl, 2006).

Testing Hypotheses and Theories

The use of scientific methods and analysis in applied psychology parallels that in many other areas, with applied biological sciences such as medicine providing perhaps the clearest equivalent. Practice in psychology should draw extensively from the emerging evidence base in statistics. However, it has increasingly diverged from current statistical theory and practice, a trend that contrasts markedly with many other sciences.

The dominant paradigm within psychology is, and has been for more than half a century, Null Hypothesis Significance Testing (NHST), sometimes described as the Null Hypothesis Decision procedure (NHD) (Hogben, 1957; Rozeboom, 1960). Orthodoxy within psychology suggests that passing judgement on a scientific theory depends on the acceptance or rejection of a null hypothesis, dependent on whether the calculated value of a statistical test falls within a 'rejection region' of a distribution of scores. This approach became especially popular in the biological sciences, reaching a peak of use in the 1950s (Fidler, 2006). However, it has been extensively criticised, with concerns expressed about its use and misuse from an early stage by both advocates and critics of the method (Boring, 1919; Fisher, 1955; Hogben, 1957; Meehl, 1967; Rozeboom, 1960).

Traditional Null Hypothesis Significance Testing (NHST)[2] was, from the 1950s onwards, largely replaced in statistics with inferential procedures that had greater utility (Rozeboom, 1960). There are two key types of error that can be made in assessing any given hypothesis. The hypothesis can be correct but is incorrectly rejected (a Type I error) or, alternatively, it may be incorrect but is accepted as true (a Type II error). NHST lacks utility in this respect as the decision whether or not a given experimental outcome supports a hypothesis depends crucially on the experimenter's tolerance for Type I risk. Type II risks using this method are not readily assessable at all (Meehl, 1967).

Even more fundamentally, it has been argued that NHST is based on a profound misconception about the purpose of scientific experiments. Essentially the approach seems predicated on the assumption that the

231

purpose of an experiment is decision-making. A more valid view is that experiments are in fact about making appropriate rational adjustments concerning the extent that hypotheses are believable in light of accumulating evidence. Judgements in turn may then be made about the extent to which such data support broader theoretical explanations (Hogben, 1957; Meehl, 1967; Rozeboom, 1960). Clearly, this is not a dichotomous process but rather one based on judgements about likelihood. Scientific experiments therefore supply cumulative evidence which helps to increasingly support or refute conclusions that may be logically deduced from the data. Only where conclusions are logically incompatible with the data is rejection warranted (Rozeboom, 1960).

The role of scientific knowledge is thus not that of determining actions but, rather, of establishing rational beliefs on which to base decisions. NHST performs poorly in this respect. No matter how improbable an experimental hypothesis may be, it can generally be tested against a more improbable null hypothesis. This is something recognised early in the development of the method when stress was placed on the need to use null hypotheses based on credible theoretically derived values (Fisher, 1955). Yet this cautionary point has been poorly integrated into practice. Even where it is integrated and hypotheses are matched against such null hypotheses, the NHST approach still performs poorly. Science as a systematic body of probabilistic knowledge is not developed through an accumulation of binary decisions about 'truth' or 'falsity'. Brief reflection on this point suggests that bizarre results may follow from such a method. Research in the area of decision theory confirms this intuitive analysis, suggesting that such an approach has poor utility. To decide most effectively when to act or not act as though a hypothesis is correct, the probability of the hypotheses under consideration needs to be known, along with the utility of the various decision outcomes, and this is not the case with NHST (Hogben, 1957; Meehl, 1967; Rozeboom, 1960).

In psychology, a 'no effect', or nil hypothesis, has provided an easily available 'opposite' null to research hypotheses. Indeed, so tempting has this been for psychologists that it has been suggested that for most psychological researchers the nil hypothesis has become *the* null hypothesis (Grannas, 2002). There are a number of major problems with this. This form of null hypothesis generation is generally intended to be, *a priori*, false. Since it is set up for rejection, this is seldom in genuine doubt and the question becomes one of whether the researcher has collected sufficient data to demonstrate a largely predetermined result. This process of rejecting a 'straw' null hypothesis provides no new information and so permits little genuine progress. Equally, rejecting such a null or nil hypothesis does not 'prove' the research hypothesis in anything other than the weakest sense. The approach has a further fundamental flaw in not encouraging the researcher to determine the size and nature of any effects observed (Grannas, 2002).

NHST depends on the use of arbitrary decision points and these too generate a significant difficulty. In psychology, these are often set at a level of a 5 per cent chance of a Type I error using a given test statistic. Whilst this represents some degree of caution in decision-making, there is no logical reason for a value of 5 per cent, rather than 4 per cent, 6 per cent or indeed 0.001 per cent. Yet very small differences in the test statistic chosen using NHST can change the decision made on acceptance or rejection of the experimental hypothesis.[3]

NHST additionally introduces a strong bias in favour of one chosen hypothesis amongst a large number of potential and reasonable alternatives. This has been graphically described in terms of the favoured hypothesis being assumed innocent until proven guilty and the null hypothesis being presumed guilty until no choice remains but to judge it innocent (Rozeboom, 1960). This differential weighting of hypotheses results from individual choices made by the experimenter combined with the NHST method favouring one hypothesis over other possibilities. This runs counter to the evidence base derived from classical theory of inverse probability. Here all hypotheses are treated as equal in terms of *a priori* probability, with the estimated probability reflecting the credibility of hypotheses based on grounds other than the data being assessed.[4]

At a more practical level, NHST has been criticised on the grounds that it has little or no influence on practice. Rejected hypotheses are rarely given up. There are multiple examples of this in the context of psychology in prisons but perhaps the most striking relates to treatment interventions with prisoners. Here emergent data from NHST approaches are often treated in a variety of logically curious ways. Where the value of the test statistic falls within the arbitrary range for rejection, the experimental hypothesis is frequently not abandoned at all. Efforts may be made to explain away the finding as due to error or to give the experimental hypothesis further advantages over the null hypothesis, for example, by conducting multiple *post hoc* comparisons of selected data against weaker null hypotheses. Stress may also be placed on how close to the arbitrary cut-off point the exact probability value is, suggesting that the result is approaching statistical significance.[5]

This begs the question of why such a flawed research method gained such popularity and continues to predominate in psychology despite declining use elsewhere. A number of suggestions have been put forward and amongst these it seems likely that the simple and mechanistic inferential algorithm provided is one factor. NHST is also the method with which psychologists are most familiar, having been taught (or drilled in) this method, sometimes largely to the exclusion of all others, as undergraduates. NHST also has an important byproduct in appearing to estimate the probability of a given experimental outcome under the assumption that a certain hypothesis is correct. It does this under the pretext of a significance test and this effect seems so useful that psychologists, where the probability of a given hypothesis is often hard to determine, may have been slow to adopt evidence-based approaches (Hogben, 1957; Rozeboom, 1960).

Evidence-Based Approaches to Hypothesis Testing

There is a clear and increasingly pressing need for evidence-based reform within psychology in relation to training in scientific method and in statistical reporting. These are not original observations so the fact that reform within psychology has been far slower than in other areas, such as medicine, is all the more puzzling (Fidler, 2006; Kline, 2004). It has perhaps been slowest of all in prison settings which have until recently remained curiously isolated from mainstream developments (Crighton, 2006c).

A detailed discussion of these issues goes well beyond the scope of this chapter but a number of practical suggestions have consistently been made for evidence-based practice reforms. These include replacement of the NHST approach entirely, advocated by some. Others have cautioned against 'throwing the baby out with the bathwater', seeing a limited continuing role for NHST (Grannas, 2002). There is, though, a broad consensus in the evidence base that current practice is inappropriate and lacking in statistical and methodological rigour. It has also been stressed that reforms to statistical reporting in psychology need to be substantive, reflecting deeper understanding, rather than simply replacing one mechanistic approach with another (Meehl, 1967, 1997).

The reporting of effect sizes and confidence intervals[6] as used in biomedical research has been extensively and convincingly advocated (Cumming and Finch, 2001, 2005; Fidler, 2006; Meehl, 1967; Rozeboom, 1960). This has become central to reporting in areas such as public health and has clear value within applied psychology in prisons (Rothman & Greenland, 1998).

Other reforms advocated include:

- greater use of graphic representation of statistical information;
- greater use of likelihood ratios;

234

- more consideration of the clinical and practical implications of findings;
- better consideration of the impact of sample size influences;
- greater appreciation of meta-analysis and the issues associated with the methodology;
- the need to see scientific results as cumulative in nature; and
- more effective assessment of trends and patterns going beyond dichotomous decision (Fidler, 2006; Rozeboom, 1960).

It is difficult to see rational reasons to contest such reforms. Within medical research, such changes have been effectively driven forward since the 1980s (Rothman, 1988). In psychology, despite concerted efforts from some (Kendall, 1997; Kline, 2004; Loftus, 1993), such reforms have made very limited progress. In an assessment of statistical reporting in the journal *Epidemiology* for example, it was reported that 90 per cent of articles reported confidence intervals (Fidler, Thomason, Cumming *et al.*, 2004). In contrast, an analysis of the *American Journal of Psychology* found that 94 per cent of articles simply used probability testing (Hubbard & Ryan, 2000).

There is also a need for much greater precision and caution in line with scientific approaches. This might be simply explained as not going beyond the data. Nowhere is this more clearly illustrated than in the approach taken to causation by a number of psychologists in prison settings. Until the twentieth century, it had been suggested that causality involved three assumptions described by Born (1949). First, that there are laws by which the occurrence of an entity B of a certain class depends on the occurrence of an entity A of another class, where the word entity means any physical object, phenomenon, situation, or event, where A is called the cause and B the effect. Second, that there must be antecedence, where A occurs prior to or at least simultaneous with, B. Third, that cause and effect must be in spatial contact or connected by a chain of intermediate things in contact (Born, 1949, as cited in Sowa, 2000). Developments from the twentieth century onwards mean that these assumptions no longer appear accurate as exact statements about some events (Sowa, 1999, 2000).Within applied psychology, however, they remain generally adequate.

The need for such relatively high levels of evidence for causation has had limited impact on some applied psychology as evidenced by very imprecise and misleading thinking. Terms such as 'criminogenic' are illustrative of this. This term has been used extensively and quite successfully in the marketing of some interventions within prisons and beyond. It is widely used in a number of imprecise and often conflicting ways. These include references to correlates of criminal behaviour. The term is also sometimes used to refer to 'risk factors' or correlates antecedent to a specified event. It is also sometimes used to suggest a causal relationship, analogous to terms such as pathogenic implying effect, antecedence and contiguity. In fact, the use of such language is pseudoscientific, creating a superficial appearance of scientific understanding with little real substance. A key plank of the reforms needed in applied psychology in prisons is the abandonment of such imprecise thinking and replacement with clearly specified meaningful concepts (Crighton, 2006c; Towl, 2004b).[7]

Evidence-Based Practice (EBP)

Evidence-based practice refers to efforts to use scientifically gathered evaluative evidence to inform and develop effective practice. It is not a new idea having been convincingly advocated in the context of medicine for many years (Cochrane, 1999[1972], 1979, 1989). Before the 1950s, it was noted that there was little interest within medicine in the evaluation of interventions. Decisions about treatments were effectively dependent on informal and closed networks of 'eminent' practitioners (Cochrane, 1972; Fidler, 2006). Moves towards more systematic evaluation followed the advent of new 'miracle' drugs such as antibiotics and steroids in the 1950s. Further impetus came from pioneering thinkers such as Cochrane (1972). These ideas have steadily gained ground across much of health care. Psychology has also increasingly adopted these reforms but in prisons relative isolation from mainstream developments was the norm until the beginning of this century and progress has continued to be slow.

One argument against such reforms within psychology is that the 'objectivity' of science is illusory and that it does not reflect some incontrovertible external state. At a philosophical level, many may not argue against this. Scientific knowledge is essentially about intersubjectivity. Indeed, science has been eloquently described as 'nothing but enlightened and responsible common sense – common sense broadened by imaginative critical thinking.' (Popper, 1983). Such observations seem so obvious that they are rarely addressed. Yet a great deal of research and practice in psychology is undertaken and reported with an apparent delusion of 'objectivity'.

The move towards using evidence-based practice has also been subject to a number of 'pragmatic' criticisms. Perhaps the most powerful of these is that the work of professional groups accounts for only a small fraction of the variance in outcomes. This is evident in relation to a wide range of health and criminal justice outcomes. Factors such as poverty, stress levels, environmental conditions, behaviours and genetic makeup interact to

236

account for by far the largest part of such outcomes. This has been most extensively studied in the area of public health, where it has raised the question of why so much effort is expended on refining healthcare interventions rather than addressing other factors with greater impacts. One reason suggested for this is that healthcare interventions are highly profitable industries and, like any industry, they will seek to stay in business and maximise profits (Cochrane, 1989; Reinhardt, 2002). There is clear veracity to this argument which has clear parallels in Criminal Justice and suggests a shift of emphasis. The argument, though, can be seen as one in favour of evidence-based practice helping to shape interventions that have the best effects.

Perhaps unsurprisingly, EBP has been subject to criticism from professional interests with concerns expressed about its role in centrally determining clinical practice. In the USA this has taken the form of unease about the role of managed care organisations (MCOs) and in the UK about organisations such as the National Institute for Health and Clinical Excellence (NICE). Such bodies raise concerns about professional practice being dictated and the exclusion of assessments and interventions that have not been empirically validated (Levant, 2004). Such arguments may appear to be simply interest group lobbying and indeed it is difficult to see the rational case for using assessments and interventions that are not empirically validated outside the context of experimental trials. A more subtle disquiet here is perhaps the use of inadequate evidence under the guise of EBP to make decisions going beyond the data.

More persuasively, it has been suggested that there are as yet unresolved difficulties with the extent that EBP findings generalise across populations. Findings predominantly based on white middle-class samples may, for example, have less relevance to black working-class populations (Levant, 2004). It is also evident that some approaches are less easily suited to empirical evaluation than others. Short-term protocol-based psychological interventions lend themselves to straightforward evaluation more obviously than long-term humanistic psychological therapies. Such criticisms have some salience but do seem largely concerned with limitations in the evidence base and research methodologies, rather than being a fundamental critique of drawing on scientific evidence to guide practice.

Evaluation of Treatment Effects

Methodology serves to reduce and codify sources of error that may impact on evaluations. Where sources of such error are not controlled, then the interpretation of findings becomes unclear, since they may be due to genuine

237

effects, or error, or both. Effective methodology also helpfully codifies many of the solutions to questions under consideration, helping to ensure the validity of any inferences being drawn. As highlighted above, appropriate methodology also contributes to the goal of treating scientific evidence as cumulative.

Removal of possible alternative explanations is perhaps the greatest challenge in conducting scientific evaluations in prisons. A large number and variety of threats to the validity of any evaluation are present and many of these are poorly understood. Evaluations in prisons face a number of potential period, age and cohort effects (Fabio, Loeber, Balasubramani *et al.*, 2006). It is also highly unlikely that prisoners will experience one and only one intervention whilst in custody. In combination, this suggests a clear need to consider differential effects. Such examples could be multiplied but the essential point is that, common to many applied settings, it is seldom possible (or ultimately necessarily desirable) to adequately control all the potential factors which could affect the validity of evaluation.

Fortunately, there are powerful methodological approaches which help to circumvent such difficulties. Randomised control trials (RCTs) are a group of such experimental paradigms. They involve randomly allocating individuals to different intervention conditions and ideally allow assessment of outcomes by researchers who have no knowledge of the intervention conditions. This method has been extensively used in a range of applied settings but is perhaps best known in the field of health where it has been extensively used to evaluate treatment effects since the 1950s. RCTs have significant advantages as they rule out many threats to the validity of a study. As a result, such approaches are rated highly in most attempts to categorise experimental quality such as the Maryland Scale (Sherman, Gottfredson, MacKenzie *et al.*, 2000). Such methods do not provide a panacea. They are not immune to threats to validity. It is also notable that around 30 per cent of those in the 'placebo' condition of an RCT may respond positively and it seems clear that such things as contact with others who show care and concern is itself in fact a form of intervention. There is also some evidence of an increasing 'placebo response' across randomised trials. In RCTs looking at interventions in depression, for example, a correlation of +0.43 between this and year of publication (compared to a correlation of +0.26 between drug response and year of publication) has been reported (Walsh, Stuart, Seidman *et al.*, 2002). In addition, spontaneous recovery may occur and is known to be greater in less severe cases and generally RCTs will involve those with less severe problems as exclusion criteria may remove those with more severe problems from study (Khan *et al.*, 2002).

238

Whilst RCTs are one method of gathering cumulative scientific data, they represent a powerful approach with good utility. In turn, they lend themselves to meta-analytic techniques that 'pool' data from multiple sources (Campbell & Fiske, 1959). This facilitates the identification of small or unusual intervention effects and side effects. It is surprising and deeply regrettable that this method has been so little used in prisons. A potential explanation for this is that rigorous approaches are in some way, perhaps for ethical or practical reasons, unsuited to use in prison settings. Such explanations might appear to gain some support from the shortage of RCTs undertaken in prisons. Yet there are a number of examples of ethically and methodologically sound RCTs in parallel areas of criminal justice. These have included studies of child and family interventions to reduce delinquency (Farrington & Welsh, 2006; Lösel & Beelman, 2006); restorative justice (Strang & Sherman, 2006); intensive supervision under probation and parole (Petersilia & Turner, 1993) and drug testing (Britt, Gottfredson & Goldkamp, 1992). This suggests that any claimed ethical and technical barriers to the use of these powerful methods can and have been effectively addressed elsewhere.

Objections to the use of RCT methodology have been put forward on the basis that prisoners should not be denied treatments known to be effective and in turn the public should not be put at risk from untreated offenders in this way (Thornton, personal communication, 2000). Such an argument would be persuasive if true. It is less than convincing where the evidence of effectiveness is absent, as in the family of manualised groupwork interventions in prisons, collectively known as 'accredited offending behaviour programmes'. Such interventions are clearly experimental and the evidence base in support is generally limited and often of poor quality. Here the suggestion that any treatments have demonstrated definitive effectiveness is at very best unscientific, with less still known about the possibility of negative (side) effects (Crighton & Towl, 2007; Harper & Chitty, 2005; Thomas-Peter, 2006a, 2006b; Towl, 2004b, 2006).

A rigorous approach to evaluation has potential consequences for service provision. Often a key difficulty can be the assumption that research is in place to 'prove' that a particular intervention is effective, rather than to test effect size and utility incrementally. This is evident in some of the research into manualised 'offending behaviour programmes'. Here, at times, there appears to be a resolute unwillingness to consider data adequately which does not support the approach (Latissa, Cullen & Gendreau, 2002; Mann, 2004). Clearly, approaches such as this do not appear to respond to emerging findings or rational argument and as such lack scientific credibility.

A more pragmatic argument against using RCT approaches has been one of equity and fairness. It is not, so the argument goes, fair or equitable to deny someone treatment that may help them. Such sentiments appear laudable but they represent something of a utopian vision and one comparatively rarely seen in prison or other applied settings.[8] Resources in prisons are generally limited and prisoners' needs are unlikely to be universally met. It can convincingly be argued that, in settings with such severely limited resources, random allocation is in fact the most equitable and fair method of allocation (Lösel, personal communication, 2007).

Systematic Reviews

Systematic reviews represent an effort to rationally integrate data from multiple sources. They can be broadly divided into quantitative approaches (meta-analysis) and qualitative approaches, where reviews are undertaken using specific criteria, such as National Centre for Health and Clinical Excellence (NICE) reviews in the UK (National Institute for Health and Clinical Excellence, 2007a).

Meta-analysis

Meta-analysis involves combining data from a number of sources and has a number of advantages and disadvantages. It allows the pooling of large amounts of data, making it possible to identify weak or rare effects. In addition, differential effects that might not otherwise become evident may be seen and evaluated, such as differing treatment effects across social or ethnic groups (Lösel, personal communication, 2007).

However, the method does depend entirely on the quality of studies included. The method was developed initially for pooling high quality data, such as that from double-blind randomised control trials. Here the quality of the data being input tends to be uniformly high. In psychology, meta-analytic techniques have been extended to the pooling of quasi-experimental and non-randomised studies primarily using NHST. This is associated with greater heterogeneity in the data being analysed. The use of meta-analyses in this way has been more contentious and has yielded mixed results. It has at times resulted in conclusions being drawn based on pooled data from unacceptably weak studies (Hanson & Morton-Bourgon, 2004). The results of such pooling lack scientific rigour and the old computing maxim of 'garbage in, garbage out' is perhaps applicable here. The undoubted power of the method is not designed to address inclusion of inadequate data. The poor state of the evidence base in many of the areas of interest to applied psychologists in prisons means that the use of meta-analysis at this stage may often be inappropriate and potentially misleading.

Qualitative Reviews

Qualitative reviews similarly aim for a synthesis of data. Methods vary but in order to be scientifically rigorous need to be rational and systematic. Examples of such reviews in the context of health and related areas include National Institute for Health and Clinical Excellence (NICE) (National Institute for Health and Clinical Excellence, 2007b) reviews and Cochrane Collaboration reviews (Cochrane Collaboration, 2007).

The strengths of such approaches are that they produce summaries of findings in a form that is generally useful in informing practice. At its best, the method can integrate a wide range of data (including RCTs and meta-analyses), giving an effective summary of the current state of a given field and emerging trends. The main weakness of the approach is the scope for the introduction of biases. As with meta-analyses, it is also crucially dependent on the quality of data that is available for inclusion. The development of qualitative reviews in the criminal justice sector have been slower to develop than in health but progress has begun with the development of the Campbell Collaboration to parallel that of the Cochrane Collaboration (Campbell Collaboration, 2007).

Evaluating Interventions in Prisons

Interventions within prisons over the last decade have been largely characterised by an increasingly 'one size fits all' approach. This has been based on a narrow and limited reading of a largely methodologically weak evidence base (Bailey, 2006; Crighton and Bailey, 2006; Lösel, personal communication, 2007; Thomas-Peter, 2006a; Towl, 2006). 'One size fits all' approaches have been increasingly challenged with reassertion of the importance of both risk and functional issues in targeting interventions and also in the effective evaluation of treatment effects (Crighton, 2004, 2005c, 2005d; Crighton & Towl, 2007; Lösel, personal communication, 2007).

A striking example of this is the suggested relationship between risk, treatment design and treatment impacts: analogous perhaps to the relationship between the severity of an illness and treatment impact. This suggests that those who present 'low' risk may be unlikely to need intervention. They will tend to be more likely to 'remit' or desist from criminal behaviour in the absence of external intervention and efforts to provide treatment are thus less likely to yield positive results. This accords with findings of lower treatment impact with lower risk groups (Farrington & Welsh, 2003; Lipsey, 2007; Lösel & Bender, 2006). Indeed, the situation may be more stark than this with treatment directed at those of lower risk, particularly where undertaken in undifferentiated group settings or by relatively unskilled practitioners, producing potentially counter therapeutic effects (Crighton & Towl, 2007; Thomas-Peter, 2006a, 2006b).[9]

In terms of functional issues, it seems clear that differential outcomes are the rule rather than the exception, yet these have generally not been considered in prisons (Lösel & Bender, 2006; Towl, 2006). For example, an RCT study of the use of restorative justice approaches suggests overall positive effects but with less impact for minority (primarily Australian aboriginal) groups (Strang & Sherman, 2006). It is possible here to speculate about the role in outcomes of factors such as social exclusion and group memberships. Evidence drawing on social psychology research into social identity suggests the centrality of individual interpretations of others: yet such research has been poorly integrated into practice in prison settings (Tajfel, 1982; Zimbardo, 2007).

A key point is perhaps that, whatever the promise of individual interventions, they need to be targeted in a differential, timely and flexible manner. The approach to date in prisons has largely failed to address these, stressing instead 'throughput' targets, delivery of consistent (largely undifferentiated) interventions, delivery of interventions by staff with characteristics very different from participants and compliance with delivery specified in written manuals. The focus on total numbers undertaking interventions in prisons, rather than on outcomes as measures of success, seems at odds with the expressed primary purpose of such activities. Appropriate matching of individuals to interventions and better consideration of what might be termed 'process' seems crucial to achieving positive evaluations.

Measuring Outcomes

A central issue in evaluation is choice of outcome measures. In prisons, the focus has been very largely on official reconviction rates. Efforts to use other measures have strongly focused on proxy measures in the form of psychometric assessments. These have been used in an effort to estimate treatment effects. Both these measures raise significant concerns.

Reconvictions are of clear importance and in all probability have an ongoing role to play in evaluation. There are, though, good grounds to suggest that this measure has distorting effects, not least because of low rates of detection and conviction for many types of offence (Towl, 2006). Multi-setting and multi-informant approaches to evaluation are generally advocated as good practice (Lösel, personal communication, 2007). The challenge of developing such evaluative measures in prisons has generally not been addressed as well as it could have been. It seems likely that this has had a number of adverse impacts, not least of which is the obscuring of a number of possible treatment, differential and side effects (Lösel, personal communication, 2007; Towl, 2006).

The use of proxy measures in the form of psychometric assessments creates an often false appearance of broader-based evaluation. The manner in which these techniques have been used in prisons, though, is less than convincing. Many of the measures used have had inadequate psychometric properties. The extent of use may to some degree have been economically driven. Such assessments appear relatively cheap to administer but can also be profitably marketed. Yet the association between scores on many of these assessments and subsequent outcomes is often, at best, unclear. In the context of prisons, many of the assessments used suffer from poor standardisation of those being assessed and there is often a lack of baseline data from the community and relevant subpopulations, making meaningful interpretation difficult (Crighton & Towl, 2007). Even where the quality of psychometric assessments is less in doubt, clinical utility often is. The relationship between changes on psychometric measures and clinically significant change is unclear. In parallel, there has been a very disappointing and marked tendency to neglect simpler, more cost-effective and straightforward measures, such as 'improved' versus 'not improved' (Crighton & Towl, 2007; Kenworthy, Adams, Bilby et al., 2003).[10]

Models for Future Evaluation

Models for future evaluation and research in this area need to have a central focus on ethical practice. Recent historical examples highlight the importance of conducting evaluative research in accordance with high ethical standards. Consideration of ethical issues in the context of prisons needs to go beyond simple listing of 'ethical issues' and the use of written 'consent' forms. Ethical conduct needs to be fundamental to the way psychologists think about all aspects of practice. Statutory regulation of psychologists

243

seems likely to add significantly to the existing impetus for improving standards within applied psychology by putting in place strong sanctions, making psychologists clearly and individually accountable for their professional acts both of commission and omission (British Psychological Society, 2006).

Evaluation research will also increasingly need to demonstrate credibility within the broad professional community. A key challenge for reform here is the issue of conflicts of interest. Psychology is not unique in this and it is a problem that faces biomedical researchers more generally but it has been an area of growing concern. Curiously, this has, to date, scarcely been formally acknowledged. As well as independence, evaluation research needs to effectively demonstrate validity and utility. In achieving, this evaluation research needs to become methodologically 'fit for purpose'. Research that simply demonstrates changes on psychometric measures, based on quasi-experimental NHST approaches, is generally inadequate and inappropriate to such a task. Likewise, studies exclusively addressing official reconviction rates seem unfit, alone, for purpose, addressing as they do only a small proportion of actual offending.

There is a pressing case in prisons to start to make use of available powerful methodological approaches, most particularly RCT methods and to increase the range of researchers involved in this important area of work. These methods need to draw on multiple measures and multiple sources of data in combination with clinically relevant measures. There is some potential discomfort for practitioners here since such measures may identify existing interventions that are ineffective or even actively harmful, with associated professional and economic costs. The alternative, however, is to continue to put the public at risk, inappropriately detaining prisoners, maintaining sectional interests and wasting public resources, something which is wholly untenable.[11]

Summary

- Scientific approaches share a number of fundamental characteristics. Most critically, they involve rational approaches to gathering and evaluating evidence in order to develop a cumulative probability-based evidence base. Psychology has often gone astray in this respect with the use of inappropriate methods out of step with the evidence base. Such weaknesses have often been masked by the use of unhelpful pseudoscientific jargon. Work in prisons has suffered from this; such practices serve only to detract from improving understanding.

- Evidence-based practice refers to efforts to use such scientifically gathered evidence to inform and develop more effective practice. This is not a new idea but it is one that has gained significant ground in recent years, primarily in health settings. The adoption of EBP in prisons has been relatively slow and patchy. Properly implemented, EBP provides protection for people against interventions that are ineffective or indeed actively harmful and as such unethical.

- Ethical issues need to be central to all areas of practice, not least evaluation. The advent of statutory registration seems likely to accelerate positive developments in this respect, with psychologists becoming directly and individually accountable for acts of commission and omission.

- There is a clear need to use powerful methodological approaches available to evaluate practice. Most strikingly, randomised control trials (RCTs), where individuals are randomly assigned to different intervention conditions, provides an effective technique for evaluation. This method eliminates many threats to the validity of evaluation inherent in other less powerful methods. RCTs have been used in some degree in evaluating interventions across criminal justice settings but to a disappointly limited extent in prisons.

- Interventions within prisons over the last decade or so have been largely characterised by an increasingly 'one size fits all' approach. This is surprising, given that marked individual differences in responses to treatment are well-known and clearly evident. As a result, it seems that such an approach may serve to disguise true treatment effects.

- A central issue in evaluation in prisons is the choice of outcome measures. Here there has been a strong focus on official reconviction rates and on proxy measures in the form of psychometric assessments. The use of psychometric assessments as proxy measures is less than convincing. The association between such assessments and subsequent outcomes are at best unclear. In parallel, there has been a marked and curious tendency to neglect simpler and more cost effective clinical measures of impact.

- Multi-setting and multi-informant approaches to evaluation are generally advocated as good practice yet evaluation in prisons has generally used single-source and single-criterion measures. It seems likely that this has had a number of adverse impacts, including obscuring a number of possible treatment effects.

- Offenders themselves have a great deal to tell us about what interventions are likely to be helpful and effective. Even so, it is clear that some

245

practitioners and policy makers have reservations about evaluations using this kind of information.

Notes

1   There are numerous examples that could be chosen to illustrate this point. A relatively recent example in the UK was the period 1922–1967 when between 5000 and 10,000 children with an average age of 8 years and 9 months were sent to Australia (a total of around 150,000 were resettled across former 'dominion' nations). Most were sent, as part of a policy of settling the 'Dominions' with 'good white stock', to charitable and religious institutions. As part of this process, children in care were lied to, misled and deceived about the nature of the relocation. Some were told their parents had died when they had not. As a result of such unethical conduct, many were sent to institutions where they were subjected to systematic physical and sexual abuse (House of Commons, 1998).

2   Rozeboom (1960) in his paper on this subject preferred the term Null Hypothesis Decision procedure (NHD). Although in many respects more technically accurate this term has not gained wide currency and the more widely used term Null Hypothesis Significance Testing is used here.

3   The arbitrary nature of such decisions perhaps explains why psychologists technically inaccurately refer to results going in the 'right' direction when, for example, the risk of a Type I error is 6 per cent or 7 per cent rather than 5 per cent. Such thinking suggests a fundamental misunderstanding of the NHST process they have chosen to use.

4   A full discussion of the mathematics involved is beyond the scope of this chapter but a very readable summary of the key points is given by Rozeboom (1960).

5   In the context of prisons in the UK, this curious approach to hypothesis testing has had significant and potentially negative practical effects. In the 1990s, a diverse range of public sector interventions with prisoners was abandoned on the basis that they had failed to show statistical significance when tested using NHST. These were replaced by centrally designed manual-based interventions, many of which were bought in full or partly from for profit subcontractors. These have since performed equivocally on NHST evaluations but efforts have often been made to reinterpret these later findings.

6 A detailed consideration of the advantages of using confidence intervals rather than NHST goes beyond the scope of this chapter. Two of the main advantages are that the approach is not biased towards one favoured hypothesis in the way that NHST is. In addition, the approach does not depend on an arbitrary cut-off point. CI information at 95 per cent and 99 per cent levels involves different ways of conveying the same information. Information on both can be sensibly reported (indeed, perhaps should be reported) without creating logically incompatible results.

7 In concrete terms, this would suggest such things as a return to talking about 'correlates' of criminal behaviour and, where antecedence can be demonstrated, 'risk factors' and 'protective factors'. Such language has the added advantage of being more readily understood by scientific and non-scientific audiences alike.

8 It is also at odds with the portrayal of some interventions in criminal justice settings that, it has been argued, are sometimes framed almost as additional punishments rather than efforts to help offenders which also protect others from subsequent harm. Thomas-Peter (2006a, 2006b) provides a detailed discussion of such orthodoxies.

9 Here, the recent growth of manualised group-based interventions in prisons raises particular issues. The model can be characterised as very managerial, or indeed 'managerialist', in approach, adopting a 'one size fits all' philosophy on an almost industrial scale. The aim here can degenerate into one of meeting input targets. For those on the frontline of the system, the task therefore becomes one of getting large numbers of prisoners to enter and remain in standardised group interventions, largely regardless of need or effects (Thomas-Peter, 2006a, 2006b).

10 Partly this might be explained by the poor take-up of RCT methodology. Within such experimental designs, simpler 'blind' ratings can be made in this way. With less robust designs, this is often not possible. In this respect, the use of poor methodology and psychometrics may often have had an unhelpful and symbiotic relationship.

11 Such changes represent a shift of emphasis away from targets for treatment throughput to a more experimental approach to treatments. Whilst this generates initial costs in health economic terms, this is likely to lead to more cost-effective use of resources and improved public protection.

References

Abel, G.G., Becker, J.V., Mittleman, M.S. *et al.* (1987) Self-reported sex crimes of nonincarcerated paraphiliacs. *Journal of Interpersonal Violence*, 2(6), 3–25.

Abel, G.G. and Rouleau, J-L. (1990) The nature and extent of sexual assault. In W.L. Marshall, D.R. Laws and H.E. Barbaree (Eds.) *Handbook of sexual assault*. New York: Plenum Press.

Adler, A. (1992) *Understanding human nature* (trans. Colin Brett). Oxford, UK: Oneworld Publications.

Ainsworth, M.D.S., Blehar, M.C., Waters, E. and Wall, S. (1978) *Patterns of attachment: A psychological study of the strange situation*. Hillsdale, NJ: Erlbaum.

Alder, C. and Polk, K. (2001) *Child victims of homicide*. Cambridge: Cambridge University Press.

Allard, R., Marshall, M. and Plante, M.C. (1992) Intensive follow up does not decrease the risk of repeat suicide attempts. *Suicide and Life Threatening Behaviour*, 22(3), 303–14.

Altshukler, L.L., Bauer, M., Frye, M.A. *et al.* (2001) Does thyroid supplementation accelerate tricyclic antidepressant response? A review and meta-analysis of the literature. *American Journal of Psychiatry*, 158, 1617–22.

American Psychiatric Association (1952) *Diagnostic and statistical manual of mental disorders*. Washington, DC: American Psychiatric Association.

American Psychiatric Association (1980) *Diagnostic and statistical manual of mental disorders* (3rd edn). Washington, DC: American Psychiatric Association.

American Psychiatric Association (1987) *Diagnostic and statistical manual of mental disorders* (3rd edn, revised). Washington, DC: American Psychiatric Association.

American Psychiatric Association (1994) *Diagnostic and statistical manual of mental disorders* (4th edn). Washington, DC: American Psychiatric Association.

American Psychiatric Association (2000) *Diagnostic and statistical manual of mental disorders* (4th edn, text revision). Washington: American Psychiatric Association.

References

Anderson, E. (1990) *Streetwise: Race, class, and change in an urban community.* Chicago, IL: University of Chicago Press.

Anderson-Varney, T.J. (1991) An evaluation of a treatment programme for imprisoned child sex offenders. Unpublished dissertation, Michigan State University.

Angst, J., Gamma, A., Gatspar, M. *et al.* (2002) Gender differences in depression: Epidemiological findings from the European Depression I and II Studies. *European Archives of Psychiatry and Clinical Neuroscience, 252,* 201–9.

Aos, S., Barnowski, R. and Lee, R. (1998) Preventive programs for young offenders: effective and cost-effective. *Overcrowded Times, 9*(2), 1–11.

Aos, S., Phipps, P., Barnoski, R. *et al.* (2001) *The comparative costs and benefits of programs to reduce crime (version 4).* Washington, DC: Washington State Institute for Public Policy.

Applebaum, P.S., Clark Robbins, P. and Monahan, J. (2000) Violence and delusions: Data from the MacArthur Violence Risk Assessment Study. *American Journal of Psychiatry, 157*(4), 566–72.

Argyle, M. (1994) *The psychology of social class.* London: Routledge.

Arnett, J. (1999) Adolescent storm and stress reconsidered. *American Psychologist, 54,* 317–26.

Aronson, E. (2003) *The Social Animal* (9th edn). New York: W.H. Freeman.

Åsberg, M., Traskman, L. and Thoren, P. (1975) 5-HIAA in the cerebrospinal fluid: a biochemical suicide predictor? *Archives of General Psychiatry, 33,* 1193–7.

Ashman, L. and Duggan, L. (2002) Interventions for learning disabled sex offenders. *The Cochrane Database of Systematic Reviews 2002, Issue2. Art. No.: CD003682. DOI: 10.1002/14651858.CD003682.*

Asmundson, G.J., Frombach, I., McQuaid, J. *et al.* (2000) Dimensionality of post-traumatic stress symptoms: a confirmatory factor analysis of DSM-IV symptom clusters and other symptom models. *Behaviour Research and Therapy, 38*(2), 203–14.

Avery, D. and Winokur, G. (1976) Mortality in depressed patients treated with electroconvulsive therapy and antidepressants. *Archives of General Psychiatry, 33,* 1029–37.

Aytes, K.E., Olsen, S.S., Zakrajsek, T. *et al.* (2001) Cognitive/behavioural treatment for sexual offenders: An examination of recidivism. *Sexual Abuse: A Journal of Research and Treatment, 13,* 223–31.

Bailey, J. (2006) Life sentence prisoners in England and Wales: An empirical study. PhD dissertation. ARU, Cambridge, UK.

Baker, A.W. and Duncan, S.P. (1985) Child sexual abuse: a study of prevalence in Great Britain. *Child Abuse and Neglect, 9,* 457–67.

Ban, T. (2000) From DSM-III to DSM-IV: progress or standstill? In E. Franzck, G.S. Ungvari. E. Ruther and H. Beckman (Eds.) *Progress in Differentiated Psychopathology.* Wuerzburg, Germany: International Werniche-Kleist-Leonhard Society.

Bardens, D. (2004) *Elizabeth Fry: Britain's second lady on the five-pound note.* London: Chanadon Publications.

References

Barker, D.J.P. (2001) Preface. *British Medical Bulletin, 60,* 1–3.

Barlow, D.H., Hayes, S.C. and Nelson, R.C. (1984) *The scientist practitioner.* Oxford, UK: Pergamon.

Barnard, K.E. and Eyres, S.J. (1979) *Child health assessment. Part 2: The first year of life.* Washington, DC: Government Printing Office.

Baron, S.W. and Hartnagel, T.F. (1997) Attributions, affect, and crime: Street youths' reactions to unemployment. *Criminology, 35*(3), 409–34.

Barrett-Conner, E., von Muhlen, D., Laughlin, G.A. and Kripke, A. (1999) Endogenous levels of dehydroepiandrosterone sulfate, but not other sex hormones, are associated with depressed mood in older women: The Rancho Bernardo study. *Journal of the American Geriatric Society, 47,* 685–91.

Basoglu, M., Livanou, M., Crnobaric, C. *et al.* (2005) Psychiatric and cognitive effects of war in former Yugoslavia. *Journal of the American Medical Association, 294,* 580–90.

Baumrind, D. (1980) New directions in socialization research. *American Psychologist, 35,* 639–52.

Bear, D. (1991) Neurological perspectives on aggressive behavior. *Journal of Neuropsychiatry and Clinical Neuroscience, 3,* 3–8.

Beard, G. (1869) Neurasthenia or nervous exhaustion. *Boston Medical and Surgical Journal, 3,* 217–21.

Bebbington, P. (2004) The classification and epidemiology of unipolar depression. In M. Power (Ed.) *Mood Disorders: A Handbook of Science and Practice.* Chichester, UK: John Wiley and Sons.

Beck, A.T., Ward, C. and Mendelson, M. (1961) Beck Depression Inventory (BDI). *Archives of General Psychiatry, 4,* 561–71.

Beck, A.T., Ward, C.H., Mendelson, M. *et al.* (1962) Reliability of psychiatric diagnoses: 2. A study of consistency of clinical judgements and ratings. *American Journal of Psychiatry, 119,* 351–7.

Beckett, H., Heap, J., McArdle, P. *et al.* (2004) *Understanding problem drug use among young people accessing drug services: a multivariate approach using statistical modelling techniques Home Office Online Report 15/04.* London: Home Office. Retrieved on 29 June 2007 available from http://www.homeoffice.gov.uk/rds/pdfs04/rdsolr1504.pdf

Beelmann, A., Pfingsten, U. and Lösel, F. (1994) Effects of training social competence in children: A meta-analysis of recent evaluation studies. *Journal of Clinical Child Psychology 23*(3), 260–71.

Begg, C., Cho, M., Eastwood, S. *et al.* (1996) Improving the quality of reporting of randomized controlled trials. The CONSORT statement. *Journal of the American Medical Association, 276*(8), 637–9.

Benson, J. (2001) *Working More Creatively with Groups* (2nd edn). London: Routledge.

Berliner, L., Schram, D., Miller, L.L. *et al.* (1995) A sentencing alternative for sex offenders: A study of decision making and recidivism. *Journal of Interpersonal Violence, 10,* 487–502.

References

Berndt, T.J. and Keefe, K. (1995) Friends' influence on adolescents' adjustment to school. *Child Development, 66,* 1312–29.

Bevan, W. (1991) Contemporary psychology: A tour inside the onion. *American Psychologist, 46,* 475–83.

Bevan, W. and Kessel, F. (1994) Plain truths and home cooking: Thoughts on the making and remaking of psychology. *American Psychologist, 49*(60), 505.

Bisson, J.I., Shepherd, J.P., Joy, D. *et al.* (2004) Early cognitive-behavioural therapy for post-traumatic stress symptoms after physical injury. The British Journal of Psychiatry, *184,* 63–9.

Björkvist, K., Österman, K. and Kaukiainen, A. (2000) Social intelligence – empathy = aggression? *Aggression and Violent Behaviour, 5,* 191–200.

Blackburn, R. (1988) On moral judgements and personality disorders: The myth of the psychopathic personality revisited. *British Journal of Psychiatry, 153,* 505–12.

Bogue, J. and Power, K. (1995) Suicide in Scottish prisons: 1976–1993. *The Journal of Forensic Psychiatry, 6*(3), 527–40.

Boring, E.G. (1919) Mathematical versus statistical importance. *Psychological Bulletin, 16,* 335–8.

Born, M. (1949) *Natural Philosophy of Cause and Chance.* New York: Dover Publications.

Bottoms A.E. (2003) 'Theoretical reflections on the evaluation of a penal policy initiative'. In Zedner, L. and Ashworth, A. (Eds.) *The criminological foundations of penal policy.* Oxford, UK: Oxford University Press.

Bottoms, A.E. (2005) Methodology matters. *Safer Society. Summer 2005,* 10–12. Retrieved 23 June 2007, available from http://www.nacro.org.uk/safersociety/SS25%20Bottoms%20article.pdf

Bottoms, A.E., Gelsthorpe, L. and Rex, S. (Eds.) (2001) *Community penalties.* Cullompton, UK: Willan.

Boulton, M., Trueman, M. and Chan, C. (1999) Concurrent and longitudinal links between friendship and peer victimization: Implications for befriending interventions. *Journal of Adolescence, 22,* 461–6.

Bowlby, J. (1969) *Attachment and loss: Attachment (Vol. 1).* New York: Basic Books.

Bowles, S. and Gintis, H. (1976) *Schooling in capitalist America: Educational reform and the contradictions of economic life.* NewYork: Basic Books.

Bowles, S. and Gintis, H. (2001) Schooling in capitalist America revisited. Retrieved 11 May 2005 available from http://www.umass.edu/preferen/gintis/soced.pdf

Bregin, P.R. (2004) Suicidality, violence and mania caused by selective serotonin reuptake inhibitors (SSRIs): A review and analysis. *International Journal of Risk and Safety in Medicine, 16*(1), 31–49.

Breslau, N. (2002). Epidemiological studies of trauma, posttraumatic stress disorder, and other psychiatric disorders. *Canadian Journal of Psychiatry, 47,* 923–9.

Breslau, N., Chilcoat, H.D., Kessler, R.C. *et al.* (1999) Previous exposure to trauma and PTSD effects of subsequent trauma: Results from the Detroit Area Survey of Trauma. *American Journal of Psychiatry, 156,* 902–7.

References

Brettle, R.P., Davidson, J., Davidson, S.J. *et al.* (1986) HTLV-III Antibodies in an Edinburgh Clinic. *Lancet, 1,* 1099.

Bricklin,A., Van Hasselt, V.B. and Hersen, M. (1999) Overview. In V.B. Van Hasselt and M. Hersen (Eds.) *Handbook of psychological approaches with violent offenders: Contemporary strategies and issues.* New York: Plenum.

Bridgwood, A. and Malbon, G. (1995) *Survey of the physical health of prisoners 1994. A survey of sentenced male prisoners in England and Wales by the Social Survey Division of OPCS on behalf of the Prison Service Health Care Directorate.* London: HMSO.

Briere, J. (1997) *Psychological assessment of adult posttraumatic status.* Washington, DC: American Psychiatric Association.

British Psychological Society (2000) *Recent advances in understanding mental illness and psychotic experiences.* Leicester: British Psychological Society.

British Psychological Society (2004) *A review of the current scientific status and fields of application of polygraphic deception detection.* Leicester: British Psychological Society.

British Psychological Society (2006) *Code of ethics and conduct.* Leicester: British Psychological Society.

British Psychological Society (2007) *Division of forensic psychology guidance for working towards chartership.* Leicester: British Psychological Society.

Britt, C.L., Gottfredson, M.R. and Goldkamp, J.S. (1992) Drug testing and pre-trial misconduct: An experiment on the specific deterrent effects of drug monitoring defendants on pre-trial release. *Journal of Research in Crime and Delinquency, 29*(1), 62–78.

Bronfenbrenner, U. (1979) *The ecology of human development.* Cambridge, MA: Harvard University Press.

Bronfenbrenner, U. and Ceci, S.J. (1994) Nature–nurture reconceptualized in developmental perspective: a bioecological model. *Psychological Review, 101,* 568–86.

Brown, A. (1994) *Groupwork* (3rd edn). Aldershot, UK: Ashgate.

Brown, G.L., Goodwin, F.K., Ballenger, J.C. *et al.* (1979) Aggression in humans correlates with cerebrospinal fluid amine metabolites. *Psychiatry Research, 1,* 131–9.

Brown, G.W. and Harris, T.O. (Eds.) (1978) *Social origins of depression: A study of psychiatric disorder in women.* London; Tavistock. Brown, G.W., Bifulco, A. and Harris, T.O. (1987). Life events, vulnerability and onset of depression: Some refinements. *British Journal of Psychiatry, 150,* 30–42.

Brown, G.W., Harris, T.O. and Bifulco, A. (1986) Long-term effects of early loss of parent. In M. Rutter, C.E. Izard and P.B. Read (Eds.) *Depression in young people: Developmental and Clinical Perspectives.* New York: Guilford.

Bureau of Justice (1998) Bureau of Justice Statistics. US Department of Justice Criminal Offender Statistics. Retrieved 30 June 2007 available from http://www.ojp.usdoj.gov/bjs/crimoff.htm#sex1998

Buros, D.K. (Ed.) (1978) *The VIII mental measurements yearbook.* Highland Park: Gryphon Press.

References

Burton, R. (2001) *The anatomy of melancholy*. New York: New York Review of Books.

Cabinet Office (2005) Professional skills for government. Retrieved 17 May 2007 from http://psg.civilservice.gov.uk/

Campbell Collaboration (2007) retrieved on 20 May 2007 from http://www.campbellcollaboration.org/index.asp

Campbell, D.T. and Fiske, D.W. (1959) Convergent and discriminant validation by the mutlitrait-multimethod matrix. *Psychological Bulletin*, 56, 81–105.

Carlisle, P. and Loveday, P. (2007) Performance management and the demise of leadership. *International Journal of Leadership in Public Services*, 3(2), 18–26.

Carlson, E.A. (1998) A prospective longitudinal study of attachment disorganization/disorientation. Child Development, 69, 1107–28.

Carney, R.M., Freedland, K.E., Sheline, Y.I. *et al.* (1997) Depression and coronary heart disease: a review for cardiologists. *Clinical Cardiology*, 20(3), 196–200.

Carter, P. (2003) *Managing offenders, reducing crime correctional services review (The Carter Report)*. London: Home Office.

Carter, G. and Polger, P. (1986) A 20-year summary of National Weather Service verification results for temperature and precipitation (Technical Memorandum NWS FCST 31). Washington, DC: National Oceanic and Atmospheric Administration.

Caspi, A. (2000) The child is father of the man: Personality continuities from childhood to adulthood. *Journal of Personality and Social Psychology*, 78, 158–72.

Cattell, R.B. and Warburton, F.W. (1967) *Objective personality and motivation tests*. Urbana, IL: University of Illinois Press.

Cawson P., Wattam, C., Brooker, S. *et al.* (2000). *Child maltreatment in the United Kingdom: A study of the prevalence of child abuse and neglect*. London: National Society for the Prevention of Cruelty to Children.

Cerletti, U. (1940) L'Elettroshock. *Rivista Sperimentale di Frenatria*, I, 209–310.

Charlton, J. (1995) Trends and patterns in suicide in England and Wales. *International Journal of Epidemiology*, 24, 42–5.

Cherlin, A.J., Furstenberg, F.F., Chase-Lonsdale, P. *et al.* (1991) Longitudinal studies of effects of divorce on children in Great Britain and the United States. *Science*, 252, 1386–9.

Chess, S. and Thomas, A. (1996) *Temperament: Theory and practice (basic principles into practice)*. New York: Brunner Mazel.

Chowdhury, N., Hicks, R.C. and Kreitman, N. (1973) Evaluation for an aftercare service for parasuicide (attempted suicide) patients. *Social Psychiatry*, 8(2), 67–81.

Cinamon, H. and Bradshaw, R. (2005) Prison health in England. *British Journal of Forensic Practice*, 7(4), 8–13.

Clarke, J. and Newman, J. (1997) *The managerialist state*. London: Sage.

Cleare, A.J. (2002) Biological models of unipolar depression. In M. Power (Ed.) *Mood disorders: A handbook of science and practice*. Chichester: John Wiley and Sons.

References

Cochrane A.L. (1972) Effectiveness and efficiency: Random reflections on health services. London: Nuffield Provincial Hospitals Trust. (Reprinted in 1999 for Nuffield Trust by the Royal Society of Medicine Press, London).

Cochrane A.L. (1979) 1931–1971: A critical review, with particular reference to the medical profession. In *Medicines for the Year 2000*. London: Office of Health Economics.

Cochrane A.L. (1989) Foreword. In I. Chalmers, M. Enkin and M.J.N.C. Keirse (Eds.) *Effective care in pregnancy and childbirth*. Oxford: Oxford University Press.

Cochrane Collaboration (2007) What is the Cochrane Collaboration? Retrieved on 20 May 2007 available from http://www.cochrane.org/docs/descrip.htm

Coleman, J.C. (1980) *The nature of adolescence*. London: Methuen.

Collins, D. and Lapsley, H. (2002) *Counting the cost: Estimates of the social costs of drug abuse in Australia, 1998–9. Monograph 49*. Canberra: Australian Government Department of Health and Ageing.

Conduct Problems Prevention Research Group (2002) Evaluation of the first three years of the Fast Track prevention trial with children at high-risk for adolescent conduct problems. *Journal of Abnormal Child Psychology, 30*(1), 19–35.

Connolly, T., Arkes, H.R. and Hammond, K.R. (2000) *Judgement and Decision Making* (2nd edn). Cambridge: Cambridge University Press.

Cooper, A. (1995) Review of the role of antilibinal drugs in the treatment of sex offenders with mental retardation. *Mental Retardation, 33*(1), 42–8.

Coryell, W. and Sehlesser, M. (2001) The dexamethasone suppression test in suicide prediction. *American Journal of Psychiatry, 158*, 748–53.

Cotgrove, A.J., Zirinsky, L., Black, D. *et al.* (1995) Secondary prevention of attempted suicide in adolescence. *Journal of Adolescence, 18*(5), 569–77.

Cowie, H., Naylor, P., Talamelli, L. *et al.* (2002) Knowledge and attitudes towards peer support: A two-year follow-up to the Prince's Trust. *Journal of Adolescence, 25*, 453–67.

Craissati, J. and McClurg, G. (1997) The Challenge Project: A treatment programme evaluation for perpetrators of child sexual abuse. *Child Abuse and Neglect, 21*, 637–48.

Cravchick, A. and Goldman, D. (2000) Genetic diversity among human dopamine and serotonin receptors and transporters. *Archives of General Psychiatry, 57*, 1105–14.

Creed, F. (1981) Life events and appendicectomy. *Lancet, 1* (82350), 1381–5.

Creed, F. (1985) Life events and physical illness. *Journal of Psychosomatic Research, 1985, 29*(2), 113–23.

Creighton, S. (1995) *Voices from childhood: A survey of childhood experiences and attitudes to child rearing among adults in the United Kingdom*. London: National Society for the Prevention of Cruelty to Children.

Creighton, S. and Noyes, P. (1989) *Child abuse trends in England and Wales 1983–1987*. London: National Society for the Prevention of Cruelty to Children.

Crighton, D.A. (1997a) Risk assessment in the prison service. *Prison Service Journal, 113*, 2–4.

References

Crighton, D.A. (1997b) The psychology of suicide. In G.J. Towl (Ed.) *Suicide and self-injury in prisons.* Leicester: British Psychological Society.

Crighton, D.A. (1999) Risk assessment in forensic mental health. *British Journal of Forensic Practice, 1*(1), 16–18.

Crighton, D.A. (2000a) Reflections on risk assessment: suicide in prisons. *British Journal of Forensic Practice, 2*(1), 23–30.

Crighton, D.A. (2000b) Suicide in prisons: a critique of UK research. In G.J. Towl, L. Snow and M.J. McHugh (Eds.) *Suicide in prisons.* Oxford, UK: Blackwell.

Crighton, D.A. (2000c) Suicide in prisons in England and Wales 1988–1998: An empirical study. Unpublished PhD dissertation. ARU, Cambridge, UK.

Crighton, D.A. (2000d) Editorial – Special Issue on suicide in prisons. *British Journal of Forensic Practice, 2*(1), 2–3.

Crighton, D.A. (2002a) Suicide in prisons: a critique of UK research. In G.J. Towl, L. Snow and M.J. McHugh (Eds.) *Suicide in prisons.* Oxford, UK: Blackwell.

Crighton, D.A. (2004) Risk assessment. In A.P.C. Needs and G.J.Towl (Eds.) *Applying psychology to forensic practice.* Oxford: Blackwell.

Crighton, D.A. (2005a) Applied psychological services. *British Journal of Forensic Practice, 7*(4), 49–55.

Crighton, D.A (2005b) Psychological research into sexual offenders. In G.J. Towl (Ed.) *Psychological Research in Prisons.* Oxford: Blackwell.

Crighton, D.A. (2005c) Risk assessment. In D.A. Crighton and G.J. Towl (Eds.) *Psychology in Probation Services.* Oxford: Blackwell.

Crighton, D.A. (2005d) Applied psychological services. *British Journal of Forensic Practice, 7*(4), 49–55.

Crighton, D.A. (2006a) Methodological issues in psychological research in prisons. In G.J. Towl (Ed.) *Psychological research in prisons.* Oxford: Blackwell.

Crighton, D.A. (2006b) Psychological research into reducing suicides. In G.J. Towl (Ed.) *Psychological research in prisons.* Oxford: Blackwell.

Crighton, D.A. (2006c) Psychological research into sexual offenders. In G.J. Towl (Ed.) *Psychological research in prisons.* Oxford: Blackwell.

Crighton, D.A. and Bailey, J.E. (2006) Psychological research into life sentence offenders. In G.J. Towl (Ed.) *Psychological research in prisons.* Oxford: Blackwell.

Crighton, D.A. and Towl, G.J. (1995) Evaluation issues in groupwork. In G.J. Towl (Ed.) *Groupwork in prisons.* Leicester, UK: British Psychological Society.

Crighton, D.A. and Towl, G.J. (1997) Self inflicted deaths in England and Wales, 1988–90 and 1994–5. In G.J. Towl (Ed.) *Suicide and self-injury in prisons.* Leicester: British Psychological Society.

Crighton, D.A. and Towl, G.J. (2002) Intentional self-injury. In G.J. Towl, L. Snow and M.J. McHugh (Eds.) *Suicide in prisons.* Oxford: Blackwell.

Crighton, D.A. and Towl, G.J. (Eds.) (2005) *Psychology in probation services.* Oxford: Blackwell.

Crighton, D.A. and Towl, G.J. (2007) Experimental interventions with sex offenders: A brief review of their efficacy. *Evidence Based Mental Health, 10,* 35–7.

References

Crisp, D. and Stanko, E. (2001) Domestic violence: A healthcare issue, In J. Shepherd (Ed.) *Violence in healthcare, understanding, preventing and surviving violence: A practical guide for health professionals*. Oxford: Oxford University Press.

Crittenden, P.M. (1985) Social networks, quality of parenting, and child development. *Child Development*, 56, 1299–1313.

Crittenden, P.M. (1997) Toward an integrative theory of trauma: A dynamic-maturational approach. In D. Cicchetti and S. Toth (Eds.) *The Rochester Symposium on Developmental Psychopathology, Vol. 10: Risk, Trauma, and Mental Processes*. Rochester, NY: University of Rochester Press.

Crittenden, P.M. (1998) Distorted patterns of relationships in maltreating families: the role of internal representational models. *Journal of Reproductive and Infant Psychology*, 6, 183–99.

Crittenden, P.M. (1999) *Attaccamento in età adulta. L'approccio dinamico-maturativo alla Adult Attachment Interview*. Milano, Cortina.

Crittenden, P.M. (2000) A dynamic-maturational model of the function, development and organisation of human relationships. In R.S.L. Mills and S. Duck (Eds.), *The developmental psychology of personal relationships*. Chichester: John Wiley.

Crittenden, P.M. (2005) The origins of physical punishment: An ethological/attachment perspective on the use of punishment by human parents. In M. Crittenden, P. M. and Claussen, A. H. (Eds.) (2000) *The organization of attachment relationships*. New York: Cambridge University Press.

Crittenden, P. M., Claussen, A.H. and Kozlowska, K. (2007) Choosing a valid assessment of attachment for clinical use: A comparative study. *Australia New Zealand Journal of Family Therapy*, 28, 78–87.

Crittenden, P.M. and Craig, S. (1990) Developmental trends in child homicide. *Journal of Interpersonal Violence*, 5, 202–16.

Cronbach, L.J. and Meehl, P.E. (1955) Construct validity in psychological tests. *Psychological Bulletin*, 52, 281–302.

Cumming, G. and Finch, S. (2001) A primer on the understanding, use and calculation of confidence intervals based on central and noncentral distributions. *Educational and Psychological Measurement*, 61, 530–72.

Cumming, G. and Finch, S. (2005) Inference by eye: Confidence intervals, and how to read pictures of data. *American Psychologist*, 60, 170–80.

Cummings, E.M. and Davies, P.T. (1994) Maternal deprivation and child development. *Journal of Child Psychology and Psychiatry*, 35, 73–112.

Cunningham, P.B. and Henggler, S.W. (1999) Engaging multiproblem families in treatment: lessons learned throughout the development of multisystemic therapy. *Family Process*, 38, 265–81.

Curran, L., McHugh, M.J. and Nooney, K. (1989) HIV counselling in prisons. *Aids Care 1*(1), 11–25.

Dabbs, J.M., Carr, T.S., Frady, R.L. *et al.* (1995) Testosterone, crime, and misbehavior among 692 male prison inmates. *Personality and Individual Differences 1995*, 18, 627–33.

References

Daley, S.E., Hammen, C., Davila, J. and Burge, D. (1998) Axis II symptomatology, depression and life stress during the transition from adolescence to adulthood. *Journal of Consulting and Clinical Psychology, 66,* 595–603.

Daly, M. and Wilson, M.I. (1994). Some differential attributes of lethal assaults on small children by stepfathers versus genetic fathers. *Ethology and Sociobiology, 15,* 207–17.

Daly, M. and Wilson, M. (1996) Violence against stepchildren. *Current Directions in Psychological Science, 5,* 77–81.

Damasio, A.R. (1994) *Descartes' error: Emotion, reason, and the human brain.* New York: Avon Books.

Darke, J.L. (1990) Sexual aggression: achieving power through humiliation. In W. Marshall, D.R. Laws and H.E. Barbaree (Eds.) *Handbook of sexual assault: Issues, theories and treatment of the offender.* New York: Plenum Press.

Davis, K.E. and Jones, E.E. (1960) Changes in interpersonal perception as a means of reducing cognitive dissonance. *Journal of Abnormal and Social Psychology, 61,* 402–10.

Dawson, A. and Tylee, A. (Eds.) (2001) *Depression: Social and economic timebomb.* London: BMJ Books.

Day, K. (1994) Male mentally handicapped sex offenders. *British Journal of Psychiatry, 165,* 630–9.

D'Cruze, S. (Ed.) (2000) *Everyday violence in Britain, 1850–1950: Gender and class, women and men in history.* London: Longman.

DeMarco, R.R. (2000) The epidemiology of major depression: Implications of occurrence, recurrence, and stress in a Canadian community sample. *Canadian Journal of Psychiatry, 45,* 67–74.

Dent, M. and Barry, J. (2004) New public management and the professions in the UK: Reconfiguring control? In M. Dent, J. Chandler and J. Barry (Eds.) *Questioning the new public management.* Aldershot, UK: Ashgate.

Department of Health (1992) *The health of the nation: A strategy for health in England.* London: HMSO.

Department of Health (1996) NHS psychotherapy services in England: review of strategic policy. London: Department of Health.

Department of Health (2001) *Statistical bulletin: statistics on alcohol. England, 1978 onwards.* London: The Stationery Office.

Department of Health (2004) Organising and delivering psychological therapies. London: Department of Health.

Department of Health (2005) *Joint statement issued by Department of Health, NHS Employers and Trade Unions on Agenda for Change (England only).* London: Department of Health. Retrieved on 27 May 2007 available from http://www.dh.gov.uk/en/Policyandguidance/Humanresourcesandtraining/Modernisingpay/Agendaforchange/index.htm

Department of Health (2006) *Health Secretary announces new architecture of the local NHS. Reference number: 2006/0142.* London: Department of Health.

References

Dexter, P. and Towl, G.J. (1995) An investigation into suicidal behaviours in prison. *Issues in Criminological and Legal Psychology, 22*, 45–53.

DiFazio, R., Abracen, J. and Looman, J. (2001) Group versus individual treatment of sexual offenders: A comparison. *Forum on Corrections Research 13*, 56–9.

Dodd, T., Nicholas, S., Povey, D. *et al.* (2004) *Crime in England and Wales 2003/2004.* London: Home Office.

Doel, M. (2006) *Using groupwork.* London: Routledge.

Doel, M. and Sawdon, C. (2005) *The essential groupworker.* London: Jessica Kingsley.

Donnelly and M. A. Strauss (Eds.) *Corporal punishment of children in theoretical perspective.* New Haven, CT: Yale University Press.

Dooley, E. (1990) Prison suicide in England and Wales, 1972–87. *British Journal of Psychiatry, 156*, 40–5.

Double, D. (2002) The limits of psychiatry. *British Medical Journal, 324*, 900–4.

Douglas, K., Ogloff, J., Nichols, T. *et al.* (1999) Assessing risk for violence among psychiatric patients: The HCR-20 Violence Risk Assessment Scheme and Psychopathy Checklist: Screening version. *Journal of Consulting and Clinical Psychology, 67*, 917–30.

Duffy, M., Gillespie, K. and Clark, D.M. (2007) Post-traumatic stress disorder in the context of terrorism and other civil conflict in Northern Ireland: randomised controlled trial. *British Medical Journal, 334*, 1147–50.

Duguid, S. (1986) Selective ethics and integrity: Moral development and prison education. *Journal of Correctional Education, 37*(2), 60–4.

Duncan, B.L. and Miller, S.D. (2000) *The heroic client.* San Francisco: Jossey Bass.

D'Unger, A.V., Land, K.C., McCall, P.L. and Nagan, D.S. (1998) How many latent classes of delinquent/criminal careers? Results from mixed Poisson regression analysis. *American Journal of Sociology, 103*, 1593–1620.

Dunn, J. (1992) Siblings and development. *Current directions in psychological Science, 1*, 6–9.

Dunn, J. and Kendrick, C. (1982) *Siblings: Love, envy and understanding.* Oxford: Basil Blackwell.

Durkheim, E. (1952) *Suicide.* London: Routledge, Kegan Paul.

Durkheim, E. (1953) *Sociology and philosophy.* New York: The Free Press.

Egger, M. and Smith, G.D. (1995) Misleading meta analysis. *British Medical Journal, 310*, 752–4.

Eibl-Eibesfeldt, I. (1989) *Human ethology.* New York: Aldine de Gruyter.

Elkin, I., Shea, M.T., Watkins, J. *et al.* (1989) National Institute of Mental Health Treatment of Depression Collaborative Research Programme. General effectiveness of treatments. *Archives of General Psychiatry, 46*(11), 971–82.

Elliott, D. S., Huizinga, D. and Morse, B. J. (1986) Self-reported violent offending: A descriptive analysis of juvenile violent offenders and their offending careers. *Journal of Interpersonal Violence, 1*, 472–514.

Elzinger, B.M. and Bremner, J.D. (2002) Are the neural substrates of memory the final common pathway in posttraumatic stress disorder (PTSD)? *Journal of Affective Disorders, 70*, 1–17.

References

Erikson, E. (1968) *Identity: Youth and crisis.* London: Faber.

Essex, M.J., Klein, M.H., Cho, E. *et al.* (2002) Maternal stress beginning in infancy may sensitize children to later stress exposure: effects on cortisol and behavior. *Biological Psychiatry, 52*(8), 776–84.

Evans, K., Tyrer, P., Catalan, J. *et al.* (1999) Manual-assisted cognitive behaviour therapy (MACT): A randomized controlled trial of a brief intervention with a bibliotherapy in the treatment of recurrent deliberate self-harm. *Psychological Medicine, 29*(1), 19–25.

Ewing, C. P. (1997) *Fatal families: The dynamics of intra-familial homicide.* Thousand Oaks, CA: Sage.

Fabio, A., Loeber, R., Balasubramani *et al.* (2006) Why some generations are more violent than others: Assessment of age, period, and cohort effects. *American Journal of Epidemiology, 164*(2), 151–60.

Falshaw, L., Friendship, C. and Bates, A. (2003) *Sexual offenders: Measuring reconviction, reoffending and recidivism. Research development and statistics directorate: Findings Report 183.* London: Home Office.

Falshaw, L., Friendship, C., Travers, R. and Nugent, F. (2004) Searching for 'what works': HM Prison Service accredited cognitive skills programmes. *The British Journal of Forensic Practice, 6*(2), 3–11.

Farrington, D.P. (1989) Early predictors of adolescent aggression and adult violence. *Violence and Victims, 4*, 79–100.

Farrington, D.P. (1991) Childhood aggression and adult violence: Early precursors and later life outcomes, In D.J. Pepler and K.H. Rubin (Eds.) *The development and treatment of childhood aggression.* Hillsdale, NJ: Lawrence Erlbaum.

Farrington, D.P. (1993) Understanding and preventing bullying. In M. Tonny and N. Morris (Eds.) *Crime and Justice, 17.* Chicago: University of Chicago Press.

Farrington, D.P. (1994) Early developmental prevention of juvenile delinquency. *Criminal Behaviour and Mental Health, 4*, 204–27.

Farrington, D.P. (1995) The Twelfth Jack Tizard Memorial Lecture: The development of offending and antisocial behaviour from childhood: Key findings from the Cambridge Study in Delinquent Development. *Journal of Child Psychology and Psychiatry 36*(6), 929–64.

Farrington, D.P. (1997) Early prediction of violent and non-violent youthful offending. *European Journal of Criminal Policy and Research, 5*(2), 51–66.

Farrington, D.P. (1998) Predictors, causes and correlates of male youth violence. *Crime and Justice: A Review of Research, 24*, 421–75.

Farrington, D.P. (2001) The causes and prevention of violence. In J. Shepherd (Ed.) *Violence in health care, understanding, preventing and surviving violence; A practical guide for health professionals.* Oxford, UK: Oxford University Press.

Farrington, D.P. (2003) Advancing knowledge about the early prevention of adult antisocial behaviour. In D.P. Farrington and J. Coid (Eds.) *Early prevention of adult antisocial behaviour, Cambridge Studies in Criminology.* Cambridge, UK: Cambridge University Press.

References

Farrington, D.P. and Coid, J.W. (2003) Conclusions and the way forward. In D.P Farrington and J.W. Coid (Eds.) *Early prevention of Adult Antisocial Behaviour.* Cambridge, UK: Cambridge University Press.

Farrington, D.P., Hancock, G., Livingston *et al.* (2000) *Evaluation of Intensive Regimes for Young Offenders. Research Findings 121.* London: Home Office Research, Development and Statistics Directorate, London.

Farrington, D.P. and Jolliffe, D. (2002) *Feasibility study into using a randomised controlled trial to evaluate treatment pilots at HMP Whitemoor (RDS/01/250),* Institute of Criminology, University of Cambridge.

Farrington, D.P. and Loeber, R. (Eds.) (1998) *Serious and violent offenders: Risk factors and successful interventions.* Thousand Oaks, CA: Sage, California.

Farrington, D.P., Loeber, R. and Van Kammen, W.B. (1990) Long-term criminal outcomes of hyperactivity-impulsivity, attention deficit and conduct problems in childhood. In L.N. Robins and M. Rutter (Eds.) *Straight and devious pathways from childhood to adulthood.* Cambridge: Cambridge University Press.

Farrington, D.P. and Welsh, B. (2003) Family-based prevention of offending: A meta-analysis. *Australian and New Zealand Journal of Criminology, 26,* 127–51.

Farrington, D.P. and Welsh, B. (2006) *Saving children from a life of crime: Early risk factors and effective interventions.* Oxford: Oxford University Press.

Farrington, D.P. and West, D.J. (1990) The Cambridge study in delinquent development: a long-term follow-up of 411 London males. In H.J. Kerner and G. Kaiser (Eds.) *Criminality: personality, behaviour, life history.* Berlin: Springer Verlag.

Faulkner, D. (2006a) Foreword. In G.J. Towl (Ed.) *Psychological research in prisons.* Oxford, UK: Blackwell.

Faulkner, D. (2006b) *Crime, state and citizen: A field full of folk* (2nd edn). Cullompton, UK: Waterside Press.

Faulkner, D. (2007) Prospects for progress in penal reform. *Criminology and Criminal Justice, 7*(2), 135–52.

Fergusson, D.M., Horwood, L.J. and Lynskey, M.T. (1995) Maternal depressive symptoms and depressive symptoms in adolescents. *Journal of Child Psychology and Psychiatry, 36,* 1161–78.

Festinger, L. (1957) *A Theory of cognitive dissonance.* Stanford, CA: Stanford University Press.

Festinger, L. and Carlsmith, J.M. (1959) Cognitive consequences of forced compliance. *Journal of Abnormal and Social Psychology, 58,* 203–10.

Feyerabend, P. (1999) Knowledge, science and relativism. In J. Preston (Ed.) *Philosophical papers, Vol. 3.* Cambridge: Cambridge University Press.

Fidler, F. (2006) Should psychology abandon p values and teach CIs instead? Evidence-based reforms in statistics education. Retrieved 21 September 2007 from http://www.stat.auckland.ac.nz/~iase/publications/17/5E4_FIDL.pdf

Fidler, F., Thomason, N., Cumming, G., Finch, S. and Leeman, J. (2004) Editors can lead researchers to confidence intervals but they can't make them think: Statistical reform lessons from medicine. *Psychological Science, 15,* 119–26.

Finkelhor, D. (1979) *Sexually victimised children.* New York: Free Press.

References

Finkelhor, D. (1984) *Child sexual abuse: new theory and research.* New York: Free Press.

Finkelhor, D. (1997). The homicide of children and youth: A developmental perspective. In G. Kaufman Kantor and J. Jasinski (Eds.). *Out of the darkness: Contemporary perspectives on family violence.* Thousand Oaks, CA: Sage.

Finkelhor, D., Hotaling, G., Lewis, I.A. and Smith, C. (1990) Sexual abuse in a national survey of adult men and women: Prevalence, characteristics and risk factors. *Child Abuse and Neglect, 14,* 19–28.

Fisher, D. (1995) The therapeutic impact of sex offender treatment programmes. *Probation Journal 42,* 2–7.

Fisher, R.A. (1955). Statistical methods and scientific induction. *Journal of the Royal Statistical Society. Series B (Methodological), 17*(1), 69–78.

Flouri, E. (2005). Post-traumatic stress disorder (PTSD): What we have learned and what we still have not found out. *Journal of Interpersonal Violence, 20,* 373–9.

Foa, E.B., Steketee, G. and Rothbaum, B.O. (1989) Behavioral/cognitive conceptualization of post-traumatic stress disorder. *Behavior Therapy, 20,* 155–76.

Fonagy, P., Steele, M., Steele, H., Higgitt, A. and Target, M. (1994) The theory and practice of resilience. *Journal of Child Psychology and Psychiatry, 35*(2), 231–7.

Ford, D.E., Mead, L.A., Chang, P.P. *et al.* (1998). Depression is a risk factor for coronary artery disease in men: The precursors study. *Archives of Internal Medicine, 158*(13), 1422–6.

Free, M. (2002) *Cognitive therapy in groups.* Chichester, UK: John Wiley and Sons.

Freeman, H., Arikian, S. and Lenox–Smith, A. (2000). Pharmacoeconomic analysis of antidepressants for major depressive disorder in the UK. *Pharmacoeconomics, 18*(2), 143–8.

Friendship, C., Beech, A. and Browne, K.D. (2002) Reconviction as an outcome measure in research. A methodological note. *British Journal of Criminology, 42,* 442–4.

Friendship, C., Falshaw, L. and Beech, A. (2003) Measuring the real impact of accredited offending behaviour programmes. *Legal and Criminological Psychology, 8,* 115–27.

Friendship, C., Mann, R. and Beech, A. (2003) *The prison-based sex offender treatment programme – an evaluation. Home Office Research Findings, 205.* London: Home Office.

Frommberger, U., Stieglitz, R. D., Nyberg, E. *et al.* (2004) Comparison between paroxetine and behaviour therapy in patients with posttraumatic stress disorder (PTSD): a pilot study. *International Journal of Psychiatry in Clinical Practice, 8,* 19–23.

Furby, L., Weintrott, M. and Blackshaw, L. (1989) Sex offender recidivism: a review. *Psychological Bulletin 105,* 3–30.

Garb, H. (1998) *Studying the clinician: Judgement research and psychological assessment.* Washington, DC; American Psychological Association.

Geddes, J., Carney, S., Cowen, P. *et al.* (2003) Efficacy and safety of electroconvulsive therapy in depressive disorders: A systematic review and meta-analysis. *Lancet, 361*(9360), 799–808.

References

Geddes, J.R., Carney, S.M., Davies, C. *et al.* (2003) Relapse prevention with antidepressant drug treatment in depressive disorders: A systematic review. *Lancet, 361*(9358), 653–61.

Geddes, J.R., Freemantle, N., Mason, J. *et al.* (2002) *Selective serotonin reuptake inhibitors (SSRIs) for depression (Cochrane Review).* Cochrane Library, Issue 1. Oxford, UK: Update Software.

Geddes, J.R. and Juszczak, E. (1995) Period trends in the rate of suicide in the first 28 days after discharge from psychiatric hospital in Scotland, 1968–92. *British Medical Journal, 311,* 357–60.

Geddes, J.R., Juszczak, E., O'Brien, F. *et al.* (1997) Suicide in the 12 months after discharge from psychiatric inpatient care, Scotland 1968–92. *Journal of Epidemiology and Community Health 51,* 430–4.

Gelles, R.J. (1972) It takes two: The role of victim and offender. In R.J. Gelles (Ed.) *The violent home: A study of physical aggression between husbands and wives.* Newbury Park, CA: Sage.

Gelles, R.J. (1989) Child abuse and violence in single-parent families: Parent absence and economic deprivation. *American Journal of Orthopsychiatry, 59,* 492–501.

George, C., Kaplan, N. and Main, M. (1985) Adult attachment interview: Interview protocol. University of California, Berkeley.

Gerra, G., Zaimovic, A., Avanzinmi P. *et al.* (1997) Neurotransmitter-neuroendocrine responses to experimentally induced aggression in humans: influence of personality variable. *Psychiatry Research, 66,* 33–43.

Gibbons, J.S., Butler, J., Urwin, P. *et al.* (1978) Evaluation of a social work service for self-poisoning patients. *British Journal of Psychiatry, 133,* 111–18.

Gigerenzer, G. (2002) *Reckoning with risk: Learning to live with uncertainty.* Harmondsworth, UK: Penguin.

Glassman, A.H. and Shapiro, P.A. (1998) Depression and the course of coronary artery disease. *American Journal of Psychiatry, 155*(1), 4–11.

Glassman, A.H., O'Connor, C.M., Califf, R.M. *et al.* (2002). Sertraline treatment of major depression in patients with acute MI or unstable angina. *Journal of the American Medical Association, 288*(6), 701–9.

Godfrey, C., Toumbourou, J.W., Rowland, B. *et al.* (2002) *Drug education approaches in primary schools. Technical Report 4.* Melbourne, AUS: Australian Drug Foundation Clearing House.

Goldman, R. and Goldman, J. (1982) *Children's sexual thinking.* London: Routledge and Kegan Paul.

Goleman, E. (1996) *Emotional intelligence.* London: Bloomsbury.

Golombok, S. and Fivush, R. (1994) *Gender development.* Cambridge, UK: Cambridge University Press.

Good, D.A. and Watts, F.N. (1989) Qualitative research. In G. Parry and F.N. Watts (Eds.) *Behavioural and mental health research: A handbook of skills and methods.* Hove, UK: Lawrence Erlbaum Associates.

References

Goodyer, I.M. and Altman, P.M.E. (1991) Lifetime exit events and recent social and family adversities in anxious and depressed school-age children and adolescents. I. *Journal of Affective Disorders, 21,* 219–28.

Goodyer, I.M., Herbert, J., Tamplin, A. *et al.* (1997) Short-term outcome of major depression. II. Life events, family dysfunction, and friendship difficulties as predictors of persistent disorder. *Journal of the American Academy of Child and Adolescent Psychiatry, 36,* 474–80.

Gorman, K., Gregory, M., Hayles, M. and Parton, N. (Eds.) (2006) *Constructive work with offenders.* London: Jessica Kingsley.

Gospodarevskaya, E.V., Goergen, S.K., Harris, A.H., Chan, T., de Campo, J.F., Wolfe, R., Gan, E.T., Wheeler, M.B. and McKay, J. (2006) *Economic evaluation of a clinical protocol for diagnosing emergency patients with suspected pulmonary embolism. Cost effectiveness and resource allocation 2006, 4:12 doi:10.1186/1478-7547-4-12.* Retrieved 28 May 2007. Available from http://www.resource-allocation.com/content/4/1/12

Graham, J. and Bowling, B. (1995) *Young people and crime.* London: Home Office.

Grannas, M. (2002) Hypothesis testing in psychology: Throwing the baby out with the bathwater? Online paper retrieved on 14 May 2007 from http://www.stat.auckland.ac.nz/~iase/publications/1/3m1_gran.pdf

Gregory, R. (1998) Snapshots from a decade of the brain: Brainy mind. *British Medical Journal, 317,* 1693–5.

Grisso, T. and Applebaum, P. (1998) *Assessing competence to consent to treatment: A guide for physicians and other health professionals.* New York: Oxford University Press.

Gross, J.J. and Levenson, R.W. (1993) Hiding feelings: The acute effects of inhibiting negative and positive emotion. *Journal of Abnormal Psychology, 106*(1), 95–103.

Grove, W. and Meehl, P. (1996) Comparative efficacy of informal (subjective, impressionistic) and formal (mechanical, algorithmic) prediction procedures: The clinical-statistical controversy. *Psychology, Public Policy and Law, 2,* 293–323.

Grusec, J.E., Saas-Kortsaak, P. and Simutis, Z.M. (1978) The role of example and moral exhortation in the training of altruism. *Child Development, 49,* 920–3.

Grusec, J.E., Davidoff, V.M. and Lundell, L. (2002) Prosocial and helping behaviour. In P.K. Smith and C. Hart (Eds.) *Handbook of child social development.* Malden, MA: Blackwell.

Grusec, J.E. and Godnow, J.J. (1994) Impact of parental discipline methods on the child's internalisation of values: a reconceptualization of current points of view. *Developmental Psychology, 30,* 4–19.

Gunn, J. (1998) Psychopathy: An elusive concept with moral overtones. In T. Millon, E. Simonsen, M. Birket-Smith and R.D. Davis (Eds.) *Psychopathy: Antisocial, criminal and violent behaviour.* New York: Guilford Press.

Gunn, J. (2000) Future directions for treatment in forensic psychiatry. *British Journal of Psychiatry, 176,* 332–8.

Habermann, U. (1990) Self-help groups: A minefield for professionals. *Groupwork, 3*(3), 221–35.

References

Haddad, P.M. (2001) Antidepressant discontinuation syndromes. *Drug Safety*, 24, 183–97.

Hall, D. (2001) Reflecting on Redfern: What can we learn from the Alder Hey story? *Archives of Disease in Childhood*, 84, 455–6.

Hamilton, M. (1960) A rating scale for depression. *Journal of Neurology, Neurosurgery and Psychiatry*, 23, 56–62.

Hankoff, L.D. (1980) Prisoner suicide. *International Journal of Offender Therapy and Comparative Criminology*, 24(2), 162–6.

Hanson, R. (1998) What do we know about sex offender risk assessment? *Psychology, Public Policy and Law*, 4, 50–72.

Hanson, R.K. and Bussiere, M.T. (1998) Predicting relapse: a meta-analysis of sexual offender recidivism studies. *Journal of Consulting and Clinical Psychology*, 66, 348–62.

Hanson, R.K. and Morton-Bourgon, K. (2004) *Predictors of sexual recidivism: an updated meta-analysis*. Ottawa, CA: Public Safety and Emergency Preparedness Canada.

Hanson, R.K. and Thornton, D. (2000) Improving risk assessments for sexual offenders: a comparison of three actuarial scales. *Law and Human Behaviour*, 24, 119–36.

Hanson, R.K., Broom, I. and Stephenson, M. (2004) Evaluating community sex offender programmes: A 12-year follow-up of 724 offenders. *Canadian Journal of Behavioural Science*, 36(2), 85–94.

Hanson, R.K., Gordon, A., Harris, A.J.R. *et al.* (2002) First report of the Collaborative Outcome Data Project on the effectiveness of treatment for sex offenders. *Sexual Abuse: A Journal of Research and Treatment*, 14, 169–94.

Hanson, R.K., Steffy, R.A. and Gauthier, R. (1993) Long-term recidivism of child molesters. *Journal of Consulting and Clinical Psychology*, 61, 646–52.

Harlow, L.L. (1997). Significance testing in introduction and overview. In L.L. Harlow, S.A. Muliak and J.H. Steiger (Eds.) *What if there were no significance tests?* Mahwah, New Jersey: Lawrence Erlbaum Associates.

Harper, G. and Chitty, C. (2005) *The impact of corrections on re-offending: A review of 'what works'* (2nd edn). *Home Office Research Study*, 291. London: Home Office.

Harre, R. (1984) *Personal being: A theory for individual psychology*. Cambridge, MA: Harvard University Press.

Harrington, R.C., Fudge, H., Rutter, M. *et al.* (1991) Adult outcomes of childhood and adolescent depression. II. Risk for antisocial disorders. *Journal of the American Academy of Child and Adolescent Psychiatry*, 30, 434–9.

Harris, G., Rice, M. and Quinsey, V. (1993) Violent recidivism of mentally disordered offenders: The development of a statistical prediction instrument. Criminal Justice and Behaviour, 20, 315.

Harrow, M., MacDonald, A.W., Sands, J.R. and Silverstein, M.L. (1995). Vulnerability to delusions over time in schizophrenia and affective disorders. *Schizophrenia Bulletin*, 21, 95–109.

References

Hart, S., Cox, D. and Hare, R. (1995) *The Hare Psychopathy Checklist: Screening version.* Toronto, CAN: Multi-Health Systems.

Hatty, S. and Walker, J. (1986) *Deaths in Australian prisons.* Canberra: Australian Institute of Criminology.

Hawk, G., Rosenfield, B. and Warren, J. (1993) Prevalence of sexual offences amongst mentally retarded criminal defendants. *Hospital and Community Psychiatry, 44*(8), 784–6.

Hawkins, J.D., Catalano, R.F. and Miller, J.Y. (1992) Risk and protective factors for alcohol and other drug problems in adolescence and early adulthood: implications for substance abuse prevention. *Psychological Bulletin, 112,* 64–105.

Hawton, K., Bancroft, J., Catalan, J. *et al.* (1981) Domiciliary and out-patient treatment of self-poisoning patients by medical and non-medical staff. *Psychological Medicine, 11,* 169–77.

Hawton, K., McKeown, S., Day, A. *et al.* (1987) Evaluation of out-patient counselling compared with general practitioner care following over-doses. *Psychological Medicine, 17,* 751–61.

Hawton, K., Salkovskis, P.M., Kirk, J. *et al.* (Eds.) (1989) *Cognitive behavioural therapy for psychiatric problems: a practical guide.* Oxford, UK: Oxford University Press.

Hawton, K., Townsend, E., Arensman, E. *et al.* (2007). Psychosocial and pharmacological treatments for deliberate self harm (Review) Issue 2. Cochrane Database of Systematic Reviews CD001764. Retrieved on 30 June 2007 available from http://www.mrw.interscience.wiley.com/cochrane/clsysrev/articles/CD001764/pdf_fs.html

Hayes, R.A. (2004) Introduction to evidence-based practices. In C.E. Stout and R.A. Haynes (Eds.) *The evidence-based practice: Methods, models and tools for mental health professionals.* Hoboken, NJ: John Wiley.

Hayles, M. (2006) Constructing Safety: A Collaborative Approach to Managing Risk and Building Responsibility. In K. Gorman, M. Gregory, M. Hayles and N. Parton (Eds.) *Constructive work with offenders.* London: Jessica Kingsley.

Head, H. (1916) A discussion on shell shock. *Lancet, 1,* 306–7.

Healy, D. (1997) *The antidepressant era.* Cambridge, MA: Harvard University Press.

Hecker, J.E. and Thorpe, G. (2003) *Introduction to clinical psychology.* Boston, MA: Pearson.

Hedderman, C. (2007) Rediscovering resettlement: narrowing the gap between policy rhetoric and practice reality. In A. Hucklesby and L. Hagley-Dickenson (Eds.) *Prisoner resettlement: policy and practice.* Collumpton, UK: Willan.

Heider, F. (1958) *The psychology of interpersonal relations.* New York: John Wiley and Sons.

Heim, C., Newport, D.J., Heit, S. *et al.* (2000) Pituitary-adrenal and autonomic responses to stress in women after sexual and physical abuse in childhood. *Journal of the American Medical Association, 284,* 592–7.

Henning, K.R. and Freuh, B.C. (1996) Cognitive-behavioural treatment of incarcerated offenders: An evaluation of the Vermont department of corrections' cognitive self-change programme. *Criminal Justice and Behaviour, 23,* 523–41.

References

Henry, J.B. (2001) *Clinical diagnosis and management by laboratory methods* (20th edn). Philadelphia, PA: Saunders.

Herman, J.L. (1992) *Trauma and recovery: The aftermath of violence – from domestic abuse to political terror.* New York: Basic Books.

Hesse, E. (1996) Discourse, memory, and the Adult Attachment Interview: A note with emphasis on the emerging Cannot Classify category. *Infant Mental Health Journal, 17,* 4–11.

Hester, M. and Westmarland, N. (2005) Tackling domestic violence: Effective interventions and approaches. *Home Office Research Study, 290.* London: Home Office.

Hetherington, E.M. (1989) Coping with family transitions: winners, losers, and survivors. *Child Development, 60,* 1–14.

Hetherington, E.M., Cox, M. and Cox, R. (1982) Effects of divorce on parents and children. In M. Lamb (Ed.) *Nontraditional families.* Hillsdale, NJ: Erlbaum.

Hinde, R.A. and Dennis, A. (1986) Categorizing individuals: An alternative to linear analysis. *International Journal of Behavioral Development, 9*(1), 105–19.

Hinde, R.A. and Stevenson-Hinde, J. (Eds.) (1973) *Constraints on learning: Limitations and predispositions.* London and New York: Academic Press.

Hirschfield, R.M.A. and Weissman, M.M. (2002) Risk factors for major depression and bipolar disorder. In K.L. Davies, D. Charney, J.T. Coyle and C. Nemeroff (Eds.) *Neuropsychopharmacology: The fifth generation of progress.* Philadelphia, PA: Lipincott, Williams and Wilkins.

HM Inspectorate of Prisons (1999) *Suicide in prisons – thematic review.* London: Home Office.

HM Inspectorate of Probation (2002) *Annual report 2001–2002.* London: Home Office.

HM Prison Service and National Probation Service (2003) *Driving delivery: A strategic framework for psychological services in prisons and probation.* London: HM Prison and National Probation Service.

HM Prison Service (2004) *Prison Service Order (7035) Research Applications and Ethics Panel.* London: HMPS.

HM Prison Service (2005) *Prison Service Order (7035 revised) Research Applications and Ethics Panel.* London: HMPS.

HM Treasury (2003) *Every child matters. House of Commons Command Paper Cm 5860.* London: HM Treasury. Retrieved 14 May 2007 available from http://publications.everychildmatters.gov.uk/eOrderingDownload/CM5860.pdf

Hodge, J. and Renwick, S.J. (2002) Motivating mentally abnormal offenders. In M. McMurran (Ed.) *Motivating offenders to change: A guide to engagement in therapy.* Chichester, UK: John Wiley and Sons.

Hogben, L. (1957) *Statistical Theory: The relationship of probability, credibility, and error: An examination of the contemporary crisis in statistical theory from a behaviourist viewpoint.* London: Allen and Unwin.

Holcombe, H.R. (1996) Just-so stories and inference to the best explanation in evolutionary psychology. *Minds and Machines, 6*(4), 525–40.

References

Holder, H.D. (1997) *A community systems approach to alcohol problem prevention.* Cambridge: Cambridge University Press.

Hollin, C.R. (2002) Risk-needs assessment and the allocation to offender programmes. In J. McGuire (Ed.) *Offender rehabilitation and treatment: Effective programmes and policies to reduce re-offending.* Chichester, UK: John Wiley and Sons.

Holmes, T.H. and Rahe, R.H. (1967) The social readjustment rating scale. *Journal of Psychomatic Research, 11,* 213–17.

Home Office (2003) Drug strategy. Retrieved on 29 June 2007, available from http://www.drugs.gov.uk/drug-strategy/overview/

Home Office (2004) *Reducing crime – changing lives.* London: Home Office.

Hood, C. (1991) A public management for all seasons. *Public Administration, 69,* 3–9.

Hood, R., Shute, S., Feilzer, M. *et al.* (2002) *Reconviction rates of serious sex offenders and assessments of their risk. Home Office Research Findings No. 164.* London: Home Office.

House of Commons (1998) *The welfare of former British child migrants. Select Committee on Health Third Report.* London: The Stationery Office. Retrieved on 14 May 2007 from http://www.parliament.the-stationery-office.co.uk/pa/cm199798/cmselect/cmhealth/755/75503.htm#n2

House of Commons Science and Technology Committee (2006) *Drug classification: making a hash of it? Fifth Report of Session 2005–06.* London: The Stationery Office.

Houston, J., Wrench, M. and Hosking, N. (1995) Group processes in the treatment of child sex offenders. *The Journal of Forensic Psychiatry, 6*(2), 359–68.

Howe, M.J.A. (1988) Intelligence as an explanation. *British Journal of Psychology, 79,* 349–60.

Howell, D.C. (1999) *Fundamental statistics for the behavioural sciences* (4th edn). Pacific Grove, CA: Duxbury Press.

Howells, K. and Day, A. (2003) Readiness for anger management: Clinical and theoretical issues. *Clinical Psychology Review, 23,* 319–37.

Howells, K., Day, A., Bubner, S. *et al.* (2002) Anger management and violence prevention: Improving effectiveness. *Trends and Issues in Crime and Criminal Justice, 207.* Canberra, AUS: Australian Institute of Criminology.

Hubbard, R. and Ryan, P.A. (2000) The historical growth of statistical significance testing in psychology – and its future prospects. *Educational and Psychological Measurement, 60,* 661–81.

Huizinga, D., Loeber, R. and Thornberry, T.P. (1995) *Recent findings from the program of research on the causes and correlates of delinquency (U.S. Department of Justice, Office of Justice Programs, Office of Juvenile Justice and Delinquency Prevention, NCJ 159042).* Washington, DC: US Government Printing Office.

Iadicola, P. and Shupe, A. (2003) *Inequality and human freedom.* Lanham, MD: Rowman and Littlefield.

Jadad, A.R. (1998) *Randomised control trials: A user's guide.* London: BMJ Books.

References

Jenkins, R., Bebbington, P.E., Brugha, T. *et al.* (1997) The National Psychiatric Morbidity Surveys of Great Britain – strategy and methods. *Psychological Medicine*, 27, 765–74.

Jenkins, R. and Singh, B. (2000) Policy and practice in suicide prevention. *British Journal of Forensic Practice*, 2(1), 3–11.

Jick, H., Kaye, J.A. and Jick, S.S. (2004) Antidepressants and the risk or suicidal behaviours. *Journal of the American Medical Association*, 292(3), 338–43.

Johnson, J., Howarth, E. and Weissman, M.M. (1991) The validity of major depression with psychotic features based on a community sample. *Archives of General Psychiatry*, 48(12), 1075–81.

Jones, E.E., Kannouse, D.E., Kelley, H.H. *et al.* (Eds.) (1972) *Attribution: Perceiving the Causes of Behavior.* Morristown, NJ: General Learning Press.

Jones, J. (1990) *Violent statistics, American Psychological Association Monitor,* 4. Washington, DC: American Psychological Association.

Jones, L. (2004) Offence paralleling behaviour (OPB) as a framework for assessment and interventions with offenders. In A.P.C. Needs and G.J. Towl (Eds.) *Applying psychology to forensic practice.* Oxford, UK: Blackwell.

Jones-Webb R., Toomey, T.L., Short, B. *et al.* (1997) Relationships among alcohol availability, drinking location, alcohol consumption, and drinking problems in adolescents. *Substance Use and Misuse*, 32(10), 1261–85.

Joudo, J. (2006) *Deaths in custody in Australia: National Deaths in Custody Program annual report 2005. Technical and background paper series, no. 21 (online only).* Canberra, AUS: Australian Institute of Criminology. Retrieved on 30 June 2007 from http://www.aic.gov.au/publications/tbp/tbp021/

Judd, L.L., Akiskal, H.S., Maser, J.L. *et al.* (1998) A prospective 12-year study of subsyndromal and syndromal depressive symptoms in unipolar major depressive disorders. *Archives of General Psychiatry*, 55, 694–700.

Kandel, D.B. and Davies, M. (1986) Adult sequelae of adolescent depressive symptoms. *Archives of General Psychiatry*, 43, 255–62.

Kazdin, A.E. (2003) Psychotherapy for children and adolescents. *Annual Review of Psychology*, 54, 253–76.

Keane, T.M. and Wolfe, L.J. (1990) Comorbidity in post-traumatic stress disorder: An analysis of community and clinical studies. *Journal of Applied Social Psychology*, 20, 1776–88.

Keller, M.B., McCullough, J.P., Klein, D.N. *et al.* (2000). A comparison of nefazodone, the cognitive behavioural-analysis system of psychotherapy, and their combination for the treatment of chronic depression. *New England Journal of Medicine*, 342(20), 1462–70.

Kelly, S. and Bunting, J. (1998) *Trends in suicide in England and Wales, 1982–96.* London: Office of National Statistics.

Kendall, P.C. (1997). Editorial. *Journal of Consulting and Clinical Psychology*, 65, 3–5.

Kendler, K.S. and Prescott, C.A. (1999) A population-based twin study of lifetime major depression in men and women. *Archives of General Psychiatry*, 56, 39–44.

References

Kendler, K.S., Thornton, L.M. and Gardner, C.O. (2000) Stressful life events and previous episodes in the etiology of major depression in women: An evaluation of the 'kindling' hypothesis. *American Journal of Psychiatry*, *157*, 1243–51.

Kenworthy, T., Adams, C.E., Bilby, C. *et al.* (2003) Psychological interventions for those who have sexually offended or are at risk of offending. *The Cochrane database of Systemic Reviews. Issue 4. Art. No.: CD004858. DOI: 10.1002/14651858. CD004858*

Kessler, R.C., Sonnega, A., Bromet, E. *et al.* (1995) Posttraumatic stress disorder in the National Comorbidity Survey. *Archives of General Psychiatry*, *52*(12), 1048–60.

Khan, A., Khan, S.R., Shankles, E.B. *et al.* (2002) Relative sensitivity of the Montgomery–Asberg Depression rating scale, the Hamilton Depression rating scale and the Clinical Global Impressions rating scale in antidepressant clinical trials. *International Clinical Psychopharmacology*, *17*(6), 281–5.

Kilpatrick, D.G., Resnick, H.S., Freedy, J.R. *et al.* (1998) The posttraumatic stress disorder field trial: Evaluation of the PTSD construct: Criteria A through E. In T. Widiger, A. Frances, H. Pincus *et al.* (Eds.) *DSM-1V sourcebook*. Washington, DC: American Psychiatric Press.

Kinderman, P. (2005) The applied psychology revolution. *The Psychologist*, *18*(12), 744–6.

King, R. and Alexander, E. (2002) ACLU statement for the record for the Senate Judiciary Committee hearing on prison rape prevention (7/31/2002). Retrieved on 13 June 2007 from http://www.aclu.org/prison/conditions/14676leg20020731.html

Klassen, D. and O'Connor, W. (1988) Crime, inpatient admissions, and violence among male mental patients. *International Journal of Law and Psychiatry*, *11*, 305–12.

Klassen, D. and O'Connor, W. (1990) Assessing the risk of violence in released mental patients: A cross-validation study. *Psychological Assessment: A Journal of Consulting and Clinical Psychology*, *1*, 75–81.

Kline, P. (2000) *Handbook of psychological testing* (2nd edn). London: Routledge.

Kline, R.B. (2004) *Beyond significance testing: Reforming data analysis methods in behavioral research*. Washington DC: American Psychological Association.

Koch, S. (1981) The nature and limits of psychological knowledge. *American Psychologist*, *36*, 257–9.

Kohlberg, L. (1969) *Stages in the development of moral thought and action*. New York: Holt, Rinehart and Winston.

Koren, D., Norman, D., Cohen, A. (2005) Increased PTSD risk with combat-related injury: A matched comparison study of injured and uninjured soldiers experiencing the same combat events. *American Journal of Psychiatry*, *162*, 276–82.

Kovacs, M. (1986) A developmental perspective on methods and measures in the assessment of depressive disorders: The clinical interview. In M.Rutter, C.E. Izard and R.B. Read (Eds.) *Depression in young people: Developmental and clinical perspectives*. New York: Guilford.

269

References

Kovacs, M., Feinberg, T.L., Crouse-Novak, M. *et al.* (1984) Depressive disorders in childhood. II. A longitudinal study of the risk for a subsequent major depression. *Archives of General Psychiatry*, 41, 643–9.

Kuhn, T. (1996) *The structure of scientific revolutions* (3rd edn). Chicago: Chicago University Press.

Lane-Morton, T. (2005) What health partnerships should seek to provide for offenders. *British Journal of Forensic Practice*, 7(4), 3–7.

Larson, R. and Ham, M. (1993) Stress and 'storm and stress' in early adolescence: their relationship of negative events to dysphoric affect. *Developmental Psychology*, 29, 130–40.

Larzerle, R.E. (2000) Child outcomes of nonabusive and customary physical punishment by parents: an updated literature review. *Clinical Child and Family Psychology Review*, 3, 199–221.

Latissa, E.J., Cullen, F.T. and Gendreau, P. (2002) Beyond correctional quackery – professionalism and the possibility of effective treatment. *Federal Probation*, 66, 43–9.

Laucht, M., Esser, G. and Schmidt, M.H. (1997) Developmental outcome of infants born with biological and psychosocial risks. *Journal of Child Psychology and Psychiatry*, 38, 843–53.

Laucht, M., Esser, G. and Schmidt, M.H. (2001) Differential development of infants at risk for psychopathology: the moderating role of early maternal responsivity. *Developmental Medicine and Child Neurology*, 43, 292–300.

Lea, S., Auburn, T. and Kibblewhite, K. (1999) Working with sex offenders: The perceptions and experiences of professionals and paraprofessionals. *International Journal of Offender Therapy and Comparative Criminology*, 43(1), 103–19.

Lee, M. and George, S. (2005) Drug strategy unit. *British Journal of Forensic Practice*, 7(4), 39–48.

Leff, J., Vearnals, S., Brewin, C.R. *et al.* (2000). The London Depression Intervention Trial. Randomised controlled trial of antidepressants vs. couple therapy in the treatment and maintenance of people with depression living with a partner: Clinical outcome and costs. *British Journal of Psychiatry*, 177, 95–100.

Lejoyeux, M. and Ades, J. (1997) Antidepressant discontinuation: a review of the literature. *Journal of Clinical Psychiatry*, 58, 11–15.

Levant, R. (2004) The empirically-validated treatments movement: A practitioner/educator perspective. *Clinical Psychology Science and Practice*, 11, 219–24.

Lewinsohn, P.M., Rohde, P., Klein, D.N. and Seeley, J.R. (1999) Natural course of adolescent major depressive disorder. I. Continuity into young adulthood. *Journal of the American Academy of Child and Adolescent Psychiatry*, 38, 56–63.

Lezak, M.D. (2004) *Neuropsychological assessment*. New York: Oxford University Press.

Lidz, C., Mulvey, E. and Gardner, W. (1993) The accuracy of predictions of violence to others. *Journal of the American Medical Association*, 269, 1007–11.

Liebling, A. (1992) *Suicides in prisons*. London: Routledge.

References

Liebling, A. and Krarup, H. (1993) *Suicide and self-injury in male prisons – a summary*. London: Home Office.

Linehan, M.M., Armstrong, H.E., Suarez, A. *et al.* (1991) Cognitive-behavioral treatment of chronically parasuicidal borderline patients. *Archives of General Psychiatry*, 48, 1060–4.

Lipsey, M.W. (2007) Unjustified inferences about meta-analysis. *Journal of Experimental Criminology*, 3(3), 271–9.

Lipton, D., Martinson, R. and Wilkes, J. (1975) *The effectiveness of correctional treatment: A survey of treatment evaluation studies*. New York: Praeger.

Litz, B.T., Orsillo, S.M., Kaloupek, D. *et al.* (2002) Emotional processing in posttraumatic stress disorder. *Journal of Abnormal Psychology*, 109, 26–39.

Loeber and Farrington, D.P. (Eds.) (1998) *Serious and violent juvenile offenders: Risk factors and successful interventions*. Thousand Oaks, CA: Sage.

Loeber, R., Farrington, D.P. and Waschbusch, D.A. (1998) Serious and violent juvenile offenders. In R. Loeber and D.P. Farrington (Eds.) *Serious and violent juvenile offenders: Risk factors and successful interventions*. Thousand Oaks, CA: Sage.

Loftus, G.R. (1993) Editorial comment. *Memory and Cognition*, 21, 1–3.

Lonczak, H.S., Abbott, R.D., Hawkins, J.D. *et al.* (2002) Effects of the Seattle Social Development Project on sexual behaviour, pregnancy, birth, and sexually transmitted disease outcomes by age 21 years. *Archives of Pediatrics and Adolescent Medicine*, 156(5), 438–47.

Looman, J., Abracen, J. and Nicholaichuk, T.P. (2000) Recidivism among treated sexual offenders and matched controls: Data from the regional treatment centre (Ontario). *Journal of Interpersonal Violence*, 15, 279–90.

Lorant, V., Croux, C., Weich, S. *et al.* (2007) Depression and socio-economic risk factors: 7-year longitudinal population study. *British Journal of Psychiatry*, 190, 293–8.

Lorenz, K.Z. (1981) *The foundations of ethology*. Vienna: Springer-Verlag.

Lösel, F. (1998) Treatment and management of psychopaths. In D. Cooke, A. Forth and R. Hare (Eds.) *Psychopathy: Theory, research and implications for society*. Dordrecht, NL: Kluwer Academic.

Lösel, F. and Beelman, A. (2006) Child social skills training. In B.C. Welsh and D.P. Farrington (Eds.) *Preventing crime: What works for children, offenders, victims and places*. Dordrecht, NL: Springer.

Lösel, F. and Bender, D. (2003) Protective factors and resilience. In D.P. Farrington and J. Coid (Eds.) *Early prevention of adult antisocial behaviour, Cambridge Studies in Criminology*. Cambridge, UK: Cambridge University Press.

Lösel, F. and Bender, D. (2006) Risk factors for serious and violent antisocial behaviour in children and youth. In A. Hagell and R. Jeyarajah-Dent (Eds.) *Children who commit acts of serious interpersonal violence; Messages for best practice*. London: Jessica Kingsley.

Lösel, F. and Schmucker, M. (2005) The effectiveness of treatment for sexual offenders: A comprehensive meta-analysis. *Journal of Experimental Criminology*, 1, 117–46.

References

Lovejoy, C.O. (1981) The origin of man. *Science, 211*, 341–50.

Loxley, W., Toumbourou, J., Stockwell, T.R. *et al.* (2004) *The prevention of substance use, risk and harm in Australia: A review of the evidence.* Canberra, AUS: Australian Government Department of Health and Ageing.

Lucas, C.P., Fisher, P., Piacentini, J. *et al.* (1999) Interview questions associated with attenuation of symptom reports. *Journal of Abnormal Child Psychology, 27*(6), 429–37.

Luciana, M. (2003) Cognitive development in children born preterm: implications for theories of brain plasticity following early injury. *Developmental Psychopathology, 15*(4), 1017–47.

Luepritz, D.A. (1986) A comparison of maternal, paternal and joint custody: understanding the varieties of post-divorce family life. *Journal of Divorce, 9*, 1–12.

Luo, Z.C. and Karlberg, J. (2001) Timing of birth and infant and early neonatal mortality in Sweden 1973–95: longitudinal birth register study. *British Medical Journal, 323*, 1327.

Lyman, J.M., McGwin, G., Jr, Malone, D.E. *et al.* (2003) Epidemiology of child homicide in Jefferson County, AL. *Child Abuse and Neglect, 27*, 1063–73.

Maccoby, E.E. (1998) *The two sexes: Growing up apart, coming together.* Cambridge, MA: Belknap Press.

Maccoby, E.E. and Martin, J.A. (1983) Socialization in the context of the family: parent–child interaction. In P.H. Mussen (Ed.) *Handbook of child psychology: Vol. 4. Socialization, personality and social development.* New York: Wiley.

MacIntyre, A. (1985) How psychology makes itself true – or false. In S. Koch and D.E. Leary (Eds.) *A century of psychology as science.* New York: McGraw-Hill.

Macleod, A.D. (2004) Shell shock, Gordon Holmes and the Great War. *Journal of the Royal Society of Medicine, 97*, 86–9.

Main, M. and Goldwyn, R. (1984) Adult attachment scoring and classification systems. Unpublished manuscript, University of California, Berkeley.

Main, M. and Hesse, E. (1990) Parents' unresolved traumatic experiences are related to infant disorganized attachment status: Is frightened and/or frightening parental behavior the linking mechanism? In M.T. Greenberg, D. Cicchetti and E.M. Cumming (Eds.) *Attachment in the preschool years. Theory, research, and intervention.* Chicago, IL: University of Chicago Press.

Main, M., Kaplan, N. and Cassidy, J. (1985) Security in infancy, childhood and adulthood: a move to the level of representation. In I. Bretherton and E. Waters (Eds.) *Growing points of attachment theory and research. Monographs of the Society for Research in Child Development, 50*, Nos. 1–2.

Main, M. and Solomon, J. (1986) Discovery of a new, insecure disorganized/disoriented attachment pattern. In T.B. Brazelton and M.Yogman (Eds.) *Affective development in infancy.* Norwood, NJ: Ablex.

Mair, G. (2004) The origins of What Works in England and Wales: A house built on sand? In G. Mair (Ed.) *What matters in probation.* Cullompton, UK: Willan.

Malinoski-Rummel, R. and Hansen, D.J. (1993) Long-term consequences of childhood physical abuse. *Psychological Bulletin, 114*, 68–79.

References

Mann, R.E. (2004) Innovations in sex offender treatment. *Journal of Sexual Aggression*, 10(2), 141–52.

Maras, P. (2007) President's column. *The Psychologist*, 20(4), 195.

Marks, D.F. and Sykes, C.M. (2002) Randomized controlled trial of cognitive behavioural therapy for smokers living in a deprived area of London: outcome at one-year follow-up. *Psychology, Health and Medicine*, 7(1), 17–24.

Marks, I., Lovell, K., Noshirvani, H. *et al.* (1998) Treatment of posttraumatic stress disorder by exposure and/or cognitive restructuring: a controlled study. *Archives of General Psychiatry*, 55, 317–25.

Marques, J.K., Day, D.M., Nelson, C. and West, M.A. (1994) Effects of cognitive-behavioural treatment on sex offender recidivism. *Criminal Justice and Behaviour*, 21, 28–54.

Marques, J.K., Wiederanders, M., Day, D.M. *et al.* (2005) Effects of a relapse prevention program on sexual recidivism: Final results from California's Sex Offender Treatment and Evaluation Project (SOTEP). *Sexual Abuse: A Journal of Research and Treatment*, 17(1), 79–107.

Marshall, T., Simpson, S. and Stevens, A. (2000) *Health care in prisons: A health care needs assessment*. Birmingham, UK: University of Birmingham.

Marshall, W.L. (1999) Diagnosis and treatment of sexual offenders. In I.B. Weiner and A.K. Hess (Eds.) *The Handbook of Forensic Psychology* (2nd edn). New York: John Wiley.

Marshall, W.L., Eccles, A. and Barbaree, H.E. (1991) The treatment of exhibitionists: A focus on sexual deviance versus cognitive relationship features. *Behaviour Research and Therapy*, 29, 129–35.

Marshall, W.L., Jones, R., Ward, A. *et al.* (1991) Treatment outcome with sex offenders. *Clinical Psychology Review*, 11, 465–85.

Marshall, W.L., Laws, D.R. and Barbaree, H.E. (Eds.) (1990) *Handbook of sexual assault: Issues, theories and treatment of the offender*. New York: Plenum.

Martinson, R. (1974) 'What works? Questions and answers about prison reform'. *The Public Interest*, 35, 243–58.

Maslow, A.H. (1970) *Motivation and personality* (2nd edn). New York: Harper and Row Publishers.

Mason, J.K. and Laurie, G.T. (2006) *Mason and McCall Smith's law and medical ethics* (7th edn). Oxford, UK: Oxford University Press.

Mazza, J.J. and Reynolds, W.M. (1999) Exposure to violence in young inner-city adolescents: Relationships with suicidal ideation, depression, and PTSD symptomatology. *Journal of Abnormal Child Psychology*, 27(3), 203–13.

McCall, M. (2004) *Deaths in custody in Australia: 2003 National Deaths in Custody Programme (NDICP) annual report*. Technical and background paper series no. 12. Canberra: Australian Institute of Criminology. Retrieved 21 September 2007 from http://www.aic.gov.au/publications/tbp/tbp012/

McConaghy, N. (1995) Are sex offenders ever 'cured'? Treatment options are limited by a lack of scientific evidence. *The Medical Journal of Australia*, 162, 397.

References

McConaghy, N., Armstrong, M.S. and Blaszcynski, A. (1988) Expectancy, covert sensitisation and imaginal desensitization in compulsive sexuality. *Acta Psychiatrica Scandinavica*, 72, 176–87.

McGrath, M., Cann, S. and Konopasky, R. (1998) New measures of defensiveness, empathy, and cognitive distortions for sexual offenders against children. *Sexual Abuse: A Journal of Research and Treatment*, 10, 25–36.

McGrath, R.J., Cumming, G., Livingstone, J. *et al.* (2003) Outcome of a treatment programme for adult sex offenders: From prison to community. *Journal of Interpersonal Violence*, 18, 3–18.

McGuire, J. (2000) Defining correctional programmes. *Forum on Correctional Research*, 12, 5–9.

McHugh, M.J. (2000) Suicide prevention in prisons: Policy and practice. *British Journal of Forensic Practice*, 2(1), 12–16.

McLaughlin, E., Muncie, J. and Hughes, G. (2001) Permanent revolution: New Labour, New public management and the modernisation of criminal justice. *Criminal Justice*, 1(3), 301–17.

McLeavey, B.C., Daly, R.J., Ludgate, J.W. *et al.* (1994) Interpersonal problem-solving skills training in the treatment of self-poisoning patients. *Suicide and Life Threatening Behavior*, 24, 382–94.

McNally, R.J. (1992) Disunity in psychology: Chaos or specialisation? *American Psychologist*, 47, 399–413.

McNally, R.J. (2003) Progress and controversy in the study of posttraumatic stress disorder. *Annual Review of Psychology*, 54, 229–52.

McNeil, D. (1998) Empirically based clinical evaluation and management of the potentially violent patient. In P. Kleespies (Ed.) *Emergencies in mental health practice: Evaluation and management*. New York: Guilford Press.

McNeil, F., Batchelor, S., Burnett, R. and Knox, J. (2005) *Reducing re-offending – key practice skills*. Glasgow, UK: SWIA and Glasgow School of Social Work. Retrieved on 23 June 2007, available from http://www.scotland.gov.uk/Resource/Doc/91931/0021949.pdf

Meehl, P.E. (1954) *Clinical versus statistical prediction: A theoretical analysis and a review of the evidence*. Minneapolis: University of Minnesota.

Meehl, P.E. (1967) Theory-testing in psychology and physics: A methodological paradox. *Philosophy of Science*, 34, 103–15.

Meehl, P.E. (1973 [1959]) Why I do not attend case conferences In P.E. Meehl, *Psychodiagnosis: Selected papers*. Minneapolis, MN: University of Minnesota Press.

Meehl, P.E. (1997) The problem is epistemology, not statistics. Replace significance tests by confidence intervals and quantify accuracy of risky numerical predictions. In L.L. Harlow, S.A. Mulaik and J.H. Steiger (Eds.) *What if there were no significance tests?* Mahwah, NJ: Lawrence Erlbaum Associates.

Meltzer, D., Tom, B.D.M., Brugha, T.S., Fryers, T. and Meltzer, H. (2002) Common mental disorder symptom counts in populations: Are there distinct case groups above epidemiological cut-offs? *Psychological Medicine*, 32, 1195–1201.

Menninger, K.A. (1938) *Man against himself*. New York: Harcourt Brace.

References

Menzies, R. and Webster, C. (1995) Construction and validation of risk assessments in a six-year follow up of forensic patients: A tridimensional analysis. *Journal of Consulting and Clinical Psychology, 63,* 766–8.

Merriam-Webster's Medical Dictionary (2002) Retrieved on 30 June 2007, available from http://www.ucsfhealth.org/adult/health_library/dictionary.html

Meyer, L.J., Cole, C. and Emroy, E. (1992) Treatment for sex offending behaviour: An evaluation of outcome. *Bulletin of the American Academy of Law, 20,* 249–53.

Mezey, G. and Robbins, I. (2001) Usefulness and validity of post-traumatic stress disorder as a psychiatric category. *British Medical Journal, 323,* 561–3.

Miethe, T.D. and McDowell, D. (1993) Contextual effects in models of criminal victimisation. *Social Forces, 71,* 741–59.

Miller, G.A. (1967) *Psychology – The science of mental life.* Harmondsworth: Pelican/ Penguin.

Mitchell, P., Spooner, C., Copeland, J. *et al.* (2001) A literature review of the role of families in the development, identification, prevention and treatment of illicit drug problems. *National Health and Medical Research Council Monograph.* Canberra, AUS: Commonwealth of Australia.

Moffitt, T.E. (1993) Adolescence-limited and life-course-persistent antisocial behavior: A developmental taxonomy. *Psychological Review, 100,* 674–701.

Monahan, J. and Steadman, H.J. (Eds.) (1994) *Violence and mental disorder: Developments in risk assessment.* Chicago, IL: University of Chicago Press. Monahan, J. and Steadman, H.J. (1996) Violent storms and violent people: How meterology can inform risk communication in mental health law. *American Psychologist, 51,* 931–98.

Monahan, J., Steadman, H.J., Applebaum, P. *et al.* (2000) Developing a clinical useful actuarial tool for assessing violence risk. *British Journal of Psychiatry, 176,* 312–19.

Monahan, J., Steadman, H., Silver, E. *et al.* (2001) *Rethinking risk assessment: The MacArthur Study of mental disorder and violence.* New York: Oxford University Press.

Monahan, J., Steadman, H., Clark Robbins, P. *et al.* (2005) An actuarial model of violence risk assessment for persons with mental disorders. *Psychiatric Services, 56,* 810–15.

Montgomery, S.A., Montgomery, D.B., Jayanthi-Rani, S. *et al.* (1979) Maintenance therapy in repeat suicidal behaviour: A placebo controlled trial. *Proceedings of the 10th International Congress for Suicide Prevention and Crisis Intervention.* Ottawa, Canada.

Mooney, C. and Duval, R. (1993) *Bootstrapping: A nonparametric approach to statistical inference.* Newbury Park, CA: Sage.

Morgan, H.G., Burns, C.C., Pocock, H. *et al.* (1975) Deliberate self-harm: clinical and socio-economic characteristics of 368 patients. *British Journal of Psychiatry, 127,* 564–74.

Morgan, R. (2005) Prevention, not detention. *The Guardian,* Wednesday 24 August 2005. Retrieved on 27 June 2007 from http://society.guardian.co.uk/thinktank/ story/0,,1554789,00.html

References

Mullen, P.E., Martin, J.L, Anderson, J.C., Romans, S.E. and Herbison, G.P. (1994) The effect of child sex abuse on social, interpersonal and sexual function in adult life. *British Journal of Psychiatry, 165*, 35–47.

Mullender, A. (2000) *Reducing domestic violence. What works? Meeting the needs of children, Home Office Briefing Note*. London: Home Office.

Mullender, A. (2004) *Tackling domestic violence: Providing support for children who have witnessed domestic violence, Home Office, Development and Practice Report, 33*. London: Home Office.

Murphy, B.E. (1997) Antiglucocorticoid therapies in major depression: A review. *Psychoneuroendocrinology, 22*, s125–s132.

Murtagh, T. (2007) *The Blantyre House affair: A modern day witch hunt*. Dorset, UK: Waterside Press.

Myers, C.S. (1940) *Shellshock in France 1914–1918*. Cambridge, UK: Cambridge University Press.

Nagin, D. and Tremblay, R.E. (1999) Trajectories of boys' physical aggression, opposition, and hyperactivity on the path to physically violent and nonviolent juvenile delinquency. *Child Development, 70*, 1181–96.

Najavits, L.M., Weiss, R.D. and Shaw, S.R. (1997) The link between substance abuse and posttraumatic stress disorder in women: a research review. *American Journal of Addictions, 6*, 273–83.

Narey, M. (2001) Evidence to the Home Affairs Select Committee, 4 December. Retrieved 12 May 2007. Available at http://www.publications.parliament.uk/pa/cm200102/cmselect/cmhaff/428/1120410.htm

Narey, M. (2002) Perrie Lecture 14 June – Prison Service College, Newbold Revel. Prison chief attacks CRE for hindering war on racism. Reported in *The Guardian*, Friday, 14 June 2002.

National Confidential Inquiry (2006) *Five year report of the National Confidential Inquiry into suicide and homicide by people with mental illness*. Manchester, UK: University of Manchester.

National Institute for Clinical Excellence (NICE) (2005) *Post-traumatic stress disorder: The management of PTSD in adults and children in primary and secondary care*. London: Gaskell.

National Institute for Health and Clinical Excellence (NICE) (2007a) *Depression: Management of depression in primary and secondary care*. London: British Psychological Society and Gaskell. Amended guideline retrieved 29 May 2007, available from http://guidance.nice.org.uk/CG23/guidance/pdf/English

National Institute for Health and Clinical Excellence (NICE) (2007b) Memorandum of evidence to the Health Select Committee. London: National Institute for Health and Clinical Excellence.

National Offender Management Service (2005) *Strategy for the management and treatment of problematic drug users within the correctional services*. London: Home Office.

Needs, A. and Towl, G.J. (2003) Series editors' preface. In G.J. Towl (Ed.) *Psychology in Prisons*. Oxford: Blackwell.

276

References

Needs, A. and Towl, G.J. (2004) Preface. In A.P.C. Needs and G.J. Towl (Eds.) *Applying psychology to forensic practice.* Oxford, UK: Blackwell.

Nelson, K.E., Saunders, E.J. and Landsman, M.J. (1993) Chronic child neglect in perspective. *Social Work, 38*(6), 661–71.

Newcombe, A.F., Bukowski, W.M. and Patee, L. (1993) Children's peer relations: A meta-analytic review of popular, rejected, neglected, controversial, and average sociometric status. *Psychological Bulletin, 113,* 99–128.

Newman, D.L., Moffitt, T.E., Caspi, A. *et al.* (1996) Psychiatric disorder in a birth cohort of young adults: Prevalence, comorbidity, clinical significance, and new case incidence from ages 11 to 21. *Journal of Consulting and Clinical Psychology, 64,* 552–62.

NICHD Early Child Care Research Network (2001) Child-care and family predictors of preschool attachment and stability from infancy. *Developmental Psychology, 37,* 847–62.

Nicholaichuk, T., Gordon, A., Gu, D. *et al.* (2000) Outcome of an institutional sexual offender treatment programme: A comparison between treated and matched untreated offenders. *Sexual Abuse: A Journal of Research and Treatment, 12,* 139–53.

Nicholas, S., Povey, D., Walker, A. *et al.* (2006) *Crime in England and Wales 2004/2005.* London: Stationery Office.

Nicholson, J.M., Fergusson, D.M. and Horwood, J. (1999) Effects on later adjustment of living in a stepfamily during childhood and adolescence. *The Journal of Child Psychology and Psychiatry and Allied Disciplines, 40,* 405–16.

Nicolas, H.R. and Molinder, I. (1984) *Multiphasic sex inventory manual.* Tacoms, WA: Nicolas and Molinder.

Noble, J.H. (2006) Meta-analysis: Methods, strengths, weaknesses, and political uses. *Journal of Laboratory and Clinical Medicine, 147*(1), 7–20.

Nolan, D.S., Amgren, A.S. and Bell, J.B. (2000) Studies of the relationship between environmental forcing and the structure and dynamics of tornado-like vortices. Retrieved on 20 June 2007 available from http://www.osti.gov/bridge/servlets/purl/782526-EYVDhc/webviewable/782526.PDF

Novaco, R. (1994) Anger as a risk factor for violence among the mentally disordered. In J. Monahan and H. Steadman (Eds.) *Violence and mental disorder: Developments in risk assessment.* Chicago, IL: University of Chicago Press.

Office of Technology Assessment (1983) *Scientific validity of polygraph testing: A research review and evaluation: A technical memorandum.* Washington, DC: United States Congress.

Olds, D.L., Henderson, C.R., Cole, R. *et al.* (1998) Long-term effects of nurse home visitation on children's criminal and antisocial behaviour: Fifteen-year follow-up of a randomized controlled trial. *Journal of the American Medical Association, 280,* 1238–44.

Olds, D.L., Henderson, C.R., Kitzman, H.J. *et al.* (1999) Prenatal and infancy home visitation by nurses: recent findings. *The Future of Children, 9*(1), 44–65.

O'Leary, K.D. and Wilson, G.T. (1975) *Behavior therapy: Application and outcome.* New York: Prentice-Hall.

References

Olfson, M., Marcus, S.C. and Pincus, H.A. (1999) Trends in office-based psychiatric practice. *American Journal of Psychiatry, 156*, 451–7.

Olweus, D. and Endresen, I.M. (1998) The importance of sex-of-stimulus objects: trends and sex differences in empathic responsiveness. *Social Development, 3*, 370–88.

Online Oxford Dictionary (2007) Retrieved on 29 June 2007 available from http://www.askoxford.com/concise_oed/drug?view=uk

Ost, J. (2005) EMDR of limited use whichever way you look at it. *Healthwatch Newsletter, 58*, 4–5.

Österman, K., Björkvist, K., Lagerspetz, K. *et al.* (1997) Sex differences in styles of conflict resolution: a developmental and cross-cultural study with data from Finland, Israel, Italy and Poland. In D. Fry and K. Björkvist (Eds.) *Cultural values in conflict resolution.* Mahwah, NJ: Lawrence Erlbaum.

Ozer, E.J., Best, S.R., Lipsey, T.L. and Weiss, D.S. (2003) Predictors of post-traumatic stress disorder and symptoms in adults: A meta-analysis. *Psychological Bulletin, 129*, 52–73.

Painter, K. and Farrington, D.P. (1999) Street lighting and crime: Diffusion of benefits in the Stoke on Trent Project. *Crime Prevention Studies, 10*, 77–122.

Patterson, G.R. and Bank, L. (1989) Some amplifying mechanisms for pathological processes in families. In M.R. Gunnar and E. Thelen (Eds.) *Minnesota Symposia on Child Psychology: Vol. 22.* Hillsdale, NJ: Erlbaum.

Patterson, G.R. and Yoerger, K. (1997). A developmental model for late-onset delinquency. In D.W. Osgood (Ed.) *Motivation and delinquency.* Lincoln, NE: Nebraska Symposium on Motivation.

Pattison, E.M. and Kahan, J. (1983) The deliberate self-harm syndrome. *American Journal of Psychiatry, 140*, 867–72.

Pearce, J.B. (1978) The recognition of depressive disorder in children. *Journal of the Royal Society of Medicine, 71*, 494–500.

Petersilia, J. and Turner, S. (1993) *Evaluating intensive supervision probation/parole: Results of a nationwide experiment.* Washington, DC: US Department of Justice.

Piaget, J. (1977[1932]) *The moral judgement of the child.* Harmondsworth: Penguin.

Pickles, A., Rowe, R., Simonoff, E. *et al.* (2001) Child psychiatric symptoms and psychosocial impairment: Relationship and prognostic significance. *British Journal of Psychiatry, 179*, 230–5.

Pinel, P. and Maudsley, H. (1977) Treatise on insanity: Responsibility in mental disease: Two works series Medical Psychology. In D.N. Robinson (Ed.) *Significant contributions to the history of psychology 1750–1920: Vol. III.* Frederick, MD: University Publications of America.

Piquero, A.R., Farrington, D.P. and Blumstein, A. (2007) *Key issues in criminal career research: New analyses of the Cambridge Study in Delinquent Development.* New York: Cambridge University Press.

Plake, B.S. and Spies, R.A. (2005) *Mental measurements yearbook.* Lincoln, NE: University of Nebraska Press.

References

Plutchik, R. (1980) *Emotion: A psychoevolutionary synthesis.* New York: Harper Row.

Plutchik, R. (1994) *The psychology and biology of emotions.* New York: Harper Collins.

Plutchik, R. (1997) Suicide and violence: the two-stage model of countervailing forces. In A.J. Botsis, C.R. Soldatos and C.N. Stefanis (Eds.) *Suicide: Biopsychosocial Approaches.* Amsterdam: Elsevier.

Podmore, J. (2004) Leadership and management in the criminal justice system: an exploration of the management of change in a 'failing prison'. *British Journal of Forensic Practice, 6*(3), 30–5.

Popper, K.R. (1983) *Realism and the aim of science: From the postscript to the logic of scientific discovery.* London: Routledge.

Popper, K.R. (2004[1968]) *The logic of scientific discovery.* London: Routledge Classics.

Post, R.M. (1992) Transduction of psychosocial stress into the neurobiology of recurrent affective disorder. *American Journal of Psychiatry, 149*, 999–1010.

Post, R.M., Weiss, S.R.B., Leverich, G.S. *et al.* (1996) Developmental psychobiology of cyclic affective illness: Implications for early therapeutic intervention. *Development and Psychopathology, 8*, 273–305.

Powell, G. (2005) The president's column. *The Psychologist, 18*(5), 259.

Pratt, D., Piper, M., Appleby, L. *et al.* (2006) Suicide in recently released prisoners: a population-based cohort study. *The Lancet, 368*(9530), 119–23.

Pratt, L.A., Ford, D.F., Crum, R.M. *et al.* (1996) Depression, psychotropic medication, and risk of myocardial infarction. Prospective data from the Baltimore ECA follow-up. *Circulation, 94*(12), 3123–9.

Preston-Shoot, M. (1987) *Effective groupwork.* London: British Association of Social Work and MacMillan Press.

Proctor, E. (1996) A five-year outcome evaluation of a community based treatment programme for convicted sexual offenders run by the probation service. *Journal of Sexual Aggression, 2*, 3–16.

Prudo, R., Brown, G.W., Harris, T. *et al.* (1981) Psychiatric disorder in a rural and urban population: 2. Sensitivity to loss. *Psychological Medicine, 11*(3), 601–16.

Punamäki, R-L., Qouta, S. and El-Sarraj, E. (2001) Resiliency factors predicting psychological adjustment after political violence among Palestinian children. *Journal of Behavioral Development, 25*(3), 256–67.

Qin, P. and Nordentoft, M. (2005) Suicide risk in relation to psychiatric hospitalisation: evidence based on longitudinal registers. *Archives of General Psychiatry 62*, 427–32.

Quinsey, V.L., Harris, G.T., Rice, M.E. *et al.* (1993) Assessing treatment efficacy in outcome studies. *Journal of Interpersonal Violence, 8*, 512–23.

Quinsey, V., Harris, G., Rice, M.E. *et al.* (1998) *Violent offenders: Appraising and managing risk.* Washington, DC: American Psychological Association.

Reinhardt (2002) Doctors are more interested in having high incomes than providing better health care. *British Medical Journal, 324*, 1335.

References

Reinhardt, U.E., Hussey, P.S. and Anderson, G.F. (2003) US health care spending in an international context. *Health Affairs* 23(3), 10–25.

Resick, P.A., Nishith, P., Weaver, T.L. *et al.* (2002) A comparison of cognitive processing therapy with prolonged exposure and a waiting condition for the treatment of chronic posttraumatic stress disorder in female rape victims. *Journal of Consulting and Clinical Psychology, 70,* 867–79.

Riala, K., Alaraisanen, A., Taanila, A. *et al.* (2007) Regular daily smoking among 14-year-old adolescents increases the subsequent risk for suicide: The Northern Finland 1966 Birth Cohort Study. *Journal of Clinical Psychiatry, 68,* 775–80.

Rice, M.E., Quinsey, V.L. and Harris, G.T. (1991) Sexual recidivism among child molesters released from a maximum security institution. *Journal of Consulting and Clinical Psychology, 59,* 381–6.

Richardson, J., Coid, J., Petruckevitch, A. *et al.* (2002) Identifying domestic violence: cross-sectional study in primary care. *British Medical Journal, 324,* 1–6.

Ringer, F. and Crittenden, P. (2007) Eating disorders and attachment: The effects of hidden processes on eating disorders. *European Eating Disorders Review. 15,* 119–30.

Roberts, I., Li, L. and Barker, M. (1998) Trends in intentional injury deaths in children and teenagers (1980–1995). *Journal of Public Health, 20*(4), 463–6.

Rohde, P., Lewinsohn, P.M. and Seeley, J.R. (1990) Are people changed by the experience of having an episode of depression? A further test of the scar hypothesis. *Journal of Abnormal Psychology, 99,* 264–71.

Roid, G.H. (2003) *Stanford Binet intelligence scales.* Itasca, IL: Riverside Publishing.

Romans, S., Martin, J. and Mullen, P. (1996) Women's self-esteem: A community study of women who report and do not report childhood sexual abuse. *British Journal of Psychiatry, 169,* 696–704.

Romero, J.J. and Williams, L.M. (1983) Group psychotherapy and intensive probation supervision with sex offenders. *Federal Probation, 47,* 36–42.

Rooth, F.G. and Marks, I.M. (1974) Persistent exhibitionism: short-term response to aversion, self-regulation and relaxation treatments. *Archives of Sexual Behaviour, 3*(3), 227–49.

Rose, S., Bisson, J., Churchill, R. and Wessely, S. (2002) *Psychological debriefing for preventing post traumatic stress disorder (PTSD).* Cochrane Database of Systematic Reviews 2002, Issue 2. Art. No.: CD000560. DOI: 10.1002/14651858. CD000560.

Rosenhan, D.L. and Seligman, M.E.P. (1989) *Abnormal psychology* (2nd edn). New York: W.W. Norton.

Rothman, K.J. (1988) *Modern epidemiology.* Philadelphia, PA: Lippincott Williams and Wilkins.

Rothman, K.J. and Greenland, S. (1998) *Modern epidemiology* (2nd edn). Philadelphia, PA: Lippincott-Raven.

Roy, A. (1982) Risk factors for suicide in psychiatric patients. *Archives of General Psychiatry, 39,* 1089–95.

References

Royal College of Psychiatrists (2002) *Suicide in prisons*. London: Royal College of Psychiatrists.

Royce, J.R. (1970) *Toward unification in psychology. The first Banff Conference on Theoretical Psychology*. Toronto: University of Toronto Press.

Rozeboom, W.W. (1960) The fallacy of the null-hypothesis significance test. *Psychological Bulletin*, 57, 416–28.

Ruggiero, K.J., Morris, T.L. and Scotti, J.R. (2001). Treatment for children with posttraumatic stress disorder: Current status and future directions. *Clinical Psychology: Science and Practice*, 8, 210–27.

Rutter, M., Graham, P., Chadwick, O. *et al.* (1976) Adolescent turmoil: fact or fiction? *Journal of Child Psychology and Psychiatry*, 17, 35–56.

Rutter, M. and Sroufe, L.A. (2000) Developmental psychopathology: Concepts and challenges. *Development and Psychopathology*, 12, 265–96.

Sackheim, H.A., Prudic, J., Devanand, D.P. *et al.* (2000) A prospective, randomized, double-blind comparison of bilateral and right unilateral electroconvulsive therapy at different stimulus intensities. *Archives of General Psychiatry*, 57(5), 425–34.

Saladin, M.E., Brady, K.T., Dansky, B.S. *et al.* (1995) Understanding comorbidity between PTSD and substance use disorders: two preliminary investigations. *Addictive Behaviors*, 5, 643–55.

Salekin, R., Rogers, R. and Sewell, K. (1996) A review and meta-analysis of the Psychopathy Checklist and Psychopathy Checklist (Revised): Predictive validity of dangerousness. *Clinical Psychology: Science and Practice*, 3, 203–15.

Salkovskis, P., Atha, C. and Storer, D. (1990) Cognitive behavioural problem-solving in the treatment of patients who repeatedly attempt suicide. A controlled trial. *British Journal of Psychiatry*, 157, 871–6.

Sampson, R.J., Raudenbusch, S.W. and Earls, F. (1997) Neighbourhoods and violent crime: A multilevel study of collective efficacy. *Science*, 277, 918–24.

Sanders, M.R., Turner, K.M.T. and Markie-Dadds, C. (2002) The development and dissemination of the Triple P – Positive Parenting Program: A multilevel, evidence-based system of parenting and family support. *Prevention Science*, 3(3), 173–89.

Sandstrom, M.J. and Coie, J.D. (1999) A developmental perspective on peer rejection: Mechanisms of stability and change. *Child Development* 70(4), 955–66.

Scarr, S. (1992) Developmental theories for the 1990s: Development and individual differences. *Child Development*, 63(1), 1–19.

Schacter, D.L. and Tulving, E. (1994) What are the memory systems of 1994? In D.L. Schacter and E. Tulving (Eds.) *Memory systems*. Cambridge, MA: Bradford.

Schaffer, H.R. and Emerson, P.E. (1964) The development of social attachments in infancy. *Monographs of Social Research in Child Development*, 29(94).

Scheela, R.A. (1992) Sex offenders in treatment: variations in remodeling and their therapeutic implications. *Journal of Offender Rehabilitation*, 23, 157–77.

Schweinhart, L.J. and Weikart, D.P. (1997) The High/Scope preschool curriculum comparison study through age 23. *Early Childhood Research Quarterly*, 12(2), 117–43.

References

Scott, A.I.F. and Freeman, C.P.L. (1992). Edinburgh primary care depression study: Treatment outcome, patient satisfaction, and cost after 16 weeks. *British Medical Journal*, *304*(6831), 883–7.

Scott, J., Moon, C.A.L., Blacker, C.V.R. *et al.* (1994) A.I.F. Scott and C.P.L. Freeman's 'Edinburgh Primary Care Depression Study'. *British Journal of Psychiatry*, *164*(3), 410–15.

Scottish Executive (1999) *Report of the Advisory Group on Youth Crime.* Edinburgh: Scottish Executive.

Sedlak, A.J. and Broadhurst, D.D. (1996) *Third national incidence study of child abuse and neglect: Final report.* Washington, DC: US Dept. of Health and Human Services.

Sepejak, D., Menzies, R., Webster, C. *et al.* (1983) Clinical prediction of dangerousness: Two-year follow-up of 408 pre-trial forensic cases. *Bulletin of the American Academy of Psychiatry and Law*, *11*, 171–81.

Serin, R. and Amos, N. (1995) The role of psychopathy in the assessment of dangerousness. *International Journal of Law and Psychiatry*, *18*, 231–8.

Shah, S. (1978) Dangerousness and mental illness: Some conceptual, prediction, and policy dilemmas. In C. Frederick (Ed.) *Dangerous behavior: A problem in law and mental health.* Washington, DC: Government Printing Office.

Shapiro, F. (2001) *Eye movement desensitisation and reprocessing: Basic principles, protocols, and procedures* (2nd edn). New York: Guilford Press.

Shapiro, M.B. (1961) The single case in fundamental psychological research. *British Journal of Medical Psychology*, *34*, 255–62.

Sharry, J. (2006) *Solution-focussed groupwork.* London: Sage.

Shaw, J. (2007) *Suicide in mentally disordered offenders (National Study of Suicide in Recently Released Prisoners). The Research Findings Register. Summary number 1785.* Retrieved 14 May 2007 available from http://www.ReFeR.nhs.uk/ViewRecord.asp?ID=1785

Shaw, M. and Hannah-Moffat, K. (2004) How cognitive skills forgot about gender and diversity. In G. Mair (Ed.) *What matters in probation.* Cullompton, UK: Willan.

Shaw, T.A., Herkov, M.J. and Greer, R.A. (1995) Examination of treatment completion and predicted outcome among incarcerated sex offenders. *Bulletin of the American Academy of Psychiatry and Law*, *23*, 35–41.

Sheline, Y.I. and Minyun, M.A. (2002) Structural and functional imaging of affective disorders. In K.L. Davies, D. Charney, J.T. Coyle and C. Nemeroff (Eds.) *Neuropsychopharmacology. The fifth generation of progress.* Philadelphia, PA: Lippincott, Williams and Wilkins.

Shepherd, J. (Ed.) (2001) *Violence in health care, understanding, preventing and surviving violence: A practical guide for health professionals.* Oxford, UK: Oxford University Press.

Shepherd, J.P and Farrington, D.P (1995) Preventing crime and violence. *British Medical Journal*, *310*, 271–2.

References

Sherman, L., Gottfredson, D., MacKenzie, D. *et al.* (1997) *Preventing crime: What works, what doesn't, what's promising. Report to the US Congress*, Washington, DC: United States Congress.

Shorter, E. (2001) Historical review of diagnosis and treatment of depression. In A. Dawson and A. Tylee (Eds.) *Depression: Social and economic timebomb*. London: BMJ Books.

Sibert, J.R, Payne, E.H, Kemp, A.M. *et al.* (2002) The incidence of severe physical child abuse in Wales. *Child Abuse and Neglect, 26*(3), 267–76.

Singh, B. and Jenkins, R. (2000) Suicide prevention strategies – an international perspective. *International Review of Psychiatry. 12*, 7–14.

Singleton, N., Bumpstead, R., O'Brien, M. *et al.* (2001) *The prevalence of psychiatric morbidity among adults living in private households, 2000*. London: HMSO.

Singleton, N., Meltzer, H., Gatward, R. *et al.* (1998) *Psychiatric morbidity among prisoners in England and Wales: a survey carried out in 1997 by the Social Survey Division of ONS on behalf of the Department of Health*. London: The Stationery Office.

Singleton, N., Pendry E., Taylor, C. *et al.* (2003) Drug related mortality among newly released offenders. *Research Findings, 183*. London: Home Office.

Skeem, J.L. and Mulvey, E.P. (2001) Psychopathy and community violence among civil psychiatric patients: Results from the MacArthur Violence Risk Assessment Study. *Journal of Consulting and Clinical Psychology, 69*(3), 358–74.

Smith, A. (1905) *The Wealth of Nations* (5th edn). E. Cannan (Ed.). London: Methuen.

Smith, G.D. and Egger, M. (1998) Meta-analysis: Unresolved issues and future developments. *British Medical Journal, 316*, 221–5.

Smith, P.K., Cowie, H. and Blades, M. (2004) *Understanding children's development*. Oxford: Blackwell.

Snow, L. (1997) A pilot study of self-injury amongst women prisoners. In G.J. Towl (Ed.) *Suicide and Self-Injury in Prisons*. Leicester: British Psychological Society.

Snow, L. (2006) Psychological understanding of self-injury and attempted suicide in prisons. In G.J. Towl (Ed.) *Psychological research in prisons*. Oxford, UK: Blackwell.

Social Exclusion Unit (2002) *Reducing re-offending by ex-prisoners*. London: The Stationery Office.

Soothill, K.L. (1976) Rape: a twenty-two year cohort study. *Medicine, Science and the Law, 16*(1), 62–9.

Sowa, J.F. (1999) *Knowledge representation: Logical, philosophical, and computational foundations*. Pacific Grove, CA: Brooks Cole Publishing.

Sowa, J.F. (2000) Processes and causality. Online paper retrieved on 17 May 2007 available from http://www.jfsowa.com/ontology/causal.htm

Spieker, S J. and Crittenden, P.M. (2007) Preschool attachment and child care research: Comparison of two theories. Poster presentation at the biennial meeting of the Society for Research in Child Development, Boston, MA.

References

Spitzer, R.L. (1983) Psychiatric diagnosis: are clinicians still necessary? *Comprehensive Psychiatry*, 24(5), 399–411.

Squire, L.R., Chace, P.M. and Slater, P.C. (1976) Retrograde amnesia following electroconvulsive therapy. *Nature 260*, 775–7.

Staats, A.W. (1991). Unified positivism and unification psychology. *American Psychologist*, 46, 899–912.

Stanko, E. (2000) Foreword. In S. D'Cruze (Ed.) *Everyday violence in Britain, 1850–1950: Gender and class, women and men in history*. London: Longman.

Stanko, E. (2001) Re-conceptualising the policing of hatred: Confessions and worrying dilemmas of a consultant. *Law and Critique, 12*(3), 309–29.

Stanko, E., Crisp, D., Hale, C. *et al.* (1998) *Counting the costs: Estimating the impact of domestic violence in the London borough of Hackney*. London: London Borough of Hackney.

Stattin, H. and Magnusson, D. (1996) Antisocial development: A holistic approach. *Development and Psychopathology, 8*, 617–45.

Steadman, H.J. and Silver, E. (2000) Immediate precursors to violence among persons with mental illness: A return to a situational perspective. In S. Hodgis (Ed.) *Effective prevention of crime and violence among the mentally ill*. Dordrecht, NL: Kluwer Academic.

Steinberg, L., Lambourn, S.D., Dornbusch, S.M. and Darling, N. (1992) Impact of parenting practices on adolescent achievement: authoritative parenting, school involvement, and encouragement to succeed. *Child Development, 63*, 1266–81.

Steinmetz, S.K. (1999) Sociological theories of violence. In V.B. van Hasselt and M. Hersen (Eds.) *Handbook of psychological approaches with violent offenders: Contemporary strategies and issues*. New York: Plenum.

Sternberg, R.J. and Grigorenko, E.L. (2003) *The psychology of abilities, competencies, and expertise*. New York: Cambridge University Press.

Sternberg, R.J. and Wagner, R., K. (Eds.) (1994) *Mind in context: Interactionist perspectives on human intelligence*. New York: Cambridge University Press.

Sternberg, R.J., Wagner, R.K. and Okagaki, L. (1993) Practical intelligence: The nature and role of tacit knowledge in work and at school. In H. Reese and J. Puckett (Eds.) *Advances in lifespan development*. Hillsdale, NJ: Erlbaum.

Sternberg, R.J., Wagner, R.K., Williams, W.M. and Horvath, J.A. (1995) Testing common sense. *American Psychologist, 50*(11), 912–27.

Stockton, W. and Crighton, D.A. (2003) Sex-offender groupwork. In G.J. Towl (Ed.) *Psychology in prisons*. Oxford: Blackwell.

Stockwell, T., Gruenewald, P.J., Toumbourou, J.W. *et al.* (Eds.) (2005) *Preventing harmful substance abuse: The evidence base for policy and practice*. Chichester: John Wiley.

Stout, C.E. (2004) Controversies and Caveats. In C.E. Stout and R.A. Haynes (Eds.) *The evidence-based practice: Methods, models and tools for mental health professionals*. New York: John Wiley.

Strang, H. (1995) Child abuse homicides in Australia: Incidence, circumstances, prevention and control. In D. Chappell and S. Egger (Eds.) *Australian violence:*

References

Contemporary perspectives II. Canberra, AUS: Australian Institute of Criminology.

Strang, H. and Sherman, L. (2006) Restorative justice to reduce victimization. In B.C. Welsh and D.P. Farrington (Eds.) *Preventing crime: What works for children, offenders, victims, and places*. Dordrecht, NL: Springer.

Straus, M.A., Gelles, R.J. and Steinmetz, S.K. (1980) *Behind closed doors: Violence in the American family*. New York: Praeger.

Strauss, J.S. (1969). Hallucinations and delusions as points on continua functioning: rating scale evidence. *Archives of General Psychiatry, 21*, 581–6.

Summerfield, D. (2001) The invention of post-traumatic stress disorder and the social usefulness of a psychiatric category. *British Medical Journal, 322*, 95–8.

Summerfledt, L.J. and Antony, M.M. (2002) Structured and semistructured diagnostic interviews. In M.M. Antony and D.H. Barlow (Eds.) *Handbook of assessment and treatment planning*. New York: Guilford Press.

Sumpter, R.E. and McMillan, T. (2005) Misdiagnosis of post-traumatic stress disorder following severe traumatic brain injury. *British Journal of Psychiatry, 186*, 423–6.

Svanberg, P.O. (1998) Attachment, resilience and prevention. *Journal of Mental Health, 7(6)*, 543–78.

Swets, J. (1988) Measuring the accuracy of diagnostic systems. *Science, 240*, 1285–93.

Swets, J., Dawes, R. and Monahan, J. (2000) Psychological science can improve diagnostic decisions. *Psychological Science in the Public Interest, 1*, 1–26.

Tajfel, H. (1982). Social psychology of intergroup relations. *Annual Review of Psychology, 33*, 1–39.

Takahashi, K. (1990) Are the key assumptions of the 'Strange Situation' procedure universal? A view from Japanese research. *Human Development, 33*, 23–30.

Tanner, J.M. (1973) Growing up. *Scientific American, 229 (Sept.)*, 35–43.

Taylor, R. (2001) A study of neurasthenia at the National Hospital for the relief and cure of the paralysed and epileptic, Queen Square, London, 1870–1932. *British Journal of Psychiatry, 179*, 550–7.

Taylor, J., McGue, M. and Iacono, W.G. (2000) Sex differences, assortative mating, and cultural transmission effects on adolescent delinquency: a twin family study. *Journal of Child Psychology and Psychiatry, 41*, 433–40.

Taylor, S., Fedoroff, I.C., Koch, W.E.J. *et al.* (2001) Posttraumatic stress disorder arising after road traffic collisions: patterns of response to cognitive-behavior therapy. *Journal of Clinical and Consulting Psychology, 69*, 541–51.

Taylor, S., Thordarson, D.S., Maxfield, L. *et al.* (2003) Comparative efficacy, speed, and adverse effects of three PTSD treatments: exposure therapy, EMDR and relaxation training. *Journal of Consulting and Clinical Psychology, 71*, 330–8.

Teeson, M., Degenhardt, L., Hall, W. *et al.* (2005) Substance abuse and mental health in longitudinal perspective. In T. Stockwell, P.J. Gruenewald, J.W. Toumbourou and W. Loxley (Eds.) *Preventing harmful substance abuse: The evidence base for policy and practice*. Chichester, UK: John Wiley.

References

Terman, L.M. and Merill, M.A. (1960) *Stanford-Binet intelligence scale*. New York: Houghton Mifflin.

Tessier, R., Nadeau, L., Boivin, M. and Tremblay, R.E. (1997) The social behaviour of 11- to 12-year-old children born as low birth weight and/or premature infants. *International Journal of Behavioural Development, 21*, 795–811.

Thase, M.E., Dube, S., Bowler, K. *et al.* (1996) Hypothalamic-pituitary-adrenocortical activity and response to cognitive behaviour therapy in unmedicated, hospitalised depressed patients. *American Journal of Psychiatry, 153*, 886–91.

Thomas-Peter, B. (2006a) The modern context of psychology in corrections: Influences, limitations and values of 'what works'. In G.J. Towl (Ed.) *Psychological research in prisons*. Oxford, UK: Blackwell.

Thomas-Peter, B. (2006b) The needs of offenders and the process of changing them. In G.J. Towl (Ed.) *Psychological research in prisons*. Oxford, UK: Blackwell.

Thompson, C., Kinmonth, A.L., Stevens, L. *et al.* (2000). Effects of good practice guidelines and practice-based education on the detection and treatment of depression in primary care. Hampshire Depression Project randomised controlled trial. *Lancet, 355*(9199), 185–91.

Thorogood, M., Cowen, P., Mann, J. *et al.* (1992). Fatal myocardial infarction and use of psychotropic drugs in young women. *Lancet, 340*(8827), 1067–8.

Toch, H. (1998) Psychopathy or antisocial personality in forensic settings. In T. Millon, E. Simonsen, M. Birket-Smith *et al.* (Eds.) *Psychopathy: Anti-social, criminal and violent behaviour*. New York: Guilford Press.

Tolan, P.H. (1987) Implications of onset for delinquency risk identification. *Journal of Abnormal Child Psychology, 15*, 47–65.

Tolan, P.H. and Gorman-Smith, D. (1998) Development of serious and violent offending careers. In R. Loeber and D.P. Farrington (Eds.) *Serious and violent juvenile offenders: Risk factors and successful interventions*. Thousand Oaks, CA: Sage.

Tong, L.S. and Farrington, D.P. (2004) *How effective is the 'reasoning and rehabilitation' programme in reducing reoffending? A meta-analysis of evaluations in four countries*. Cambridge, UK: Institute of Criminology, University of Cambridge.

Topp, D.O. (1979) Suicide in prison. *British Journal of Psychiatry, 134*, 24–7.

Torhorst, A., Moller, H.J., Schmid-Bode, K.W. *et al.* (1988) Comparing a 3-month and a 12-month-outpatient aftercare program for parasuicide repeaters. In H.J. Moller, A. Schmidtke and R. Welz (Eds.) *Current issues of suicidology*. Berlin: Springer-Verlag.

Toumbourou, J.W. and Gregg, M.E. (2002) Impact of an empowerment-based parent education programme on the reduction of youth suicide risk factors. *Journal of Adolescent Health, 31*(3), 279–87.

Toumbourou, J.W., Williams, J., Waters, E. *et al.* (2005) In T. Stockwell, P.J. Gruenewald, J.W. Toumbourou and W. Loxley (Eds.) *Preventing harmful substance abuse: The evidence base for policy and practice*. Chichester, UK: John Wiley.

Towl, G.J. (1993) Anger control groupwork in practice. In G.M. Stephenson and N.K. Clark (Eds.) *Children, evidence and procedure*. Leicester, UK: British Psychological Society.

References

Towl, G.J. (1994) Ethical issues in forensic psychology. *Forensic Update 39*, 23–6.

Towl, G.J. (1995) Anger management groupwork. In G.J. Towl (Ed.) *Groupwork in prisons*. Leicester, UK: British Psychological Society.

Towl, G.J. (2000) Suicide in prisons. In G.J. Towl, L. Snow and M.J. McHugh (Eds.) *Suicide in prisons*. Oxford: Blackwell.

Towl, G.J. (2004a) Applied psychological services in HM Prison Services and the National Probation Services. In A.P.C. Needs and G.J. Towl (Eds.) *Applying psychology to forensic practice*. Oxford, UK: Blackwell.

Towl, G.J. (2004b) Applied psychological services in prisons and probation. In J. Adler (Ed.) *Forensic psychology, concepts, debates and practice*. Cullompton: Willan.

Towl, G.J. (2005a) National offender management services: Implications for applied psychological services in probation and prisons. *Forensic Update, 81*, 22–6.

Towl, G.J. (2005b) Risk assessment in evidence based mental health. Risk assessment. Evidence-Based Mental Health, *8*, 91–3.

Towl, G.J. (2006) Drug misuse intervention work. In G.J. Towl (Ed.) *Psychological research in prisons*. Oxford, UK: Blackwell.

Towl, G.J. and Bailey, J. (1995) Groupwork in prisons: An overview. In G.J. Towl (Ed.) *Groupwork in prisons*. Leicester, UK: British Psychological Society.

Towl, G.J. and Crighton, D.A. (1996) *The handbook of psychology for forensic practitioners*. London: Routledge.

Towl, G. and Crighton, D. (1997) Risk assessment with offenders. *International Review of Psychiatry, 9*, 187–93.

Towl, G.J. and Crighton, D.A. (1998) Suicide in prisons in England and Wales from 1988 to 1995. *Criminal Behaviour and Mental Health, 8*, 184–92.

Towl, G.J. and Crighton, D.A. (2005) Applied psychological services in the national probation service for England and Wales. In D.A. Crighton and G.J. Towl (Eds.) *Psychology in probation services*. Oxford: Blackwell.

Towl, G.J. and Crighton, D.A. (2000) Risk assessment and management. In G.J. Towl, L. Snow and M.J. McHugh (Eds.) *Suicide in prisons*. Oxford: Blackwell.

Towl, G.J. and Crighton, D.A. (2006) Distributed leadership for distributed services: Offender management and public protection. *British Journal of Leadership in Public Services, 1*(1), 49–55.

Towl, G.J. and Crighton, D.A. (2007a) Psychologists in prisons. In J. Bennett, B. Crewe and A. Wahadin (Eds.) *Understanding prison staff*. Cullompton, UK: Willan.

Towl, G.J. and Crighton, D.A. (2007b) Psychological services in prisons in England and Wales. In B. Ax and T. Fagan (Eds.) *Corrections, Mental Health and Social Policy*. Springfield, IL: Charles C. Thomas.

Towl, G.J. and Dexter, P.M. (1994) Anger management with prisoners: An empirical evaluation. *Groupwork, 7*(3), 256–69.

Towl, G.J., Snow, L. and McHugh, M.J. (Eds.) *Suicide in prisons*. Oxford: Blackwell.

Townsend, P., Donaldson, N. and Whitehead, M. (1990) *Inequalities in health: The Black Report and the health divide*. London: Penguin.

287

References

Tumim, S. (1990) *Report of a review by Her Majesty's Chief Inspector of Prisons for England and Wales of suicide and self-harm in prison service establishments in England and Wales.* London: HMSO.

Turiel, E. (1998) The development of morality. *Handbook of child psychology, Vol. 3* (5th edn). New York: Wiley and Sons.

Turner, B.W., Bingham, J.E. and Andrasik, F. (2000) Short-term community based treatment for sexual offenders: Enhancing effectiveness. *Sexual Addiction and Compulsivity, 7,* 211–24.

Tversky, A. and Kahneman, D. (1982) Judgment under uncertainty: Heuristics and biases. In D. Kahneman and A. Tversky (Eds.) *Judgment under uncertainty: Heuristics and biases.* Cambridge, UK: Cambridge University Press.

Vaillant, G.E. (1998) *Adaptation to life.* Cambridge, MA: Harvard University Press.

van der Kolk, B.A. (1997) The psychobiology of posttraumatic stress disorder. *Journal of Clinical Psychiatry, 58*(9), s16–s24.

van der Sande, R., van Rooijen, E., Buskens, E. *et al.* (1997) Intensive in-patient and community intervention versus routine care after attempted suicide: A randomised controlled intervention. *British Journal of Psychiatry, 171,* 35–41.

van Heeringen, C., Jannes, S., Buylaert, W. *et al.* (1995) The management of non-compliance with referral to out-patient after-care among attempted suicide patients: a controlled intervention study. *Psychological Medicine, 25,* 963–70.

van Os, J., Jones, P., Lewis, G. *et al.* (1997) Developmental precursors of affective illness in a general population birth cohort. *Archives of General Psychiatry, 54,* 625–31.

Vaughan, B., Egeland, B., Sroufe, L.A. and Waters, E. (1979) Individual differences in infant-mother attachment at 12 and 18 months: stability and change in families under stress. *Child Development, 50,* 971–5.

Verkes, R.J., Van der Mast, R.C., Hengeveld, M. *et al.* (1998) Reduction by paroxetine of suicidal behavior in patients with repeated suicide attempts but not major depression. *American Journal of Psychiatry, 55,* 543–7.

Vernon, P.E. (1961) *The measurement of abilities. London: University of London Press.*

Volavka, J. (1999) The neurobiology of violence. *Journal of Neuropsychiatry and Clinical Neuroscience, 11,* 307–14.

Wald, M.S. and Woolverton, M. (1990). Risk assessment: The emperor's new clothes? *Child Welfare, 64*(6), 483–511.

Walker, A., Kershaw, C. and Nicholas, S. (2006) *Home Office Statistical Bulletin 12/06 Crime in England and Wales 2005/06.* London: Home Office. Retrieved 14 May 2007 from http://www.homeoffice.gov.uk/rds/pdfs06/hosb1206.pdf

Walsh, B.R., Stuart, M.D., Siedman, N. *et al.* (2002) Placebo response in studies of major depression: variable, substantial and growing. *Journal of the American Medical Association, 287,* 1840–7.

Waterhouse, J. and Platt, S. (1990) General hospital admission in the management of parasuicide: A randomised controlled trial. *British Journal of Psychiatry, 156,* 236–42.

References

Watson, R. and Stermac, L. (1994) Cognitive group counselling for sexual offenders. *International Journal of Offender Therapy and Comparative Criminology*, *38*, 259–70.

Wechsler, D. (1975) Intelligence defined and undefined: a relativistic appraisal. *American Psychologist*, *30*, 135–9.

Wechsler, D. (1997) *Wechsler Adult Intelligence scale* (3rd edn). San Antonio, TX: The Psychological Corporation.

Weiner, B. (1974) *Achievement motivation and attribution theory.* Morristown, N.J.: General Learning Press.

Weiner, B. (1980) *Human motivation.* New York: Holt, Rinehart and Winston.

Weiner, B. (1986) *An attributional theory of motivation and emotion.* New York: Springer-Verlag.

Weissman, M.M., Bland, R.D., Canino, G.J. *et al.* (1996) Cross natural epidemiology of major depression and bipolar disorder. *Journal of the American Medical Association*, *276*, 292–9.

Welsh, B.C. and Farrington, D.P. (2007) Scientific support for early prevention of delinquency and later offending. *Victims and Offenders*, *2*(2), 125–40.

Welu, T.C. (1977) A follow-up program for suicide attempters: Evaluation of effectiveness. *Suicide and Life Threatening Behavior*, *7*, 17–30.

White, P., Bradley, C., Ferriter, M. and Hatzipetrou, L. (1998) Management of people with disorders of sexual preference and for convicted sexual offenders. *The Cochrane Database of Systematic Reviews*, Issue 4. Art. No.: CD000251. DOI: 10.1002/14651858.CD000251.

Whiting, B.B. and Whiting, J.W.M. (1975) *Children of six cultures: a psycho-cultural analysis.* Cambridge, MA: Harvard University Press.

Williams, R.J. and Chang, S.Y. (2000) A comprehensive and comparative review of adolescent substance abuse treatment outcome. *Clinical Psychology: Science and Practice*, *7*(2), 138–66.

Wilson, E.O. (2000) *Sociobiology: The new synthesis.* New York: John Wiley.

Wilson, J.J. (2000) *Safe from the start: Taking action on children exposed to violence.* Washington DC: Office of Juvenile Justice and Delinquency Prevention.

Wolfson, A.R. and Carskadon, M.A. (1998) Sleep schedules and daytime functioning in adolescents. *Child Development*, *69*, 875–87.

Wolke, D. (1998) Psychosocial development in prematurely born children. *Archives of Disease in Childhood*, *78*, 567–70.

Woodward, L.J. and Fergusson, D.M. (2000) Childhood peer relationship problems and later rsks of educational under-achievement and unemployment. *The Journal of Child Psychology and Psychiatry and Allied Disciplines*, *41*, 191–201.

World Health Organization (2007) ICD 10 Online. Retrieved on 30 June 2007 available from http://www.who.int/classifications/apps/icd/icd10online/

Wright, J., Binney, V. and Smith, P.K. (1995) Security of attachment in 8–12-year-olds: a revised version of the Separation Anxiety Test, its psychometric properties and clinical interpretation. *Journal of Child Psychology and Psychiatry*, *36*, 757–74.

References

Wright, L., Borrill, J., Teers, R. *et al.* (2006) The mental health consequences of dealing with self-inflicted death in custody. *Journal Counselling Psychology Quarterly, 19*(2), 165–80.

Yalom, I. (1985) *The theory and practice of group psychotherapy* (3rd edn). New York: Basic Books.

Yesavage, J., Becker, J., Werner, P. *et al.* (1983) Family conflict, psychopathology, and dangerous behaviour by schizophrenic inpatients. *Psychiatry Research, 8,* 271–80.

Young, A.H., Gallagher, P. and Porter, R.J. (2002) Elevation of the cortisol-dehydroepiandrosterone ratio in drug-free depressed patients. *American Journal of Psychiatry, 159,* 1237–9.

Youth Justice Board (2003) *Substance misuse: Key elements of effective practice.* London: Youth Justice Board.

Youth Justice Board (2007) *Annual report and accounts.* London: Youth Justice Board.

Zimbardo, P.G. (2003) Phantom menace: Is Washington terrorizing us more than Al Qaeda? *Psychology Today, 36,* 34–6.

Zimbardo, P.G. (2007) Understanding how good people turn evil. Interview transcript. *Democracy Now!* (March 30, 2007). Retrieved 21 May 2007, available from http://www.democracynow.org/article.pl?sid=07/03/30/1335257

Index

Note: page numbers in italic denote tables or figures separated from their textual reference.

291

Index

Index

Index

detoxification 162–3
developmental factors 135–7, 171
developmental psychology 11, 34, 57–8, 113, 135–7
developmental psychopathology 129–30, 146
dexamethasone suppression test (DST) 140
diabetes 134
Diagnostic and Statistical Manual of Mental Disorders 175, 183n1
  DSM I 131
  DSM III 131, 168
  DSM IV 63, 69, 75, 92n3, 132, 172
dialectical behaviour therapy (DBT) 197–8
diathesis stress model 169, 170, 181–2
disorganised pattern of behaviour 40–2, 44
dissonance: see cognitive dissonance
diversity 31, 32n5, 106
Division of Criminological and Legal Psychology 19
Division of Forensic Psychology (DFP) 19–21, 30
divorce 45
DMM: see Dynamic-Maturational Model
domestic violence 204–6
Douglas, K. 110, 113
Down's syndrome 36, 56n1
Drucker, P. 5
drug misuse in prisons xi, 68, 151–2
  adolescence 158, 165
  community care 162
  community resources 159
  detoxification 162–3
  family factors 155–6
  harm 154–5, 161
  interventions 65, 158–9, 164–5
  mental health 62, 64
  mothers 165
  parent education 158

pre-birth factors 155
pregnancy 155, 156–7
preschool interventions 165
prevalence 153, 159–61, 165, 201n4
prevention 154–5
risk factors 155–6
school-based studies 158
temperament 155
drug testing 160, 239
drugs 151, *153*
  evaluation 236
  legal status 152–3, 154, 156–9, 164
DSM: *see* Diagnostic and Statistical Manual of Mental Disorders
dual-diagnosis 133
Durkheim, E. 188
Dynamic-Maturational Model 40–1, 42, 43–4, 55
dysfunctional responses 168, 183n4
dysphoria 130, 136, 148n1

ecological context 35, 54, 71
educational achievement 48–9, 67
educational deficits 32n8, 59
educational psychology services 32
effect sizes 234–5
electroconvulsive therapy 130, 141, 145, 146, 148
embryonic development 37–8
EMDR: *see* eye movement desensitisation and reprocessing
emotional states, negative 190
empathy 49–50
employment status 67
endocrine changes 52
Epidemiological Catchment Study 145
epidemiology
  depression 132, 134–5, 137
  suicide in prisons 186–90
  trauma 170–3
Epidemiology journal 235

Index

Index

298

Index

Index

Index

Index